SIT AND CRY
TWO YEARS IN THE LAND OF SMILES

For Steve,
If you hadn't lied to me
FBI and told them what a great
guy I was — I'd never have
been accepted by Peace Corps —
and this book would
never have been written!

Enjoy, my friend —

B Maloy

Sit and Cry

Two Years in the Land of Smiles

Burgess Needle

Burgess Needle (signature)

Ripton, VT
5/8/07

Wren Song Press
Middlebury, Vermont

Sit and Cry: Two Years in the Land of Smiles

First Edition, April 2017

Interior and cover design by Winslow Colwell/Wren Song Design

Published in the United States by Wren Song Press
1 Lower Plains Road, Middlebury, Vermont 05753

The text of this publication was set in Minion.

ISBN: 978-0-9753706-9-8

Library of Congress Catalog No. 2017906474

To my roommate Wisut Pinyovanichka
and to the Students of Nangrong School

11/67   Borneo

INTRODUCTION

S*it And Cry* has the format of a journal, the texture of a memoir, and the narrative thrust of fiction because it is based on letters that have been enlarged due to Monday-morning reflections and edited from the perspective of a story teller.

Everything within these pages happened and every person represented has an existence. Events have sometimes been abridged or expanded for narrative impact and in a few instances names have been changed where I felt there was potential for embarrassment.

This book's roots go back to Thailand; but, the first melding of letters and journal entries began in Newton, Massachusetts where I lived for a while after I returned to America. Later, when I moved to Tucson, boxes of pages traveled with me where every eight years or so I'd attempt to re-assess and tweak the material into a coherent whole. Over several decades, I've written a number of short stories and twenty-five poems based on these entries and letters.

I need to thank all the kind and patient souls who've read the book and offered advice. Karen Dahood, one of my earliest readers, gave me much guidance with narrative focus. Nancy Ozeri's keen copy editing captured dangling participles and herded wandering syntax. Gayle Jandrey reminded me to offer more developed classroom scenes and to share how I felt inside about the war raging along Thailand's borders.

Thom Huebner, a Thailand Peace Corps Volunteer himself who went on to become a professor at Chulalongkorn University in Bangkok, identified errors having to do with Thai culture, language, government and food.

Wisut Pinyowanichka, my best friend and roommate during two years in Thailand, allowed me far more access to the land and people of that country than I ever would have managed on my own. He is my friend for life and I pray there is nothing in this work that embarrasses him.

Win Colwell, of Wren Song Press, used his expertise to seamlessly fuse the text with the photographs. The results are not only attractive to the eye, but more importantly, directly appeal to the heart.

While the occasional felicitous phrases are mine to wear with pride, I must also claim credit for whatever errors, great or small, exist in the narrative.

left: First photo of Burgess in Bangkok, 1967.

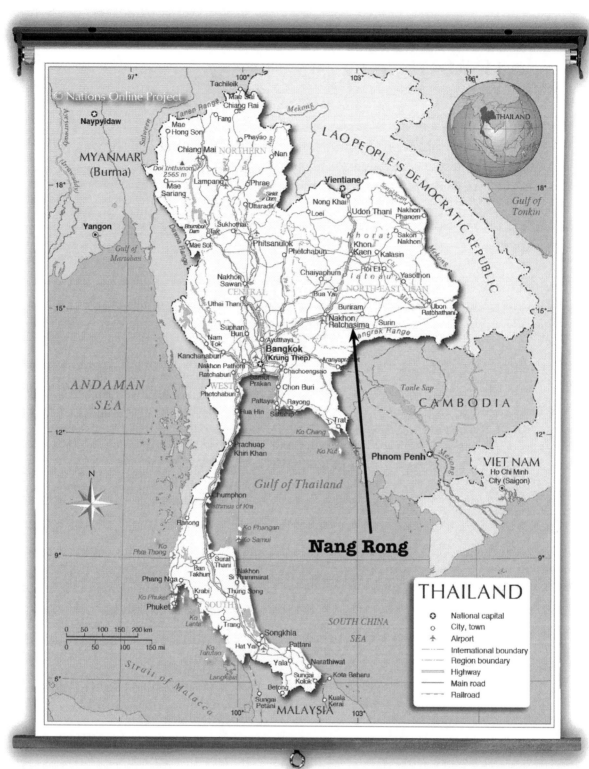

PRELUDE

My headmaster and I sat up front. It was called the Death Seat. If the bus crashed, the driver always managed to leap to safety, but everyone else in the front was crushed. Our driver sat with one foot extended out to the running board, as if primed for a hasty escape. Meanwhile, we remained stationary. The hood was up. A man in a blue uniform kicked a few tires, then stepped back and studied the situation. He leaned under the hood and I heard him spit several times. The driver yelled something, the man in blue stepped back and the engine roared to life with an ominous grinding noise. A black cloud billowed exhaust as the driver cautiously released the clutch. The mechanic slammed the hood shut and swung easily onto the very edge of the front seat. We backed away from the wooden platform and into an obnoxious cloud of exhaust and dust. Then, with a frightening groan of metal on metal, we moved from reverse into first and lurched ahead toward Nang Rong Village. We were tightly packed across the bench: a small boy clung to the outside, the driver hunched over the wheel, then the mechanic squeezed in next to me and the headmaster and, finally, a silent monk in saffron robes. Wheezing and coughing, the bus bounced over deep ruts as we headed out of Buriram Province in northeast Thailand. The wind whistled as the driver jammed the gas, played with the gears and murmured to the engine in tones as urgent as a jockey to a recalcitrant pony. Behind me, I heard the other passengers chatting, but up front all was quiet. I surreptitiously glanced at the monk. His head was smooth-shaven and a pair of delicate wire-rimmed glasses perched on his nose. I realized he was staring at my shirt pocket where a pack of Thai cigarettes peeked out. Did monks smoke? Was it de rigeur to offer a monk a cigarette? Taking a chance, I pulled out the pack and offered him a smoke. He accepted it gravely, turned sour when he saw the brand and politely handed it back. "I thought they were Salem," he said in perfect English, and turned back to stare at the road.

It began to rain. The road disappeared and the bus slid and swayed through a red quagmire and watery ruts made by farmers' carts drawn by enormous water buffalo. Undaunted by rain or road, the driver forged ahead at a steady 40 kilometers per hour. The roof leaked right above my lap. Too bad about my Thai silk suit. Beads of water clung to the monk's head like rain drops on the hood of a waxed car. Every 15 minutes or so the bus stalled. The mechanic got out and spit under the hood. It worked each time. And while the mechanic spat on the engine, the driver crumpled up several cigarettes and rubbed tobacco strands over the outside of the windshield. Since there was no windshield wiper, maybe he thought the tobacco would absorb or repel the water. Eventually, the windshield was laced with soggy strands of tobacco, making it hard to see anything. I tried to imagine what awaited me at the last stop, Nang Rong Village, where I'd been assigned to teach English for two years by the Peace Corps.

May 5, 1967
THAILAND

I had my first glimpse of Bangkok, whose full name in Thai includes the appellation 'City of Angels.' It appeared beneath my Boeing 707 as an endless brown and green city crisscrossed with canals that gripped the estuary of the Chao Phrya River.

We were greeted by officials from the Thai Ministry of Education, fitted with sweet-scented leis of local blossoms and escorted into the Ministry's main auditorium.

I was one of 50 volunteers in Thailand XVIII sent to the Land of Smiles, where an English governess instructed the children of King Mongkut and later wrote about her experiences in a book called *Anna and the King of Siam*. Although the author, Anna Leonowens, fictionally placed herself near the center of the country's royal court and as a confident of the king, Thai records barely make mention of her presence. I thought I had a better sense of my own minuscule place in the grand scheme of Thai culture and society.

Thailand, the only country in Southeast Asia never to have been colonized by a Western power, found itself in 1967 trapped between the hostile forces of North Vietnam and the suffocating embrace of the American military machine. Enormous U.S. airbases had been established adjacent to major Thai cities: Udorn, Korat and Sattahip. For the first time in the history of its foreign affairs a Thai government found itself with no way to easily shift foreign policy back and forth depending on circumstances.

We had been told during training that there were rumors some volunteers were CIA surrogates. Disguised as foreign language teachers from middle class backgrounds, we were identified by our own left-of-center cousins as purveyors of information for the CIA data banks in Langley, Virginia. If the CIA had any plans for me, I was unaware of them. All I could think of when I first disembarked was how the heat and humidity caused my entire body to sweat most of its fluids into my clothing.

I was a 25-year-old recent college graduate with a B.A. in English literature from the University of Massachusetts, who came across a Peace Corps recruiting table on campus that lured me over with a banner that read "PEACE CORPS GOES TO PARADISE." The table was manned by former volunteers who told me the agency was looking for college graduates to work in America's Trust Territories in the Pacific. They had a newly-abbreviated application form, only four pages long.

At that particular point in time, I'd somehow managed to earn a series of academic deferments and passed three pre-induction physicals, but now that a mid-year graduation loomed ahead I saw myself as a prime candidate for basic training at Fort Dix, New Jersey. Going to paradise as a Peace Corps volunteer seemed an infinitely better deal. I soon received a fat letter from Peace Corps, Washington telling me that I'd been accepted into a program for…not the Trust Territories, but Thailand! And, that my three month training program would take place in Hawaii! I would be going to paradise after all. All I had to do was convince my draft board it was okay for me to leave the continental United States.

Although my initial petition was rejected, when I told them I would be teaching English in Thailand they changed their minds and stamped the necessary papers. I was simultaneously relieved and filled with anxiety. What did my draft board know that I did not? My first thought upon hearing I was being released, at least temporarily, from the draft, was "What if I get lost between here and there?" This was not merely some vague, neurotic concern. I once read of a character who lacked a moral compass. I, however, lacked an old-fashioned geographical compass. Basically, I rarely *ever* knew where I was in relation to anything else. The simple truth is I always will be on the verge of -- or in the midst of -- being totally lost. Government investigators who interviewed my friends, teachers and employers apparently never came across that little blip on my profile.

After three months of Thai language training and lectures about Thai culture, we were flown first to Manila and, finally, Bangkok. At the airport we were loaded on a bus and taken to the dormitory of a Teacher Training College. The shock of seeing dozens of Esso gasoline trucks careening along the highway impressed upon my romantic imagination the fact that Thailand had a firm financial umbilicus to my own country.

We spent several days in Bangkok and were briefed by American and Thai government officials. An American army captain actually named James Bond lectured our group on security. Mr. Kukrit, the editor and owner of Siam-Rath, a politically influential newspaper, told us, "In a land of nervous smiles, I alone will give you straight facts with a straight face." I later learned some of his self-assurance derived from his relationship to the royal family. His brother, Prime Minister, Seni Pramoj, was doing his best to turn his government into a true constitutional monarchy, but was meeting major resistance from the military powers that were accustomed to running things. The country was then ruled by a tapestry of forces representing the military, business, Buddhism and King Bhumipol. Thailand's political and social infrastructures were constantly stressed by the incongruence of priorities among these major power brokers.

Thailand XVIII was a fairly sedate group with a few nervous giggles as we sat in the auditorium waiting for a representative from the Ministry of Education. When he walked across the stage, holding a long, wooden cue, we leaned forward in anticipation. Speaking slowly and clearly into a microphone, he gestured with his pointer to a large map of Thailand. Name by name, he indicated and identified the site where each of us would be spending the next two years of our lives.

"Burgess Needle!"

I took a deep breath and held it.

"You have been assigned to the town of Nang Rong in the northeast."

He touched a portion of the map that seemed to be right on the border, then turned to face me.

"Nang Rong is located in Buriram Province. Buriram is the poorest province in Thailand, but Nang Rong is the richest district in the province."

I nodded, a smile frozen on my face, as I tried to assimilate the fact I'd soon be setting up housekeeping in the richest district of the poorest province.

"You will be approximately 30 kilometers from the Cambodian border. You will discover that many of the farmers in this region speak Cambodian as well as Thai. This will be an opportunity for you to learn *two* languages."

There was some muted laughter. Every Friday during training the Thai language instructors posted all our names in order of our language proficiency. Out of 50 slots, I was usually number 50. Thai alone would be enough of a challenge for me. I didn't need Cambodian. The minister smiled in my direction and continued.

"I believe it is interesting to note that the name Nang Rong means 'To Sit and Cry.' Perhaps you will discover the origins of that name during the next two years."

"However, do not despair," the speaker continued, "because Buriram means 'City of Happiness.' Perhaps you will discoverer why there is a place called 'Sit and Cry' in a province called 'City of Happiness.' "

That afternoon, we were warned about the hazards of uncooked salads, various recipes that contained raw blood and trichinosis in the water. The doctor presenting this medical lecture then asked the women to wait outside because he had something he had to tell the men. This prompted moans and groans, but the women eventually left. The doctor proceeded to tell us that venereal diseases were rampant and cautioned to always use a condom. He said that several times. He then mentioned that if anyone did contract VD we were to immediately send a telegram to his medical office in Bangkok with a message that we would be arriving soon for treatment of foot problems. That would be the code for letting them know we had picked up something and needed antibiotics.

"Why would we say foot problems?" someone called out.

"Because whatever you get would eventually begin to drip on to your foot," he said, smiling. "The important thing is to be treated as soon as possible. Some of you may naively think these things will eventually just go away on their own – they won't. And, the longer you wait, the more difficult it will be to affect a cure. Okay, that's it. You can go. Tell the women they can come in now."

We quietly left, but on the way out I signaled to one of the women that I'd be waiting for her after the lecture. She nodded. Soon, they too emerged.

"What did he tell you?" I asked her.

"He told us to be extremely cautious and think twice before sleeping with any of you because some of you will pick up gonorrhea."

"Really?"

"Yes," she said, backing away. "Really."

"No, come on! Did he actually say that?"

"Burgess, basically what he told us was that some of you guys might catch some form of VD while you're living alone in some isolated village and that we should be careful ourselves. That's all."

"Wow! That's kind of a heavy message. Want to get something to eat?"

"No, thank you."

May 13, 1967

The train slowly pulled out of Bangkok's Hua Lumpong Station and left in its wake vendors who ran alongside my window holding up plastic baggies of sweetened colored water, pieces of fruit and grilled chicken legs. The first class compartments were thinly occupied by upper-level government officials and rich businessmen who sat behind sealed windows in air-conditioned comfort. Extremely wrinkled women with betel nut-stained teeth carried straw baskets in the third class sections. Savoring the middle kingdom, I waved from my second class window at the more energetic hawkers who ran the length of the station in hope of one last sale.

Finally, I was traveling up-country through the early morning haze on the rapid train out of Bangkok. Sensory impressions of the capitol: the stink of garbage mixed with the scent of spices, an aura of perfume from tourist shops, food vendors spooning out noodle soup, open clothing arcades by government buildings, a flower stall near the lines of people outside *Wat Pra Keo* – The Temple of the Emerald Buddha, piles of shoes neatly stacked near monasteries and crisp, uniformed guards standing at attention by various ministries. Traffic was grid-locked, an enormous Pepsi Cola billboard loomed ahead and a man rode an elephant that plodded its way out of town.

My train headed northeast toward Buriram Province. From there I'd go by bus to Nang Rong. Accompanying me, for the first eight hours of her ride, was Susan, another volunteer, heading for a town even further up-country than mine. As the mist cleared we became less interested in the passing scenery and nibbled on slices of bread and sipped warm soft drinks. All green outside the window, as the open spaces of a Thailand we had yet to meet blurred by.

My stomach tightened and my throat dried up. Susan and I regarded each other nervously. During training we hadn't said more than a dozen words to each other.

The train whistled from station to station, their names printed black-on-white and in Thai and English: Lopburi, Saraburi, Ayuthya…but, I kept repeating the only name that was meaningful for me: Buriram! Buriram! Buriram!

Susan and I were afraid to eat anything more than bread. Opposite us, a large family broke open rattan baskets and gorged themselves on guavas, bananas, watermelons and oranges. A train steward walked down the aisle selling cardboard plates of fried rice and fish sauce. I turned away and stared at passing coconut trees. Every time we stopped, no matter how small the station, dozens of small children rushed up waving pieces of fried chicken on sticks and more colored drinks. They screamed and cajoled up at our windows.

The other passengers regarded us quietly. Susan had to use the bathroom. She hesitantly asked directions. Smiles all around. The two foreigners had human needs just like them. After Susan found her way back, several passengers crowded close to us and asked questions. The sum of our combined vocabularies was barely enough to understand a fraction of each question.

"Are you married?"

Both of us understood that one and Susan blushed as I shook my head. We gradually understood they wanted to know how long we had been in their country and how long we planned to stay.

"This is so frustrating," I said to her. "I can barely count to 10 and ask where the bathroom is."

Someone offered her a banana, so she pressed her palms together in a *wai* and murmured "*Khop khun, kha.*"

Her little "Thank you" was worth a round of applause and so it went for a few hours more until someone called out, "Buriram! Next stop is Buriram!"

We'd been told to expect very brief stops and to make sure the nearest window was kept open in case we had to literally throw our luggage out on the platform. The dry air that rolled through the window as the train slowed was murderously hot. Wearing my new Thai silk suit that I'd purchased in the capital on a whim seemed to have been an act of lunacy. My forehead was streaked with red dust. There was a pool of sweat running the circumference of my belt. The train lurched to a stop.

Half the passengers seemed in a hurry to get off together. Produce packed in bamboo baskets was lowered out windows. Aisles were jammed with adults and children. Where was my suitcase? I began to tremble. What if I was unable to get off in time and ended up in another city? How would I ever find my way back?

"Hey! Come on! Get off the train. We already have your suitcase!" someone called out to me.

There were several young Americans standing alongside the train waving at me. During my moment of catatonia Susan and several passengers had already handed off all my belongings.

"Thank you…" I started to say, but they just pushed me to the door.

Taking deep breaths, I heard a voice inside my head say, "Go! Go!" and I made it to the door, took three steps down and felt solid ground as the train abruptly shuddered and began to move behind me. I turned to say one last goodbye and saw Susan leaning out the window handing my small Pan Am bag out to people on the platform. A whistle blew and I felt a growing wind behind me as the train picked up steam, leaving me in a cloud of red dust.

Two guys who turned out to be community development volunteers walked over and introduced themselves as Frank and Ralph. An attractive Asian woman stood off to one side, looked back at me and smiled. I smiled back. She introduced herself as Sharon Lim from California, a teacher at the Girls' Secondary School in Buriram.

I kept looking around nervously for my headmaster. My regional Peace Corps director told me he received a telegraph from the headmaster saying he'd be in Buriram to meet me when I got off the train. Sharon told me not to worry and she joined Frank and Ralph in dragging me away to a small restaurant where I met the owner, Miss Pensee, a petite woman with an easy smile. Ralph ordered four Cokes with ice.

"I thought we weren't supposed to have any ice with our drinks," I said.

"If you want to drink warm Coke that's okay with me," he shrugged. "The trick is to suck up your drink the instant the ice cools it but before too many of the pathogens have a chance to melt."

Four frosty glasses filled with ice and Coke were placed before us. Without a second thought I grabbed one of them and sucked it dry. Delicious!

Outside the restaurant, the sun was beginning to sink, but the air was still quite warm. Clouds of red dust rose and fell along the street. I saw taxis being driven slowly up and down the street as their drivers shouted out where they were headed. *Samlaws*, the Thai version of a pedicab, swarmed in every direction. In shops across the street the wares were stacked in windows, on shelves and right to the edge of the sidewalk. Passing customers stared in at us obliquely. One middle-aged man in a khaki uniform glared at me with jaundiced eyes. I forced myself to look away.

Ralph said he was from New Jersey and Frank from upper New York state. They all wanted to know various pieces of minutiae about America. After a while I got the impression they weren't interested in what I was saying, just excited at tuning in to another voice speaking English. I wondered how long it would take me to become like that. The Thai man continued to stare at me intently. Ralph asked me if I wanted anything to eat. I nodded. They began to order food. I said something to Sharon about the man who observed my every move. She looked his way, flushed, then quickly turned back to me.

"That's your headmaster!" she exclaimed. "You better go over right away and introduce yourself."

Introduce myself? I tried to recall the formal phrases of greeting someone. How should I address him? If he were just another adult I'd use the common "*khun*" form, kind of like "mister." Wait a minute! What was a headmaster called? "*Adjan yai.*" That's it! I lurched to my feet and walked up to him. He seemed to view my approach with hostile resignation.

"My name is Burgess Needle," I said in halting Thai. "Are you the headmaster of Nang Rong School?"

His face broke into hundreds of tiny wrinkles. It was a smile! He slowly got to his feet and extended his right hand.

"I am very glad to meet *you*!" his voice rose on the last word.

As our hands tightened their grip around each other, all I could think was, *Thank you God … he can speak English*!

I looked back at the others. Sharon bowed her head slightly toward my headmaster. He motioned for them to approach. Suddenly, everyone around me was speaking Thai very quickly. I had a sinking sensation in my gut. In very short order I would be leaving these three volunteers behind and left only to my own limited linguistic devices in some small village. Wait a minute! That sinking sensation was a literal roller-coaster taking off somewhere deep in my stomach. I had to find a bathroom, fast! Sharon gently touched my elbow.

"Are you okay? You suddenly turned really pale."

I told her what was going on and she quickly explained to everyone else. Was that *kind* laughter? Miss Pensee showed me where to go. The tiny bathroom had only a squat-john in the middle of the floor. Somehow I managed to balance myself against a wall and not soil my clothes. Old Thai newspapers made for an untidy finale. Was this happening to me because of the ice I had with my drink? Were all those stories true about local ice possibly being made with canal water, mixed with run-off from God knows where, formed into not-too-clean ice vats, dragged through the back of pick-up trucks by hemp ropes, transported on mounds of dirty sawdust and finally crushed and cut with rusty picks? Could be.

It was time to say goodbye to Ralph, Frank and Sharon and walk with Adjan Suraporn, my headmaster, to the Nang Rong bus, a converted Fargo truck decorated with flowers, drawings of animals and abstract art in vivid colors. Flags and pennants waved from the luggage railing on top. This would be open-air traveling. No glass windows, only wooden bars. The bus seemed to be already full. Several of the men wore uniforms similar to the headmaster's. They all saluted him. Naked babies crawled on the floor. Nodding to themselves, a number of elderly women chewed betel nut leaves. Several younger women suckled babies. The aisles were packed with baskets, cardboard boxes and rattan cases of produce and chickens. There was no possible place to sit. The driver greeted us with great deference and gently urged two passengers from the front seat to move to the back where they squatted on the floor.

My headmaster sat next to me on the front seat and after half an hour or so he turned to me and asked, in Thai, "Are you comfortable, Khun Burgess?"

I racked my brain for a suitable answer. I finally managed to come up with, "Yes, it is fun!"

He looked at me quizzically, then down at his nails.

I pondered long and hard, then told him, "I think it is enjoyable to ride on a Thai bus."

The headmaster guffawed and shouted what I just said to the driver. The bus swerved almost over the edge of the road as the driver burst out laughing.

I thought I recalled that the verb "to ride" in Thai sounds like "*khee*" with a falling tone. Hmmm. Is it possible I used a tone that meant "to shit" instead of "to ride?" Had I just told him that I found it enjoyable to shit on a Thai bus? Maybe using a *low* tone makes it *ride* and using a *falling* tone means taking a *shit*. Too confusing.

The monk smiled at me as he threw his third cigarette into the rain. Wind whipped palm fronds in a frenzy, tobacco pieces collected into the corners of the windshield and the monk seemed to desire a conversation.

"How many people live in Nang Rong," I asked him, in Thai.

He told me there were 3,000 or 30,000 or 300,000 people. I needed to work on my numbers.

"Do you know about Buddhism?" he asked, in English.

"No, not much," I admitted.

"Good," he said. "Then you will not have to forget all the wrong things people often say about Buddhism."

He seemed to be waiting for a response.

"Ah, good," I replied.

"Good," he repeated.

Everything was good except the weather. The bus made a sharp turn, skidded halfway across the road, righted itself and pulled into a tiny hamlet with nothing much in view except a water-buffalo, several men on bicycles and a very fat man on a motorcycle. Suddenly, the rain stopped, the clouds parted and an absolutely smooth patch of road appeared before us. The clay and gravel pavement seemed to hover above and between submerged rice paddies. Tall coconut palms gracefully swayed alongside the road. I stared out at green miles of water-filled squares filled with new rice stalks. Occasional trees off in the distance added a dimensional sense of distance. Above, the sky was now deep blue with faint cumulus clouds scattered about. No matter whether I turned to the left or right, the land was flat, with not the slightest elevation to be seen. A tiny junction ahead contained a shack made of sticks and banana fronds. A small girl standing before it held out a bunch of bananas as the bus paused as if for breath and I leaned out the window to read the white lettering on blue background of a sign planted next to the stand. It read: NANG RONG in Thai and English letters.

The road deteriorated as we approached the village. There was a flash of brown, wooden buildings on stilts, a few run-down shops, then a market area with a bus stop of wooden counters, tall pilings and an iron awning. People, *samlaws* and dogs crowded together and lunged ahead as the bus slowly ground to a halt.

Chickens squawked and dogs howled. Above, the sky shimmered an absolute blue. Puddles of water indicated the storm we'd passed through had also hit Nang Rong. The air was warm and sweet. From my vantage point I saw that none of the village's buildings were more than three stories high and all were made of dark-stained wood, possibly local teak. I stepped down and unfurled myself. I was a lot taller than anyone else in sight. The monk from the bus was met by a contingent of other monks, all carrying black umbrellas. They brought an extra one for him. Walking away so close together that their umbrellas kissed with soft clicks, the monks allowed their robes freedom to flow against each other and rustled softly in the late afternoon breeze. Their leaving presented a saffron tapestry punctuated with ebony parasols.

The bus driver broke my reverie by asking me something in rapid-fire Thai. I smiled and gave a dumb shrug. Again, he asked me a question, only this time carefully articulating each word.

"How long will you be in Thailand?" I understood him to say.

"Two years," I replied, in Thai.

He pressed his palms together and bowed his head.

"Welcome to Thailand," he said. "You are very smart."

He turned away and helped unload luggage from the roof of his bus. My headmaster touched me gently on the shoulder and, waving across the area before us with his other arm, said, "This is for you. This is Nang Rong."

Three *samlaws* skidded to a halt before us. All my belongings went in one. The headmaster and I each had one to ourselves. Young drivers, who wore blue shorts, faded khaki shirts and white pith helmets, strained hard on the pedals and we were off. Settling back in my seat I stared at my driver's incredibly large calf muscles as he valiantly pumped up a slight incline away from the market district. We passed through the center of town and then by an open-front store. Small children spotted me and ducked behind their mothers. The mothers smiled and waved. I tried to keep track of where we were going in relation to the bus stop, but there were few landmarks for me to focus on and remember. Three wooden buildings past the fly-speckled water-buffalo? No, that wasn't any good. Obviously, the buffalo was in transit. Right turn by the very tall coconut palm tree. Hmmm. There were only about 10,000 coconut palms around.

Our convoy skirted a large field and my driver's muscles bulged and strained as we hit another hill scarred with ruts and pocked with water holes. Another turn and we picked up speed, past two concrete pillars supporting barbed wire. Ahead were two large brown wooden buildings. As we drove by them I managed to read the sign over the larger of the two – NANG RONG SCHOOL. We sped between the buildings and stopped in front of a newly-painted house that rested high atop concrete columns. It was the only painted house in town.

"Khun Burgess, this is your house. This is where you will live.

I was stunned. It was beautiful. Where was the wooden shanty I'd imagined? Our drivers hauled my suitcases up into the house and we followed. I wandered from room to room as the headmaster settled up with the drivers.

I smelled fresh paint, then realized the windows had neither glass nor screens. The two-by-fours that framed the house were clearly visible. There was no insulation, plasterboard, electricity or plumbing. A light breeze gently pushed a wooden shutter away from the wall. There was no furniture except for a twisted metal cot and a folded mattress in what could be a bedroom.

I stood in the middle of the largest, most central area and turned in circles. The headmaster followed me with a fixed smile. Footsteps. Three uniformed men entered.

"Khun Burgess, these are some of the other teachers at Nang Rong School."

The three men examined me with some caution, then nodded their heads.

I raised my hands, palms together before my face and gave the traditional *wai*. They laughed and each insisted on pumping my right hand.

"My name is Prayun," said the first. "I am the other English teacher. This is Mr. Preeda, the history teacher, and this is Mr. Gimyong who teaches many subjects (he paused to translate for Mr. Gimyong who smiled broadly) and he is also the, ah, vice-headmaster. Is that correct?"

"Assistant-headmaster?" I suggested.

"Yes, yes, of course!" he exclaimed. "You are the assistant-headmaster," he said to Mr. Gimyong, who smiled back.

"I am happy to be here," I said. "I am happy to meet everyone."

They all smiled.

"I think you are very handsome," Preeda said.

I was unable to come up with a response to that, so I just kept smiling. Everyone beamed. The Land of Smiles.

"Did you know Miss Charlotte?" asked Preeda. "She was also from Peace Corps."

"No," I said. "I'm sorry, but I didn't know her."

"She was from Clearwater, Florida."

"Uh huh, and I'm from Boston, Massachusetts."

They looked shocked.

"The King of Thailand went to school in Boston," Prayun said. "You must be very smart."

"Well, not too smart," I said, modestly. "Where did the king go to school?"

"Do you know about Harvard? He went to Harvard."

"Yes," I said. "I know all about Harvard. I think the king is a great deal smarter than I am."

"Yes," Prayun said. "He is. But, you also come from Boston. Miss Charlotte spoke Thai very well and she knew how to cook Thai meals and eat very spicy food."

Before I could respond the headmaster broke and asked, "You are hungry?"

"Yes, I am hungry."

"You can eat hot, Thai food?" he asked, in Thai.

"Yes, I can eat hot, Thai food," I replied in Thai.

They all applauded and I felt myself blush. Preeda and Prayun stepped aside and let Gimyong and myself pass between them through the door and down the stairs into the soft, early evening air where the sky behind the school buildings still held a delicate pink hue. We marched in an uneven procession, skirted the school's fence and cut across the field to the market area. Several buffalo carts passed us, their drivers seemingly asleep over their reins. Creaking and groaning, their large, wooden wheels struggled for a grip on the moist earth. Preeda saw me staring and asked me if America had anything like that. I shook my head. I felt as if I had fallen into some tropical past unfamiliar to my most distant ancestors.

We stopped in the middle of town before a small restaurant that was haphazardly filled with odd tables and chairs. The side facing the street was open except for a drawn metal grate. They led me up the few steps to a cool interior, through the main room, to a small courtyard out back. A long table surrounded by a dozen or so chairs awaited us. Gravely, they motioned for me to pick a chair before they all seated themselves. At once, the owner bustled out shaking a white, cotton table cloth which he carefully draped over the table. No one spoke to him, but as if following former orders he quickly brought out tray after tray of food, two cases of soda water, several quarts of cold beer and a very large bottle of Thai whiskey labeled "Mekhong" in prominent script.

I was exhausted. My eyes kept slitting shut no matter how hard I tried to keep them open. My tarnished suit hung on me like a wet rag. I pinched myself over and over under the table and tried to remain attentive.

The owner returned carrying an enormous covered platter which he carefully placed dead center before me. Conversation stopped as he grasped the handle and in one smooth movement lifted the cover in a cloud of steam to reveal an entire massive leg of a pig roasted in its own juices. A number of dark bristles protruded through the skin. Several plates of cooked vegetables surrounded the platter, including one I recognized as fried morning-glory leaves.

Alongside each chair stood small end-tables each carrying large bowls of steamed white rice. A large wooden bucket off to one side was filled with (oh no!) crushed ice. We each downed a few glasses of chilled beer and nibbled on roast pork. Beneath the rough skin was the most delicious, succulent meat I'd ever tasted. Another large plate was brought out with fried beef in oyster sauce, another of hot cashews, then two bowls of soup (one with chicken, the other with meat balls), celery and asparagus stalks resting on ice, and as much *larb* as anyone wanted (I was told during training that larb was a common dish throughout the northeast made of chicken, beef, fish, pork or even mushrooms minced with chili and mint. It was seasoned with fish sauce and lime juice. The only cautionary note was that sometimes the meat was raw so there was a possibility of parasites).

The headmaster gestured toward a shallow bowl to my right. I scooped up a small mound and dropped it on my plate. It looked like sauerkraut.

"Miss Charlotte like it very much," someone said.

I brought a small spoonful to my mouth and started to chew. They all watched me intently. Wow! It was insanely hot. I looked up, startled and flushed. They laughed and laughed.

"Too spicy for you?" The headmaster asked.

"No," I coughed. "It's very good! What is it?"

"Papaya, lime, fish sauce and…" he paused and turned to one of the other teachers and whispered something. The other teacher whispered back. "…and garlic. This is a food from here, from Isaan. It is called *somdam*."

After that, each teacher made a point of placing a different kind of food on my plate. I sampled it all and told them, in all candor, it all tasted fine, even though some of the salad dishes seemed particularly sour to me. Soon, the beer was gone and the owner of the restaurant returned to open the whiskey bottle.

"Do you have this in your country?" the headmaster asked me, as he handed over the bottle.

I shook my head. It looked like regular whiskey. I turned the bottle around and saw some printing in English. It read "May 1, 1967." That was only a few weeks ago!

New glasses were delivered and each teacher filled his glass with ice and soda. I did the same. The headmaster nodded to Prayun who poured healthy slugs all around. We weren't going to drink the whole bottle, were we? Diluted with soda, Mekhong whiskey tasted like a mild, sweet American rye. After a while, the ice and soda were gone. As the last drops of Mekhong were released, the owner brought out another bottle. Gimyong swayed in his seat and Preeda appeared to be dozing. I was drunker than I had ever been in my life and I'd lost my sense of touch. It didn't matter how hard I pinched my leg under the table, I felt nothing. The headmaster and Prayun seemed as alert as ever, although their eyes had begun to turn scarlet around the pupils.

Possibly at some secret signal by the headmaster, the others pushed their chairs away and tried to stand. We managed to leave without knocking over any chairs and stumbled through the restaurant to the street. I heard two empty whiskey bottles roll off the table and smash onto the concrete patio.

Miraculously, we managed to walk back to my new house in the dark, although I did walk directly into two telegraph poles, wrenched my ankle in a pot-hole and slid over one wide gravel patch into a split that should have popped the seam of my crotch.

We climbed the stairs and I found myself standing, once again, in the middle of the largest room. Stiffly erect, his red eyes gleaming under the dim light of one small overhead bulb, Adjan Suraporn seemed to be pondering a difficult decision.

"Khun Burgess," he began. "Now, you will take the bath and then we shall have the initiation."

Initiation? Was that really the word he wanted? A bath? Where could I possibly take a bath? Not that I didn't want one, but there didn't appear to be any plumbing.

Preeda led me to a small room toward the back. Inside, I saw an enormous water jar filled with clear water and a few dead mosquito larvae bobbing on the surface. Next to that was a squat-john surrounded by clean, white tiles.

Preeda smiled as he pantomimed filling a large dipper with water and emptying it over his head. Okay. Fine. I walked back to the room with the broken cot and peeled off my suit. Underneath, I wore a short-sleeved shirt. Where the sleeves ended, my arms were dyed blue by the wet silk of my new suit. I opened my shaving kit and looked at myself in the tiny mirror. Rimmed with red dust and clotted with particles of sand among red veins, my eyes revealed themselves. I remembered the bottle of Southern Comfort I'd been carrying since Bangkok, stepped out modestly wearing a towel, and retrieved it. They stared at me in silence. Gimyong suddenly reached out and gingerly patted my right bicep.

"White…white," he said, then stepped back quickly as the headmaster angrily shook his head.

Prayun moved in closer and peered below the spot Gimyong touched.

"Oho!" he exclaimed. "Blue! He is the blue man!"

At that, even the headmaster rolled his eyes, unable to hide a grin.

I held out the Southern Comfort, hoping they'd interpret that as a polite gesture. Adjan Suraporn accepted it, hefted its weight, unscrewed the top, sniffed it and gave a big smile! He took quite a long pull and after touching his watering eyes, he handed it to Prayun. That seemed like a good time to leave them for my bath. I threw several buckets of freezing water over my head and shocked myself back to fear and trembling.

Shivering, I dried off and zipped back to my suitcase. The teachers were all sitting on the floor looking kind of dazed. I politely closed the door behind me, rubbed my hair with a towel, patted myself dry, threw on some after-shave, got dressed and peeked out to see how things were going.

They were all flat out on the floor staring at the ceiling. I saw the empty Southern Comfort bottle by the headmaster's head. I squatted by Gimyong to sort of get close and the noise from my crackling knees startled the headmaster who sat up with a jolt. He managed to force out a smile. The others slowly got to their feet.

"You do not look like Khun Burgess," Adjan Suraporn said.

As I tried to figure out what he meant, he pulled out a scrap of paper that had my picture on it and a brief biographical sketch. It had been taken toward the end of training.

"We thought you had a beard," he said, pointing to the dark shading beneath my chin.

It was a very bad Xerox copy that also made me appear to have small pox and broken teeth.

He went on to tell me that they were all relieved to see that I was not a "hippy." They'd had some fears I would frighten the students. I started to laugh, but stopped when he abruptly pulled himself to full attention.

"Khun Burgess," he said. "We shall now have the initiation."

He cleared his throat and began to speak. After a few seconds I realized it was simply his formal welcome speech to me. Sober, I never would have managed it, but since I was drunk I interrupted him and asked, "Can you wait a minute while I get something?"

As he stared at me in utter incomprehension I ran back into the room, pulled out my portable tape recorder, popped in the microphone, turned it on and ran back to hold it close to his mouth.

He smiled. Everything was okay. He officially welcomed me in a formal Thai speech, which I only dimly understood. I gathered he made some reference to the long relationship between his country and mine. Based on the expressions of the other teachers it was a fantastic speech. As he reached the finale, he grasped my right hand and pulled me toward him and switched to English.

"….and you will do your duty to this school!" he concluded.

He slammed his arms to his side, stood at even stiffer attention, made eye contact with the others and they shouted "*Chayo!*" and applauded.

Not knowing what else to do, I pulled in my stomach, stuck out my chest and saluted them all. My initiation was over.

May 14, 1967

I woke up to the sound of roosters crowing. Boston was 12,000 miles and a few hundred years away. Intense sunlight poured into my room. For some reason hundreds of scraps of magazines and newspapers were scattered around my house, so I worked my way out of my morning's daze by stumbling around picking them up. My stomach felt queasy. I drank quite a bit of water from the rain barrel (they did say *rain* barrel, didn't they?). At noon, someone from the school came by and asked if I would like to walk with him to the market. He seemed to be so familiar with me I was too embarrassed to ask his name. I threw some water on my face, slicked back my hair and walked with him through my new green world to the shops. I bought an iron, a radio, a shirt and a very solid bicycle. Even after forking over the equivalent of $35 worth of baht I still felt rich. The shopkeepers seemed undecided about what degree of deference I deserved, but they were certainly friendly and laughing with my fellow teacher. In all the conversations I heard that morning, I identified no more than a few nouns.

Even though there were dogs barking, children laughing and the wheels of buffalo carts squeaking around me, there was also a strange stillness I didn't recognize at first: no traffic, no horns, no planes.

As I pushed my new bicycle back home I came face to face with a small crowd of officials, including: the Buriram Police Chief, the commander of the border patrol, the Nang Rong Police Chief, his lieutenant and a few other local officials who all seemed eager to shake my hand. With the exception of the lieutenant, everyone spoke to me in a mixture of Bangkok Thai, local slang and what I took to be Cambodian. I just kept nodding my head and saying *thank you.* Eventually, most of them took off and I was left with the lieutenant who said, "They are all very happy you will go to the party at the Police Chief's house."

"I will?"

I was not at all happy with this turn of events because I didn't want the townspeople to associate me with either police or military.

"Yes," he said. "You told them you would be happy to go and you thanked them very politely. They think you are very smart."

"I'm afraid I didn't really understand everything they said," I admitted.

"Don't worry. *Mai pen rai.* Do you know what that means?"

"Yes, it means 'never mind.'"

"Yes, and it's true. Don't worry about anything. Everybody likes you."

A policeman came by later that evening and escorted me to the chief's house. About a dozen or so officials were already there, along with the headmaster and many from the police force, and they all insisted I have a drink. From the back of the room, my headmaster seemed to stare right through me. I tried to keep the whiskey as diluted as possible with soda water and ice. The chief shouted for everyone to be quiet through a microphone connected to a pair of huge loudspeakers. He pointed to me and I think he said a few nice things about Peace Corps and how smart I was. Everyone applauded.

"The party is for his birthday," the lieutenant whispered in my ear. "Hold up your glass and say something and I will translate."

I held up my glass, the lieutenant got everyone's attention and I toasted the chief his good health and happy birthday.

The translation took much longer. Much, much longer! Big applause. The chief walked over and gave me a great, big hug. We all retreated to another room where tables were already loaded with food. I sat with the lieutenant, the chief and a group of civilians, which might have included the *nai amphur* or mayor. There was fried chicken (okay), bamboo shoot soup (edible), something that looked like chicken livers, something that looked like cabbage, but burned off the outer layer of my palate. Then, I remembered it was called *som tam*.

The headmaster looked at the others then back at me as if explaining it all to me for the first time.

"This is made from green papaya crushed with a handful of palm sugar, lime, fish sauce, peanuts and chilies." He said that *this* is different from the Bangkok type because people in the northeast add *pla ra* (pickled fish sauce). I chugged a glass of water with lots of ice, then went back to more Mekhong whiskey which began to taste pretty good.

"*Som tam* is a special plate because of what is in it," the headmaster said. "The dish has the five main tastes of all Paak Isaan cooking: *sour* lime, *hot* chili, *salty* and *savory* fish sauce, and *sweetness* from palm sugar."

"I did not understand all of that," the chief said to the headmaster. "You are very smart with English."

"That is why he is *Adjan Yay*," the lieutenant said to his boss.

As if he suddenly realized he might have insulted him, the lieutenant gave a slight nod, quickly got to his feet and walked away.

I pointed to some gray and blue orbs that looked like eggs and asked the headmaster if these were the famous 100-year-old eggs I'd heard about in America. He translated and everyone laughed.

"What are they called in Thai?" I asked him.

"Ah, I think you do not have this in America. There are no words. If I told you the Thai words it would sound unusual."

"Please try."

"These eggs are preserved in clay, ash, salt, lime and rice hulls for a long time, but not 100 years!"

"What are they preserved in?"

"The Thai words for this are *khai yeo maa*. It means *egg urine horse*. I think you must eat some more."

He explained to the others and they watched as I carefully cut an egg into quarters, raised it to my mouth and gagged as a powerful smell of ammonia hit me. I put it in my mouth then grabbed a glass of whiskey and swallowed it like a pill: a big, greasy, foul-smelling pill. They all applauded.

"Do you like *ahan Isaan*?" the headmaster asked. "The part of Thailand you are in now is called Paak Isaan, so the food on this table is called *ahan* (food) Isaan."

"Yes," I said in Thai. "It is delicious."

Everyone applauded then suddenly quieted down and I realized the chief was holding out his microphone to me.

"You will please sing a song for us," he said.

"Excuse me?"

"Please sing a song. Do you know '500 Miles?' Miss Charlotte used to sing it."

So, that's what the former volunteer sang at parties, but I had no singing talent. I coughed. The speakers boomed my cough around the room. Chairs moved so everyone now faced me directly.

"...*if you miss the train I'm on*
you will know that I am gone..."

They applauded and asked for more. These were undoubtedly the most polite people in the world. I remembered a Thai song we practiced during training called "*Nam San Dyyn.*" I only knew a few lines, but they all quickly joined in when I began. Everyone beamed.

"You are very smart."

I took another swallow of Mekhong and sighed. The party lasted until two, at which time a small group left for the local red light district and I bicycled home. Every pothole sucked me in and I was positive every shadow held a cobra ready to strike. There were no street lights or house lights except for a few dim kerosene lanterns. I skidded on a soft shoulder and fell. No damage, but I almost shrieked at the feel of vines on my face. I scrambled back on my bike, made it home, ran into the bathroom where I threw water on my face and crashed on my little cot. Rolling over, I turned on my radio and picked up the U.S. Armed Forces station in Pleikou, Vietnam and fell asleep to the Rolling Stones singing "Ruby Tuesday."

Within an hour I sat up and waved off a cloud of mosquitoes. Back in the bathroom I peered at my face in the cracked mirror and saw my cheeks were swollen and pocked with dozens of tiny red welts. I found some ragged and torn mosquito netting in a corner, wrapped it all around my head, sneezed several times and fell into a fitful sleep. Although it must have been at least 90 degrees in the room, I kept several loose blankets over most of my body for protection. Roosters yanked me back to consciousness at dawn's first light.

I began to have thoughts about my immediate future. School started in a few days. What will I do then? I have this horrible feeling that I'm perpetrating some terrible fraud on everyone here. What will I possibly be capable of doing in a room filled with Thai students who probably know as much English as I know Thai? What if they don't know any English at all? What will I do then?

May 15, 1967

As Alice said, "Things are certainly very peculiar…" Every time I attempted to initiate a conversation in Thai I ended up in Wonderland. I tried plain and simple English and got riddles in return. I said, "Hello, how are you this morning?" They replied, "Man Thai people have rice for breakfast. You want?"

There were two secondary schools in town; one was private, the other was run by the government. Ostensibly, all education in Thailand through secondary school was under the Ministry of Education, but there were quite a few private schools. By and large, in the up-country districts, such as Buriram, government schools were better staffed and had higher educational standards. Bangkok had a few private schools that were better than anything the government had to offer, but they were expensive. There was a system of quotas and quality control. If a poor student was unable to pass the entrance exam to the next level or applied too late in the year, he ended up attending a private school. I picked up a few hints indicating that wealth and/or power equaled entry into a government school, regardless of brains. I wondered how things would turn out if a headmaster's son wasn't too bright.

Adjan Suraporn, the headmaster, invited me to his home for dinner. I planned to ask him questions about the differences between the two school systems. His house was a massive teak building with rooms that seem to have been added on as the need arose. Judging from the age groups I saw, three generations called the place home.

Outside, children played *takraw,* where they all stood in a circle and passed a bamboo rattan ball around with everything except their hands. On the steps, a few teenagers read books. Under the house, which rested on wooden pilings, young girls played with babies. Beside the front stairs old women sat chewing betel nut leaves. Riding around the perimeter on bicycles, teenage boys shouted and whistled.

I stepped through the front door and saw Adjan Suraporn sitting in a lotus position on the floor with an open bottle of Mekhong whiskey and two empty glasses beside him. The teak floor planks gleamed from having been rubbed for hours with coconut husks. I gave him a fairly high *wai* as a sign of respect; he threw me a perfunctory one back and motioned for me to sit down across from him on a thin mat. A young woman quickly brought in a bucket of ice and several bottles of soda water. After several drinks in silence, more food was brought in: fried pork strips, chicken soup, fried chicken, fish stew, the inevitable *larb*, vegetables, mounds of rice, beef stew, fiery *som tam* and fried morning glory leaves.

Delicious as it all tasted, I was extremely uncomfortable in the position and before long my thighs and back were killing me. Some older people drifted in and stared at me from time to time as everyone dug into the food. I'm certain they talked about me. Occasionally, Suraporn translated a word or two, but I basically had no idea what was being said.

Suraporn abruptly asked me if I was homesick, but before I could answer he went on to say that his house was my house and any time I felt lonely or in need of company to just drop by. He went on to say that his wife wanted very much to visit America some day. I wrote down my home address and telephone number and handed it to him with an invitation to drop by any time. He smiled and the rest of them nodded as the translation came through.

The headmaster spoke about problems at Nang Rong School and in the community. His vocabulary was fairly extensive, but he obviously hadn't had much practice and didn't like having to search for words. I brought up the subject of the town's private school. He nodded and calmly said he owned it! It turned out he had been the first teacher at Nang Rong School and he had single-handedly built up its staff and reputation. He also owned large chunks of real estate that included the access road from the city of Korat (the site of an enormous United States Air Force base), which could one day be worth a bundle if federal money ever came through to pave it.

A few children crawled over and touched my arm, gently plucking the hair and exclaiming at my *fur*. The remainder of the food was taken away and more whiskey came in. No more ice or soda, but we kept drinking. If it was supposed to be some sort of endurance contest I had no hope of winning; I was a rank amateur up against a pro. Tiny lights flickered above us, then went out. Candles were lit and I started to fall forward. A small hand scratched my back as the headmaster yawned and stretched then suddenly shouted something at a small girl whose fingers were wandering up to my shoulders. I think he told her to go to bed. More whiskey. Just before I passed out, Suraporn got up with the agility of a gymnast and said something like, "…pleasant dreams…"

Wearily, and with great difficulty, I made it back down the stairs to my bicycle and wobbled home, falling only once.

....

May 17, 1967

After I finished my first day of teaching I went into the teachers' lounge and collapsed into a chair. Adjan Suraporn sat in front of me reading a newspaper while the rest of the faculty corrected papers. Communication between myself and the rest of the staff was limited by my knowledge of Thai. Was I in a kind of "see if he bites" phase?

Nang Rong School had grades: MS–1, MS–2 and MS–3 which I was told were roughly equivalent to 8th, 9th and 10th grades (or maybe 4th, 5th and 6th grades, I wasn't too sure about this). Student placement was not necessarily by age, but rather by subject level. The smaller students in an MS–1 class seemed very young. Attending secondary school for the first time, they wandered about in a dazed fear of doing something wrong. They arrived at the school by bike or on foot. Many came from poor families that eked out a subsistence living cultivating rice. Most of these children would not advance beyond MS–3.

Road to Nangrong.

Nangrong on the day I arrived.

Photo of my new home a few days after I arrived.

Inside my MS-1 classroom.

Local boy scouts cook their own rice.

Local children in water hole on the road to Prakhonchai.

Med techs guarded by soldiers during malaria blood tests.

Phanom Rung ruins with cobras of Kali.

Nang Rong students in costume for Loy Kratong Festival.

King Chulalungkorn Day in Nang Rong.

Weekend classes beneath my house.

Scenes from Camp Thai-Am Peter Pan play.

With Mr. Wasan (on my left) the local weatherman.

The meat section of Nangrong's market.

During training I was taught that MS–1 students were the most malleable because they had the least to "un-learn" in terms of poor English acquired from barely-trained Thai teachers. When the Ministry of Education passed a law making English a mandatory subject, the nation's school districts did not have anywhere near an adequate supply of trained teachers. However, since Thailand has a federalized system of education, teachers teach whatever they are instructed to teach, with little or no say of their own. Whatever problems they may have pronouncing English are passed directly to their students. I hoped for at least one MS–1 class of my own. Miss Charlotte had done such a fine job of convincing the headmaster that a volunteer could best be utilized handling one entire class that he offered me *all* of the MS–1 English sections – a total teaching load of 18 hours a week. I sensed an air of "Let's see how well you do with this package before we give you any more." They offered me the authority to write and administer my own tests, assign grades and even take a hand in extra-curricular activities.

I had been told that Peace Corps policy strongly advised host country schools not to simply plug volunteers into teaching slots, as if they were nothing more than members of a foreign teachers pool. The perspective had been that volunteers were available to teach *others* how to teach English by example and model.

My plan was to establish workshops for the other English teachers where I could demonstrate ways of presenting pronunciation drills, grammar and composition. Host schools may receive no more than three Peace Corps Volunteers sequentially. The premise is that three generations of volunteers should be ample opportunity to demonstrate good methodology.

The first piece of mail I received was from Scott Duncan, Peace Corps regional director for the northeast. The envelope included a voucher to use on the railroad system and a list of books I could borrow from his lending library. The attached list included such titles as: *Bamboo Building Materials, Dr. Salisbury's Poultry Disease Manual, Germs, Worms and You* and *Fifty-five Tin Can Projects.*

My first major problem emerged when Adjan Suraporn handed me a list of all my students' names – in Thai! I desperately tried to spell them out one letter at a time, but finally gave up. During training we'd only learned the most rudimentary aspects of the Thai written language, focusing almost all our time and energy on oral drills, memorization of common phrases and numerous ways in which a declarative sentence could be turned into a question. During the first few periods I let the students get used to my very existence. When I tried a few sentences on them in their own language they simply looked bewildered. Eventually, it became apparent they could follow more of what I said if I spoke to them in a kind of pidgin English. No one from the staff ever looked in to see how I was doing.

On the second day I called each quaking student up to my desk, asked them to point to their name on my roll and say their name out loud. Once they did that I transliterated each name into its English equivalent. It usually took me four or five repetitions before I came up with something in my own alphabet I could pronounce back to them closely enough so that they nodded in agreement. They *did* have interesting names: Sunee, Wisit, Bamnet, Choy, Satit, Bunchu, Tuasuk, Sangpet, Sangiap, Jaruayporn and Somchai. They also had nicknames, usually the last syllable of their full name. Jaruaypon, for example, is usually just called *Pon* by her friends. There were several boys in each class named Somchai. It must be the same as Joe.

During a break on the second day, the headmaster took me aside and said I had to go with him immediately on an important visit. Don't worry about your classes, he told me, someone would cover them. We ended up at the Office of Education for Nang Rong District where Suraporn presented me to the director, a man who spoke no English at all. With my headmaster translating, I answered that I was 26 years old, my name was Burgess Needle, yes, I could eat rice and, well, yes, I was sort of homesick.

I saw my first Thai movie. There was only one theater in town, one movie a week and most of the town seemed to appear for the event. I walked through the market with Wisai, one of my MS–3 students, and he purchased tickets for us. We stumbled over plank benches in the dim light and climbed rickety stairs to the middle section of a back row.

As long as the screen remained blank, everyone looked at me. Since the two previous Peace Corps volunteers had been women, I might have been the first white male they'd ever seen.

Suddenly, the few dim lights went out and the screen came to life and that's when I realized whatever projector they had behind us did not come equipped with sound. All the male roles in the film were spoken by a man sitting behind a microphone and all the female and children's voices were dubbed by a woman sitting next to him. Musical interludes, usually car chases, were played with 45 rpm records on a tiny phonograph. I vaguely followed the plot through images and a few lines that struck a familiar chord from training: What's your name? Where are you going? Are you hungry? Obviously, I missed the deeper themes.

The audience laughed throughout, whether people were being shot, making love or running from the law. We all sucked and chewed on salted watermelon seeds. At the end of the film we stood for the King's Anthem and I almost disabled myself by sliding on a mound of chewed-up, soggy sunflower seeds scattered down the stairs.

May 18, 1967

Prayun, a highly-respected member of the faculty, dropped by just before dark and asked if I'd like to *pai teo* [go out for fun]. Handsome as a movie star, with shiny, black hair and sensitive eyes, Prayun also spoke a modicum of English.

We bicycled through town with dogs nipping at our heels. I was still getting used to living in this rural, tropical environment where rows of tall palms lined every path, shimmering rice paddies extended toward the horizon and, except for an occasional bus or military jeep, traffic consisted of carts being pulled by water buffalos. I stared in wonder at the enormous fronds and inhaled an evening breeze that carried the scent of the open Thai landscape, a wisp of smoke from kerosene lanterns and the pungent smell of livestock. Prayun, in his spotless, starched white shirt, creased trousers and glistening hair was also a part of that scene.

A light attached to my front bumper attracted huge flying insects whose wings brushed my face as we sped along. Giant moths left a powdery reside on my eye-lids, cheeks and forehead. We stopped for Fantas and a few cookies at a tiny general store. I looked over the display of cigarettes and purchased a pack of *Sai Fon* (Falling Rain) for 30 cents. The package stated that these cigarettes were made by the Thai Tobacco Monopoly.

After circling the town, we returned to the school grounds and on to the edge of what's called *Nong Tamu*, a pond of clear water half-covered with water lilies and lotus blossoms. Sitting close to the water's edge, we sipped our drinks and stared at the last, maroon vestige of the sun as it was extinguished by some distant rice paddy. After a while, Prayun got to his feet, stretched and turned toward his bicycle.

"You are very polite," he said, "but you must study more Thai language. Many people wish to talk with you, but they are afraid."

"Why are they afraid?"

"They think if they ask you something in Thai and you do not understand, then it might make you feel foolish or sad or something and they do not want to do that."

"Thank you, Prayun, for explaining that to me."

"There are many other people in Nang Rong you do not know. You know the mayor, who is elected, but you do not know the head man, who is very wise and to whom people go for advice. You know the doctor, but you do not know the barber. Study more Thai language and many of the others will talk with you. Goodbye, I must go to my home."

The next morning I got up earlier than usual and wandered along the banks of *Nong Tamu* again. In the clear light of morning, the water was perfectly still, broken only by the light touch of skimming insects. As an emerging sun burned off the morning haze I saw dozens of butterflies slowly stretch their wings and preen themselves. I was told that there was good fishing here, but others warned me that the water was a government preserve and no fishing was allowed. I spotted the first student of the morning. He appeared painfully skinny to my eyes, but he also appeared to be enjoying himself as he followed a path along the water. He wore a white pith helmet, white short-sleeved shirt and blue shorts. Since Thais address each other with a polite "*khun*" [mister] before their first names, my students all call me Mr. Burgess. Except for the headmaster, Adjan Suraporn Khamonchai, I don't think I heard anyone's last name.

The student spotted me and cheerfully called out, "Mr. Burgess! Where you go?"

Mr. Burgess! I felt like a plantation owner. Back at the school, I walked up to the edge of my classroom doorway and nodded to my class leader. He stood at attention and yelled, "*Nakhrien, trong*!" [Class, stand!]. Once they were ready, I entered the room.

28

The first business of every class was to take attendance, but each name was a formidable obstacle. If I didn't know any better I'd swear some of the students changed their names from one day to the next. I spent a lot of time on pronunciation drills.

What *am* I doing here? How many of these students will ever have a reason or opportunity to speak English?

Meanwhile, not an hour went by, either in the teacher's lounge or in the town, where someone didn't take me aside and ask, "Do American people eat rice?"

"Yes!" I wanted to scream. "They eat rice. They can eat rice. They are eating rice even as we speak and they will eat rice forever!"

I missed my family's sandwich business and the warm cellar filled with hanging salamis, loaves of warm bread and bags of hot, fresh rolls. I missed speaking English at a normal pace. The teachers told me that no Americans ever came through Nang Rong District. Soldiers? Doubtful. I was on the edge of some barely traveled world. Buriram City, the provincial capital, was only about 40 miles away, but it seemed like a remote kingdom. I was terrified of leaving this town on a bus and never finding my way back. Three months to go before the first break.

May 20, 1967

Several radios outside played loud music: flamenco-like guitar sequence came from Cambodia; Radio Laos had a French opera going; Radio Peking broadcasts martial music as a backdrop to quotations from Chairman Mao. Most of the Thai stations beamed something that sounded remarkably like American big band sounds from the 1950s. Stations from North and South Vietnam played what sounded like soft guitar strums.

Lying in my bed, listening to the sounds of strange insects, I was aware over and over again that I was as far away from my home as I could geographically be. In Hawaii, I had my first taste of being a member of a minority, but here I was the only American, period. I knew that when I woke up the next day, before opening my eyes I'd hear roosters crowing and sense the shadow of a mosquito net hanging loosely about me. The chattering voices I'd hear outside my window would be undecipherable to me. I had put off taking formal lessons in Thai. Was I in a weird sense of denial? As much as I wanted to get here and as difficult as the training program was, it was as if my life here were a dream-state. One hour, suddenly, I would wake up and the palm trees and the ragged little girl who hauled water to my door once a week would disappear.

Shopping was a constant frustration. My limited vocabulary led me into pantomime in order to find something as simple as a can opener. Evenings, I was obsessed with fantasies of milk shakes and cheeseburgers. I bought a small, kerosene-operated burner and hoped to figure out a way to bake something with flour.

Later on Wisai, one of the local students and a kind of house boy for Preeda, stood beside me ironing clothes. Preeda didn't have an iron of his own so he loaned out Wisai to do his clothes and mine.

Sharon, the volunteer I first met when I got off the train, telegraphed me to say she would visit me tomorrow. She had been here over a year and seemed to be quite proficient in Thai. I felt inadequate enough without a fluent visitor for comparison. Still, just to be able to jabber away in English with someone would be great.

The police chief asked me to teach his men English. Is this commensurate with Peace Corps policy? I didn't want to get involved with the police or military, even though they were all quite outgoing and friendly.

I casually mentioned to Wisut, my roommate, that the local police seemed okay. He thought about that for a minute then said, "Yes, some are good. But, they are still policemen." I liked this guy. He had learned English from a previous volunteer and I was sure he'd help me fit in.

As a respected foreigner, I was treated with greater deference than ordinary citizens. Maybe the police, along with the townspeople, had yet to figure out where I was positioned in the local social register. Except for the chief, all the policemen I met were incredibly young and extremely polite. Maybe this was part of their training to look up to authority figures. I really disliked the way they kept saluting me in the marketplace. Maybe I would ask Wisut about getting them to stop.

I had lunch today in town with several teachers. They ordered a ton of food and refused to allow me to pay for anything. I couldn't imagine they ate like this on a regular basis. Did I need to be more assertive in grabbing the check?

Every dish held something wonderful: long, shallow bowls of stew, deep dishes of soup, warmed nuts, some kind of fried green leaves and a pitcher of iced tea. I kept asking them to identify the various foods.

Nothing I managed to order on my own vaguely resembled what other people ate. I keep looking for some sort of snack food to keep in my house. The headmaster served me delicious, crisp, candied-fried pork strips. What was it called? I saw a shop that had a huge platter covered with strips of meat, dotted with dozens of black flies. I asked Wisut about it and he said it was the meat the headmaster served me before frying. Oh good, at least that's *before* frying!

May 22, 1967

I found an old copy of Mad Magazine and went through it with Wisut. It had an illustrated feature called "Shadows" in which people are shown doing one action while their shadows did something quite different. One example was of a man gazing mournfully at a coffin, while his shadow kicked its heels in glee. Wisut glanced at a few segments and burst out laughing. I was relieved to find that the two of us laughed at the same thing. I heard later he shared the magazine with the other teachers.

When Preeda asked me if I liked the school lunch that day, I told him I thought it was delicious. He shook his head, smiled and asked, "Ah, but what does your shadow say?"

I showed photographs of my family to the faculty and they seemed particularly impressed with interior shots of the house. They were also extremely interested in pictures of my grandparents. Something about the image of elderly Americans intrigued them. Maybe they'd never seen any. They thought my two sisters were beautiful, although they guessed their ages to be much higher than they were.

I received a book on programmed Thai language instruction from my rep in Korat. If I studied it enough maybe I'd eventually be able to decipher the local newspapers. Reading Thai aloud was still impossible for me. There seemed to be so many rules for tone and inflection, I didn't know if I'd ever memorize them enough to actually apply them.

I heard that two volunteers from my group were being treated in Bangkok for amoebic dysentery. My own health remained good and I thought I might even start teaching PE for the fun of it.

Wisut and Preeda sat in my living room chatting. The words "kitchen," "living room" and "bedroom" were merely labels I attached to spaces in the house. Apart from the metal cot in one area there was no clear distinction between one space and another. I sent away to a California company for some rock star posters to put on my walls.

Wisut returned last night drunk as a skunk.

I managed to ask him in Thai if he was drunk and he reeled around, stared at me glassy-eyed and said, in English, "You speak Thai very smart!"

"Thank you," I said.

"You know about something…" he began, then paused as if considering his words. "You know that some teachers do not drink Mekhong?"

"Really?"

"Yes, it is true. They do not drink Mekhong or smoke or go to the… to visit the women. You know about that? The women?"

"Yes, I know about the women. So, some teachers do not do that?"

"Yes, some teachers do not do that. What do you think about that?"

"I think we can do whatever we want."

"Yes! We can do whatever we want. Good. But, some things we not talk about with other teachers because maybe not a good idea. What do you think about that?"

"I agree with that," I said.

"Good," he said. "Good answer. You are my friend. Good night. I will see you tomorrow."

A few days ago I attempted to use a black metal box a neighbor brought over that had been used by the previous volunteer as an oven. I rigged it up on wires so that it hung over a kerosene burner. It had a cheap thermostat that seemed to skip up or down 100 degrees at a time. I took a chance and tried to follow a recipe for plain white cake. It turned out okay, but created a new problem: ants! The little devils were everywhere! I tried to keep things out of their reach, but they were implacable explorers. I had to throw out much of the sugar I bought because the morning after I made the cake, ants had invaded the bags. Whenever I sat down to read they crawled up my legs. Next plan was to fill small tins of water and place one under every table leg.

I tried to explain to a few teachers what my parents did for a living, but the concept of getting by on making several hundred sandwiches every morning and delivering them to drugstores, factories and barrooms didn't seem to translate. Thinking of the family business, I ended up having dreams of all the food I've ever left on a table and nightmares of how I used to casually throw away leftovers. I thought about asking my family to fold up the tablecloth next time they finished eating and send it to me special delivery.

I was just sitting down to read late at night when I heard the sound of a heavy truck pulling up outside. A truck! I leaped to my feet, ran out the back door and stared into the night. All I could make out was a large, military-type vehicle. I could hear men speaking to each other in English.

"Hello!" I called out to them. "Hello! I'm up here."

"Hey, man," a voice answered. "Where's the chick?"

Then, they came into view—four American soldiers decked out in commando garb. I'd forgotten how big Americans can get. They seemed incredibly heavy and lumbering in their movements. Do I seem that way to the Thais?

They carefully walked up the wooden steps and entered my living room. As they cautiously leaned their rifles against the wall, they explained they'd heard rumors of a Peace Corps woman who lived in the town of Nang Rong.

"Sorry, she left about four months ago."

"Well, shit!" one of them exclaimed. "So, what you're saying is, you're it."

"Sorry, but you're right."

"Hey, don't mind him," one of the others spoke up. "He's just breaking your balls. Pretty skimpy quarters you got here."

"Yeah, pretty skimpy," I agreed.

They went on to tell me they were working as a kind of mobile advisory unit near the village of Hinkondom, close by the Cambodian border. As they took turns telling me about their activities I noticed the machetes, small knives, hand guns and coiled pieces of rope tucked into side pockets or strapped to their thighs. They wore Australian-type bush hats and one had a peacock feather dangling from the side.

I boiled water for instant coffee as we continued to chat. It was wonderful just to be able to speak English at a natural speed. They told me they'd worked on roads, bridges and some buildings in the area, but didn't speak much Thai.

"So, you guys are regular army?" I asked.

"Well, no, we're actually...[he paused to glance at the others]...Seabees!"

Were they for real? I didn't care. They unrolled a geodesic map and located their camp and said if I ever "...had a hankerin' for American food to just drop on by."

"What kind of stuff do you have?"

"All kinds of canned goods. If you can put it in a can, then we're got some."

I handed them each small cups of black coffee which they instinctively sniffed as if accustomed to being handed unknown liquids.

"Yeah, we'll be glad to share, just make sure you don't, you know, sort of sneak up on us too quietly."

They all laughed. I could just imagine what happened to people who moved in on the camp too quietly.

All this time, another man stood silently in the doorway. I gestured to him and they explained he was their translator. I noticed he kept glancing at his watch.

"So, how long you planning to live here?" one of them asked.

"I'll be teaching here at Nang Rong School for two years."

"Two fucking years in this place?" one of them stared at me incredulous. "What do you do here all the time? We've only been at the camp for three months are we are totally stir-crazy. We got a couple weeks of R & R coming up in Australia and you can bet your ass we'll be glad to get there."

"It's actually kind of nice here. I'm just beginning to understand enough of the language to get by and maybe I'll even be able to eat more after my stomach adjusts to the food."

"Yeah, man. You look like you could use a few good sit-down meals, you know what I mean? Hey! Who's that?!!"

They all immediately reached for their rifles as Wisut and Preeda casually walked in, gave a brief hello to the translator and waited to be introduced. The soldiers were awkward with them, as if they were potential enemies. Wisut and Preeda, in turn, were more than a little stiff in their presence. I could easily see why Peace Corps told us not to associate with military or police any more than we had to. I didn't give that warning a thought when I heard them speaking English. Loneliness easily trumped policy. I only saw them as fellow Americans.

Only a few minutes after everyone had been introduced to everyone else, the soldiers stretched, picked up their rifles and headed for the door. I followed them down the stairs to their vehicle, which still had its auxiliary lights on. I could see some lettering stenciled on the side. Breaking it down syllable by syllable, it read: *EEN LAKE FLEEN*

I asked the interpreter what it meant in English.

"That not Thai, that English," he said.

English? I repeated the syllables over and over. Suddenly, it dawned on me, "In like Flynn!"

I said the words out loud and the soldiers laughed.

"Do you know what it means?" I asked the translator.

"They tell me, but I cannot say. I think it impolite."

He stared at the ground, obviously embarrassed.

Suddenly, it dawned on me that the words *in like Flynn* didn't just mean 'You've got it made!'

"Thank you for visiting me," I said in Thai, and a magnificent smile appeared on his face. He saluted me and got in with the soldiers who quickly turned on their high-beam lights, backed up until they were on the road, and roared off into the night. A piece of my America had just passed through.

May 23, 1967

I biked over to the market to buy a notebook and ended up in a restaurant watching the local world pass. People walked by who who waved in my direction. Little children ran out into the street to catch a glimpse of me. I sat there for close to an hour smoking and staring at the cracked, wooden sidewalk, the general merchandise store across the street with kerosene lanterns hanging in the window, the dirt street fairly dry now but contributing to a light red haze that perpetually hung over the area and the occasional water buffalo hauling a wooden cart.

Wonderful, warm showers arrived sporadically. The longer I sat at my table, the more black flies buzzed me and several dogs of a type that usually inspire nightmares kept trying to curl up at my feet. They all had extensive mange, puss-dripping eyes and froth at the mouth. The town crier strolled by and hit a heavy, metal gong four times.

I had grown accustomed to what little of the local food I knew how to order, but I was still uneasy about having chicken soup for breakfast. It seemed like everything I was eating recently was very bland. Were the cooks watching out for me or did I just happen to order bland food? Soon after the gong man passed, I stubbed out my cigarette, stretched and headed for home.

Wisai came by later in the evening. He claimed to be 17, but had the appearance of a junior high student. Miss Charlotte must have worked with him quite a bit since he spoke English very well. His diction was extremely slow, but also remarkably clear. All our conversations so far were about food, the heat and whether I was still homesick. He was extraordinarily polite and deferential.

Shortly after Wisai left, the mosquitoes arrived. It was quite hot inside the house, but even hotter outside. I was afraid if I opened the wooden shutters to let in a little breeze, more insects would join me. Anything with wings in this neck of the woods seemed to like my blood.

Later, Wisai went shopping for me and brought back a bag of very roughly-textured sugar, two cans of evaporated milk and six duck eggs. I tried out the oven again and managed to make a fairly edible cake. But I could not figure out why the frosting didn't harden. Could it be the heat?

After I put everything away, I showed Wisai how to play dominos. He really got into the game and I pondered the irony of playing a game called 'dominos' in a country that is described as a domino itself.

Most of the Thais I spoke with seemed not to take a political stand, but I wasn't sure if they were being polite or unwilling to say anything until they knew me better. The maps they used in social studies classes emphasized southeast Asia with a very prominent Thailand usually colored red.

Everyone referred to me as *farang,* though not to my face. I'm not sure if there is an exact equivalent to *farang* in other languages. I was called a *haole* in Hawaii, but I think that only refers to Caucasians.

When I returned home last night I took a corner on the wrong side of the road and smashed into Wisai. My enormous bike was barely dusted, but Wisai's sustained major damage. I had to keep reminding myself to drive on the left and look to the right before crossing streets. Over his not-too-strenuous objections, I forced 40 baht into his hand and told him to let me know if his bike cost more to fix.

May 24, 1967

Buriram is a poor cousin to the surrounding provinces, ranking lowest in per capita income. Nang Rong, is the richest district in Buriram Province due its fertile land, available water and central location on the local highway network. While cities like Korat got the troops and heavy capital investment required to feed, clothe, shelter and entertain them, towns like Nang Rong went along pretty much as they had for generations. Even though Buriram had a rail line and train station, Nang Rong would soon have improved roads leading straight to Korat and Surin. Perhaps the ease of access to other markets would bring future prosperity to the citizens of Nang Rong.

I brought home a large wall map of Thailand and found where other members of my group were located. None were within easy traveling distance. My friend Roger was in Wapipatum which, on the map, seemed only inches away, but when I asked teachers how to get there they all began with, "First you go to Bangkok…" Seemed that all the rail lines ran north-south and there were no connecting roads running east-west between Buriram and Wapipatum.

Sharon, the volunteer from the Girls School in Buriram, along with Ralph, a poultry and swine expert, and Jack, who knew about civil engineering, came by for a visit. I found Sharon's stories about teaching English as a foreign language reassuring. Ralph talked about becoming fluent in Thai at the same time he introduced innovative swine-raising techniques to local farmers. Jack, who struck me as being as fluent in Thai as in English, described his working relationships with his host road engineers and how his advice contributed to local roads becoming better graded, less likely to develop potholes and angled in such a way so that water run-off during the rainy season kept them more navigable. After they left, I felt terribly depressed about my mundane role here and the half-assed job I felt I was doing.

A few days later, I decided to swallow my fear about never finding the town again, and took a bus to Buriram. Once again, a monk sat beside me, but he was far less communicative. He expressed no interest in my cigarettes.

The open-air converted Fargo truck that passed for a bus, bounced over hardened ruts with colored pennants flying in the wind. I thought of Rimbaud's poem where he linked every vowel with a color—"Vowels: A black, E white, I red, U green, O blue…" The colors that flashed by me seemed more vivid than in any previous experience: the black tires of the bus rolled me into the unknown, stray white puffs of clouds above so incongruous in this dry heat, red metal decorations cut to resemble animals from the Ramayana clung riveted to the wood just below my hanging right arm, a green blur of gigantic banana fronds and the stark omega-blue of the sky that chilled me even in the 100 degree heat. Rimbaud referred to "The Omega – the ray of violet in One's eyes." But to me, feeling alien and afraid, the entire blue horizon seemed part of God's own iris.

I stayed the night at Jack's, talking with him until early morning, playing chess and exchanging science-fiction stories. He struck me as totally dedicated and happily surprised at how well the Thais accepted and liked him. I had a sense he envisioned himself back in the States as a far more ordinary citizen than the unique and desired person he was here. He had no plans to return. We shared a breakfast of scrambled duck eggs and chopped pork pieces over a mound of white rice flavored with peppery fish sauce instead of salt. I envied him the obvious status he enjoyed as he nodded to various men who stopped to salute him. Would I ever get to feel the easy comfort he exuded in the restaurant before my two years were up? He waved me off from the bus station with a casual hand as my bus bounced back over the same road, returning me to Amphur Nang Rong.

Someone from the Jeem-Jeem [Smile-Smile] Restaurant sent a young child over every evening with a meal that usually included fried rice and fish sauce. Someone must have told the school staff how boring my food was, because I suddenly began to get pieces of meat or fish with the rice.

I found myself looking forward to being home alone with a paperback in English. Preeda dropped by and when I complained about being hot and thirsty but tired of Fanta soft drinks, he sent a student up a nearby coconut tree. I was astonished at the child's skill and with what alacrity he scampered up the tree to dislodge a few coconuts. Squatting beside me he casually used a small machete on the dark-green fruit, cutting away the stem and making a neat opening clear through to the delicious liquid and delicately-flavored meat inside. I thought I had tasted coconut before, but it had obviously been some cheap imitation.

I found out that another volunteer from my group had given up and went home early. We started with 61 trainees in Hawaii, and we are now down to 43 teachers, four secretaries and two nurses. Will I be here for the full two years? I'm beginning to think I will.

....

May 27, 1967

Wisut came by at 5:30 to take me to the morning market as he'd promised, but I felt too groggy and sick to go. He promised to bring back some food for me from the market.

Smiling, as if I'd just complimented him on something, Wisut said, "Never mind. We'll go another time." I didn't want him to think I wasn't interested in going to the market in his company, but there was simply no way I could have found the energy. Roosters crowed outside and I couldn't fall back asleep. The air felt fetid and sticky even this early, making it hard for me to guess if I also had a fever. A student appeared with duck eggs, sugar and fried rice. I thanked him then forced myself up and managed to make a small cake in the steel box over the kerosene burner. Once again, I was unable to get the frosting to peak.

By noon, it was much hotter. Fleas and mosquitoes hopped all over me and ants had invaded everything. The fried rice felt like a lead ball in my stomach and my head felt on fire with fever. I staggered to a kitchen window, flung the wood shutters open and threw the rice out. It immediately attracted a pack of mangy dogs who fought over every grain.

Despite my illness I couldn't help but notice how fresh and clear it was outside. Outside my kitchen window all was green, green and more green. Radios blared from nearby houses: Cambodian news reports, Mamas and the Papas and Chairman Mao. I knew I should start on my weekly lesson plan and memorize my students' names, but it was too hot inside, so I headed for the shade beneath my house. Time to find a student nimble enough to bring down some more coconuts.

May 28, 1967

I fell into a deep sleep last night only to continually wake up with agonizing stomach cramps. By morning's rooster crow I'd already vomited three times out a window, but when I peeked down later there was nothing to be seen. Dogs? I was too dizzy to stand for more than a few minutes. Wisai came with the usual rice and soup, but this time the soup seemed greasy and unappetizing. I threw it out the window the minute he left. My temperature was around 102 and every bone in my body ached. I checked my medical sheet for an illness that fit my symptoms and a few of them, such as something called dengue fever, came from mosquito bites. Well, that certainly seemed possible. There were millions of dead insects lying inside and outside the house. I had dusted the entire area with DDT. After a sweat-drenched nap I tried to eat again, but couldn't swallow, then had the dry heaves. Wisai returned with a large bowl of freshly-made chicken broth. I tried a spoonful, and gagged. Could I have poisoned myself with DDT? I might as well stop all the dusting since there are a billion more insects waiting to replenish the ranks of the dead.

A butterfly sailed in through my bedroom window and settled on a few drops of honey on my desk. A friend in Boston asked if I could send her a few Thai butterflies for her collection, so I trapped this one under an empty water glass. Wisut, who dropped by to try and get me to nibble on some sweets, managed to get me laughing with stories about the school. Then, he noticed the orange and black winged butterfly fanning itself against the smooth sides of the glass.

"Some people say that when you allow a bird or an animal its freedom you receive good luck for your next life. Do you know about that?" he asked me.

I shook my head.

"Some people say," he went on, "that if you do a good thing when you are sick, then you must feel better soon. Do you know about that?"

"No," I croaked. "I didn't know about that."

He shrugged and left me alone with the greasy soup and a dying butterfly.

I remembered reading about the vendors in Bangkok's Lumpini Park who have dozens of small birds packed in wicker cages that they will release for a small sum. People regularly pass by to pay a few baht for a bird to be freed and by that action to gain a bit of merit for the next life.

I rolled over on my side, reached out and tipped the glass on to its side. The butterfly fluttered in place for another moment then slowly sailed out the window. I fell back, exhausted, and stared at the ceiling. What had I just done? Was that my first step toward enlightenment?

I continued to sweat from every pore. Even the soles of my feet were wet. My hands shook when I tried to hold them in front of my face. My mattress and linens were soaked and stank. Two more aspirin didn't seem to do anything. Later, as I stared up at the ceiling, I heard someone giggling under my house. When I peered out the window I saw three girls in blue skirts, white blouses and pith helmets staring up at me. I can't imagine what I looked like, but they bolted when they saw me. I felt tired, worn out and old.

May 29, 1967

I woke this morning with a vague sense of having had a lengthy, horrible dream, but no specific memories. Then, it hit me: I didn't feel sick. My temperature was back to normal. When Wisut came by with a cup of Ovaltine, two soft-boiled eggs and *patongos* (deep-fried dough, like donuts) I ate it all. We talked for a few minutes and Wisut commented on how much better I looked since I'd released the butterfly. Suddenly, severe cramps returned. Several polymagma tablets didn't help. Wisut left and Wisai arrived with my regular breakfast of rice and soup. When I was alone, I threw it all out the window. The dogs looked much healthier since I arrived.

Back on my bed, I tried the radio. Nothing. I must have lost at least 10 or 15 pounds just in the past week. There were wrinkles on my stomach as if I'd just given birth. Outside, I heard the students reciting their lessons. Dozens of birds were in the mango trees twittering. My bedroom and kitchen were littered with paper, rags and scraps of food. There was no more DDT.

I received a letter from my sister Clare expressing concern about my northeast location. She'd done some reading about the ancient enmity between Thailand and Cambodia. However, this hostility has gone on for so long the locals take it for granted. If calling wandering bands of outlaws 'Communists' gets more federal aid, then that's what the locals call them. Seemed as if buffalo thieves and Communists all fell under the same generic umbrella.

The few local reports of actual fighting I've heard of originated in the small village of Lahansai, about ten 10 miles east of Nang Rong. Teachers told me the federal government was convinced there are were both Cambodian insurgents and Communist infiltrators scouting the area. Living conditions in Lahansai were were so poor I didn't doubt that the locals were willing to align themselves with any force offering a change in the status quo. While most Thais base their diet on rice, the people of Lahansai have to supplement their meals with surplus ground corn from the United States. They hate the texture and taste of this imported *meal.* Wisut said the soil lacks many of the trace minerals and organic compounds necessary for growing anything but guava and banana trees. Some government agricultural specialists appeared at irregular intervals, but they only treated the symptoms – i.e. telling the farmers what the local soil needed. Bangkok needed to send much more federal aid so to complete irrigation projects and provide subsidized fertilizers. The per capita income was very low. Farmers in Lahansai never have had good years; they only have subsistence years and starvation years.

Although I was beginning to enjoy my status as a teacher, I was still *not* accustomed to using students as errand boys. The rest of the teachers thought nothing of sending a student here or there to buy personal items or deliver messages. I tried to give Wisai change after he brought back a soft drink for me from the market. He cried when I made the gesture.

Students who arrived late to my class waited in the doorway until I noticed them, then bowed low before entering the room. Children everywhere in town lept to their feet and stood at attention when I rode by on my bicycle. I asked the headmaster's permission to leave school to mail a letter, but he looked at me as if I was insane. He shouted for a student to come over and told *him* to mail the letter. If Wisut heard that there was not enough water in my barrel, he called out to any passing student to bring tins of water to the house. A water girl filled six used kerosene cans from the well and hauled them half a mile to the house for two bath. That service costed 10 cents!

So what did I spend money on beside the barest of essentials? The sole commercial outlets for entertainment, besides drinking or visiting the red light district, were one new movie a week at the local theater or sitting in the middle of the municipal field with the other peasants to chew fried bananas and watch re-runs of Japanese commercials. The only English language reading material I found was a stack of Mad Magazines and Reader's Digests. I could take a *samlaw* ride across town for 15 cents, but the seats were made for skinnier butts than mine and there were no shock absorbers to smooth over the ruts. I waited for a long-promised paperback booklocker that Peace Corps gave all volunteers. I had almost nothing left in my medical kit. Nothing remotely connected to digestive problems was left.

Before I became sick, Wisut took me to a small party where a woman read my future with a deck of cards. She told me I'd have many girl friends, but would not marry until late in life. The men cheered and the women laughed. I was relieved to hear nothing about a premature death.

Like oxygen molecules, the ants were everywhere. I put all my sugar and flour in small plastic bags and hung them from the ceiling. In the morning, I found ants crawling up the walls, across the ceiling and down the strings like tiny firemen. Even with the shutters closed, mosquitoes slipped in. The floors and walls were slippery with squashed bugs. The outside paint on the house was turning gray from some sort of insidious mold. Apparently, some local fungus attacked the oil-based paint.

It took about two hours for me to do my own laundry, primarily to rinse out the suds. Maybe Wisut could find someone from the market who could do this for me.

I wished there were another volunteer near by.

May 30, 1967

The lilacs must have beeen out by now in Boston. Everything was green and blooming *here* all the time. I sure didn't yearn for snow, but this lushness was beginning to get on my nerves. Sometimes I sat in the shade beneath my house, stared out at the flora and wondered when it all got a chance to rest. A good percentage of my daily food was green. Soon, perhaps, like some creature from a Marvel Comic, I would begin to turn green myself.

This evening, the rains arrived and cool winds prevailed. The teachers warned me about their idea of a cold season. After changing their dire predictions from Centigrade to Fahrenheit I estimated it might get as low as 65 F. Maybe by the time it happened 65 *would* seem like freezing to me.

I decided to share a few of my homemade cakes with other teachers and they loved them! They all asked for a second piece.

My monthly living allowance hadn't arrived yet, but if I had any left over at the end of June maybe I would open a savings account. Everything went through the post office, but Wisut promised me Nang Rong would soon have its own bank.

I discovered another local restaurant delicacy similar to the delicious roast pork leg I had the first day I arrived; it's pig leg soup. I admit although I loved the taste of the soup, I still gagged slightly at bristles on the skin.

Looking back at my journal notes I realized I never mentioned or explained how it was that I ended up with Wisut as my roommate. What happened was my headmaster kept asking me if I was comfortable living alone. He occasionally varied the wording so that one day it was, "Mr. Burgess, are you very lonely in your home?" The next day He might ask, "Mr. Burgess, would you like to have someone live with you?" I was dimly aware that Thai culture viewed living alone as a form of punishment and I began to factor that awareness into the significance of the headmaster's constant questions. After the fourth or fifth time he queried me, I admitted I wouldn't mind having someone live with me. The next day (!) Wisut showed up with all his personal belongings. I was delighted. If I'd only known who It was the headmaster had in mind, I would've acquiesced in a second.

Although my first few classes this morning went fairly well, I was suddenly hit with cramps and had to go home and curl up on my bed. I thought I had gotten much thinner than when I arrived, but there was no scale to prove it, only the loose skin on my stomach.

Rumors in the teacher's lounge said Nang Rong might soon have electricity 24 hours a day. It was lights out at 10:00 PM But, even before that, the amperage was extremely erratic and my light bulbs suddenly went from bright to a barely perceptible red glow. Good thing no one was plugging in any appliances.

This afternoon the roosters crowed, the birds in the mango tree trilled their little heads off and children yelled back and forth on their way home from school. A young lady from the restaurant delivered an enamel container of food. She said the teachers at the school were worried about me so they chipped in to get me some soup. After I thanked her, she said, "Well, you can't speak too much Thai now, but Khun Charlotte learned to speak and you will, too."

First optimistic words I'd heard in a while.

June 1, 1967

It was very hot from early morning on and I spent most of it under my house nibbling coconut meat and sipping Ovaltine. I never once dreamed I'd drink Ovaltine again and here I was in northeast Thailand not only taking it in, but thinking, "Hey, not bad!" Many Thais have it for breakfast along with six teaspoons of sugar and a healthy dollop of sweetened evaporated milk. Almost the entire day went by without a cramp or a dry-heave, and I remained hungry. It was time to increase my food vocabulary.

A letter arrived from my parents warning me of a cholera epidemic they'd read about in the New York Times. Coincidentally, a federal inoculation team came through here a few days ago. I'd already been inoculated by Peace Corps doctors and been told to make sure no one from any of these traveling teams inoculated me. Seems their not-quite-perfect sanitation methods could lead to hepatitis.

My mother ended her letter by reminding me to always boil the water before drinking. Great. If I could only figure out a way to boil the ice before I put it in my soft drinks I'd be all set.

June 2, 1967

When I rode my bike through town this morning I suddenly realized it was beginning to look familiar! The idea that I'd be living here for the next 22 months no longer filled me with anxiety, fear and depression. A few people waved in my direction and I realized I *knew* them. I felt strangely reassured. There was such a stillness to an up-country Thai village, a kind of inner tranquility quite new to me. I felt a wonderful comfort as I took in the scent of every breeze: fresh vegetables and smoked fish from the morning market, the slight humidity and sweetness from the rice paddies, and lotus blossoms and acrid red clay dust from the main road.

By 10:00 this morning Wisut had finished moving in. This was the culmination of a continuous flow of small packages and roughly strung together cardboard boxes delivered over the past several days. As my new roommate sat in his room listening to a tape recording of the previous volunteer's voice, I wondered if I would ever escape the ghost of Ms. Charlotte. It was strange to hear her voice careening off the walls, a kind of drone against the staccato rhythm of the insects. Outside, a gentle wind brought a hint of coolness from the north. The mango tree out front lost a few leaves, the school's janitor picked some thyme from my back yard, three small birds were trapped briefly in my room before they found an open shutter, a small lizard fell on my head while I was reading this afternoon and made me spill tea on the desk, and the blue, clear sky over Nang Rong was warm and friendly.

Wisut took me to visit his uncle, nicknamed Pon, who came out to greet and inspect me. We stared at each other for a few minutes. He was tall and heavy-set for a Thai with skin coloring a bit darker than most of the teachers. Perhaps some distant ancestor had marched with the ancient Khmers. His eyes had the same rheumy cast as the headmaster's, but Pon's hair was pure white, a rarity in these parts, and cut in a ragged crewcut. His legs were massive, gnarled with heavy blue veins and bulging calf muscles above large feet that rested flatly on the fine sand. His toe nails were thick, dark and cracked, while his swollen ankles seemed appropriate for someone who had wielded authority for more years than I have memories.

He stood still as if waiting for me to act, so I pressed my palms together before my face in a formal *wai*. In Thai culture, the higher up the *wai* the higher sign of respect. I tried to place my hands at a level worthy of a mayor, but slightly below that of a provincial governor. His immediate response was a *wai* even higher than my own – his idea of a joke. Wisut giggled. Pon burst into a hearty belly-laugh and threw his arms about me in a tight bear hug. His skin felt like smooth leather. With a gruff shout he threw me off and held me at arm's length. I started to say something to Wisut when Pon reached out and captured my hand in a crushing grip and began pumping it up and down, hoarsely repeating the words, "America... *dee maak*! [America is very good!]".

He repeated this several times and only stopped when I broke in to say the same thing about Thailand. He laughed, slapped me on the back hard enough to shake a few vertebrae loose and turned to Wisut for help in translating.

After Wisut helped me with a brief dialogue about homesickness and Thai food, he left to pick up packages from the bus station.

Left alone with Pon and his wife, I could only mumble idiotic phrases that left him staring at me in gracious pity. His wife settled herself back into a comfortable corner and stuffed a few more betel leaves in her mouth. She was a large woman with three or four red-stained teeth showing through betel-stained gums and lips. Her body swayed easily against a loose blouse that sallied casually over her *pasin* (a traditional Thai dress or skirt that's basically a band of cotton cloth wrapped neatly just below the arm pits).

Pon's house was large and airy with the same random plan as the headmaster's. Rooms attached to other rooms jut outside and back. A porch slanted toward a dusty road. Just as I leaned back to see what else was on the road, a young girl came through the doorway and, in that incredibly graceful way Thais have of crouching low when passing between others or presenting a gift, she held out a tray of freshly plucked bananas. Pon and I sat on woven mats across from each other, he in a comfortable lotus position and I with my stiff knees protruding up and out.

The Thai language was a jumble in my head and phrases leaped up only to be drowned by French sentences, which in turn became confused with fragments of Hebrew.

"America bomb Vietnam," he told me in clear English.

I stiffened, expecting an anti-American tirade.

"Good!" he exclaimed. "Kill communists... Vietnam people [a slur of Thai words]... Cambodian people *mai dee* [no good]," he finished, satisfied he'd made his point.

I told him the bananas were delicious. He cocked his head and I repeated again, in Thai, how much I liked Thai bananas. He chuckled and nodded. I could tell it was evident to him that the United States had sent a moron to his country. If only I knew the Thai words for "imperialism" or "balance of power."

Thankfully, Wisut re-appeared and began translating again.

"Uncle asks if you know what Thai people say to each other when they meet?"

"No," I shook my head. "I don't."

Once again Wisut translated.

"He said because our country has been attacked many times and because there have been many wars Thai people have to keep moving. So, now, when we meet we always ask, "Where are you going?"

I nodded.

"The Chinese," he continued, "are always hungry. They are always thinking about food. So, when the Chinese people meet each other they always ask, "Have you had rice, yet?" What do Americans say when they meet each other?"

After Wisut explained the question, I replied, "We say, 'How are you?'"

He looked at me, puzzled.

"Why do they ask that? Is there much sickness in America?"

"No," I said. "I think it is just being polite."

He was obviously puzzled, but let it drop.

Wisut returned and diverted Pon's attention with one joke or another. They spoke at length about the high cultural qualities of Thais as opposed to the negative aspects of Vietnamese (too warlike), Laotians (viewed as bargain-basement Thais), Cambodians (stupid) and Burmese (cheaters who want to steal Thai land). The feuding between Thailand and these countries has been going on for hundreds of years and dovetailed neatly in the context of the Vietnam War. Pon spoke in one breath of buffalo thieves who slip across the border from Cambodia and in the other of dropping H-bombs on the whole country.

Foreign affairs were eventually dropped in favor of food: Thai, European and American.

"Can you eat rice?" he asked me.

"Yes, I like rice."

"You are very smart."

"Thank you. I like bananas, too."

"He told me that already," Pon said, looking over at Wisut. "Why does he keep telling me he likes bananas? Are they unknown in his country?"

"I don't know," Wisut told him.

Meanwhile, we gorged on more bananas. When the bananas were gone, bottles of Mekhong whiskey were brought in. Nice, warm whiskey served neat in small porcelain cups. After a dozen refills I noticed the scratches on the teak floor resembled clever sketches of famous Hollywood personalities.

"Look," I said to Wisut, "there's Bob Hope."

Wisut got up and said some pleasantry about what a nice time we had, but it was time to go home. Click! His words reminded me of a pattern of sentences we had to memorize during training that had to do with saying goodbye at social functions. Before I knew what I was doing, I blurted out a formal response for taking departure with the intent of meeting again soon.

They both stared at me in shock.

"How do you know about saying that?" Wisut asked.

"He can speak Thai after all," Pon murmured.

I shrugged. What else could I say? That I didn't even know exactly what I had just said? That I was like some trained seal squeezing the proper horns on cue?

"You are very smart," Pon repeated.

I bowed to him and I carefully backed away. As I turned to go out the door, he called out my name. I looked around to see that he was reaching out to me with something in his hand.

"Here," he said, "take some bananas."

The teachers have been overly conscious whenever I fail to smile. Even a neutral expression causes them to frown and ask if I'm homesick, girl sick or just sick. As I discovered during Peace Corps training, Thai people are extremely empathetic, sometimes to the point of feeling someone else's pain when there's no pain to begin with.

When Wisut and I returned to the house we exchanged life stories. He was originally from southern Thailand, but grew up in Bangkok where the rest of his family lived. His father, who was Chinese, died at an early age of hard work, hard drink and too many cigarettes. Wisut maintained that no one else in his family drank or smoked, but (with a laugh) he pointed to himself and admitted he might be making up for the rest of them.

Although he hadn't sampled much Western food, his tastes were different from that of the typical Nang Rong citizen. He missed fresh saltwater fish, fried shrimp and dishes made with kelp. He ended up in Nang Rong after taking the national teacher's exam in Bangkok and then being assigned here. He said he'd barely heard of Buriram, never mind Nang Rong, and at first refused to go. His mother convinced him to take whatever was offered. He countered by telling her he was considering the police academy. She reminded him of police brutality against his father's family. So, that was that. He moved to Nang Rong.

After three years in Nang Rong, Wisut said he'd become accustomed to the demands and pace of life in a small northeast Thai village and had no plans to leave. The school certainly made full use of his talents. He's fixed broken machinery, constructed art projects and worked with the headmaster on blueprints for future building plans.

His English was fairly basic, but nowhere near as limited as my Thai. We continued to amaze ourselves by the creative range of our communicative efforts.

The school was scheduled to have a *Wai Khru* (Honor the Teachers) ceremony on Thursday, where the faculty sits before the student body, who sing their praises and present them with gifts. Wisut explained that this was done annually (as is another ceremony that honors the students) and that he eagerly looked forward to Thursday.

"Do you think you will receive many gifts?" I asked.

"Only one big one," he replied.

"What's that?"

"On that day I will not have to work."

We laughed together like small kids sharing a secret.

Wisut made about 900 baht a month as compared to my own 1,400 (the exchange rate was 20 baht to the dollar). He didn't have a university degree, but if he did our salaries would be comparable.

After several weeks of Thai food I am down to about 150 pounds, from my normal 175. Wisut, on the other hand, was about five feet tall and weighed something less than 100 pounds. His complexion was absolutely smooth and clear. His coloring, possibly because of his half-Chinese parentage, was lighter than that of many Thais even in Bangkok and certainly fairer than Thais who have Cambodian blood somewhere in their lineage.

Wisut loved to talk, joke, gossip, sing and entertain, whether in Thai, English, Chinese or even scraps of Cambodian.

At first, the two of us kept the house immaculate. Then, a shirt was left here, a book left there, dirty laundry began to pile up in corners and dirty dishes stacked up in the kitchen. Truthfully, we began to know each other for the slobs we were.

Mosquitoes again invaded the house and there was a constant buzz in my ears as I sat still trying not to think about the newest addition to our household.

I first heard him/her/it one evening in the form of a sudden shriek in the middle of the night that yanked me awake with a pounding pulse. The initial burst of sound was followed by a slightly lower echo of the first and then another and another until it finally faded away in descending volume. I asked Wisut the following morning what made that sound. Some sort of bird? Not bothering to look up from his book, he nodded and said, yes, that's what it must be.

Then, just last night when we returned home late from the market and stepped through the door, I turned quickly in the dark and clicked on the lights. There was a loud scratching sound above my head. We both looked up to see an immense lizard, a sort of small *dragon* with lumpy skin, mottled green and brown coloring, scurrying swiftly across the ceiling, upside down, pushing its foot through a hole in the ceiling that led to… the bathroom.

"What the hell was that?"

"Oho!" he cried. "Now, we have good luck! That is a *dookeh*! It makes a noise like… DOOKEH… DOOookeh…Dooookeh…you know? Like that."

He made a perfect imitation of the sound I'd heard during the night. Great, I thought. Now, every time I use the bathroom I will know with certainty that a dookeh will be looking down on me.

Wisut explained that the silver lining to having a dookeh live with us is that if its air bladder is full enough to make its inimitable sound more than eight times in a row, then good luck is sure to follow. The problem is that by the time I woke up I didn't know how many "dookehs" were already sounded. And so, I pictured myself waking with a start at an explosion of sound, only to mentally focus on the number of "dookehs" I heard.

As I pondered this situation, Wisut walked around the house picking up his things and mine, examining them briefly, then placing them back down. Music from The King and I was playing. The movie is banned here because of liberties taken with the dramatization of King Mongkut (played by Yul Brynner). Wisut liked the music.

King Mongkut's reign was contemporaneous with that of Abraham Lincoln. There is a record of their correspondence at the Smithsonian. Apparently, when the king heard of Lincoln's problems with the southern states, he felt great empathy, saying something to the effect that he, too, had always had problems with his southern provinces. After thinking it over, the king offered Lincoln some warrior elephants to help the Union Army turn the tide of battle. The offer was politely refused on grounds of inclement weather and scarcity of proper forage.

I finally looked up *dookeh* in my *Mary Haas Thai-English Dictionary* and discovered that it translates as "gecko."

With Wisut's help I began to use longer Thai phrases in the market. This evening while we were in town, a woman stopped to ask Wisut some questions. I was happy to realize I actually kept up with most of what she was saying, until I suddenly grasped that she *wanted* me to understand and was intentionally speaking slowly with a small vocabulary. Oh well, I still felt pretty good about it.

June 4, 1967

I was calmly sitting in my living room with an old, rayon bedspread wrapped around my lower body, wondering what to do with my time. I followed a teaching schedule, but I was sure I wasn't living up to Peace Corps expectations.

There was a slight breeze from the east and the sky was barely overcast. The air was warm and not too humid. Fronds of large green palms and coconut trees made a hissing sound as they rubbed against each other. My laundry, recently hung to dry, occasionally gave a sharp "snap." Now and then, the haze broke to allow a ray of sunlight to settle on some small shrub or spice plant, giving it a faint aura. Several hundred feet from me, students played ping pong and the nick-nock of the plastic ball was like the ticking of a grandfather clock set in an enormous greenhouse.

Bicyclists pedaled along the path by my house. The jingle of their bells caused a flock of birds pecking at the rice I threw out my window to scurry back and forth, rise a few feet before settling back to the grim task of staying alive.

Staying alive was a grim task for all fauna in this region. Dogs, especially, had it rough. Most of them suffered from mange and were covered with scabs. I could see one panting in the shade of a mango tree. It was a favorite tree for local dogs. There were usually one or two feeble beasts rubbing against the bark in a vain attempt to rid their sore hides of fleas and ticks that would certainly follow them to death. Bad as the dogs had it, at least they were still here, which is more than could be said of cats. I thought that was strange, thinking, as I was, of Siamese cats. I hadn't seen any cats since I left Bangkok. One of the teachers told me that the World Health Organization delivered tons of DDT to kill mosquitoes and halt the spread of malaria, but after massive spraying and dusting all the cats crept off to die. They'd rubbed against DDT tainted walls, licked themselves clean and perished. The same almost happened to the valuable silk worms, but someone must have finally connected the dots and DDT sprayers were more carefully trained.

Construction on a nearby temple was slow and the hammer beats were so infrequent each one caused me to sit up and look around. The sound of wind chimes and Pali prayers, faintly audible, lapped at the edge of my consciousness.

The wooden shutters of my house had broken loose from their clasps and slammed, in no discernible rhythm, against the side walls.

Wisut woke me this morning at 6:00 and we walked over to the market. It was my first visit to the kind of active commerce typical for a small, Thai village. As I started to ask Wisut when we would reach it, I was suddenly aware that portions of the market had already erupted around me. Women from outlying hamlets were in town to do their daily shopping. Among the stalls, I saw several girls from my classes selling vegetables, duck eggs and small pastries. Large blocks of ice with pieces of straw sticking to them were stacked here and there keeping some items cool. Because electrical power only ran about 10 hours a day, no one had a refrigerator and shopping for food was a daily event. The duck eggs were always fresh and a myriad of stands had dainty desserts wrapped in banana leaves sealed with wooden slivers. I saw noodles, crisp fried crullers called *pa thong go,* coconuts and coconut drinks, slabs of beef, pig heads that stared out at oblivion, piles of new and used clothing, trays of fake jewelry, cap pistols – and throngs of people. Everyone was haggling, cajoling, straining to finish their business before the final tolling of the temple gong and the last name of God was uttered.

I loomed over the vendors like some awkward Gulliver. Wisut and I drank coffee and nibbled *pa thong go* in a small restaurant that opened out to the street. We watched the people mingle, break off into eddies by exits and finally flow on to the street.

At the rear of the restaurant, farmers sat hunched over cracked tables, fondling their morning start of Mekhong whiskey, and, with their gnarled hands folding and unfolding, they discussed the events of their world.

We strolled back to the house for a more satisfying breakfast of fried duck eggs and Ovaltine. Then, it was time for laundry. We piled our dirty clothes into a tub and trudged over to the well. Wisut carried a steel bucket and long lines of nylon rope, while I carried the wash tub, clothes and a box of detergent.

Wisut attached the rope to the bucket, dropped it down the well, then hauled it back up with a long-handled pole. Straining with effort, he brought up one bucketful after another, then poured the water into the basin. We pounded and soaked the clothes then ran them through clear water again and again until the bubbles ran in a frenzy about our feet and the clothes were clean. It struck me that every time my family ran a load of laundry back in Boston the machine probably generated more water than Wisut and I would have hauled in several days. We walked back to the house to take down the dry wash from the lines and put up the wet.

Later, we cleared a few square yards of ground behind the house for a badminton court. Our neighbors came out to watch the *farang* hit the ground with a sharp-edged hoe as if he knew what he was doing. Tired after only an hour, we knocked down some coconuts and cut off the ends with a machete. The inside liquid was cool and sweet. I slipped back into the house and fell asleep under my mosquito net. The sounds of Nang Rong Village lulled me away. When I awoke, I had a meal of chicken stew, Ovaltine, more *pa thong go* and two slices of the cake Wisut and I baked last night. The frosting still wasn't coming out right. I threw the remainder of the meal out the window and the dogs came crawling over to fight and bark over it.

I found out a few days ago that all teachers are required to stay in the school buildings as long as classes are in session. I had been leaving whenever I had free time. Wisut told me the headmaster didn't want to say anything to the foreigner who had traveled 12,000 miles to teach at his school. Still, I had an idea Wisut didn't bring this to my attention spontaneously.

A word I heard every day was *diyo...diyo...* It translates as "...soon...I'll get it done soon." That's how I felt about organizing an English Club and taking Thai language lessons with Prayun.

June 6, 1967

Radio Peking just claimed "... an attack has been made by the imperialist forces of Great Britain, the United States and its running dog, Israel, against the forces of the United Arab Republic ... many Israeli planes attacked Cairo and were shot out of the sky while the Egyptian army is making wide gains on the ground sweeping ahead with the armed forces of Jordan and Syria ... killing many Israeli troops and bombing Tel Aviv."

After 20 minutes of searching the airwaves I picked up the Voice of America and heard that Israeli forces were victorious everywhere and making tremendous gains in the Sinai desert. I couldn't help feeling a tremendous sense of pride in being Jewish. I knew there's a distinction between being Jewish and being Israeli, but at a time when Israel was under attack I felt a kinship with all its citizens.

June 7, 1967

I glanced at the front page of the local Thai language newspaper and saw pictures of the fighting in the Middle East. Thai radio stations said the Israelis attacked first. VOA stated the Arabs were about to attack and that this was a pre-emptive strike. The Thais assumed I had a fixed bias for Israel because the United States is its ally, so they smiled and changed the subject when I asked their opinion of what was happening.

I received my first month's living allowance of 1,400 baht. I told the Peace Corps to send a money order because I would have problems cashing a check, necessitating a long bus ride to Buriram. The money order was made out to a bank in Buriram so I had to go there anyway. One of the teachers heard about my money order situation and said that since he was going to Buriram he could cash it for me.

Buriram's governor dropped by the school today for what I gathered was an unexpected visit. When his convoy was spotted on the outskirts of town, somehow word was passed to the headmaster. I had *no* idea how they did that. Adjan Suraporn dashed into the teachers' lounge and ordered everyone to quickly clean their desks, coil up the speaker wires of the PA system, hide extra books behind filing cabinets and blow dust off all desk tops. The visit itself was uneventful except that he slowed his inspection down long enough to have a few words with me. His command of English was way beyond my abilities in Thai, but I still hated the attention.

I had to throw out the sugar because the ants overcame all the barriers and infiltrated every bag. Ovaltine, locked securely in a can, was surrounded and about to be penetrated. I sprinkled DDT powder around the water supply in hopes of checking their forays. The following morning I found tiny ant corpses everywhere, scattered between the water jar and a tiny hole in the wall.

As I wrote these words in the early evening, my dinner was delivered from the Jeem-Jeem Restaurant. I had one more wash to do. My drinking water was running low. I'd have to boil some more. What little remained in the large, clay container had clumps of dead mosquito larvae. Good that they were dead; bad, because I didn't know what killed them. Maybe I was scattering a little too much DDT. Where was my little water-girl? The rainy season appeared to have petered out and the past week was hotter than the ninth circle of Hell.

June 9, 1967

Several months ago, while still undergoing training in Hawaii, I wondered what my relations would be like with Thai women. During one of the information sessions a returned volunteer told us that he had remained celibate during his two years in-country. To the expression of disbelief this statement prompted, he went on to describe the vicious strains of VD common in what would be our host country. Someone asked him about using condoms, and he laughed and made a joke to the effect that Thai latex was so thick you weren't able to feel anything during the act so why bother. Someone else asked him why not simply get a girlfriend. He said it was possible, but unlikely given the strict codes of conduct followed by the average Thai women we were likely to come in contact with. "Why didn't you become a monk?" someone shouted. There was no answer.

The Peace Corps women at that session bridled at the suggestion they were looser in their sexual behavior than the Thai women.

The guest speaker told us that, "Both of our cultures have a double standard when it comes to sexual acts. Males can screw around all they want and may even enhance their reputation (in a way), but the women's reputation gets nailed. Same thing in Thailand. The point is that most of you will be stationed in very small Thai villages where everyone knows everyone else and what everyone else is doing. Once a Thai woman gets known as someone who sleeps with Farangs, her chances of ever marrying a respectable Thai male drops way off."

We discussed what going on a date might be like and how young Thai men and women usually double or triple date even when going to dances or movies. Language facility would obviously be a major factor. If all a volunteer could do is ask where the bathroom is located, his chances of getting to know a woman on a more intimate level would not be too good.

My own fluency, after three months of training and several weeks in-country, certainly ruled out any immediate close friendships with women. The female teachers maintained their distance from me, but remained friendly and often asked questions about America. Wisut was the only teacher I felt I was getting to know. Late one evening, after he returned from a party and a little drunk, he admitted that he was afraid he might "…do the bad thing…"

A few nights ago he brought up the subject of sex and burst out laughing when I expressed enthusiasm. He said maybe some day someone might offer me a trip to the red light district and that it would cost 10 baht (about 50 cents). He warned me that because Nang Rong was so small and isolated the women might not be too pretty.

Using the first Thai phrase I'd ever learned, I said, *Mai pen rai*. Never mind!

Meanwhile, the damn mosquitoes kept dying in my Ovaltine before it cooled off enough to drink it.

Not very long after that little talk, when I was reading a Henry James novel, I heard my name called.

I stepped out on to my little porch and saw Mr. Boonsuk, a teacher from one of the private schools, sitting glassy-eyed on his bicycle.

"Hey you, we go get girls," he shouted. "You come with us for see Susie Wong and then drink Thai beer. Okay?"

"Okay," I said. "Right now?"

"What?"

"Never mind. I'll be right out."

"Good. I go get some Thai beer and be back for to get you. You be here?"

"Yes, I'll be here."

He awkwardly turned his bicycle around, collided with a coconut tree, then set off in wobbly fashion for town.

I pulled on a pair of pants, slipped into a loose shirt, loafers, made sure I had a condom in my pocket and waited. And, waited.

Three hours later, when it was pitch dark, he returned with friends. I was already well back into James when their bicycles smashed into the concrete supports of my house. I stepped out and waited as they peeled themselves free and dusted off.

"Okay," Boonsuck said in a hoarse whisper. "We go now."

I saw my porch light reflect briefly off his friends' faces as they smiled in hopeful agreement. I got on my own bike and off we went along a thin path through the woods. After we'd traveled about a hundred yards Boonsuk suddenly swerved off to the side and violently vomited into a patch of wild marijuana plants. Trying hard to give me a big smile when he finished, he motioned me over to his side.

"I not feel too good. Maybe if I go get more Thai beer I feel better. I bring you some at that place. My best friend is man in blue shirt. His name is Winit. Go with him. I see you later at that place (he laughed)."

It began to rain. Boonsuk disappeared and I joined the others to merrily splash over potholes along the muddy trail. Winit looked over at me.

"Is my first time talk with you, is right?"

"Yes, first time."

"Soon," he grinned, "rain come like the cat and the dog. Is sa-lang?"

"Yes," I panted, trying hard to keep up. "That's slang."

We passed through town, by the empty market stalls and the bus stand, until nothing was left around us but the imprint of former bicycle tires for us to follow. I wobbled over the occasional buffalo-cart rut and cursed at myself for going along on such a stupid trip.

Ahead, gleamed the faint rays of a red porch light. Behind it stood a weathered, leaning house. I followed Boonsul's friends past a parked teak truck and zig-zagged through a maze of standing bicycles.

Faces appeared from around corners and stared at the insane foreigner who arrived at a Thai whorehouse in the dead of night, on a bike, in the rain.

I cautiously walked up the front steps that sagged under my weight. Squatting on the outer perimeter of the main room was a small, heavily-powdered woman. Four guys were crouched around her, resting on the balls of their feet and quietly chatting when I appeared. They looked up in shock. I was speechless, but wished I could think of something disarming to say in Thai or English. One of them motioned for me to sit near them. Where was Boonsuk? Winit grabbed for the trailing dress of a passing, diminutive women who had just left one of the cubicles with a smiling customer. Yanking her over to me, he said, "Oho, here is a pretty one for the farang. Here (to me) this one is for you. Tell her how pretty she is."

"You're very pretty," I mumbled, in Thai, and they all laughed, except the woman, who pulled herself away.

I remembered the word for 'pretty' is very similar to another word that means 'unlucky.' Had I used the right one?

52

Undaunted, Winit drew another woman over and hissed a few words to her and then slapped her behind before pushing her in my direction. The whole adventure had turned sour and all I wanted was out.

"They all afraid of you," he said. "Too tall, they say. Maybe too big."

He laughed hysterically and the others picked it up, laughter that spread from man to man like a crown fire. What was going on under all the gaity?

I was told once that the only time a Thai male reveals his true feelings is when he's drunk. These guys were certainly all drunk and I sure didn't like the true feelings they were expressing. I noticed they were all staring at an exposed portion of my right leg. I wasn't wearing any socks and there wasn't much to see except for my hairy shin. One of the men leaned over and gently brushed the hair.

"Look!" he exclaimed. "He has so much hair. Like an animal. Feel it."

The word he used actually translates as "pelt." I let it ride. The others moved in closer and soon several palms were rubbing my leg. I began to seriously consider offering myself for sale.

"The women think because you have so much hair that you have some thing bad inside of you. How you say?"

"Disease?" I ventured.

"Yes, disease."

Just then one of Winit's friends called out, "Noi! Ma nii noi." (Noi come over here).

She was the first woman I'd spotted near the door. All this time she'd been sitting quietly watching the action, but making no play herself.

Winit drew her over to me and whispered, "She says she will go with you, but it will cost more because she is afraid."

I stood up, shaking, sweat pouring off my face, down my chest, from between my legs and down on to my pelt. I nodded. She nodded back. Side-by-side, not touching, we walked into one of the cubicles.

The four walls enclosed an area slightly larger than a standard American closet and surrounded a miniature bed made of strapped bamboo poles and a straw mat.

Within the confines of that tiny place, with the flickering light of kerosene lanterns barely illuminating her face, Miss Noi looked prettier than before, but when I reached out to touch her arm she shivered with barely-contained fear.

Talking rapidly to herself, she stepped back and pulled loose a few vital knots that allowed her pasin to drop around her feet. She had the body of a chubby girl with no visible body hair. She tugged lightly at my shirt, pressed her nose close to mine and sniffed sharply. I sniffed back. It seemed important. She slipped a small hand between my legs and made a twittering sound. Someone laughed close against a nearby wall. Were they all staring at us through the cracks? It was all too much for me. I stepped away. She grabbed my shirt again and gave a strong yank at the fabric. I reached into my back pocket, pulled out all the loose baht I had and handed them to her in a crumpled ball of paper. She quickly hid it all within some small compartment of the bamboo bed then fell back down and spread her legs.

I was turned on and petrified at the same time. I turned and reached for my pants which had a condom in the back pocket. Too late. I was on top of her, holding my upper body away from her with my elbows and looked at her face. She smiled, wrapped her legs around my waist and before I knew it I was inside her and having an orgasm all at once. I heard more laughter from the other side of the wall. She gave a tentative movement against me, but I quickly withdrew, rolled over and grabbed my clothes.

As I tucked my shirt back in, she re-attached her pasin. We emerged into the glare of the public eye, holding hands. Both of us had our heads bowed and looked away from each as the men applauded. Noi gave my hand a final squeeze and retreated to sit at the feet of an older woman who'd made a late appearance. I sat back next to Winit who told me Boonsuk would not arrive after all, having passed out somewhere in the night, and would I please be a good guy by allowing him to accompany me home? I nodded.

"*Yin dee donrup Prathet Thai*," the old woman proclaimed (Welcome to Thailand). Everyone laughed. I saw Noi whisper a few words to the other woman who in turn said something to Winit.

"She wants 50 baht," he told me, apologetically.

"Fifty baht? I already gave her a lot of money. Why so much money anyway?"

"She say you ask for something…not regular. Need more money."

Something not regular? What was I even doing there in the first place? I was supposed to be teaching English, for God's sakes. I pulled out my wallet, found one, smooth 20 baht note and held it out.

"Tell her that's all I have left."

It seemed to be acceptable. We all gave each other a brief nod and I was back outside in the rain, on my bicycle and off into the forest trail. Winit and I were totally soaked by the time we reached my house. He didn't seem interested in a visit and I wasn't feeling much up for company.

Standing alone, naked in my little bathroom, feeling drained, depressed and relieved all at once, I threw buckets of cold water over myself. After drying off, I wrapped a towel loosely around my waist, walked into the kitchen and made some Ovaltine.

June 11, 1967

The headmaster asked me what my religion was. I told him I was Jewish.

"No, Khun Burgess," he shook his head. "What religion are you?" He repeated himself, but with precise diction.

"I'm Jewish."

"Khun Burgess," he sighed. "Are you Catholic or Christian?"

I understood him to mean: was I Roman Catholic or did I belong to a branch of one of the many evangelical Christian missionaries doing work in Thailand.

"I'm Jewish," I insisted, "like … ah, Moses."

"You are Jewish like Shylock?" he asked, stunned.

Shylock? Where did *that* come from?

He walked over to a wall map of the world.

"This is Israel," he pointed.

"Yes," I agreed. "That's Israel."

"These are all Jews?"

"Well, yes, mostly Jews."

Then, with a look that radiated victory he asked, "Khun Burgess, what are you?"

I pointed to the United States.

"Here are six million Jews," I told him.

I thought his eyes were going to pop out of his head.

"Six million Jews?"

I saw him glance back and forth from Israel to the United States. Then, as if a great light suddenly had gone off in his head, he turned to face me and said, "Israel and Thailand are the same."

"What?"

"Both countries are surrounded by enemies and America helps them both."

"Yes," I said, cautiously.

"Now I know more of why you are here, Khun Burgess," he concluded. "You are Jew and from America. America understands about Israel and America understands about Thailand. You are here because of friendship like that."

"Yes, something like that, but not like Shylock."

"No, no," he quickly agreed. "Not like Shylock."

I heard that two more volunteers from my group returned to the States; one caught malaria and the other severely strained his back trying to uproot a tree stump. Several others are in Bangkok being treated for amoebic dysentery.

At Wisut's inistence, I dropped by a local tailor and was measured for some slacks. My waist was down from 34 to 31.

Our badminton court was almost finished and I discovered that Ovaltine with ice cubes tasted just like a milkshake, or, at least how I remembered a milkshake tasted.

I wished it would cool off, even if only for a few days. I never thought I'd miss snow, but this endless summer was getting on my nerves.

I'm writing these words despite a blinding headache and such dizziness I can hardly see straight. Several hours ago, when the sound of Wisut's flute playing stopped, I thought he'd gone to sleep. Just as I thought of lying down myself, a small boy appeared at my door with a scribbled note that read: "Dear Burgess, would you mind if I want you come for to get something to drink??? Wisut"

Apparently, he'd given up his flute in frustration and walked over to a friend's house to join a party. Naturally, thinking of me suffering in loneliness, he invited me over.

By the time we left, the waterbuffalo we passed blurred in and out of focus, although their pungent scent remained. Wisut kept marching steadily in front of me, mindlessly avoiding deep ruts and seemingly oblivious to clouds of mosquitoes. He shook me awake the following morning just before he hurried off to school, but I was still late because I had to apply lotion over the swollen insect bites that covered my arms, face and neck.

The headmaster wanted me to concentrate primarily on rhetoric and grammar so the students would score high on the standardized government tests. Peace Corps training emphasized lesson plans that use Berlitz-style drills geared toward oral proficiency and understanding. Headmaster Suraporn reminded me to do more work with parts of speech and glared at me through the classroom door when he heard me doing minimal pair drills for pronunciation and substitution drills for familiarity with common English phrases. Stuck between my immediate supervisor's push for grammar and Peace Corp's desire to present English as a living and usable tool, I developed mini-grammar plans I could drop into place as the need arose. Immediate goals were often bollixed, as when the boss suddenly loomed over my desk in the lounge, as he did the other day, and declared, "Khun Burgess, you will teach gerunds today!"

Gerunds! I worked on simple, declarative sentences and basic parts of speech: nouns, verbs and adjectives. Prepositional phrases were about the most complex subjects I'd even considered. Gerunds? I wished the students didn't have to take those damn tests whose only function seemed to be to fail as many test-takers as possible.

Regardless of the headmaster's edict, I still devoted a portion of every class to minimal pair drills. Since there were several sounds in English that did not appear in Thai, These drills were an opportunity for Thai spealers to *hear* these new sounds by way of comparison and contrast. There were many single syllable words in English that sounded alike to Thai ears, but were actually different. For example: CHIP and SHIP. As far as Thai speakers were concerned, these words sounded exactly the same. The trick was to figure out how to make them hear the difference.

I wrote those two words on the board, pointed at them and said each one aloud as clearly as I was able, making sure to emphasize the sound of the first two letters. Then, I turned to the class and asked Jaruaypon, a bright and attentive eleven year old girl, "Do these words sound the same?"

"Yes, my teacher, they are the same."

The other students nodded in agreement.

"Thank you, Jaruaypon," I said, took a breath and asked, "Who can tell me what sound this is?"

Leaning forward, I pursed my lips, raised my tongue in my mouth and exhaled as loudly as I could to make a sound imitating a steam engine slowly pulling into the station, beginning with "…ch…ch…ch…" and then gradually changing it to "…shhhh… shhhh…shhhh…"

They all laughed and a few pounded their desks. I felt a rivulet of sweat wend its way down my back. My students' clothes were all well-pressed, sharply contrasted in blue bottoms and white tops.

"Is that funny?"

"Yes, my teacher, it is funny."

"Am I funny, Pinit?" I asked a small student up front.

He stared at me. Another student tugged at his shirt and whispered something urgently to him in Thai.

"Am I funny?" I asked, again.

"Yes, my teacher," he murmured. "You are funny."

Everyone laughed.

I held up a picture of a steam engine.

"Here's the train," I said. "Listen to it come into the station…ch….ch….ch…shhhh… shhhh….shhhhhhhhh. Can *you* make that sound, too? Can everyone in the room make that sound? Ready? Okay, everyone together…ch….ch….ch….shhhhhh…shhhh…. shhhhhhh."

The room was filled with the sound of steam engines and I orchestrated their loudness by raising and lowering my hands until all thirty-two little engines were giggling and laughing.

"That was very good," I told them. "Who can tell me if that was one sound or two different sounds?"

The room went suddenly silent.

"How about you, Sangiap. What do you think?"

"I think there are two sounds."

"Yes, there are two different sound! Now, Sangiap, look at the two words on the board. Do they sound the same?"

"Yes, my teacher."

"Okay, how do you say the first word?" I asked, pointing at CHIP.

"Chip," he said, clearly.

Very good, and what about the second word?" I asked pointing at SHIP.

"Chip," he repeated himself.

"Hmmm, really?" I made a face. "I think this one (pointing to SHIP) is like the train slowing down before it stops. You know, like when everyone said…shhh…shhhhh… shhhhhhhhhh."

He looked confused.

"The first word is chip. You got that right. But, the second word is like the train slowing down…shhhhh…shhhhhh….shhhhhhip… Ship… Can you say that?"

"Shhhhip," said. "Sshhhhhip… Shhhip.   Ship!"

"Yes, " cried. "That's good. Sangiap is right. Let's see if everyone can say that word like Sangiap. Read? One. Two. Three…Shhhhip. Good!   Ship! Ship! Good!"

I stepped back and took a deep breath.

"Jaruaypon, please stand up."

She stood up and waited.

"How do you say that word?" I asked, pointing to CHIP.

"Chip, my teacher."

"Yes, good! And how do you say the other word?" I asked, pointing at SHIP.

Her eyes widened. She looked left, then right, inhaled and said SHHHIP!"

"Yes," I said, happily. "It is ship. Everybody, say it with me…SHIP…SHIP…"

I clapped my hands. They clapped theirs.

"Class," I said, pointing to the first word. "How do you say that?"

"Chip!" They cried out.

"And, how do you say the other word?"

"SHHHHIP!"

"Yes," I said. "You are all very smart. Now I want everyone to say the words together… CHIP….SHHHIP….CHIP….SHIP…good!"

I held up my hands for silence. They foled their own hands quietly on their desks and waited.

"Class, please look at the two words on the board," I pointed. "One is CHIP and the other is SHIP. Are they the same?"

There was a momentary pause, then as one, they all shouted, "No, my teacher, They are not the same!"

I took a bow.

Oral substitution drills can also be fun. Initially, the class repeats the same basic sentence over and over again until the teacher is sure they have it right. Then, the teacher begins to change the model slightly by, for example, making substitutions in the noun slot. I might begin a sentence such as:

The book is on the table.

Here we have an article, a noun (which is also the subject of the sentence), a verb, a preposition (which is part of a prepositional phrase), and another noun (which is the object of the preposition). Once they have repeated the sentence correctly, at least half a dozen times, I might substitute "chair" for "table." If the drill has been set-up properly, the students will then say:

The book is on the chair.

Yesterday, I introduced the model sentence:

The boy is going to the market.

Teacher: Class, repeat after me, 'The boy is going to the market.'

Class: The boy is going to the market.

Teacher: field

Class: The boy is going to the field.

Teacher: house

Class: The boy is going to the house.

Teacher: school

Class: The boy is going to the school.

It's easy to see how changes can be made. However, it is very important that the teacher pays close attention to the answers he receives from the class. If you don't stay focused you could end up with what happened to me.

I said: The girl is going to the field.

The class repeated: The girl is going to the field.

Teacher: WENT

Class: The girl WENT to the field.

Teacher: WE

Class: The girl WE went to the field.

Teacher: HOME

Class: The girl we went home field.

All of a suddent I was lost and so were they!

Teacher: STOP!

This could take years. Right now, I'm concentrating on daily greetings because every morning I'm hit with, "My teacher, where you go?"

Walking to school one day, feeling terribly hung over, a student called out to me, "Mr. Burgess, where you go?"

I screamed at him, "Where are you *going*?"

"I go market," he replied, with a sad expression. "Where *you* go?"

"I am *going* to the market," I shouted into his puzzled little face.

"I go market, too," he said, softly. "You go market with me?"

What could I say, except, "Okay, I go market with you. We go market together."

....

June 12, 1967
Early morning thoughts...

The teachers arrived at school in form-fitted, starched and ironed uniforms, perfectly coiffed and remained amazingly dry, even in the heat of mid-day and in classrooms that were cooled only when a stray breeze passed through the open doors.

The trim, attractive unmarried women on the staff smiled at me even though a vast social, cultural and linguistic gulf separated us. We nodded to each other and murmured polite greetings, but we walked around each other as if a touch would burn. I deeply missed physical contact with a woman, but I hadn't a clue how to get any closer to them. Maybe part of my problem was that I had an abiding fear of becoming really involved with someone. In such a small community, everyone and his sister would be aware of each nuanced aspect of a budding romance. Did that mean everyone already knew about my trip to the house in the woods? Probably. Were the women at school keeping more of a distance from me because they knew? I couldn't even tell.

Wisut and I got up at 5:30 this morning and walked to the market through an early haze. Opening my front door and stepping down nine stairs to the ground I was once again enveloped by a strange, green land. Drooping banana fronds brushed against me as I followed Wisut to the path that led to the market. I turned and looked up in the direction of a "knock…knock…knock" sound and saw a gray-headed woodpecker hammering away against a telegraph pole. The smell of *pa thong go* frying in oil greeted us at the edge of the morning market. Rickety food stalls displayed fresh fruits, vegetables and salads. Elderly women with betel-nut stained teeth crouched on bamboo mats that held rattan baskets of tiny salted and dried shellfish, leeks and duck eggs. We ordered several *pa thong go* and carried them over to a restaurant where we also ordered fried eggs and Ovaltine. I actually chatted with the restaurant owner, much to Wisut's delight.

After breakfast, we drifted back through the market like a couple of kids, looking at everything as if for the first time. I asked one of the vendors how much two of her duck eggs cost, she gave me a gap-toothed smile and held up two fingers. I looked at Wisut, who shook his head. I gave her two baht anyway, which she stared at, then tucked six eggs into a little woven basket. I guess the two fingers must have meant two of something other than baht. I bought several more *pa thong go* for later, green onions, sweetened and dried pork ribs, a can of evaporated milk and two rice desserts wrapped in banana leaves.

Oxen teams came in from outlying districts with a variety of fruits, a truck from Buriram loaded with milled grain stopped at the bus station to be unloaded, motorcycles revved-up as municipal workers began their short haul back to their offices. Several teachers from the school were there and we chatted in the gathering heat. Wisut, in typical Thai fashion, lightly clutched the little finger of my right hand. Women passed in pairs, while men lounged in the shade or strolled by holding hands loosely and everyone seemed to be laughing for no particular reason.

My trunk arrived yesterday and I discovered it did not contain magical devices, science-fiction novels and a cheeseburgers, after all! There *was* a cookbook and, following the directions for biscuits, I made a batch that came out tender and flaky.

The headmaster commissioned Wisut to do a painting of a Thai soldier in full battle array charging across the plains. I asked Wisut where he was charging to.

"Don't ask me," he said. "Ask the soldier."

He then neatly divided a huge sheet of plywood into penciled squares to help with perspective. Within a few hours he'd sketched in the outlines of a soldier, complete with battle gear charging straight ahead. The day was blindingly hot and we kept looking out the window for our little water girls who finally arrived dragging six kerosene tins of cool water on their rusty red wagon. Even though the water was okay, Wisut sent Sompong, a local student, out to get us some coconuts for a more satisfying drink.

Last night, while I was in the market, the Great Blackout of June hit Nang Rong Village. All lights went out. Portable generators sputtered into action. I bought a flashlight and joined Wisut to wend our way back to our house which we lit with candles. In the morning I could still smell smoky wicks.

June 13, 1967

"You have the friend … the visitor," Wisut called out to me.

I was already in bed, propped up reading a two-year-old magazine, when I heard the sound of a heavy vehicle stop near my house. Assuming it was some border patrol jeep passing through town, I didn't pay attention. The visitor? Who could it be?

I quickly jumped out of bed, got dressed and got to the door just as a tall, thin figure appeared with Wisut. In the dim light, his features were unclear. I automatically *wai*-ed and heard him laugh as Wisut ushered him inside. It was then I realized it was a heavily-tanned Westerner, about middle-age, with a huge, warm smile on his face. Bubbling over to see someone new, I must have asked seven questions before I realized he was shaking his head, rolling his eyes all seeming to indicate he wasn't keeping up.

"Who are you?" I asked, slowly.

"I do not speak English much," he replied, hesitantly. "But, I can speak Thai and Cambodian. If you speak Thai, *ah mon Dieu*, please, yes, speak Thai if you may."

"*Je parle francais…*" I began, but got no further because he was already upon me, jabbering away in speed-French and I knew I'd made an ass of myself. The French I remembered from college was no match for this conversation. I motioned for Wisut to get closer because it was apparent to me, if not the Frenchman, that an intermediary was needed.

My visitor quickly understood where my language abilities were and heaved an enormous sigh of regret. We tried to communicate in Thai, but my vocabulary was too slim to get much past names and home cities. Wisut went into the kitchen to make tea. Eventually, we settled down and began what was the most frustrating yet fascinating conversation I'd ever had. There we were: Wisut, Preeda (who also dropped in), Henri (the Frenchman), a friend of his from the market, and myself – all speaking at once, in several languages. Henri's friend was Thai-Chinese and reverted to some strain of Cantonese with Wisut. Preeda asked Henri if he came from the border area. When he replied that he did, he and Preeda switched to Cambodian.

Occasionally, Henri looked in my direction and tried some Thai, and if that didn't work, a bit of French. My own thoughts were in chaotic English. Gradually, it came out that Henri was a Catholic missionary working out of a small town about 25 kilometers from Nang Rong.

"He wants to know what religion you are," Wisut said.

I think he understood me to say I was Jewish before Wisut even tried to translate because he immediately burst out laughing. Henri's summation of the situation, which I eventually pieced together, was:

"I came here because I heard there was an American woman. I find a man. I speak French. He speaks English. I know Thai. He knows very little. I am fluent in Cambodian. He knows none at all. I came as a Catholic missionary hoping to give confession. He is Jewish. *C'est formidable!*"

After an hour the room filled with cigarette smoke and Wisut's delicate tea service was soon overflowing with ashes. Someone opened the wooden shutters and several grasshoppers hopped in. Henri caught a few and examined them closely. I waited for a verdict.

"*Aroi maak,*" he said (Very delicious) and popped a few in his mouth.

I gave a strangled laugh.

"*C'est vrai. Ils sont tres bon,*" he said.

We each had one more cigarette, then Henri and his friend got up to leave. Wisut explained to me that the two of them had hitched a ride on the back of a teak truck and now it was time for them to rendezvous with the truck. We all shook hands and hugged each other farewell.

Later, Wisut said that Henri told him that he'd seen many irregular troops on patrols from the Cambodian side of the border. Many of them, he said, crossed over into Thailand not so much as an armed force, but as a political force to sow dissent among the farmers, whose poverty and lack of contact with Bangkok's central government made them receptive listeners to people preaching a form of socialism guaranteed, they promised, to spread the wealth.

I had the impression that many border Thai think of themselves only vaguely as Thai. They speak Cambodian in every situation except schools and district offices. Quite a few students do not know how to read Thai, but are kept in schools as long as possible, hopefully picking up some sense of being a part of a nation called Thailand. As long as they are in school they're not playing near the stagnant canals which breed parasites and malarial mosquitoes.

June 14, 1967

I was teaching 25 hours a week using the workbook of lesson plans supplied by the school. The hoped-for chances to supplement my standard plans with what I thought were relevant sentence pattern drills and practice dialogues were few and far between. It was the rainy season and I needed a lot of energy to make my voice heard over the sound of water falling on a galvanized roof.

Wisut asked me if I wanted to go to the movies with him, but I'd already made plans with another teacher. For some reason, maybe thinking I would hurt his feelings if I told him the truth, I said, "I'd love to go with you, but I don't have time." He looked at me, puzzled. "But, you always have time," he replied. "You always have enough time to do whatever you want to do." I did not have an answer to that.

Everyone in town was excited about a big party in honor of the border patrol. Wisut's painting of a charging Thai soldier would be displayed in the official welcoming ceremony. The festivities were scheduled to begin on June 19, my 26th birthday.

I hoped I'd feel well enough to take part. My digestive system still periodically rebelled against local bacteria and I was regularly hit with bouts of diarrhea and loss of appetite. Perhaps I was ingesting too many strange spices. Or, maybe it had to do with contaminated ice I kept telling myself not to use. Then again, I was drinking way more alcohol than I ever had before. Too many possibilities to think about.

The rainy season regularly threw monsoon downpours over the area, dumping an inch or more at a time, turning the mud and clay hardened roads into quagmires. Then, the sun appeared and hardened the ruts into ridges. Bus rides became torture. I spent hours sitting on the school's porch that extends out from the lounge, staring at palm trees and convolutions of clouds. Because there were no buildings or hills in my line of sight, just endless rice fields lined with stands of trees, I felt as if I *saw* differently. My former life offered only a two-dimensional vision and now I had to get my bearings all over again for this constant sense of depth.

Five "communists" were conveniently captured near a government-sponsored rally, but that was the only news from the shifting front. None of the staff seemed interested about the fighting in either Vietnam or the Middle East. I heard rumors of guerilla activity in southern Thailand where Muslim insurgents crossed over from Malaysia.

The editor of the news journal Siam-Rath, Mr. Kukrit, who spoke to my group during our Bangkok orientation, seemed more concerned over southern skirmishes than what was happening here in Issan (as most people referred to the northeast). Kukrit was involved with his brother, Seni Pramoj, in drafting a new constitution. Since they were relatives of the revered queen, their perspective was important. They had been working on that constitution for more than 10 years. I thought the autocrats in power, like General Prapas, hoped work on the constitution would continue like Penelope's weaving, with always one more strand to work in.

This afternoon, while standing with Wisut in front of the school, I asked him if that thunder we heard coming from the east meant more rain. He cocked his head, then said, "Not thunder. Bombs. Sometimes planes come back from Vietnam and still have bombs. I think they drop them in Cambodia."

Could that be true? That's the direction Henri came from.

A plane flew overhead yesterday with olive-green markings, traveling very low, heading in the direction of the Seabee camp near the village of Hingkhondong. Reports came into town that a plane crashed at the Seabee landing strip about 80 kilometers from here. No report of casualties. Many helicopters flew back and forth all day. Maybe its part of the show the Thai border patrol is putting on for their American advisors.

After five helicopters hovered above us for a long time, red flares were suddenly ignited in the government drill field and parachutes began dropping from the sky. An unexpected wind caused havoc with the first drop. Men landed on coconut trees, shops in the market, and on the roof of the meteorology building. Succeeding drops were better executed.

The final performance involved a multi-colored chute and a gymnast who did body contortions all the way down to land right next to the flare. All the voices around me said, "That must be the American." He turned out to be the tallest Thai soldier anyone had ever seen. The local crowd was ecstatic.

Everyone praised Wisut's portrait of the Thai soldier, including the headmaster. Back at our house, after all the celebrating, Wisut took out a beautiful tea pot and two small cups. He explained there was a whole ritual to presenting and drinking tea correctly, but he did not feel like going into all that – he only wanted us to drink tea together in honor of my 26th birthday. I had not wanted to bring up my birthday with the headmaster, considering everything else that was going on, so I'd pretty much accepted the fact nothing would happen. Wisut, however, had not forgotten and our brief tea service together brought us closer together.

June 21, 1967

My regional Peace Corp representative, Scott Duncan, paid me a visit and declared, "Nang Rong is the prettiest district in the northeast."

With its lush rice paddies, swaying coconut palms, scattered ponds, stands of banana and guava trees, the area stands out in sharp contrast to so much of the destitute Issan region.

I was there when Scott interviewed my headmaster and other teachers about my teaching abilities, but his command of the language was so fluent I lost track. One phrase I managed to catch was when Adjan Suraporn told him I had a "…good heart…" Scott later told me I really needed to get a tutor and develop my language skills.

After a tour of the school, Scott, Wisut and I sat down for some homemade cake and coffee. Scott asked Wisut if he liked the *farang* cakes and Wisut replied, "He's getting better. The first one he made tasted like stone, this one is like wood."

I'd learned during training that most Thai males join the Buddhist monkhood in their teens and stay in a monastery for varying lengths of time. Some remain monks for the rest of their lives. Yesterday morning a young man from the village entered the monkhood. His family and friends celebrated his initiation as he rode through town, head freshly shaved, white-faced (with powder), on a donkey with a large yellow umbrella shading him all the way to the temple grounds. A large crowd of family and friends trailed behind blowing trumpets and beating drums. Every time I moved in to take a photograph the procession stopped and family members jammed in together with big smiles in the hope they would be included in the shot. All the while, the serene monk-to-be patiently waited.

A middle-aged monk stood next to me and glanced in my direction when I wasn't looking. I turned toward him, gave him a formal *wai* and introduced myself, using the name the teachers at the school gave me, Panthit."

"I am Adjan Chamorn," he said in clear English accompanied by a big smile. "Are you new to Nang Rong? I only heard of a woman who taught English in the school."

"Yes, she is the one I replaced. I work at the school now myself."

"Do you know about this tradition?" he asked, pointing at the crowd.

"A little," I said. "I understand the young man is about to become a monk."

"This is the time of year when most young men become monks," he said. "The next three months during the rainy season are called Buddhist Lent in English. In the Thai language this is called *Phansa*, which means the Rains Retreat. This is also the time when the king changes the costume of the Emerald Buddha in Bangkok. Have you ever seen the Emerald Buddha? It is quite beautiful."

"No, I haven't seen it. I'll have a chance to travel soon to Bangkok and I hope to see it then. Do you belong to one the Nang Rong temples?"

"I am here to teach some of the other monks, but later I will return to Khon Kaen. I studied English there at the university and later I traveled to America and lived in Indiana."

"Indiana! What were you doing there?"

"I studied religion and philosophy at Ball State University. Then, I returned to Thailand and I stay at a large temple near Khon Kaen University."

"Will you stay here for the whole rainy season?"

"Yes, I must stay here because during this period Thai monks have to stay in their own *wats* at night to pray and meditate."

"It sounds a little like the kind of Lent Catholics have in America."

"Many Thai people try to stop drinking and smoking during this holiday and they try to be more kind in everything they do in their lives. Are the Catholics like that during their holiday?"

"I think they are. Is this the only time Thai men can become monks?"

"Yes, now when the rainy season starts, is when they become monks."

"What happens if a Thai man doesn't ever become a monk?"

"He will have problems in Thailand. Young women will never marry a man who has never been a monk. They will call him *khon dip* … I think when you say it in English it is very strange. It means an unripe person."

"Yes, that sounds funny. What's he called after he's been a monk?"

"After a man has been a monk for at least three months he's called *khon suk* or ripe one. After the man leaves the monkhood he is called *thit*. Do you know about that word?"

"No, I don't think so."

"Yes, you do," he said. "The Thai name you used when you introduced yourself to me has that word in it. *Thit* means someone who is very wise and it comes from another very old word, *Panthit*, your Thai name."

"So, I am a wise man?"

"Only your Thai name means that. I'm not sure about the rest of you."

We both laughed. While talking with Adjan Chamorn I remembered there are many ways for Thai people to gain merit for their next life. One way is to give food or clothing to monks. For the first time I realized a Westerner's use of the term *begging* to apply to a monk accepting food was completely inappropriate. Wisut had explained to me earlier that a great deal of merit is earned by a young man becoming a monk, not just for himself, but also for his parents.

"Is becoming a monk the most important thing in a man's life?" I asked Adjan Chamorn.

"The three most important things in a man's life are when he's born, when he's married and when he becomes a monk."

"Is there a name for all this? I don't mean the holiday, but this whole ceremony and tradition of a young man about to be ordained?"

"Yes, it is called *Nak*."

We stood there watching the serpentine column of celebrants blowing horns, beating drums and dancing with each other. I thought of a New Orleans funeral, then pushed it from my mind.

"Is anything else going to happen now that the rainy season is here?"

"Yes, for the next four days all villages in Nang Rong District will have a contest to see who can make the biggest and most beautiful candle."

"Will you help with Nang Rong's candle, Adjan Chamorn?"

"Nang Rong does not need my help. There will be many volunteers."

"Where will they get all the wax from?"

"From the Buriram Wax Factory."

"Really?"

"No, I'm joking. There is no wax factory. I have no idea where so much wax comes from, but it will be expensive, so villages have to raise money. I think there will be Thai boxing."

"Will I see you again, Adjan Chamorn?"

"Please visit the monastery," he said. "You will always be welcome."

Another monk approached us holding two black umbrellas, and after handing one to Adjan Chamorn, they walked away together, two twirling back circles above saffron robes.

Wisut approached just as the monks walked away.

"Wisut, were you ever a monk?"

"Yes, I was a monk in a monastery near Bangkok."

"Did you ever think about staying a monk?"

"No."

"Why not?"

"Because I cannot live like a monk. Can you?"

"No, I can't."

"Okay. Will you go to the market with me?" he asked in a sing-song tone mimicking the students.

I nodded and with our little fingers linked we went to the market.

Later, back at the house, I leafed through some books about Thai Buddhism, called Theravada, and wondered if the role of Buddhism in all his manifestations could be compared to the power of the Catholic Church during the middle ages. They both worried about the next life, whether it's heaven or hell or reincarnation. The Church used to allow purchase of a form of grace that the Thais referred to as merit for the next life. Of course, the Church told its followers they could end up in hell. Buddhism warned you could end up as a cockroach.

A little girl from the Raxana Restaurant brought over some food through a blinding rainstorm on her bicycle. Inside the stacked metal containers I spotted a bowl of puffy pork balls in light soup, three strips of dried beef, a piece of chicken breast with a fried duck egg, a full tin of rice and a bowl of coconut pastry. I can't say when I realized I was no longer missing American food so much, but laying out this little treasure of a meal I thought it looked wonderful.

Final memory of the day:

I asked Wisut what I should do about the pants I had custom made in town. They turned out far too short, as if the tailor could not bring himself to believe anyone could be that tall.

"*Nam nai*," Wisut said.

"*Nam nai*? What's that mean?"

"It means 'water gone,'" he said. "You cannot get it back."

"In English we say that's water under the bridge."

"*Nam nai* easier to say," he laughed.

A teacher from one of the private schools recently asked me if I would help him type up an English test. Although it only took me a few minutes, he was extremely grateful and asked if there was anything he could get me.

"Do you know about *ganja*?" I asked.

"Yes, I know about that," he said, looking around nervously.

I knew perfectly well marijuana was illegal and Peace Corps had strict policies against its use, but as someone who enjoyed an occasional hit I was up for it.

"I don't want you to have trouble about this," I told him. "But, if you could get me a little bit, I'd appreciate it."

He nodded, but I had the impression I wasn't going to see him again in the near future. Surprising me, he pulled up the next evening on his bicycle with a large package wrapped in newspaper attached to his basket.

"Something for you, my friend," he said, and handed it to me.

He walked with me into the house and smiled as I unwrapped it to reveal a cubic foot or more of bound marijuana plants. There was more dope there than I'd seen in my entire life.

"Is it okay?"

"Yes, it's okay," I managed to answer, thinking, 'My God, what am going to do with all this dope?'

"Thank you again for your help," he said. "Is it okay if I visit you some more?"

"Come by any time. Just don't bring any more of this."

"Okay, see you later."

Once he was gone, I ground up a few leaves, emptied the tobacco from a Falling Rain cigarette, and filled the empty paper with Thai dope. After only two or three hits I was so disoriented I almost fell down. Stumbling to my bed I literally passed out and had the most vivid dreams that seemed to last forever. I got up the next morning, still dizzy, and had a cup of Ovaltine, a few stale *patongos* and a scrambled egg. Only then did I manage to concentrate long enough to separate the leaves, buds and seeds from the stems and put the good stuff into three very large plastic baggies which I tucked under my mattress. Then, I walked over to the nearest window, popped open the shutters and threw up on to the cement below.

I thought it would be a good idea to get a professional shave in honor of the big Border Patrol celebration, so while Wisut was shopping for art supplies I strolled into the town's only barbershop. The one customer already being served swiveled his head around as I entered, removed his sheet covering, gave me a half bow and ran out of the store. The barber just shrugged and motioned for me to fill the empty space. I lay back, relaxed, ready for the comfortable feeling of having someone make small talk as they piled steamy towels over my face to soften my beard. No hot towel appeared, but I noticed a small crowd had gathered on the sidewalk peering in at the *farang* about to get a shave. When typical entertainment in an area involves watching Japanese detergent commercials, seeing some American get shaved attracts attention.

As the chair tilted back and I looked up into the neutral, dark eyes of the barber, I realized I didn't know him at all. This man who was about to slide a razor up and down my face could have hated Americans all his life, and at last he had his chance.

The barber dipped his hand into a bowl of cool water then rubbed a tiny piece of soap against his palm until he'd managed to work up a small pile of lather. Somehow, he was able to cover one entire side of my face with a fine stratum of suds. Then, he took a straight razor and began to slap it against an ancient leather strap. Carefully, he pressed a glob of free soap residue from my right sideburn and slowly scraped the razor down my right cheek. I felt as if every whisker was being yanked out by its roots. Had that thing ever been sharpened on a whetstone? Assuming he'd already taken away all available skin and hair follicles, I was startled to feel him start all over again, only this time shaving *up*. Eeeeeee. He then attempted, the operant word here being *attempted*, to cut a few stray hairs he'd spotted in my nostrils, but I resisted. Smiling, he displayed a two-foot long q-tip that had seen better days and prepared to ream out my right ear. No, no and no. I held up my wrist watch and indicated time was running out. Just had to go. He rubbed his hands over my scalp, so I stayed for the haircut, which wasn't bad. Cost of half a shave and one haircut – only 3 baht. Only 15 cents for a permanent depilation.

No one commented on my new haircut and shave because they were too busy polishing everything in sight. The front balcony sagged from the weight of flowered wreaths and bouquets

The governor and several other high provincial officials dropped by to say good things about the soldiers guarding the border with Cambodia. During a ceremony inside the school's auditorium a messenger arrived from the post office with a telegram for me. As I ripped it open, all eyes were on me. It turned out to be a birthday greeting from a girl I knew in the states. I felt my face turning red and I tried to jam the message into my pocket, but everyone called out, wanting to know what it said.

"Birthday for me ..." I managed to croak and was immediately inundated with hundreds of *choke dee* (good luck) wishes from around the hall.

That evening the town held a really big party for the Home Guard. More of a crowd gathered in front of the *nai amphur's* office (the mayor) than I'd ever seen in one place before. On a large, wooden platform set up in the field, Mr. Prayun, the teacher who kept trying to give me Thai language lessons, played the drums and bass while Mr. Preeda played jazz drum and trumpet. My own talent went on display when I sang "500 Miles" in a daze of alcohol.

One of my favorite students, Miss Sombat, performed a little dance and gracefully accepted a prize from the *nai amphur*. More presentations were made and I broke away with Wisut to grab a few roasted bananas. By the time we returned, there was a Thai boxing match going on which is called *Muay Thai*. We had a brief lecture during training about *muay Thai* during which we were told it was called 'The Art of Eight Limbs' because it made use of punches, kicks, knee strikes and elbows, instead of the two points (fists) that Americans were familiar with. After the boxing matches, the platform was turned into a stage for dancing and I was persuaded to do a dance called the *ramwong* with a strikingly attractive woman who politely said she was not interested in getting to know me any better than she already did.

June 24, 1967

The constant *Ommmmmmm* coming from the monks across the field in the temple began to sound like any other background sound of nature. Birds trill, bees buzz and monks Ommmmm. Outside, the air was clear, hot and heavy with moisture. Enormous banana leaves were speckled with dew. In the direct sun, most vegetation was parched yellow, but in the shade of the mango tree all was cool and damp.

I just heard from one of the few volunteers from my group who studied Thai before Peace Corps. He decided to leave. In his telegram he said he didn't like being shown off to visitors as if he were some kind of puppy. He wasn't bitter, just sad to discover he wasn't needed for more than pronunciation drills; his students already knew English grammar better than he did. There were also a few words about his constant stomach distress. I sure identified with him on that subject.

I had begun to wonder just why the children in Nang Rong needed to learn English at all. So many of them lived on farms and once they finished the required minimum years of schooling they returned to their family plot of land. Considering how many Thai-Chinese people there were connected to the business community, I would think knowledge of Chinese would be more important.

Last night Wisut and I ate at a small restaurant on the edge of town. Each corner was filled with small parties of men and women joking, sipping beer or Fanta and laughing. When I noticed a small record player near the kitchen I pulled out the 45 rpm record I'd received in the mail and asked the owner if I could play it. Several of the customers watched me as I lowered the arm.

I was a d-d-driving to downtown L.A.
Around the midnight hour…

There didn't appear to be too many Donovan fans in the audience. I found myself tapping the table alone until I saw Wisut slowly shaking his head from side to side. As soon as I stopped the music, someone else walked over and put an old Venture's album on. Loud guitar riffs snaked out into the street. Several women smiled and began making hesitant to and fro motions with their bodies. What would poor Anna think of her Siam today?

Not much luck trying to teach my students a few songs. Between the three guitar chords I could manage and a voice that only occasionally found the tune I was a bad joke, but my students listened politely. One of them shouted out "Yankee Doodle," so I led them in a chorus or two and found myself trying to explain what a "doodle" was (they pronounced it "dooden"). The also got a kick out of "Froggie Went a-Courtin'" and "Tom Dooley." My rendition of "Hey Diddle Diddle" was met with applause and laughter. I couldn't explain what a "diddle" was either. When the class sang it, the words came out as "Hey did'n did'n, the cat and the fid'n." Time to do some more minimal pair drills.

I didn't realize the school had its own band until they magically appeared for a rehearsal yesterday afternoon. They came trooping out, beating their drums and blowing their horns and completely shocked me. They looked cute in their faded scout uniforms and bright smiles. Maybe one day they'd let me join the band and beat on a big, bass drum.

Wisut told me that his uncle enjoyed talking with me and sharing his *sato* (rice wine). I agreed that I'd liked being with his uncle myself.

"Good," he said. "So you will go with me when I visit him again this Saturday. He told me he's made another big pot of *sato* and he wants you to try it."

I tried to show some enthusiasm, although my stomach lurched at the idea.

Peace Corps sent me train tickets for the next regional seminar, but I was convinced once I left Nang Rong I'd never be able to find it again. The good news was in the form of a small note scribbled at the bottom of the notice that said if I arrived a little early the Peace Corps secretarial staff was preparing a Western-style breakfast. Could bacon and eggs be in my future?

I stayed up late with an upset stomach several nights in a row and rummaged through a stack of paperback books in English from the school's library. That led to my re-reading "A Connecticut Yankee in King Arthur's Court." After every other chapter by Mark Twain, I studied Thai language vocabulary. I compared myself to the Yankee, who found himself re-located 12,000 miles to a tiny Southeast Asian hamlet.

Wisut told me the legend of how the town of Nang Rong got its name.

Many years ago, a beautiful young woman named Oraphim was married to a handsome, but poor farmer named Padjix. They lived a happy if uneventful life in the shadow of Phnom Rung Mountain. There was food and hard work for all. Oraphim's beauty and grace were known far and wide, but she paid attention only to her husband and his land. Unfortunately, word of her charms reached the ears of nearby King Promatat, whose powers extended from the outskirts of Phii Mai to his castle atop Phnom Rung. One day, he descended from the mountain with a retinue of servants and guards to view Oraphim himself. Villagers brought word to her of his approach and his attentions. She managed to hide herself just in time within the deep recesses of a cave. Padjix, all the while, was out working his rice fields. The king and his men eventually reached the cave, but Oraphim refused to come out. They left and Oraphim returned to her home and husband who was wild with grief over his wife's disappearance. Both his neighbor's and Oraphim herself, related to him the king's desires. Hearing of that, Padjix fell on his knees and prayed to the Lord Buddha to protect them.

Some time passed and their earlier worries were forgotten. Then, news came of a large celebration to be held at the castle on Phnom Rung Mountain. King Promatat not only invited all the local farmers, but apparently with kind thoughts of his peoples' safety in mind, he also decreed that following the festivities any of those who wished to might stay the night within the palace walls. Oraphim and Padjix joined the throng that climbed the mountain. Everyone looked forward to the party and dressed in their finest clothes to make a good impression before the king. There was food and drink for all. Splendid entertainment followed. Late that evening, the sky became overcast and the way back down the mountain was obscured. Oraphim and Padjix, along with dozens of other families, decided to stay the night atop the mountain as the king indicated they might.

With the moon still hidden and the rustling of palm trees to lull them to sleep, Oraphim and Padjix fell to dreaming. Quietly, soldiers came and skillfully kidnapped the lovely Oraphim away from the very arms of her husband. He reached for her in the morning's light to find her gone. He cried and berated himself, but there was nothing he could do but return to his fields. Meanwhile, some distance away, Oraphim cried within the king's harem building. She refused to comply with the king's desires and sang instead of her unhappiness. In the time that followed, Oraphim continued to sing her melancholy songs, while in the distant fields Padjix refused food and water. As his crops went unattended, Padjix could only mourn and fast, growing thinner and thinner until the day came when the other farmers found him, lifeless, face up to the sky. No further word was ever heard of Oraphim. On the site where Padjix died a village gradually came to be built and the people, remembering the story of Oraphim and Padjix, decided to name their place 'Nang Rong' – To Sit and Cry.

June 28, 1967

Sanguan, an elementary school teacher, dropped by and asked if I'd like to go with him to the village of Paak Waan. When I said I would, he slapped me on the back and shouted "Okay!" That's just the sort of body contact Peace Corps told me Thais never do. Maybe Sanguan saw it in a cowboy movie.

He motioned for me to get behind him on his motorcycle. When he wasn't able to get it to turn over, he got off and said, slyly, "If you think you are strong enough, we could go there by bicycle."

Unable to resist a challenge, I walked with him to a neighbor's house where we borrowed a couple of bikes. The ride was terribly difficult from the start. Both bikes easily lost their chains every time we hit a bump and neither had very good brakes. Since the roads were in bad shape, it took us many stops, chain repairs and accidental slides off the road before we made it past the last Nang Rong Village sign and pushed on to Paak Waan. My skinny ass bounced and scraped over the stiff, leather seat. Before too long we were in the midst of water-filled rice paddies and approaching a wall of palm trees that Sanguan assured me was the beginning of his village. Most of the houses along the way were no more than fragile shacks. The people working the fields seemed indifferent to the heat or glare of the blinding sun. Children played in the tiny canals that criss-crossed the paddies. Some rode bravely atop massive water buffalo that browsed their lives away between sowing and harvest time. A few older men sat in the shifting shade of palm trees, staring out at the others at work and calmly chewed betel nut leaves. From under the wide brims of their thatched hats I saw quick and curious glances our way. None of those working the fields ever looked up for more than an instant.

Paying more attention to the sights than the narrow path I slid into the water a few times, but I persevered and the two of us soon clanged and puffed our way into the center of Paak Waan. First stop was the local temple where Sanguan introduced me to the abbot, then to the home of the assistant *Nai Amphur* (mayor) who offered us each a glass of Mekhong whiskey. That's when I found out Sanguan, even on pain of being impolite, did not drink alcohol.

"Now, we will visit my friend, Mr. Cheewin," Sanguan said.

Sanguan had described Cheewin earlier as a former Buriram policeman. After marrying and having a few children, and with no promotion in sight, Cheewin decided he could make more money renting some land and growing rice. That turned out to be a very bad decision.

We pulled up before a three-walled structure made of wood strips and corrugated sections of old metal. The roof was a sagging piece of sheet metal, mostly rusted away. Cheewin stood in front after we stopped, *wai'd* each other and sat down to talk. In his mid-20s and in excellent shape, Cheewin radiated a sense of energy. His expression, though slightly wary, was balanced by a pair of bright, alert eyes that examined me up and down. I must have come across as at least acceptable, because he gave a tentative smile and held out his hand for me to shake. There was something else about Cheewin I sensed as our hands separated and he motioned for us to sit down. I realized he had an air about him of total fatalism. Behind a torn sheet his wife fed the latest addition to the family. Her curiosity overcame her shyness and after she put her baby down she slipped out to meet me. She wore what I've heard described as an iron-maidenform bra which had been slightly loosened so she could feed her baby. A drab *pasin* was loosely wrapped about her waist.

"This is my wife, Adjara," I understood him to say.

Despite the humidity, heat and dust, Adjara's silky black hair fell lightly on her smooth shoulders and when she looked up at the mention of her name and saw me staring at her, she quickly glanced away.

We all squatted on the floor and asked each other questions about school, Thai food, America and work. Then, with the loveliest smile I had yet seen in Thailand, Adjara murmured something to him. He clapped his hands and told one of his children to fetch his guests some fresh coconuts. After the boy ran off, Cheewin began to wring his hands and speak faster than I could keep up. Sanguan translated that Cheewin was ashamed that he could not offer me anything more substantial than a coconut. Suddenly, there was a loud scream. Adjara leaped to her feet so quickly one breast flew free and a brown nipple with a drop of milk still clinging to it, hung away from her baby's eager mouth. Clutching the baby tightly to her, she slipped her breast back inside her bra and ran outside where she disappeared behind the rear wall of the house. Cheewin was so despondent, even this family emergency wasn't enough to move him. I began to stand, but Cheewin shook his head and motioned for me to stay seated. Adjara returned with the boy. He'd fallen from a tree and his mouth was bloody. She took him behind the curtain and whispered softly to him for the rest of my visit.

Everything was going so badly all I wanted to do was leave, but it was at that point Cheewin offered me a drink of cloudy water. Despising myself for even thinking of the water as *cloudy*, I drank it and thanked him profusely. His look implied I was acting inappropriately. I desperately wanted to do something. Then, I remembered my camera, took it out, flipped off the lens cap and set the aperture for a sunny day before asking him to look in my direction. My idea was to take a few pictures and send copies of them back to Cheewin by way of Sanguan as a present for his hospitality.

Cheewin looked down at his lap, and with his fingers fighting themselves, almost inaudibly said something to Sanguan. I paused and waited.

"He says he feels ashamed to have you take pictures of such bad things in Thailand to show your family in America," Sanguan said. "He prefers you wait. Perhaps by next year he will have a better harvest and have a chance to buy a new shirt."

Cheewin could not have been more ashamed than I was. In some clumsy fashion I made my goodbyes and we pedaled away leaving Cheewin to wait optimistically for a rich harvest.

The entire area around *Paak Waan* village appeared strikingly lush and I saw many small plots of land devoted to growing edible plants. The town of *Sweet Vegetable* must have been named for that reason. Yet, the people were absolutely destitute. Would the new constitution being drafted in Bangkok make any difference to the people of Paak Waan?

July 2, 1967

Preeda, the social studies teacher, asked me to explain then demonstrate the rules of softball to a group of Nang Rong School students. I've told many a horror story about my junior high school physical education classes, so it was ironic to find myself in this position. Mr. Eldert, my old PE teacher from Day Junior High, would have been proud of me.

I walked out to the main playing field where a group of boys waited. They grasped the basic rules very quickly and ran about the field with enthusiasm. A few minor problems quickly became apparent. These Thai children were accustomed to games that involved only feet (soccer) and something called *takraw* (passing a small, rattan ball bag and forth with every part of the body but the hands). Consequently, they were rather shy about objects that hurtled down at them from the sky – such as fly balls. Their batting practice turned out well, although most had a tendency to step a little too much away from the plate when a pitch came in. They had terrible fielding skills. Most of them prepared for pop-ups far too slowly and ended up being walloped in the chest. Another problem was first base. No one wanted to cover such a dangerous position. Short stop wasn't exactly viewed as an enviable spot either. Adjan Suraporn grunted something to me about students possibly getting hit on their sacred heads, so there's a strong possibility softball would not catch on.

Wisut invited me to go along with him to visit his Uncle Lau and try some more *sato* (fermented rice wine). I enjoyed the bicycle ride, but his uncle was not there. Wisut foraged around the cupboards, plopped a few items into a bag and off we went again, this time through field, scrublands, mud flats and more fields until we came upon Uncle Lau and a friend sitting on the edge of an ancient porch that barely remained attached to an even older house. There was nothing around us but stunted trees, tall grass, very nervous dogs, dozens of dragonflies and a scent of nearby water. Uncle Lau was happily chewing a wad of betel nut leaves and talking with his friend as we pulled up.

Wisut told me that Uncle Lau's income came from rice paddies kept him him solvent enough to maintain a large, well-stocked household. He seems to lead a casual existence of eating, smoking, chewing betel nut leaves, gossiping with friends and freely giving advice to anyone who drops by.

I *wai'd* Uncle Lau and said the few formal phrases of greeting I knew and he responded with a bellylaugh. He introduced his friend to me as Mr. Bunya, an extremely thin man with a racking smoker's cough and watery eyes. We sat in the scant shade and chatted.

Mostly, Wisut translated for me, but occasionally I was able to get in a phrase or two of my own. Mr. Bunya seemed mildly amused to hear me speak Thai, but refused to believe I could understand anything. He directed his questions for me through Wisut, who dutifully repeated them, in Thai, to me.

Uncle suggested we move to an even more secluded spot, so the four of us walked even further away from the bicycle path, until we reached a small shack that was hanging on to its last nail. Insects buzzed us, the late haze parted to allow direct sunlight to further heat the ground and a barely perceptible breeze blew pollen spores back and forth across the landscape. I did my best to stay focused in the dazzling heat, wondering: Is this real? How close am I to Vietnam? Does it matter? Where's the *sato*? Do I care?

I'd been in Thailand long enough to accept that whatever was planned, or not planned, for the afternoon would happen in its own time. Wisut opened the bag he'd filled at his uncle's and withdrew two, bright green cucumbers. He carefully peeled and sliced them into a large wooden bowl, then took out two cans of marinated sardines and sloshed them into another container. Uncle Lau stretched, yawned, and wandered about the field pulling up plants here and there in no apparent hurry or order. He pinched some, smelled others and threw them all in with the cucumbers. A man rode up on a bike to tell Uncle Lau there was no more *sato* because the PE teacher had purchased the whole lot for his own use the day before. Uncle Lau was very upset.

Attempting to mediate the conflict, I said, "Well, we already have good weather, fine food and each other's company so was there really a need for *sato*?"

Uncle examined me in much the same manner people stare at drooling infants, then turned and said something in a very hostile tone to the new arrival. The man quailed, nodded and rode off. Wisut whispered to me that Uncle Lau had suggested the world would be short one bicycle rider if some *sato* was not delivered pronto because (1) He'd already paid for it (2) He knew the rider had some he was saving for himself, and (3) There was an American guest present who should be treated with respect and that respect included some locally produced *sato*.

We returned to nibbling on delicacies. I took a spoonful of sardines, then a slice of onion and a pepper, crunched into some cucumber slices to smooth the pepper's edge, and all the while felt the warm and soothing sun melt me down into the earth.

The rider returned with a teapot full of *sato*. Uncle Lao examined it, sipped a bit, and indicated that if the man left quickly enough he might escape injury.

Uncle Lao poured everyone else half a glass, but filled mine to the brim, explaining that since I was new at this I needed to make up for lost time. It tasted extremely sour with a powerful and lingering rancid smell. I nodded politely and reached for the sardines. I figured the more food I ate, the less I would taste of the *sato* and, hopefully, a full stomach might soak up enough of the drink's alcohol to keep me awake.

After a few swallows, the *sato* began to taste much better. After chewing a few more crisp peppers, I took one last swallow and felt a rosy glow spread throughout my body. Everything about the time, place and people was wonderful.

Abruptly, Uncle Lao got to his feet and announced we had eaten enough snacks and it was time to return to his house for some real food and Mekhong whiskey. Stunned, I whispered to Wisut that I was stuffed, really full and totally satiated. In Thai you can say all of that with the phrase: *im layo.*

Wisut looked at me askance and said what we'd eaten was a mere salad and a few glasses of *sato.* Nothing. Uncle Lao would be totally insulted if we didn't return with him.

I looked back with longing at a soft pile of hay by the shack as I stood with the others, stretched and walked over to our bikes. The sun was no longer pleasantly warm and my heard throbbed as we trekked three miles back through scrub and woodland to Nang Rong and Uncle Lao's house. His wife greeted us at the door and led us inside to a floor covered with food, bottles of Mekhong, glasses of ice and soda water. I collapsed into my version of a lotus position and forced myself to nibble roast pork, fried almonds, morning glory leaves fried in oyster sauce and grilled chicken legs. My taste buds told me everything was delicious, but my stomach rebelled at every morsel I swallowed. I added as much soda to my Mekhong as I dared, felt myself beginning to fade away, but Uncle Lao wanted to discuss personal philosophies. I pinched my flesh in every secret spot I could reach to stay conscious. With Wisut's help, I understood Uncle Lao to ask:

"What do you think of a man who works hard for his money and a man who gains great wealth through mere cunning?"

When I replied that a man who worked hard slept better and awoke with a cleaner taste in his mouth he nodded.

"Do you think there is really a big difference between men and women and do you think it is a good difference?"

I said I thought women were more sensitive, men usually had more strength, but both sexes were just as smart."

"Really?" he looked at me, surprised.

"Maybe different kinds of smart," I added

I looked to Wisut for help, but he shook his head.

Uncle Lao continued to look a little uneasy.

I said that there were, of course, a few other physical differences… my voice trailed off because I didn't know what else I could say and be polite.

"Yes, yes," he nodded, "young people are happy about that. So, do you believe something happens to us after we die?"

I wanted to be honest, but I didn't want to tell him I was an atheist. I ended up mumbling something about not thinking about things like that too often, but the few times I'd really been in danger I found myself praying to something…"

Again, my voice faded out. This wasn't going well. I wanted to end it.

"If someone is bad in this world, will something bad happen to him after he dies?"

I didn't know. What did he want from me?

"I don't know if something bad will happen to him," I said. "Although I hope so. I hope they go to a very bad place."

"You should not think about that," he frowned. "That is a bad thought to have inside you."

"I really don't know what happens after we die," I admitted. "I don't think anything happens. The only important time is right now."

"Not the same as Buddhist," he said.

He turned to Wisut.

"You must tell him about Buddhism."

Wisut nodded.

We left soon after that for home.

July 6, 1967

Now that I was in the rhythm of work, knew my students names, actually liked what the janitor's wife dragged over every day for lunch, I began to allow myself a sense of finally fitting in. My weekends flashed by in a haze of *sato*, bike rides and excursions to tiny villages whose names always seemed to reflect something about their natural environment.

I kept telling myself it was time for me to start a formal study of Thai script, but myself didn't listen. Every time I thought my oral comprehension was getting better, I met someone who didn't know me, lived outside of town and spoke rapid Thai with Cambodian words thrown in and I was totally lost. Didn't they know I was an idiot and needed help? Many of the town's older citizens stopped me in the market and tried to strike up a conversation, but if the topic wandered too far from small talk, I was stumped.

When I left Massachusetts for training in Hawaii I weighed 175 pounds and I was down to 145. No matter how many plates of fried rice I ate or how many deep fried *patongos* I nibbled, there was no way I'd ever replace all the calories of Big Macs and double-thick shakes with french-fries.

Going over my accounts for this month I noticed I spent 300 baht for food, 70 baht for Pepsis, 64 baht for newspapers, 135 baht to develop film, 90 baht for Wisai who bought me eggs and various delicacies for breakfast, and 60 baht for flour, sugar and margarine. I no longer thought of a baht equaling a nickel. A baht is just a baht.

Wisut was out playing cards until late last night while I was home listening to moths hammer against the shutters and crickets searched for my clothes. I was told I had to have all my test results in early because I was leaving for a Peace Corps conference in Korat. Earlier that day, while going over my student rolls with Prayun he pointed out that I'd been calling about 70 percent of them by wrong names. I complained to Prayun that the kids always mumbled when I asked them their names and when I tried to pronounce what I thought they'd each said, they always nodded and smiled and said, "Yes, my teacher."

"They will always say, 'Yes, my teacher,' because you are the teacher," Prayun explained. "They will never tell you that you are wrong."

"But, I've been taking attendance for weeks now and they all answer to the names I called out."

"That's because they memorized the names you gave them and always raised their hands when you asked if they were present."

"I never *gave* them names," I said. "They just never gave *me* the right name."

"Well, now you know the correct names," he said. "Forget the other names you wrote down and learn the new and proper ones."

"Okay, I will."

"And, it is time for you to study more Thai. I will be your teacher. Miss Charlotte, the former volunteer, could speak and write Thai very well and she could cook Thai food, too,"

"Okay, I will."

"We shall start tomorrow right after your last class."

When I didn't answer, he just smiled at me and left the room.

July 7, 1967

I scored the reading test I gave my MS-1 students and was totally depressed. Who had been mimicking my voice all the time? The problem was these kids all had fantastic memories. They apparently parroted back whatever I said to them, but understood very little.

I became angry this afternoon when someone from the headmaster's office dropped by to tell me they were canceling classes for the rest of the day. The head of the Department of Education for the province might pay a visit, so they wanted the students to spend the rest of the afternoon cleaning the campus. Without thinking, I picked up a blackboard eraser and threw it across the room. My students sat in stunned silence. I pointed to the door.

"Go," I told them. "No school this afternoon."

Bunya, one of my smartest students, slowly got to his feet.

"My teacher," he said, slowly, "we will stay with you."

"Thank you, but you have to go outside and help clean the school grounds."

"My teacher, will you come with us?"

"Yes," I nodded, unable to hide a smile, "I'll go with you."

We trooped out of the room together, class and teacher, united as one.

I concluded that some of my students cheated on their tests. Several of the papers had exactly the same answers right down to the same spelling mistakes. I knew what I should do. At the beginning of school, Prayun gave me a bamboo switch to hit them with if they misbehaved. He disciplined students that way even if they forgot to wear their pith helmets. I had to discuss this with Wisut.

Student discipline took place every morning right after the pledge of allegiance and the national anthem. Actually, Prayun never hit any of his students very hard for minor infractions, but I saw the assistant headmaster whack a few students hard right behind their knees because they had been caught drinking alcohol.

I heard the only doctor in town had a new American medical assistant so I tried to bicycle over to see her. Since I had only a vague idea of where I was going, I soon became totally lost on one of the several dusty roads leading out of the village. Two farmers approached me and I asked them if I was heading to the doctor's office. They looked at each other, puzzled, and both asked, "Arai?" (What?) No matter how many times I asked them the same question, varying the tones on various syllables, hoping eventually to get it right, they never understood me. After they left, I got back on my bike and forced myself to continue until the wheels slipped off the road's fine sand and I collapsed at the edge of a rice paddy. The sun was a heat lamp only a few feet away from the top of my head. I pushed myself up, took hold of the bicycle and threw it with all my strength, screaming, "Fuuuuuuck!"

Since that didn't seem to help, I walked over, picked it up and slowly pushed my bike home where Wisut said the new assistant had only been in town for one day and she was already gone, probably forever.

Wisai returned from the market without the cakes I'd asked him to buy. Disappointed, I went to make some Ovaltine anyway and found the ants had invaded the water urn again and I had to throw it all out and scour the damn thing clean. Then I had to find the water girl again. At these times, I thought of all the things I took for granted back home. They say the planet has shrunk because of mass communication and jet aircraft, but the daily amenities between Nang Rong and Boston remained light years apart.

Wisai did bring me tea leaves and I heated a delicious brew in hopes of making my headache go away. The leaves were big and crisp. I crumbled them with my hands, manufactured a strainer from a piece of cloth and a coat hanger, and boiled the water over the kerosene burner. After I had my last cup of tea, but just before I went to bed, I sat at my little desk and stared at the pages of this journal. I wanted to scream about how different everything was, but it seemed that all I wrote about was ants in my kitchen and how I make tea.

Wisut left with Preeda and another friend for a party. They were already slightly drunk because they'd visited Uncle Lau earlier in the day to test a new batch of *sato*. By midnight, I was certain Wisut wasn't going to return. I was really glad I hadn't gone with them. Just before I fell asleep I heard the gecko's claws scrapping across the ceiling. It no longer cares whether anyone is awake or not and continues to startle me at night with his mournful DOOOOKEH! DOOOOKEEeeeh! DOOooookeh! Doookeeh!

I received a form from my local draft board giving me permission to leave the country. They also changed my classification from 1-A to 2-A.

Still half asleep in the fresh dawn of a new day, I stretched, and fell back into a dream of kitchen sounds: pots banging, dishes clinking, children's voices rising and falling. Was that the scent of bacon frying? A radio was playing Perry Como: Find a ring and put it round round round.

Sunlight burst into the room and I opened my eyes to the bright light of a Nang Rong morning that burned away the last vestige of my dream. The voices I heard now were Thai and the smell in the air came from charcoal fires and pots of boiling rice. Barely time for me to clean-up, dress and go to work.

After a fast breakfast, I finished grading tests and thought about what I'd pack for the trip to Korat. A telegram from Bangkok told me I'd meet with other English teachers from all over the northeast region. This would be my first chance to see the volunteers who first greeted me at the Buriram train station.

July 17, 1967

I took a bus to Buriram and walked over to Frank's house to arrange a place to crash. He was a volunteer who worked as a civil engineer for the city. Later in the day, a volunteer named Judy came in from Lamplaimart and Melinda arrived in from Satuek. I missed small talk! Walking through the city with so many Americans lifted my spirits. We had delicious coconut ice cream from a local dairy. Several of us dropped into an air-conditioned theater to see a James Garner movie, but at the last minute the theater management switched to an Italian James Bond spoof. The actors spoke Italian, with Thai dubbed in and Chinese subtitles.

Melinda spoke fluent Thai but with such a thick Brooklyn accent that one time even I had to explain something she said to a taxi driver. Her town of Satuek had such bad roads that when the rainy season arrives people settle in for months at a time. She told me her instructions upon arriving in Bangkok were to take the rapid train to Buriram, wait for a local bus to some outlying village, and then knit or macramé something until an elephant convoy passed by going her way. I counted my blessings.

Next morning Judy, Melinda, Sharon and I took the train to Korat, headed straight to the Foremost Dairy restaurant for hamburgers and banana splits. The volunteers from the northeast gathered briefly in Korat and then continued to the conference in the resort town of Khaow Yai. Because it rained the whole time we were there, swimming and hiking were out, but we played three fast football games until we were all soaked and muddy.

A peace corps volunteer named Arnie Goldstein presented an analysis of the different perspectives between Peace Corps and military personnel. As he emphasized how much more civilized and humane volunteer staff were than soldiers, someone close to the podium pointed out a contingent of special forces troops on the balcony listening intently. Goldstein quickly veered his presentation to point out the part-time teaching that soldiers were doing and how helpful they'd been in his area by lending equipment for road-building projects. It was such an abrupt digression that volunteers and soldiers all broke into laughter.

The main presentation was "PCV: Technician or Attitude Changer." Although Peace Corps volunteers were taught to be agents of change, the Thai government had accepted us on the assumption that we were primarily technicians, specialists in our fields. Result = Friction. Several community development workers delivered presentations on crop rotation, poultry and swine raising, and the notion of initiating collectives among small farms. Experience seemed to have taught the Peace Corps that collectives would be resisted primarily by two factions in the country: entrenched politicians and Chinese businessmen. The politicians were leery of collectives because they had too many connotations redolent of socialism. The businessmen, who controlled a great deal of commercial and agricultural enterprises, were loathe to give any more bargaining power to the farmers.

Peace Corps Northern Regional Representative George Papagianis was on hand to placate or enliven discussion groups with his immense knowledge of the Thai language, people and culture, not to mention his ability to read palms and prognosticate our individual futures. He said mine was too confusing and he would need to see me later when he had more charts. He did venture that "…your good luck line is so screwed-up I don't know what to say…" He cheerfully showed anyone who cared to see that his own palm showed tremendous potential. My power potential was summed up as "…meager…"

Village health and sanitation volunteers complained that various army and aid groups compromised their work. One medical volunteer said that while she was there to change Thai attitudes about personal health and sanitation, a nearby USOM (United States Operations Missions) contingent was handing out pills for every conceivable illness. The local Thai attitude became, "Why listen to Peace Corp volunteers who only urge expensive and irksome changes, when USOM offers immediate cure-alls?"

Another issue was about some volunteers in Chile who were dropped by Peace Corps because of a long protest note they sent to the New York Times regarding the war in Vietnam. Peace Corps Director of Thailand Tim Adams gave what I thought were some cursory rationales that were not satisfactory to most of those in attendance. Besides, he said, those volunteers weren't fired, they were "prematurely terminated," and not because they wrote the note, but because they signed the petition as American volunteers. Bob Ford, who appeared to be in charge of logistics for Peace Corps Thailand, complained that the selection process was all shot to hell. "…does anyone here realize that the last TEFL group didn't have *anyone* de-selected during training at all…?" Everyone gasped, except, of course, those of us from Group XVIII, who were just happy to still be in The Land of Smiles.

The conference was declared a success because of all the communication that took place between volunteers and support staff. At its conclusion, we boarded buses and began the long ride back down the mountain from Khaow Yai to Korat. Midway, my bus began to smell of burnt brake linings and several nervous souls began opening windows in order to be able to leap to safety if death appeared on the horizon. The driver managed to pause at a small shrine, got out, knelt before Buddha to say a few prayers, leaped back down the steps, hopped behind the wheel and, with a smile on his face, careened the rest of the way into the city.

I spoke with a few volunteers about local fighting near That Phanom Village in the far northeast region. They told tales of so-called Communist infiltrations, terrorist raids, and the work being done by USIS (United States Information Service), USOM, and AID workers. This was the first time I'd heard of the "Free Thai" movement and how they were rumored to be equipped with Chinese weapons. Free Thai demands land reform, a new constitution and overthrow of the royal family. Although a few Bangkok newspapers had annual crusades against corruption in high places, graft and nepotism seemed to simply be a way of doing business. Then again, I could be describing the city of Boston. One scandal involved the proliferation of diploma mills that granted teaching certificates for 6,000 to 8,000 baht. Since the average Thai worker earned about 600 baht a month and a beginning teacher got 700, many people apparently thought it was worth the risk to become a fake teacher. National colleges were churning out liberal arts and business majors faster than the civil service could absorb them. Since blue-collar jobs were viewed with disdain by anyone with more than a high school education, white-collar jobs were in big demand. Compounding the problem was the reality that most educated Thais also wanted to live and work in Bangkok, so the capital was overloaded with members of the *intelligencia* while the rest of the country suffered a brain drain.

On my brief stop in Buriram I met an American who worked for USOM under contract to build a small airfield outside of the provincial capital. When I asked him who would use it, he just rolled his eyes and shrugged. He said he was an old hand at this government contract work and had been building airfields and roads throughout Southeast Asia and the Middle East. When I asked if he thought our country was going to ship in even more men and equipment to Thailand he said it was his impression the bureaucrats in Washington now viewed Thailand as the next Vietnam. He asked me what I thought of my assignment and when I gave a positive reply he told me about four volunteers he met in Afghanistan, two women teaching English and two men doing community development work, who all told him they planned on leaving early because of the daily hardships of simply living where they were placed. He gave them all the canned goods he could spare and described their living quarters as basic shacks without any amenities, the countryside being bleak, endless plains that rolled straight out to snow-covered mountains in the far distance.

A few observations of Korat: Thai-speaking Peace Corps volunteers pay less than American soldiers for *samlaws* (pedicabs), but more than Thais; the average American soldier looked quite large next to the average volunteer, and positively huge next to the average Thai.

July 20, 1967

Wisut, Sanguan and I had a boisterous time at a party celebrating the marriage of a border patrol soldier and a local teacher. There was lots of singing, dancing and overflowing glasses of Mekhong whiskey. My students kept cheering me on every time I got up to dance. A hand with a glass of whiskey in it miraculously appeared every time I tried to leave the dance stage. Eventually, I got to sit at a small table with several other teachers who were eating something called *laap bet*. Sanguan explained it was a traditional Isaan salad that in this case contained duck, onions, chillies, roasted rice and mint leaves. I stuck a spoon in it and moved the materials around. It appeared in a kind of broth that was dark red and sticky.

"Blood?" I asked, holding my breath.

"Yes," Sanguan smiled. "Very traditional. Made with duck blood."

I allowed a very modest portion on my plate, but focused on pieces of chicken and squid. Flash bulbs went off just about every time I lifted a glass of whiskey. After a while I didn't care if the bright flashes meant I was going blind or was about to have a stroke. Finally, someone guided me up to where the newlyweds were seated and I was shown where and how to pour water on their joined hands and whisper a few words of congratulations. A local band played cha-chas, tangos, beguines and traditional Thai dances. Passing among the guests, the bride and groom pinned tiny red flowers on the lapels of the men. She giggled when she reached me, but went ahead and pinned a flower on me as well. At midnight, the band played the national anthem, everyone stood up for a final toast and we left for home.

Everyone was late to school and many of the male teachers wore dark glasses. I missed my first two classes, but my students were too shy to say anything to anyone. Apparently, they just sat there, quietly in their teacherless room until it was time for their next class. I told my head student to pass word that if any students were interested in catching up on the lesson they'd missed they could go to my house after school and I would review everything.

Several boys from my second period class dropped by in the early evening. When I invited them in, they scrambled through the main room, touching everything, oohing andahhhing at all my junk, and gazing reverently at my guitar. I showed them a colorful booklet a friend had sent me about the city of Boston. They were enchanted. None of them had even been to Bangkok, and here they were looking at the city of the king's birth. They were fascinated with scenes of the Boston Common and the Public Gardens. I tried to explain Boston's famous swan boats.

"How much does it cost to ride the swan boats?" Sunya asked.

"Six baht," I said.

They lost interest. Six baht was too much money to spend on a boat ride.

Pian noticed small ducks in the picture and happily pointed them out to the others. It was as if they were relieved to find something familiar.

"Where did the ducks come from and why do they live there?" he asked.

"I'm not sure where they came from, but I'm sure they stay there because they must know they are safe. No one will harm them, there's plenty of water and thick grasses for them to hide in and, best of all, people walking by often buy peanuts or popcorn and feed them."

They looked at me, astonished.

"Why do people feed ducks that do not belong to them?" Sangiap asked.

"Well, the ducks don't actually *belong* to anyone. They're public ducks. They belong to everyone."

They were obviously puzzled at the concept.

"Who collects the duck eggs?" Manoon asked.

Manoon's sister sold duck eggs in the morning market for the equivalent of four cents each.

"No one collects the eggs," I sighed "They just let them hatch."

Then, they all started in at once:

"What about the baby ducks?"

"Would the police be angry if the people who feed the ducks take some eggs home?"

"Why did you tell us that everyone in America is not rich?"

"They're not."

"But, you just said people throw good food to ducks that don't even belong to them. Only very rich people would do that."

They backed me into my kitchen with all their duck questions, so as a diversion I pulled down a jar of peanut butter and told them to try it. Pian sniffed a spoonful, popped some in his mouth, then gagged, ran to the window and spit it out. The others laughed. I didn't understand how it could be that they loved peanuts, but not peanut butter. Maybe I should have served it with rice.

Finally, they all left and I scooped up some old magazines that had pictures about what was going on in Vietnam. None of the teachers say very much to me about the war, but I think it's because they're not sure of my feelings and don't want to get into sensitive areas. Although I can't read Thai, I've scanned local newspapers looking for war photos, but it seemed to me the only time the war was covered was when it involved Thai troops. I have, however, seen many stories and photographs of race riots in New Jersey.

July 21, 1967

I awoke this morning to the sound of voices and giggles in the living room. Wisut and his friends were on the floor creating a poster for tomorrow's boxing match. As I brewed my Ovaltine, the rain slammed against the house and through one open shutter I saw the nearby banana fronds whipped back and forth. There was a break in the rain just as the art project hit a snag, so they ran out to get to school early. I made myself a hasty breakfast of dried biscuits, honey, fried eggs and Ovaltine.

On the edge of the school grounds most of the students were constructing a platform for the boxing match. Wisut, in a chair on the sidelines, directed the project with a cigarette dangling from his lips and a big smile on his face. Other teachers scrambled about nailing flags to wooden staffs, cutting posters, but mostly getting in the way of the students. Suddenly, the rains returned with a vengeance. Half the work crowd ran to a canopy in the field, while the other half (including me) crawled under the partially completed stage. It was hot and stuffy in the confined space, but I was surrounded by excited students who wanted me to lead them in singing a few songs. The compromise was I would sing "Five Hundred Miles from Home" if they sang a popular song I'd heard on the radio many times titled "*Pet Dat Pet*." They sang first, clapping their hands in time, and laughed as I tried to keep up with the words. I finally understood that the song came from a Thai movie "Operation Bangkok" (a take-off of the James Bond syndrome). Wisut later translated a few of lines into English.

> *Diamonds cut diamonds – always – diamonds cut diamonds*
> *Anything can happen and some lose out*
> *The cobra goes down to the mongoose*
> *The tiger eats meat, but the fish eat worms*
> *Insects sink into the water and are eaten by fish*
> *Oh, what a pity!*

The next day was fine weather for the boxing match. The sun was a blistering 91 degrees in the shade, but the fans were wild. Wisut told me they sold all the tickets either ahead of time or at the gate. Farmers and their families started pouring into town the day before in order to take part in the festivities of Buddhist Lent and many of the men purchased boxing tickets.

The day started with a long parade through town. Drums rolled and citizens gawked at Burgess the Volunteer who fulfilled a childhood dream of beating a bass drum as he marched in a parade. I heard people cry out, "Look at the foreigner! I passed by in pressed chinos, loafers, white shirt, decorated paper bag on my head, along with sunglasses. Posters were plastered on every wall advertising the boxing match. A contingent of saffron-robed monks and floats from outlying villages slowly passed by. Trailing along at the very end, were many of my students dressed in what Wisut called "interpretive costumes" but to me closely resembled the dress of American Indians.

The parade stopped at the edge of the stage grounds and a massive crowd formed, held back only by a thin strand of tightly strung barbed wire. Tickets sold briskly for one, two and five baht, depending on one's age and choice of location. The boxing was supposed to start at 1:00, but actually began at 2:30. Seven bouts were planned and in the heat of day the crowd pulsed with enthusiasm. The referee appeared and infuriated everyone by insisting the ropes that guarded the perimeter were not adequately secure and the fights would not start unless something was done. Several muscular men walked around and patted, tugged and stretched the ropes until the referee was satisfied. A bell rang and the first two contenders entered the ring. They both first bowed to Buddha, their trainers, the referee, the crowd, then closed in warily on each other. It started suddenly with a blurred kick to the groin, then an elbow to a face, then a heel to a head, a toe in an eye, a fist to the lower stomach – the referee watched closely to make sure the men committed no fouls. Boxing, Thai style, must have subtle foul rules.

Round one was barely over before one of the boxers looked up at the blazing sun, felt a bruise on his right cheek, danced to one side and then jumped out of the ring, muttering *Yung mai tyyng…ran dja tdai loei.* (I can't do it. It's hot enough to die!).

The second bout ended in similar fashion. I noticed at the end of each fight both combatants met along ringside, shook hands and laughed. It was round five before any of the pairs felt like going more than one round, but they made up for the slowness of all the previous bouts by not only pummeling each other unmercifully, but also knocking the referee out cold. The crowd jumped up and down in glee. What happened to the gentle, smiling and peaceful people I knew and loved? I spotted a bristly-faced guy a few rows into the crowd who kept holding up different finger combinations and shouting to the crowd: "… *sip-ha* …. *ha-nyyng* … *sam-song!*" (10-5 … 5-1 … 3-2!)

He was a Thai bookie. A good hard kick to the crotch was enough to immediately shift the odds from 5-1 to 1-5. If an injury caused a grimace, a rare sight, the odds shifted at lightening speed. It took a good two hours to finish all seven bouts. The last one was the best, where both boxers slugged and kicked each other for a full five rounds. The judges were so impressed they awarded prizes to both of them.

Eventually, the crowd drifted away to a local temple to see which village managed to make the largest candle. I really would have loved to take a photo of a six foot pile of wax, but I had to head home and treat a severe case of sunburn.

Wisut told me thousands of tickets had been sold even to people from distant villages. It cost 1,500 baht for the boxers (that's $75 for 14 fighters), a 100 baht fee to have a doctor present, 115 baht in taxes, 25 baht for a license fee, and a few baht here and there for construction costs and salaries of the ticket collectors. All told, they put up 2,000 baht in order to take in 10,000 baht: a profit of 8,000 baht ($400). One of the organizers whispered to me that the federal tax man was told only 3,000 tickets had been sold. My informant then asked me if this sort of thing was also done in America. When I told him it certainly was, he was delighted and invited me over to his house sometime for *sato*.

"And, don't worry about the police," he said. "They're all friends of mine. And, don't worry about the inspectors. They're the ones who made the *sato*."

Profits from the boxing matches would be used to build two more classrooms and run an electric line to the school directly from the town's generating plant. Adjan Suraporn planned to send a subsidiary line over to the school's workshop so they could finally use the power tools donated by UNICEF. Any money left after those expenditures would go toward laying a cement floor for the school's workshop.

A recent article in the *Bangkok Post* reported that two policemen were killed by frightened distillers who were in the process of making a large batch of *sato*. In their defense, the hooch makers said they thought the cops were burglars because only thieves would have smashed down the door, while real police would have knocked and asked for a bribe. They were all sentenced to death.

July 28, 1967

I spent the last four days visiting Frank, in Buriram, who told me he studied Thai for two hours every day, although he already spoke it fluently, and worked into the night on highway blueprints and cross-sections of road grading. I'm sure there are many other volunteers like Frank and they all made me feel like an indulgent dunce. He told me his rite of passage involved being thrown in with Thai road engineers from the start and even though his training as a community development worker gave him minimal training, he studied every project that was thrown his way, drew road profiles and analyzed bridge safety plans until he was satisfied. He seemed to be comfortable with his job, in his own skin and closely-bonded with many Thai friends and co-workers.

The other community development volunteer in Buriram was Ralph, an expert in poultry and swine raising. I don't know if he was an animal husbandry major in college, or not, but the last time I was with him he gleefully haggled with a farmer who wanted to buy six of Ralph's piglets. They settled on 250 baht each and both sides seemed happy.

Sharon, an English teacher at the girl's school, and one of the first to meet me at the train station, also spoke fluent Thai. Because her features were Chinese, the Thais assumed she was fluent the moment she arrived. She said even after she explained many times that she was American, just like the other volunteers, it was hard for the locals to accept she didn't at least have a genetic proclivity for the Thai language.

"So, did that motivate you to learn Thai even faster?" I asked.

"It *forced* me to learn Thai even faster," she said. "Not only that, but I think I also picked up many more idiomatic expressions because the teachers I worked with used them with me all the time."

Sharon was another volunteer who made me feel I wasn't really doing my job the way I could or should. When it came time to board the bus back to Nang Rong, my early New Year's resolution was to tell Prayun I was ready to take more Thai language lessons with him.

Just before I left, I dropped by to see Frank and say goodbye. There were a few others visiting him at the time, and all of them were concerned with Frank's appearance and general health. We all ended up walking him to the local hospital were they quickly determined he had hepatitis. The doctor explained there really wasn't anything they could give him other than vitamin shots and a prescription for rest and plenty of liquids until the illness had run its course. Frank seemed quite discouraged by the news and the last thing I heard him sharing with other volunteers was information about all the projects he was involved in that needed looking after.

Scenes from inside the hospital lingered with me even after I was back in Nang Rong: shelves weighted down with specimen bottles; clear formaldehyde jars that held animal and human embryos in various stages of development; portions of human anatomy (tumors, growths, limbs) also on display. I passed one of the operating rooms shortly after an operation and saw men mopping up blood from the rough concrete floor.

One of the female volunteers who taught at a secondary girls' school visited Buriram recently to attend a party at Frank's house before he was diagnosed with hepatitis. Even though she had planned on staying overnight, sleeping on a cot in the corner, she spotted someone from her own village at the party and decided it would be impossible for her to stay for the sake of her own reputation. Even though she was having a great time and even though it was raining outside, she decided to leave early and bicycle over to a local hotel. In the dark, her bike slid off the muddy road and she found herself in a filthy canal with a fractured arm. She managed to crawl up to the road and stagger to a farmer's house where she pounded on the door for help. The farmer, unaccustomed to night visitors and fearing it might be a robber, shouted something at her in Thai, but he spoke too fast for her to understand.

Apparently, he said something like, "Get away from my door before I shoot." Because a few seconds later that's exactly what he did. The bullets missed her, but she passed out from shock and didn't regain consciousness until the next day in a bed at the Buriram Hospital. After a day to recuperate, she was released and took a bus back to her village. The whole episode will probably never be spoken of or written about in the annals of Peace Corps experiences.

Later, back in Nang Rong, I happily returned to my old routines. One evening I walked back home with Wisut by way of a short cut through the temple grounds. Monks chanted in the background as we stepped across the shadows of pagodas sharply etched by an enormous full moon. We passed the giant gong that hung by the monks' living quarters. This was the source of a reverberating sound heard several times daily throughout the village. I heard the splash of a bucket as it hit water at the bottom of a well. The sing song murmur of Sanscrit prayers came from behind us as we neared the exit. Insects whirred through the air, some hitting my face, and I cringed. Wisut whistled and absent-mindedly kicked a stone out of his way.

A piece of wood snapped in two a few yards behind us and I started as if

shot. Wisut laughed, but it reminded me how close to consciousness my fear of being shot hung in my mind. There have been many stories of guerrilla fighters from Cambodia operating in the forests near Nang Rong.

The train from Bangkok to Buriram pushed an extended flat-bed car in front of it to set off any pressure bombs planted on the tracks before the locomotive reached it. As the war in Vietnam widened in scope, American involvement in Thai life and culture deepened. Students at my school picked up some slang from the American advisors in Korat. A few days ago I heard one student call another (darker) student a nigger.

Reports drifted my way that roads in the That Phanom area had been

mined. American special forces who were in and out of Nang Rong told me that their supply camp had been riddled with machine gun rounds.

I usually didn't think about things like that when I was out on my bicycle at night pedaling to the market or Paak Waan Village. I hadn't heard of any Americans being ambushed. Thai people who were assassinated included village headmen, school principals and border patrol police. Notes left behind said that unless cash or food was left for the guerrillas more people would be shot or held for ransom. Best not to think of that on a daily basis. All these thoughts originated from a piece of wood that snapped in a temple courtyard.

I had a fantasy of winning the national lottery for a million baht ($25,000) and paying for my family to visit me in Nang Rong. I would have loved to introduce my father to Wisut's uncle. What a team they'd have made. As I said earlier, Uncle wanted to drop atomic bombs on Cambodia and my father wanted Eldridge Cleaver for president. I'm sure they would have had a meaningful dialogue.

My family seemed even more distant to me than the map's 12,500 miles. Recent photographs I received of my sisters astounded me. They looked so big compared to my memories – or, was my sense of proportion distorted because of the diminutive Thais who surrounded me? Had anything else been distorted? Time? My values?

Wisut asked me what my father did for a living and I tried to explain that my father and my mother got up at four every morning and made several hundred sandwiches. Then my father drove a delivery route, dropping off sandwiches at drugstores, bar rooms and factories, while my mother went upstairs and made the beds, cleaned the house and prepared the salads and food for the next day's production. Oh, and she cooked all the meals, cleaned the clothes and made sure all six children were presentable before they headed off to school. Wow, just writing all that down simply reinforced how very far away I was.

July 30, 1967

I spent most of Saturday in Paak Waan Village with Sanguan exploring temples and pagodas, chatting with a few of his neighbors and trying my best not to show how utterly exhausted I was after bicycling that horrible road to their hamlet. When I entered Sanguan's home I momentarily stepped aside at the sight of an incredibly old woman chewing betel nut leaves by the door. My friend gave her a curt nod, then directed me to his collection of magazines and posters carefully collected over the years. Here was a, educated man, quite sharp in his teacher's uniform, living without inside plumbing or even occasional electricity. Nang Rong, for him, was going downtown. After an hour or so of sitting uncomfortably in a semi-yoga position on a straw mat and engaging in a limited conversation, I told him I had to return home.

"Please say goodbye to my mother," he whispered, as we stood by the door.

The ancient form on the floor, with lips stained crimson from the betel nut leaves, gazed up at me and placed her hands together in the semblance of a *wai*. I quickly returned the gesture as I lowered myself to be by her side.

"I am sorry," I said to her. "I did not know you were Sanguan's mother. How are you?"

"He speaks Thai! He speaks Thai!" she exclaimed.

Sanguan murmured a few comforting words and gradually drew me to my feet and then out the door. As I pedaled away, all I could think of was his mother's appearance. Was Sanguan himself that much older than he appeared? Did the Thais, like Dorian Gray, cling to their youth well past middle age and then suddenly collapse into a pile of wrinkles?

Back home, a student waited for me with a message that Wisut, Preeda and Prayun had all gone to the house of Adjan Gimyong (the assistant principal) to celebrate his acquiring a second stripe on his teacher's uniform. I remembered Wisut told me earlier that Gimyong's wife had been working on a fresh batch of *sato* for weeks. Tired as I was, I knew it would be too much of a social rebuff to refuse and dragged myself inside to splash some water on my face and change into fresh clothes.

"How far away is Mr. Gimyong's house?" I asked the student.

By the quizzical expression on his face I knew this was an entirely new question for him.

"About one kilometer," he guessed.

By the time we left it was dark and after half an hour I became angry and frustrated. God damn Thai culture and their sense of Time and Distance. My fresh shirt was drenched with sweat. Insects in a variety of sizes and hardness bounced off my face, arms and chest. Although the air was as humid as it could be without actually raining, I still felt dehydrated. I swallowed over and over to keep my mouth moist. Prayun, my occasional Thai language tutor, suddenly passed us going the other way.

"Thank God," I thought. "The party's over and I don't have to worry about getting stomach cramps again from too much *sato*."

But, no, he'd merely been sent to find me. The student returned home and I continued on for a few more torturous miles with Prayun until we finally reached Gimyong's house. Gimyong's wife greeted me at the door with great formality and led me through the main room to the back patio where a large contingent of teachers, already drunk, cheerfully greeted my arrival. Wisut lurched to his feet and cried out, "Hello! It is my family!" which made me smile in spite of myself. Preeda was the only sober one, but I could never determine if his sobriety was because of athletic training, religion or personal preference.

I carefully positioned myself on a large, straw mat between Wisut and Preeda. As usual, they made fun of the way my knees stayed high in the air. Centered on the mat was a large bucket of frothy *sato* surrounded by bowls of steamed rice, spicy chicken delicacies floating in puddles of peppered fish oil, an enormous mound of curry with chopped onions and pieces of water buffalo meat, warmed cashews, fried morning glory leaves in oyster sauce, an assortment of salads and several of those horse-urine eggs they knew I loved so much. They quickly filled my glass and told me to drink it all quickly because I was late and had to catch up. Thirsty from the ride, I gulped the sour liquid down until I felt a familiar warm glow form in the pit of my stomach. I have a vague recollection of Gimyong's wife staring at me as I improvised some kind of song and dance act. Unfortunately, I also remember Wisut telling me it was time to go home and me saying, "You're crazy! Go home now just when we're starting to have fun!"

I awoke around dawn, blinded by a headache and rolling over and over to escape the shrill call of nearby roosters announcing a new day over and over. Gimyong's wife stood near me offering coffee. I had a flash of all the food I consumed the previous evening as I managed to get a few sips of the heavily-sweetened coffee into my system. Outside Wisut discovered that both our bikes had flat tires, so we had to walk them home, haul them up the steps and drag them inside for safe-keeping. We fell asleep until noon.

A pounding on my front door jarred me awake and I found Mr. Sanguan outside, nervously pacing back and forth, with a reminder that I had promised him, PROMISED him to go to a party given by his headmistress. For a second I even considered the possibility then sadly broke the news I simply could not go. He left close to tears. Berating my weak body, I put on the teapot, took several aspirins and wandered aimlessly around the house until I came upon a mound of dirty laundry that had a large piece of paper balanced on top which read: "Dear Burgess – I go to play rummy at the house of Gah-goo. I come back soon. From Wisut, your family."

A few days ago Preeda, the social studies and occasional science teacher, looked up from a book he was reading about space flight and astronomy and asked me, "Do you really believe in all this?"

"All what?"

"You know, about the moon not having any air and we are all spinning through space around and around. Do you really know about that? Do you believe?"

"Yes, I believe it."

"But, how do you know?"

"I don't really know. To me, it's like religion. I just believe it to be true."

"Ahhh," he nodded, seemingly satisfied.

"Do you know where the English language books come from?" I asked him.

"What books?"

"The green books called Ladder Editions that have all those stories about the Maori people of New Zealand and how the days of the week are named after Norse and Greek gods. I mean, they have nothing to do with Thailand at all."

"The headmaster selected them," he whispered, looking back over his shoulder. "They come from Great Britain."

"Oh, then I guess that means they are the best?"

"Exactly so. The very best."

My last batch of small cakes came out so well that for the first time teachers dropped by voluntarily to have some. It was enjoyable to sit calmly with three or four of the other faculty members, make a pot of tea, serve my little cakes and accept compliments on my cooking. I could hardly wait to show off my new skills back in the States. When my family and friends ask: Did you become fluent in Thai? Were you an excellent teacher? Did you volunteer all the time for extra duty? I'll say, "No, but I learned how to make really tasty coffee cakes.

August 1, 1967

Yesterday evening was quiet, except for the insects flying in and out of the house. Things finally got so bad I crawled under my mosquito net and stayed there in the dark wondering what else to do when my student, Wisai, burst into the house, quaking with fear.

"What's wrong?" I asked him, untangling myself from the netting.

"I not able to get inside Mr. Preeda's house to sleep, so I come here in the dark. May I stay with you, my teacher?"

"Yes, of course. But, why are you so frightened?"

"Good you give me flashlight to use on way to Mr. Preeda's or else I died."

"Died?"

"Died? How?"

"Cobra in road!" he exclaimed. "I think if I not have light in my hand I must die."

"Cobra! There are cobras near here?"

"Oh yes. Many snakes now because the ground have much grass and bush for snake to hide in. You must should always walk on road or else you died."

I made a mental note to look for hip boots in town.

Again, I was under my mosquito net in the dark, this time it was not only because of all the insects, but because a thunder and lightening storm had blown into town and crippled the sole electrical generating plant in Nang Rong. Two days of darkness. I slowly began to go insane without a reading light or radio or tape player. I just could *not* go to sleep at 8:00 in the evening, even though I kept telling myself I should be able to adapt to the natural rhythms of the world around me. The reality was I collapsed on my bed, added more sweat to my meager pillow, stared helplessly as one insect after another wiggled its way into my space and waited for mosquitoes to drain me of enough blood to make me sleepy.

Another member of my group, a medical technician stationed in Bangkok, left prematurely. The story was that she felt isolated in her little office with nothing to do but fill out forms and do general clerical work. Since she could just as easily do that back in the States, she took off.

My limited language skills prevented me from keeping current on local news, gossip and rumors. When I asked Wisut why the area seemed so quiet lately he said most of the men in town were off celebrating at the border patrol building.

"What are they celebrating?" I asked, hoping I hadn't missed some big holiday.

"You know the teacher, Miss Jeri?"

"Yes."

"You do not know about her?"

"No."

"The big party is because she is marrying one of the border patrol men and everyone is happy for them. So, all teachers and all border patrol people will go to the wedding and then to the party."

"Are you going somewhere?" I asked, as he put on a fresh shirt.

"I'm going to the party. You want to go with me?"

"I didn't get invited."

"I didn't get invited either, but I'm going. I am a teacher. Miss Jeri is a teacher. So, all teachers can go. If you are border patrol, then can go, too. No invitation."

"No, thank you. I'll stay home."

"Okay, be good."

I smiled at his words. He'd just learned them from an English primer filled with possible ways of saying 'goodbye.'

As the door closed behind him, I thought about all the possible relationships in town and school that always came to me as a surprise. I never seemed to know who was related to whom. I just discovered that one of the students who came by my house for extra help is the headmaster's son. Maybe I should start asking everyone their last name, something people do not usually give out.

Soon after Wisut left another teacher came by to invite me to the party.

"I do not feel well," I told him in Thai.

"Do you want a shot?" he asked, using the English word "shot."

"What?"

"Shot," he repeated, and pulled out a small case from his pocket and opened it to reveal a hypodermic needle along with several glass vials of who knows what.

"No, thank you."

He shrugged and left for the party.

I've heard several new forms of penicillin-resistant venereal diseases have showed up lately and it's probably because people like that teacher have no compunctions about self-medicating. One of the border patrol guys told me he always gave himself a precautionary shot of penicillin before visiting a prostitute.

A woman from one of the local restaurants dropped by with my dinner. I'd actually asked Sanguan if he could pick something up for me because I wasn't feeling well, but for some reason he returned not only with some food, but also with the restaurant owner's daughter. I knew her from the market area because her small child always runs directly out to the street when he sees me, yelling, "*Farang! Farang!* (Foreigner!)." At which point, I always turn to him and loudly say, *Ja-eh!* Which is the Thai equivalent of Boo!

"Her ice is very warm," Sanguan whispered to me as the woman carefully emptied several metal containers and arranged the food on my table.

I looked up, puzzled, then back down to the small container of ice she'd brought along for my Pepsi. What was he talking about? She looked up from the table and turned to stare at me.

"Her ice," he said again. "Look into her ice."

Oh, her eyes! I looked back at her, but did not see any particular warmth in her eyes. Sanguan choked with laughter and signaled me not to say anything, but told her anyway and she playfully punched his shoulder.

After she left, Sanguan stayed with me as I ate.

"Are you full?" he asked as I pushed the last plate aside.

"Almost."

"Good, because I have special Thai food for you."

He reached under the table and pulled up a small, cloth sack I hadn't noticed. He turned it upside down over the table and a bunch of what appeared to be reddish, hairy balls rolled out. I burst out laughing just at their appearance.

"What's that?" I asked.

"These are called *ngo* .

"No?"

"No. *Ngo!*"

He carefully peeled one of the balls to reveal a whitish, soft fruit which he popped in his mouth and happily chewed. I peeled and ate one myself to experience an entirely new taste, somewhat sweet, but also utterly foreign to my experience. I pulled out my Thai-English dictionary and discovered *ngo* are called rambutan in English.

Wisai, the gentle and soft-spoken teenager who hung around the house, cautiously continued to try out his English skills with me. When I told him I planned to make some coffee cake ("sweet cake" to him) he volunteered to bicycle into town and get the eggs and milk I needed. By the time he returned I'd finished cleaning the utensils and had the rest of the ingredients out.

"Where are the eggs?" I asked.

"There were no more eggs in the market."

"Why didn't you buy a few eggs from the restaurant?"

"Too expensive! Eggs in the market are three for one baht, but eggs from the restaurant are one baht each! Too much!"

I sighed. One baht per egg was too much, but a baht was only a nickel. What the hell did I care? What was I supposed to do with all the stuff I had out on the table?

"I will go to the market tomorrow," he said. "The new morning market will have many eggs for less."

I nodded, trying hard to appear pensive instead of giving in to my baser instincts and simply strangling him on the spot.

After taking a deep breath I turned to him, smiled, and said he'd done the right thing. *Mai pen rai.* If not today, then tomorrow. He seemed to accept my lie, glanced once more at everything I had out, looked back at me for reassurance and left.

Outside, the wind was blowing in several directions at once and the heavy banana fronds tipped drunkenly left and right. I put away the coffee cake items, pulled a chair close to an open window and stared out at the almost violet sky dotted with bobbing leaves and trash. Old newspapers at my feet told of race riots in the States and about a fire on an aircraft carrier. A headline noted the US was taking a battleship out of mothballs. The following paragraph explained it would take at least 10 months to re-equip such a monstrous ship for action and concluded such a plan must mean America planned to be at war for some time to come.

A bicycle screeched to a halt beneath my house and I heard someone running up the stairs. It was Wisai.

"There are many restaurants in town," he said. "When I told one that I needed some eggs for the foreigner he sold them to me for the same as market. Here are three eggs for only one baht!"

His enormous smile made me glow. I love everyone here! On with the cakes!

August 5, 1967

I tried to write about another experience I'd had with someone at the Pink House, but when I read my own words they seemed ugly, too literal and crude. The closest I could come to describing what happened was in the form of the following poem which speaks for me and itself.

PINK HOUSE

On a drunken spree I first met her
at the Pink House where a small fee
bought time on a bamboo mat with Ms. Oy
a working girl who made me fried
morning glory leaves in oyster sauce
familiarity with place meant not annoyed by
tokays hanging from ceilings
familiarity with place meant not glancing
twice at a wandering water buffalo
months later I bonded with malaria techs
on a vector mission for tainted blood
all of us downing Mekhong whiskey beneath a gibbous
moon then headed for the Pink House where I waited
until Oy was free and by then just couldn't do it
she stayed on my mind when I visited Hindu shrines
the picnic happened months after
when I teamed with other volunteers
to play soccer against a local team
raise money for a local charity
afterwards we went out for chicken curry,
cartons of beer and fried morning glory leaves

which made me think of the Pink House
and realized I missed her so the following
Sunday afternoon my plan was a picnic
but the women were reuluctant
to move as it'd been a busy night
but Oy smiled my way and explained
the foreigners had cash, they didn't have
to work and there'd be food so we jammed
into a Land Rover with her shy on my lap
and bump along we went to a quiet lake laughing
teasing eating half-stripping near the lotus-packed
water reflecting sharp blue sky
there's a photo somewhere of me decked
with flowers lying on Oy's lap in bliss
until she quietly left me to kneel and pray
by a cracked statue of Buddha
head bowed bringing quiet all around even
silence on the return except when she surprised
me by blurting out
I do this but I good girl
for some reason I was suddenly car sick into
the red clay ruts by the side of the road and
could not wait to head home and shower
now even hearing
the word *pink* makes me tighten up
and I want to go out and drink alone

....

August 10, 1967

I stepped back inside the teachers' lounge on the second story from the porch that looked out over the school grounds and the surrounding countryside. Would I ever be bored by the sight of infinite rows of coconut palms or the flattened squares of rice paddies that flowed out to the horizon?

Although it was fairly early in the day, we seemed to have skipped the usual glorious morning haze and slipped directly into heat. Two slow-moving fans in the lounge barely moved the air in the room, but I had to stay here because final exams were coming up and since I typed faster than anyone else I was assigned the task of typing all the English language tests. I was more than a little nervous about how well (or poorly) my students would do, but I was also excited about taking the train back to Bangkok for R & R.

The tests I typed included: Reading, Expression, Literature and Comprehension. "Reading" actually involved students reading aloud to the teacher. Considering the range of the teachers' abilities, I thought grading would be very subjective. "Expression" represented grammar. "Literature" and "Comprehension" required students to read a short story and then be quizzed on the content. I asked why we needed two separate tests for what was basically the same thing, but they told me that's the way they've always done it and, by God, that's the way they will continue to do it.

I finally received a booklocker from Peace Corps, Bangkok. What a treasure chest! "Andersonville" looks very good. I also spotted the complete poems of Edgar Allen Poe, dozens of novels by contemporary authors and texts that ranged from sociology to cooking. I just finished reading Barth's "Floating Opera" and I was as happy as in the days when I used to skip high school classes to go to the public library and read whatever I wanted. I have to be careful not to lose myself with these books and skimp on my responsibilities for Nang Rong School.

I felt at that instant my future was filled with nothing but calm, teaching days, warm and clear afternoons, occasional trips to Korat and perhaps a journey to Malaysia later on. I've fallen in love with the daily chores, meals and little conversations during lunch with the other teachers. My Thai language skills have finally reached the point where I can do small talk. I found myself looking forward to every bowl of chicken curry, clear soup, sweetened evaporated milk over bananas and the occasional luxury of a cold soft drink.

Above my head hung a portrait of King Bhumipol and next to that a glorious golden image of the Buddha. Beneath them were portraits of the queen and prince. Through a side window I could see into the other buildings where students were taking tests. Around the school's brown-stained wooden buildings were green shrubs, guava trees, banana fronds and palm trees. I could easily hear a dozen different bird trills. The trees were always green and the birds were always singing, like a fertile, clockwork universe. Wisut said that the banana trees planted next to my house would bear fruit before I leave. I could already have bananas for breakfast by reaching out the window. The constant routine of duck eggs and *patongos* and Ovaltine had become boring. I thought about finding out the word for oatmeal and buying some in Bangkok, along with a can or two of Spam to have with my duck eggs. Spam as a treat?

My Aunt Eva sent me some postcards from Boston because I told her the Thais would like to see photographs from the birthplace of their king. She sent me photo-cards of big, brown pots of steaming beans with the inscription: "You don't know beans until you come to Boston."

Most of the staff were involved in the construction of a water tower and six enormous metal storage tanks. One end of a pipe was fabricated to plunge deeply into a nearby well while the other end was fitted into a newly installed hand pump that drew water into the holding tanks.

Today was the first official test. I was pretty sure they had tried it out a few times in private to make certain there would be no embarrassing failure. Everyone stood around patiently until the headmaster primed the pump, and primed it again until there was a wooshing sound from within the pipe and suddenly we heard water spilling into the

Burgess with Mr. Wason on Lake Nong Tamue.

Burgess gives impromptu lesson in his tent with students from Camp Thai-Am.

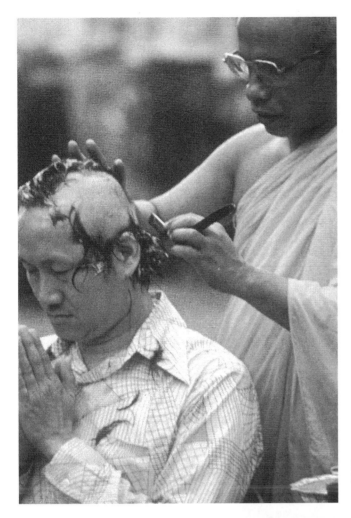

Before becoming a monk, this man had to have his head shaved.

Newly-shaved monk is presented to the public.

Entrance to Nangrong's monastery.

The end of the rainy season is a special time for offering food and clothing to monks. Giving food to a monk is one way of gaining merit for the next life.

Thanksgiving Day turkey.

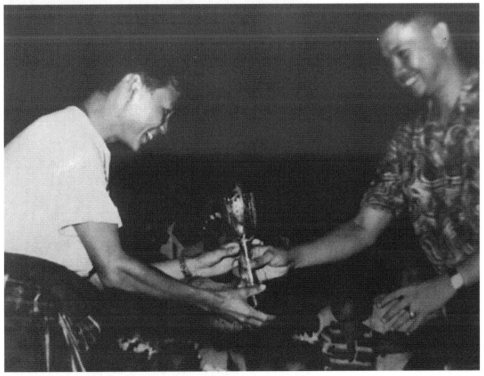

Wisut wins a prize for best traditional thai costume.

With Ms. Oy at a picnic in Buriram.

Ms. Oy praying.

storage tanks. Nang Rong's new water tower quickly filled and the students watched in wide-eyed wonder as Prayun knelt before one of the spigots and pressed down. Water exploded out on to the dusty earth, spattering his sharply pressed uniform with muddy drops. Everyone cried out, *"Chayo! Chayo Chayo!"* Prayun kept the water running, waiting until Adjan Suraporn knelt beside him and held his hands beneath the flow. Looking solemn, he rubbed his hands carefully signaling to Prayun to turn it off. The headmaster then stood before the crowd and held his hands up for all to see.

"*Sahat lao! [I'm clean!]*" he cried, and everyone shouted, *"Chayo! Chayo! Chayo!"*

A little reality check aside

One of my sisters wrote that when she was on vacation in Europe last month she thought of trying to call me from Germany. After all, she was 2,500 miles or so closer to me than from Boston. Why not try a call? But then, she confessed, she was confused by the time differences, the International Date Line; perhaps school wasn't even in session or listed in the Bangkok directory. Maybe I didn't even have a line running to my house. I shook my head as I read her kind words. Telephone line? What could she be thinking? There wasn't a telephone in the entire village, maybe not the entire province. One telegraph line connected Nang Rong to the rest of the world.

Back to the real world

My electric lights continued to flicker and blink through the evening. Just before I arrived electric service was *extended* until six in the morning. Until last February, all current ceased at 10:00 PM Melinda, a volunteer in the remote hamlet of Satuek, told me that her area still had no electricity at all after 10:00. She sounded so forlorn when she described her attempted New Year's Eve party with her Thai friends. Everybody laughed and drank and had a good time until as the lights began to dim, the crowd thinned and try as she might to keep things rolling with kerosene lanterns, it was no go. Midnight found her alone staring at her flickering shadow surrounded by empty glasses and groundout cigarettes.

August 28, 1967

Bangkok's restaurants offered a salve to my stomach's wounds from too much hot curry. I filled up on fillet mignon with baked potatoes and sour cream. The Carlton Restaurant's Russian borscht with sour cream and boiled potatoes was excellent.

I stayed at the June Hotel, a favorite stopover for minor Thai officials or maybe even a provincial governor or two. The rooms were inexpensive, but had working bathrooms with plenty of hot water. The hotel's additional attraction was a secluded parking lot out back where you could slip your vehicle in between hanging pieces of cloth, get out and walk to the rear door without anyone seeing you. A few of the volunteers I met in the lobby talked about extending their service. I heard Thailand and Nepal had the highest re-enlistment rates in Peace Corps.

My physical examination revealed a lump on the back of my head that was identified as a sebaceous cyst. I was referred to the Seventh Day Adventist Hospital for outpatient surgery. An orderly deftly shaved away part of my hair, a nurse slipped in a local anesthetic and the doctor easily removed the cyst, which he cheerfully showed me suspended in a vial of formaldehyde.

I wandered in and out of the main Peace Corps office, chatted with the secretaries and nodded in the direction of newly arrived volunteers. I later heard the new arrivals thought I'd been ambushed by Cambodian irregulars. I *wondered* why I'd been getting all those sympathetic glances.

All of the other volunteers I bumped into in Bangkok spoke far better Thai than I did and that flat out depressed me. Back at my hotel I called down to room service for their massage service, but I was unable to make myself understood. Totally embarrassing when the desk clerk showed up with a young woman who turned out to be another Peace Corps volunteer! Red-faced, I made something up about what I really wanted, too ashamed to admit the truth to her. I later found out the Thai words for "massage" and "mustache" were very similar. So, the clerk was understandably confused by the foreigner who wanted a mustache sent up to his room.

Bangkok was filled with American soldiers on R & R. All the large, air-conditioned movies were packed with American troops. I wanted to see "Gone With the Wind," but it was sold out many weeks in advance. Toward the end of my stay I picked up about $15.00 worth of packaged groceries for future treats.

Back in Nang Rong, I unpacked and worked on preparing a few lessons for the first day of school. Later, I dropped by the post office and found a cassette of "Sgt. Pepper's Lonely Hearts Club Band" and a few letters waiting for me from my family. My students loved the title song. I wished I had an 8mm movie camera with sound so I could have recorded a dozen of the boys marching up and down my classroom singing the Sgt. Pepper marching song in perfect harmony and tempo.

After school, I sat down on a chair in the shade of my house, put my head back and tried to just listen, really listen, to all the sounds around me. Enormous fronds rustled against each other in a soft breeze, distant dogs barked, the gong from the temple echoed, soft voices of students walking past hit me in an unintelligible, but warm and friendly language. Wisut's shadow passed over me and I opened my eyes.

"What are you doing?" he asked.

I tried to say that I was 'Killing time" in Thai.

He shook his head and made a face.

"Can't you say that in Thai?" I asked.

"If you say that you are killing time," he said, "then I must ask what weapons you are using?"

Sept. 1, 1967

Listening to my parents and siblings talking on a cassette tape was exciting but also depressing. It made me think of all the changes going on without me being there. My younger brother, David, was obviously entering puberty and I heard his voice changing. Everyone sounded so close and familiar, and yet so far away.

In between studying the Thai alphabet and practicing slang phrases with Wisut, I went through a bunch of Marvel comics my friend Roger loaned me. I may not be up on current news in Boston, but I'm fairly up-to-date with Thor, Dr. Strange, The Fantastic Four and Spider Man.

Wisut was out partying somewhere and the evening air was warm and humid. Nothing seemed able to deter a swarm of black ants intent on using my kitchen floor as a vast breeding ground. The temple bells rang and not too far from my house I could hear many of the townspeople heading for the *wat*. Did I miss a major religious holiday? I played the Sgt. Pepper tape again, smoked a little dope and kicked back on my bed to dream of the girl with kaleidoscope eyes. The sky in England may be marmalade, but in Nang Rong District, just before the end of twilight and the beginning of night, it is as green as Boston's summer grass.

I'd have to eat the last candy bar I brought back from Bangkok or watch it slowly melt away. After substituting dried prunes for nuts, I whipped together a Bisquick cake mix popped it into my little oven and ended up with a delicious product.

Wherever I was, in the kitchen cooking or wandering through the living room looking for my glasses, the tape-recorded voices of my family followed me. It was a little disorienting sometimes, but having the sense of family nearby was a nice cushion. I played some of the tape to a few of the teachers, but even the ones who theoretically have some knowledge of English simply laughed at the endless loop of foreign sounds. They burst out laughing when my youngest brother ended a little story to me with a *chayo*. My mother's voice drew them closer and my father's rougher tones sounding remarkably like the headmaster's, made them stand at attention.

Andy, one of the American soldiers who had visited me earlier, dropped by. He was one of the few non-Peace Corpse Americans I met who bothered to learn more than a few words of Thai. Standing over six and a half feet tall with an enormous Salvador Dali mustache, he must have made an obvious target. I loved talking with him because he seemed so genuine and spontaneous and did not seem to be guarded about any subject. I asked him if he had any interesting war stories, but he shrugged and said he didn't think it was cool to talk about stuff like that as if it were entertainment.

He told me about a locally hired Thai named Nit, who was assigned to them as a cook and who knew something about Western cuisine. When it turned out he couldn't even fry an egg they tried to fire him, only to have him reappear a week later with an official document from an American major explaining that the cook was actually working undercover for the CIA. Andy explained that since he had to keep him even though he couldn't cook he assigned him to the motor pool as a drone.

"Everything worked out real well," Andy laughed. "My captain got the CIA guys to keep paying Nit's salary and the new cook plus a per diem for both of them so we ended up with extra funds to bring in more beer from the PX in Korat."

"I thought you were the guys gathering intelligence. How come none of you knew about Nit's real assignment?"

"Are you kidding? They got so many CIA operatives here and in Laos they're always screwing up each other's jobs and sabotaging their own units. You can't believe how many fuck-ups go on."

He looked down and smiled.

"Hell, for all you know, I might be working for the agency myself and testing you to see how you respond. What do you say to that?"

He burst out laughing.

When Andy left, I kept thinking of the stories I heard in Bangkok about connections between the CIA and how they supposedly debriefed Peace Corps volunteers on information about their areas. What a joke.

I actually gained a pound to an even 150, though still far below my usual 175. A sure sign my body was beginning to adapt to curry.

Wisut returned soon after Andy left, looked around the kitchen and ate the remainder of my cake.

"Time to change your name," he said.

"To what?"

"Mr. Cook!"

When I positioned myself over the squat-john this morning, I saw a note taped to the wall in front of me. On the top were the words DO NOT TEAR and below a maze of Thai script and diagrams. I asked my student helper/house-boy, Wisai, if he knew anything about it.

"Yes, my teacher," he replied. "That is my paper. I have trouble remembering the geometry proofs, so I put them on the wall in the bathroom. Now, every time I go in there and wait for something to happen (he giggled) I read the proofs again and again. In addition to that, you have the most comfortable toilet."

If Pythagorus only knew.

One of the Seabees dropped off a copy of Life Magazine with the Beatles on the cover. I slowly read every page, all the time thinking I reminded myself of one of Somerset Maugham's South Pacific expats with my palm trees and mangos above and the London Times below.

I went with Andy and several of the other soldiers from the border patrol to a Thai boxing match. Thai soldiers never forgot I was a teacher and much to Andy's disgust they frequently told him to watch his language in front of me.

The boxing was much better than the last few I saw sponsored by the school and the meal we had in town was several notches better than anything I was accustomed to buy outside. Although border patrol guys and teachers theoretically earn the same salary, I've heard some soldiers put the squeeze on local merchants. Andy's translator actually made more. His 3,000 baht a month is double my own salary.

We continued to drink after the meal and one of the soldiers told me my first dirty joke translated from Thai. A monkey leaped from a palm tree and jammed his dingaling into a female elephant just as a bunch of enormous coconuts fell on the pachyderm's head, causing her to bellow in pain and start running through the jungle. "Take it easy, honey," yelled the monkey as he patted the giant beast's buttocks. "It only hurts the first time."

Finally, the whole crew got to their feet and talked about dropping by the local red light district at which point I made my farewells.

On his way out, Andy promised to drop off a few bottles of American whiskey to keep my taste buds accustomed to the finer things in life. It's not that I drank that much, but when I did it was Mekhong with last week's date on the bottle. I told him I didn't feel comfortable taking things for free, but he laughed and said he'd just won 80 baht during the boxing match. In any case, he was making 8,000 baht a month and other than a few R & R trips to Bangkok he had nothing to spend it on. As we stepped out on to the sidewalk he carefully checked up and down the street before continuing on to his jeep. Noticing my puzzled expression, he patted me on the back and drawled, "In case you didn't know it, there's a group out there called The Free Thai that's got a $2,000 bounty on my head – and that's dollars, son, not baht!"

I wonder what my head's worth? Probably three *sataeng*.

September 4, 1967

I still got a kick every time I approach a classroom and the head student jumped to his feet and called for everyone to stand at attention. I considered visiting some nearby villages soon. Within tiny Nang Rong there already existed the industrial crust of Western society. I wanted to see some really out of the way places that I had only glimpses of so far on my bike trips to Paak Waan Village. My Thai would have to improve considerably if I expected to go alone. Most of the hamlets surrounding Nang Rong had Cambodian-speaking populations. Cambodian uses an alphabet similar to Thai, but with a different vocabulary and is not tonal (unlike Thai, Laotian, Chinese and Vietnamese).

I wanted to do something else! See the *other* places. I'd always been afraid of the future and what I would end up doing to make a living. Some jangling nerve kept urging me to do some heroic act; that sitting there reading Henry James was wrong. The Peace Corps was supposed to give me an opportunity to drop pipe-dreams and live scared. I got unnerved when I stood before a 300-year-old pagoda or Buddhist temple whose outer walls were erected 700 years ago, or walked across rice paddies that had been under cultivation from before the time our Constitution was signed. I liked confronting these images, no matter how entangled I was with Western thought and culture (food, literature, time sense and almost instinctive drive to find work and start a family). Yet, there was something else in me that went gibbering mad at the thought of being merely successful, respected and compatible with society.

Seeing the shadow of a pagoda at night and meeting someone like Wisut was a salve for the irritation I had with being static. I was desperately afraid that I was beginning to start worrying about the future instead of leaping into it. My likes and dislikes were in a state of flux.

Would the feelings that empowered me to join the Peace Corps still be in me when I am middle-aged? Looking back at my journal entries, I re-read what I noted about the *New Yorker*, the banality of the endless ads for Steuban glass and luxury cars. Was the very weave of a mercantile culture too tight to allow real creativity? If the culture were any different would we still seek food, shelter, companionship and then, when we had it all, still end up dissatisfied? Would the next stage of human evolution be a hominid that feels no abrasion with machine-tooled happiness, even revels in it? Maybe it had already been reached. What haunted me was the knowledge I still needed a nodding approval from others for my actions.

My last night with volunteers Sharon and Frank in Buriram. They were invited out to dinner by someone I think Frank met on a road construction project. He worked for the Vennell Corporation, an American corporation which was involved with site location and development of military airfields. Our host didn't seem to mind me joining them. Although I looked forward to the food, I had some qualms about socializing too much with quasi-military types. I told myself to take it easy and just enjoy the company of other Americans. As we sat down, another guy joined us who was a parachutist stationed near Korat. Soon, the table was covered with chicken, potato salad and hot biscuits with gravy. These guys carried sizable guts and were red-faced from too much booze. Everything was delicious, including the chilled bottles of beer.

Unfortunately, the after-dinner conversation turned the food in my stomach to lead. Both of them discussed their good ol' times together and all the fun they had with the *nigras* back home. They went from there to the race riots going on now and what effects a few choice lynchings would have on calming these local "insurrectionists." I kept telling myself this was all some kind of macabre humor and the whole conversation was a form of twisted satire I would eventually comprehend. The eye signals from Frank and Sharon seemed to ask, "How can we get out of here?"

The stories got worse and I felt only revulsion that these men came from my own country and, in fact, represented the United States in Thailand. Any mention of the war in Vietnam was tied purely to American global strategic interests and not even the usual pretense of fighting for some noble cause of freedom-seeking peoples. Finally, after one more particularly obnoxious racist joke the parachutists glanced around and asked, "Hey, I haven't offended anyone, have I?"

I don't remember the signal, but we all got up at once and headed for the door.

"What's the hurry?" one of the guys asked. "We haven't even had any of that cake you all chipped in for."

Sharon mumbled something about needing to leave right away. We walked out into the humid evening air and ran into fellow volunteer, Thom Huebner, who invited us over to his house for some Benedictine he'd picked up in Hong Kong. Lying back in the darkness, we sipped black coffeee and liqeur, nibbled on popcorn and talked about the war, Peace Corps and the dinner we'd shared with two Neanderthals.

The next morning I bought a can of powerful insecticide for the trillion or so bugs intent on sharing my home. Horrible thought: would I be re-born into another phylum? Would the mosquito I kill today be related to the *me* in the year 2000?

The batch of dough I made yesterday for a loaf of white bread was a flop. Does yeast go bad if it's left out too long in this humidity? I fed the mess to the dogs. The Peace Corps cookbook has recipes for everything from fowl to cakes. I finally managed a bread dough that rose twice and baked evenly in my little oven. Tall, puffed-up loaves of white bread stood proud by my kitchen window. No dogs would get *this* bread!

Preeda, one of Nang Rong School's teachers, is planning to leave Nang Rong and move to Prakhonchai Village. That probably meant I take over his upper level English classes. I enjoyed working with the younger students, but it would be interesting to see what I could do with older kids who needed to pass the national exams at the end of their last year.

Last night was Preeda's farewell party: rivers of Mekhong and pools of soda water. Everyone in town was reeling by twilight. Restaurants were ransacked for Mekhong and an all night rummy game began.

There was so much drinking that the women stayed close to the walls and the men danced with each other. The temporary kitchen served delicacies: spicy ground meat, bowls of salad heavily seasoned and topped with ground peanuts, morning-glory leaves fried in oyster sauce, varieties of curries flavored with coconut milk and chili peppers, and beef strips boiled in pots of seasoned broth then laid on mounds of steaming white rice and small onions.

I was told that most of the teachers would accompany Preeda for his trip to Prakonchai in an enormous truck borrowed from the community development program. I had a foreboding that the good citizens of Prakonchai would be on the road to greet us with more Mekhong and food, but decided I would just have to deal with that when it happened.

Since the all-night rummy game took place in my home it looked like Verdun after the battle. No time for bread or checking the yeast. On to Prakonchai!

....

Written a few days after the Prakhonchai trip

My face was sunburned and chapped after a two day excursion to Prakonchai in the back of an open truck. The village is 30 kilometers from Nang Rong and I was a bit surprised to see many of my students heading that way on bicycles. It turned out that many of them lived more than 15 kilometers from the school, so the distance to Prakonchai is what they travel back and forth every day. I swore I'd never yell at a sleepy, drooping head again.

Wisut and I traveled in one of the two trucks that carried teachers and local dignitaries. We were loaded with bags of food (more of which was purchased at roadside stands) and bottles of Mekhong – last month's date on the label. By the time we hit the village most of the whiskey was gone. The last bump before the market made us all belch, gag and murmur "...*dja tdai loey...*" (I'm gonna die!)

Happily, we were met by the teachers and students of Prakonchai School with dozens of Pepsis for the kids and more whiskey for the grown-ups. Introductions all around and before I knew it Wisut had organized a rummy game in Preeda's new house. I sat on the fringe and tried to catch jokes, puns and friendly insults that flew around after each shuffle. After a few more sips of whiskey I was ready to pass out, when someone suggested it was time to go out and have some fun. I thought, oh Christ, I can't do this now, but I somehow roused my body up and went with the others to a local community development center. Not much to see except huge earth-moving equipment supplied by the United States. I asked one of the local agents if they planned to use the machinery to repair the road between Nang Rong and Buriram. He looked me up and down, then, with a wry expression, explained that they had already repaired that road.

The Prakonchai headmaster introduced me to the community development director, who, in turn, mentioned that he knew my friend, Frank, in Buriram and was very grateful for his help in establishing standards for grading nearby roads.

A few of us took a brief tour of the town. As we carefully walked around a fairly large hole in the middle of the street, one of the workers mentioned that Cambodians had lobbed a few mortar shells in the direction of the CD camp. Unfortunately, the shells exploded on this street instead and killed two students and a teacher who were on their way to school.

The community development director was very friendly and even bought Pepsis for the students (about 75 bottles) and also got them to join him in a few songs. He struck me as a conscientious worker, but I couldn't help remembering all the stories I'd heard about vast layers of corruption linked to the whole CD program. Many of the directors, I'd been told, had stolen from their own programs, keeping two sets of books to facilitate their actions. Because they often had large amounts of capital at their disposal, some of them became involved in gambling operations, using their funds to place bets for operations in their provincial capitals. Others became involved with Chinese businessmen in partnerships that often included the use of government equipment on land owned by both the CD directors and the businessmen. Then again, what could the Thai government expect with the low salaries they paid? Of course, coming from Boston, I knew nothing of political corruption in America (wink). Meanwhile, here in Prakonchai, a CD boss was responsible for hundreds of thousands of dollars worth of equipment and the salaries of hundreds of workers, while earning maybe $200 a month. Is it any wonder so many of them caved in? Even cabinet members in Bangkok theoretically made about $100 a month. Who believed that General Prapas lived in a palatial mansion, owned several Mercedes, sent his children to schools overseas and lived the way he did on a hundred a month? As long as American aid poured in there would be plenty for those at the top and maybe even a crumb or two for the workers at the bottom. What would happen when the money spigot was turned off?

Dateless Musings

After I returned to Nang Rong I met a local policeman who expressed interest in my impressions of Prakonchai. When I told him the story of the mortar round that killed three innocent people, he said, "I think they did not tell you the truth. It was not a mortar that killed those people, but a mine someone put under the road. Maybe they meant to kill some government official, but killed the wrong people by mistake. And, Cambodians did not do that. They do not care about that. I think it was the Free Thai group from some poor village like Baan Kruat or maybe Prakonchai itself. They have no food, no money, nothing. Many angry people live there and they get weapons from Cambodia or China and they try to hurt the government. Now, Bangkok sends *patanagon* out there with money to help, but maybe too late. That's what I think."

I tried to question him more about who might actually be involved in planting mines, but he became nervous and was obviously re-thinking the danger of what he'd just shared. I dropped the subject.

"Will Mr. Preeda like teaching in Prakonchai?" I asked.

"I think Mr. Preeda is a good person and a good teacher, but I do not understand why he wants to go to Prakonchai. Many people there speak Gampucha (Cambodian), and Mr. Preeda does not speak it. Also, it is dangerous there if you work for the government, even if you are a teacher. There are many people there fighting all the time. I know there are some people who say if you kill a teacher or a *farang*, like you, Mr. Burgess, the Communists will give you money. I think that is why all the people at Prakonchai were so happy to see you there for a visit. You showed you were not afraid and maybe they think that means things will get better for them. Baan Kruat and Prakonchai Village are two places where all the time people say 'I don't know.' Okay, maybe you don't like Communists either, so, all the time, they say the same thing, 'I don't know.' So, you ask me if I think Mr. Preeda will be happy there? Who can be happy in a place like that?"

He shrugged and walked away as I considered his words. The people were so happy to see me because I showed I was not afraid!

Sept. 24, 1967
Sunday evening

Wisai, Wisut and I strolled to the market this evening seeking entertainment. There was a big band in from Korat playing top ten Thai hits. I stayed with the crowds that encircled the band, watching the dancers and eating delicious, home-made desserts. The local movie theater was also showing a new film, so that always brought out a large crowd. Many of the little girls selling sweets near the theater were students at my school and Wisut, ever the master of sly innuendo, spoke to them.

"Oh, hello, Sombat. How are you today? Did you finish that assignment due Tuesday? Oh, look at all the candies! How much are they? For free? For me? Thank you very much. And these coconuts? Only three baht? But, they should be five! Here, I insist on giving you at least four."

And so it went down the lines of food stalls. Meanwhile, I practiced my conversational skills by chatting up people standing near me: How many Cambodians were killed in the last raid? How many border patrol police were in town now? Has the mayor finished making that batch of *sato* he promised to share? Is that woman dancing on stage *polite* or not?

We finally left the fair grounds and went to the Jeem-Jeem Restaurant where Wisut taught me how to ask for the check in Chinese. It's a nice feeling to sip a Coke in town, munch on the inside of a freshly heated coconut on the way back to the house, and then have a cup of tea with some honey cake. I felt so mellow I even practiced my Thai lettering. I'm still writing like a first grader.

Some of Wisut's friends dropped by later in the evening to prop up chairs under the house, smoke and talk with me about America. Their big interest at that moment was Dean Rusk's daughter marrying a black man. One of the men read aloud from an editorial in a Bangkok paper that pondered the idea Johnson might fire Rusk because of his daughter's new husband. The group had a generally low opinion of President Johnson. They felt he'd been far too lenient in his dealings with the North Vietnamese. They also thought he's not too …*ah*. The Thai word connotes lacking a sense of grace or style.

Sometime during 3rd week of September

Because of recent heavy rains there was enough water in the drinking and bathing tanks. I did not have to travel very far for water. Of course, once it sat around in the tank long enough it would probably acquire a milky color and I might return to the well.

Preeda came back from Prakonchai to touch base with friends. His teaching load had been reduced from 24 to 18 hours a week. He was worried, though, because the headmaster there saw him talking with me and promptly signed Preeda up to teach conversational English. Preeda was afraid he did not know enough English to do a good job, but I kept telling him, truthfully, he was certainly far and away better than anyone else they had in Prakonchai.

A few days later in September

The big news from my area concerned the arrest of the minister of agriculture for heisting hundreds of thousands of baht worth of teak logs from the national forest and selling the wood overseas. Everyone knew this practice was carried out on a small scale by local Border Patrol police, but the minister was really greedy and was drawn to others in the field with the same perspective. He got caught because the bribes he spent on local officials were not evenly distributed and smaller fish complained to the right people in Bangkok. Since the Bangkok people hadn't been getting *anything* out of the deal, Justice was abruptly awakened from her cobweb bed and pushed into action.

A fellow volunteer in Maehongsorn told me he was planning a trip to Laos and hoped to see the royal capital at Luangprapang. He mentioned that most of the Mekhong River traffic had been stopped at the government capital of Vientienne because of shoreline snipers, but he hoped a truce might be worked out before his vacation. I'd be happy to get as far as the northern Thai city of Chiengmai where the king had a summer palace and the women win international beauty contests.

Finally, I decided that I was absolutely never ever going to have my palm read again. For the third time I've been told gloom, despair and death awaited me at 35. Wisut had a book on palmistry and I decided to read my own hand. Need I say more? Yes, I could clearly see my life line was hacked to pieces somewhere mid-palm. My love-line said I'd get married at 30, have two kids, but after that it was a fade-out. Maybe I should just play it safe and live in Nang Rong for the rest of my life.

Sept. 25, 1967

I brought in an enormous cardboard clock to my class as a visual aid and tried to explain how to tell time in English. The good news is that both Western and Thai societies have a comparable military-style system that simply tells the time in 24 hour cycles. But, trying to explain our civilian version of telling time to my students proved a problem. The Thai day is split into four units of six hours each. Each segment is given a special word to indicate what part of day (or section) it belongs to. Midnight and midday have their own special words. The words used between dusk and dawn are *dtii* and *thum*. Wisut told me the words go back to when night watchmen beat out time every hour from dusk to dawn using iron bars—the word *dtii* means *to hit*. I think most of my students picked up American-style time-telling much faster than I picked up the form they use. Not only does Thai have several different words for fractions of hours (as we have "15 of" or "quarter to" or "45 minutes past"), but they also have distinctions indicating morning, afternoon and evening hours. One interesting trick I learned: if you add 543 to the current Western date you will get the date in B.E. (Buddhist Era)

The tall palms barely nod as I walk quietly through the temple grounds and listen to the monks, some chatting and others praying, and pick up the barely discernible prayer wheels tinkling. Long shadows arch out from the tips of the pagodas. In the street, children's play approaches nervous hysteria as the time approaches for them to be called home.

"*Sompong… ma nii!*" (Sompong, come here!)

Even the starving, ragged dogs are lying quietly, enjoying the first, brief coolness of the evening winds.

Even though I happily squandered hours reading "Northwest Passage," "A Death in the Family," "Quo Vadis" and "The Idiot, I also learned my second Thai song: "*Tanun Huajai*" (Heart Road). Wisut did his best to translate it for me, but there were obviously nuances of metaphor I missed. I tried my best to learn the words directly from Thai script so as to better understand the tonal inflections. Wisut also taught me the morning prayer everyone said before school while standing in formation in front of the flag pole.

Money continued to flow from my palms and I promised myself that this month I would track my spending beyond home cooked meals, restaurant meals, airmail stamps and developing black and white prints.

Teachers and students were still working on the concrete fountain and pool by the flag. I didn't know if this kind of contribution earned the same kind of merit one receives for helping build a temple or feed a monk, but everyone seemed to enjoy doing it.

My stomach still erupts occasionally, but I have a store of lomotil tablets referred to by volunteers as "cork pills" for sudden attacks of diarrhea. They may not cure the disease, but they certainly mask the symptoms.

It seemed as if everyone within earshot was suddenly playing a two-stringed instrument with a head made of a large coconut shell called a saw-u. Wisut told me the *saw-u* is the Thai version of a Chinese instrument called a *u-hu*. After much difficulty, he managed to explain to me the difference between the two is that the *u-hu* has frets along the neck and the Thai version does not. To my ears, no matter how a *saw-u* is tuned it always gives a low tone. Perhaps I haven't lived in Thailand long enough to lose my Western sense of pitch. I heard the headmaster play and as he moved his rough bow back and forth over the strings the sound was only slightly more melodious. Wisai also took up the *saw-u* and took to practicing in the precious evening hours when I yearned for quiet.

The sound of the *saw-u* followed me through town and school like the last gasp of a cat being drawn through a wine press.

On a completely different note, I received a telegram from the Peace Corps physician, Dr. Harris, that he planned to see me in Korat soon. Since I had to go to Buriram in order to get to Korat, I thought I'd spend a few days there first with other volunteers. Thank God for the new Nang Rong-Buriram taxi service that allowed anyone with a few extra baht to make the trip in about one-third the time in the relative comfort of the back seat of a Toyota. The taxi service was my greatest joy since discovering that for a ridiculously low price a local restaurant served fried beef in oyster sauce and fried morning-glory leaves. Along with a freezing bottle of Thai beer and this skinny volunteer was ready for a nap.

I tested my students on prepositional phrases and I was in shock at the horrible results. They always sat politely, nodded in agreement when I asked if they understood and then, apparently, they walked out into the world saying, "What the hell was he talking about? I have *no* idea!"

In the Thai language, the word for "foreigner" and the word for "guava" is the same – *farang*. As far as the Thais are concerned there is only one type of foreigner – i.e. anyone who is not Thai. However, there are two types of guava. One variety, larger than the other, is called simply *farang*. After birds eat *farang* the seeds pass through their digestive system and, due to some intestinal chemistry, when these seeds fall out and take root the resulting fruit is of a much smaller variety. This smaller guava is called *farang khii nok* (guava-shit-bird). Since the word *farang* also means foreigner, Thai people who try to act like Americans are sarcastically referred to as *farang-khii-nok*. Thus, they are Thais who have emerged from American assholes thinking they are fooling everyone with their newly-acquired mannerisms, but actually fooling no one. Wisut said if you called someone a *farang-khii-nok* be prepared to fight.

When I told Wisut I would be leaving town on October 11 for a conference in Korat he looked very unhappy.

"Is something wrong?"

"You will miss a very important celebration if you leave then. Wait, I must look in the dictionary."

He returned a minute later and pointed to an entry that read *Buddhist Lent*.

"Do you know about this?" he asked.

"No, what is it?"

"It is a special celebration for people who live all around here in Pak Isaan. It is the time the monks cannot travel away from their monasteries. When this holiday is at an end, then everyone celebrates, Nang Rong will have a big parade, many people make things out of wax and then we all go to the temple to give cloth and rice to the monks to earn merit for the next life."

"What about the wax part? What's that about?"

"Never mind," he shrugged. "You will not be here."

October 11, 1967

I took the bus from Nang Rong to Buriram and then took the rapid train directly to Korat. Naturally, I missed the preferred junction stop at Chira and found myself in downtown Korat. This was a bad deal for me financially since the *samlaw* fares there were quite a bit higher than they would have been on the edge. I turned away from the first five drivers who tugged at my sleeve and went off with a sharp-eyed guy who said he knew where the Peace Corps office was. I laughed at his first estimate of 15 baht for the ride, telling him I *knew* that Thais never spend more than four baht for that distance. Bad as my Thai was, he accepted my savoir-faire and said he would accept six baht for a journey that ended at the USIA office. I coughed politely and pointed out that this was not the Peace Corps! He grinned and said maybe I needed to find someone inside who spoke better Thai than I did. At that moment a staff member from USIA came out and in flawless northeast slang told my driver where to go. My language skills are not helping Peace Corp's reputation.

I found Korat confusing, chaotic and exciting mostly because I spent a great deal of time with another volunteer named Judy. We caroused around town with Rachel, a Peace Corps secretary and ended up having a great meal at Alexander's Restaurant. I felt one rush after another sitting on a cushioned seat, picking up scents of grilled steak from the kitchen and chatting it up with two *farang* women. Impossible as it seemed, Rachel abruptly announced we'd been nibbling, drinking and talking for five hours and she had to get home. Our bill came to 321 baht, a sum that catalyzed a flash of panic on each face, and we began to pull out wrinkled baht notes. Giggling, Judy and I remained behind as Rachel gathered up her things and left. Three hours and uncounted drinks later it suddenly occurred to me that I was drinking with a calm and lovely goddess. When she caught me staring, I felt my face skip back and forth from pale to blush several times in a second.

The qualities of beauty in Thai women always seemed to exist on another continuum to me. Their smooth skin with a multitude of possible hues reminded me more of dreams than reality. Part of the mystique rested upon my inability to converse on anything higher than a second grade level. On the other hand, here I was with this pale-skinned *farang* woman who seemed to have been talking non-stop for hours about Western philosophy in an animated, almost aggressive manner, and I was totally hooked. This was infatuation on a physical and intellectual plane; although, truth was, what I fervently wished to do was lightly run my hand down the front of her dress. We discussed poetry, novels, contemporary news, her family, recollections of the Connecticut River Valley, fables, mythology, sexual stereotypes, the people at the next table and dreams. We held hands, leaned over the table, looked at each other than away. I wanted to raise her up, hug her and every time the thought crossed my mind, our knees were barely touching and I lost my voice to hoarse, unspeakable emotions that left me stammering and finally silent.

We staggered from the restaurant over to the home of Scott Duncan, our Peace Corps regional director and woke him up by tripping over his porch furniture. He peered down at us from his second story bedroom window and said his front door was open. If we wanted to sleep in his living room we were welcome. My arm was around Judy's waist when I felt her stiffen at the words of invitation. I raced for sobriety, but she got there first and declined for both of us. Scott nodded and said he'd see us the next day.

A light rain began to fall. At 2:00 AM Korat was still. A lone *samlaw* driver hissed by through puddles. We called out to him, gave directions to Rachel's place where Judy was staying. Sitting tightly next to me on the *samlaw's* hard seat I felt Judy relax and I felt a wave of sexual energy. Our driver was drunk, but seemed to know where he was going as the drizzle became a downpour and the street flooded. The flimsy canvas top jammed, but we wrapped our arms about each other and, clinging tightly the whole trip, licked away heavy drops that ran down each other's faces.

Although he laughed and mumbled to himself the entire trip and weaved down alleys that seemed to turn back in on themselves, our driver eventually screeched to a stop in front of Rachel's. I gave him all the coins I had in my pocket and helped Judy down from the *samlaw*. Running through gusts of wind and rain we stumbled up the back stairs to Rachel's second-floor apartment. Judy suddenly seemed distracted, removedd, and I had no idea how to regain the initiative. After ringing the bell, she turned and embraced me, our slick faces gliding over each other, until we heard footsteps and Rachel opened her door a crack and peered through. She wearily told us she only had room for one in her bed and that one had to be Judy. Judy's hand slipped out of mine, she gave me a rueful, half-smile as I reached out for her, then the door closed and I was left alone in the rain.

I stepped dejectedly down the stairs, rounded the house to the street and found our driver, waiting and humming to himself, under the falling deluge. He didn't seem surprised to see me hop on board and as he strained down on the pedals, the rain turned back to a light mist. I told him to take me to a restaurant. He asked which one and I said anyone that was open. Humming again, he took me into the central produce market. I thanked him, shook his hand, gave him a bill from my pocket without looking at the denomination and turned to stare at the Thai version of Boston's own farmer's market.

A light mist still hung in the air and dawn was still at least an hour away as Korat's early morning market came alive. Even after all the rain, an elderly Chinese gentleman slowly walked back and forth between each stall spraying enough water in front of him to clear away any stray leaves or minute debris. A few overhead electric lights illuminated every worker's face clearly enough for me to see every gradation of skin color from the darker Cambodians to the light-skinned northern Thai and Laotians.

Fresh, green limes were carefully stacked in pyramids alongside passion fruit, pomelo, rambutan, guava and papaya. Enormous piles of bananas stood next to boxes of coconuts. Mangos seemed to be in every venders venue and I remembered all the ways in which I'd seen them prepared in Nang Rong: the not ripe ones were sliced, dipped in salt water and nibbled like pickles; at another time of the year, some mangos were boiled in a sweet syrup and eaten like candy; mangos dried in the sun turned brown and were eaten as snacks, however, my favorite way to eat mangos was when they were fully ripened and served with sticky rice and covered with coconut cream or sweetened evaporated milk.

I walked over to the banana stall and remembered Wisut explaining to me that although English had only one word for banana, Thai had many varieties of bananas and each had its own name. Some even had extremely hard, large black seeds that almost cracked my teeth. I'd seen farmers slice unripe bananas, roll them in sugar and salt and then fry them to a crisp. Every banana recipe seemed to have a story associated with it. My favorite concerned a dessert called *kluai buat chi* which translates as *banana like a nun's robe* because the bananas boiled in coconut milk and sweetened with sugar took on the same color as the clothing worn by Thai women who work in the temples.

I stood there so long staring at the bananas that a smiling clerk plucked a ripe one loose and handed it to me. I thanked him and as I peeled it and walked further along I came to the vegetable stalls: bright red and green chilies, what the Thais call *phrik yai*, looked like Christmas tree decorations hanging from wooden crates; brown and curly ginger root lay next to crisp snap peas, gleaming purple eggplants and strangely mottled pumpkins covered with bumps, then a sea of crisp kale and huge taro roots with reddish earth still clinging to them.

Shivering in the chilled and humid air, I detected the first whiff of freshly cooked soup and wandered over to see several fairly hung-over Chinese businessmen waiting for a bowl of *khao tom*, the traditional Thai hangover cure. *Khaow* means rice, and the rice in this soup is thoroughly boiled then seasoned a bit with fish oil and maybe a dash of vinegar. It sounds strange, but two large bowls of *khaow tom* straightened me out on several occasions when I had to be ready for school. It even settled my stomach!

With a bowl of soup finally in hand, I watched street kids scrounge the area for cigarette butts and *samlaw* drivers sip one last cup of Ovaltine before work. They stood near the lottery tables, calf-muscles bulging, pursing their lips between drinks for drags on limp cigarettes. I took my soup to a small table and hunched over the steaming bowl. The growing crowds walked by and stared at me with great curiosity. A Chinese waiter asked me if I wanted anything with the soup. I asked for a hot Ovaltine and a duck egg. He surprised me by bringing over a tall glass that had both ingredients stirred together. Delicious. I glanced over at the calligraphy and Thai script covering a back wall. I gathered by the numbers alongside each line that I was looking at a price list. In the middle of it all was a large, color portrait of Thailand's King Bhumipol and another portrait of Sun Yat-Sen staring out blankly at the bustling crowd. I motioned to the waiter again and when he was close I asked for the check in Cantonese. Wisut taught me the phrase. The waiter chuckled, and after returning with my change sat at my table and spoke with me in a mixture of Thai and English about his job, Nang Rong, Korat, his family, how difficult it was for him to pay for his son's education at a teacher training college in Khon Kaen and just how hard life was. We *wai*'d each other farewell and I strolled away with images of red and green chilies and the scent of damp coriander.

When I got back to the Peace Corp office, it was still early and Bangkok's heat was only beginning to rise and mingle with the heavy carbon monoxide of rush hour traffic. The Thai stenographer who slept there stared at me in dismay before coming to some private decision and let me in, laughing all the while and giggling until I made a face that asked, "What?" He kept pointing to my face then covering his mouth as he giggled some more. I walked into the men's room and looked at myself in a mirror. My hair was a rooster's thatch of black strands, loopy lipstick stains smeared my cheek and chin and a few small bruises stood out on my neck.

I washed up, then collapsed on the lobby's couch that was still warm from the stenographer's body. Scott came by soon after, but let me sleep until the lobby's traffic picked up. In his office, he leaned back and smiled at me.

"Have a good time last night?"

I felt my face blush. There was a knock on the door. Judy entered. Scott coughed politely and asked if we'd received out tetanus boosters. We both affirmed that we had.

"Well, I guess I'll catch the rapid train up to Buriram," I said, standing.

"Isn't that where you connect, Judy?" Scott asked.

"Yes," she nodded, and looked down.

We walked to the Sweet Home Bakery for coffee, pastries, scrambled eggs and orange juice. After that, we strolled to the central market and I bought a jar of peanut butter and some pop corn for my trip to Nang Rong. Judy, unusually quiet, waited for me to finish. I realized I was experiencing the residue of a feeling I didn't want to lose, that I didn't want to leave Korat's market behind me, that I didn't want to part company with Judy at all.

Once settled on our train seats and heading northeast we saw: monks chatting softly to each other; a small boy who peed on his mother's silk dress; one of Judy's former students who asked, "Miss Judy, how are you?" and a blind beggar who held a tin cup out at the sound of leather heels.

We leaned back on our first class seats and enjoyed the air conditioning. Judy set her alarm clock, and we fell asleep until the alarm came to life a few minutes before the train pulled into her town. She waved at me from the receding station and I felt a surge of self-pity as she diminished and blurred with the distance.

In Buriram, I spent the evening waiting for the American Consulate for the northeast to show up for the governor's party. He never made it, but Frank, Sharon and I had a good time eavesdropping on local political gossip.

The thought of taking the Nang Rong bus was too much for me to bear, so I splurged on a taxi back to town, found my house empty and crashed on the small cot that smelled of sweat and a pillow littered with dead mosquitoes. When I awoke, Wisut was still out. I stumbled from room to room and discovered someone had stolen my silver cigarette lighter and eaten my last piece of chocolate. I picked up my guitar, but it was so out of tune I didn't try to play.

I inhaled deeply, smelled the now familiar scent of bananas frying over charcoal and knew that meant there was going to be a gathering of some sort at the central commons area, Japanese toothpaste commercials would be shown on sheets stretched taut between bamboo poles and my students would all smile at my approach and call out to me, "Mr. Burgess… Mr. Burgess, where you go?"

......

October 17, 1967

For some time now Wisut had been creating a decorative wreath to help commemorate King Chulalongkorn Day. The king's official name in Thai is Phra Chulachom Klao Chaoyuhua or Rama V. To make matters even more complicated, Wisut told me the holiday is actually called Piyamaharaj Day. That's because the famous king was also known as Somdej Phra Piyamaharaj – King Chulalongkorn the Great. In any case, it always takes place on October 23, so it was coming up soon. I read that Chulalongkorn became king in 1868 at the age of 15 and ruled the country for the next 42 years. He's generally regarded as the driving force behind Thailand becoming a modern nation and the first monarch to travel widely. In addition to greatly expanding the entire communication infrastructure of his country, he was also the one who abolished slavery (albeit, not until 1905). Interestingly, the holiday occurs on the anniversary of his death. Along with the rest of the country, Nang Rong would have parades and a large meeting in front of the main government building. I was told all federal officials would be dressed in formal uniforms and that's where Wisut's wreath would be on display.

Just before typing this entry, I played an audio tape I received from home. The voices of my parents and siblings sounded surprisingly different than I remembered. Did they always have such pronounced Boston accents? That tiny quirk of memory just accentuated a sudden sense of loneliness.

Wisut was quite happy working on the wreath because it got him out of teaching. We laughed with each other every day. Even though Thai culture has so many differences from my own, I always felt a sense of kinship with Wisut. Since he was born and brought up in Bangkok, Nang Rong is strange to him, too. Maybe that's part of the bond we have.

Earlier today, Mr. Chop, the janitor, invited us over to help him cook some meat that came from a section of an ox he'd bought a while ago. I hadn't realized until then that Wisut had a reputation as a cook. I wished I could have filmed all of the preparations, from cutting the meat into small pieces to adding a variety of spices and vegetables to the boiling water. After a few hours, there were three bowls of *gang* (a soup with meat and vegetables), three bowls of plain, cooked meat and an enormous pot of steamed rice. During the preparations, we drank glass after glass of Mekhong whiskey diluted with soda water. Wisut added a dash of one spice here or a handful of powdered something-or-other there until everything met his standards. We nibbled on sticky rice balls and *somtam* made from pounded green papaya and lime, garlic and fish sauce. He explained to me he'd made three bowls of soup because he wasn't sure how much *heat* I could handle. I felt a little like Goldilocks as I began to sample the three bowls. Wisut had a small Thai--English dictionary and we laboriously looked up the different ingredients, which included: lemongrass, onions, lime leaves, chili and water buffalo meat. He explained that if we were doing this in the evening with plenty of time and more people then we'd be served something called *chaew hawn* that's made in separate pots and allows each person to place their own raw ingredients into the broth. The first bowl tasted simply delicious; the second had many more chili peppers in it; and one small sip from the third bowl burned my palate and made me gulp a whole glass of soda and whiskey. The others burst out laughing. Even Mr. Chop's wife, who stayed in the background with several small children, covered her mouth to hide her smile. Judged by standard Western values Mr. Chop and his family were desperately poor people, getting by on his meager janitor's salary and whatever his wife made supplying the teachers with their noon meal; however, small as his shack was and threadbare as most of the family's clothing appeared, they all seemed content.

Last night, Wisut and I bicycled to his friend's house in Nongkhi Village where we enjoyed a small feast and drank gallons of *sato*. When we were finished, they passed around a water pipe. I think this is more of a fixture in households with Chinese ancestry. Wisut picked up on my nervousness and assured me we would only be smoking *kretong* (a local tobacco). The smoke slipped into me more smoothly than from a cigarette. An old guy leaning against a wall said it was too bad there wasn't any *fin* (opium) left and all the *gancha* (marijuana) was gone, too. I couldn't tell if the smile on his face meant he was joking or merely thinking of fond memories.

Wisut saw the expression on my face and said something to the others that made them laugh. I told Wisut that I hoped some day he would be able to visit me in the states and then I'd have a chance to at least partially repay him for all that he did for me here. He shook his head.

"You help me much more," he said.

"How do I help you more?"

"You help me learn English. Pretty soon when I go to Bangkok to watch movies from America I will be able to understand everything."

"Well, you help me learn Thai."

"I wish," he said, shaking his head. "But, you are a bad student. I learn more English than you learn Thai."

"Where are you going now?" I asked, as he headed for the door.

"The headmaster wants me to look at the workers who are putting in the new flag pole and fountain in front of the school. He worries about the design."

"I think it's too bad he wants everything done in concrete and cement with straight lines. Didn't anyone talk at all about making it look more as if it's somehow connected to Thai culture? I mean, couldn't someone have come up with designs within the cement based on the designs from the walls of the temple?"

"No," he sighed. "Everyone is too afraid to say anything different. We all say, 'Yes, it is very beautiful.' Much better when the headmaster is happy."

After he left to supervise the workers I sipped some tea and chatted with Wisai,the student, who'd dropped by to practice his English.

"Are you hungry?" I asked.

"Yes, I am."

"Did you eat anything this afternoon?"

"No, I *did it*."

"Do you mean 'No, I didn't'?"

"Yes, I *DIDN'T!*" he exclaimed.

"Good. Do you want to walk with me to the market and buy a dessert?"

"Yes, thank you."

I was happy walking with Wisai through the calm evening air. As we passed through the temple grounds a spectacular full moon cast shadows from the pagodas at our feet.

"This is beautiful, isn't it?" I said.

"No, it ISN'T!" he said, emphasizing each syllable with great clarity.

"We don't have to keep practicing English pronunciation," I said. "It's okay to just go ahead and speak English without thinking about it too much. Anyway, as I was saying, it really *is* beautiful."

"I think it is very primitive."

I stared at him, shocked.

"I think that in America people do not even *see* the moon," he exclaimed. "I think that everything is so advanced there that the tall buildings and electric lights hide the moon."

It was hard for me to accept the reason behind his sadness: that he was trapped in a place where no towers shielded him from the moon.

Early in 3rd week of October

Wisut's enormous wreath celebrating King Chulalungkorn is finally finished. He created a gold temple in the middle of the design that's held in place with dozens of tiny roses on hidden wires. Strands of fine, pounded gold are interwoven through the surrounding decorations. I never saw him glance at pictures or designs of other wreaths, so I was all the more amazed at how perfectly it all came together.

Whenever I watched him work on the wreath I was struck by his concentration, coupled with an ease of motion that made me envious. There's something about the grace of most Thai actions I wished I could emulate. Even when I followed Mr. Chop walking across the school's grounds I was struck by the easy and casual manner in which he flowed through the tall grass. He wore a *pakhoma* (basically, a broad piece of colored cloth wrapped around his waist) and strolled across the field with a cigarette dangling from his lips. Although his back was always straight as a soldier's, his posture had an added nonchalance that made him seem to glide. Those were the times I felt like an ungainly beetle trapped in a land of languid butterflies.

After all the planning and anticipation, I missed the beginning of the Chulalongkorn celebration! The story began a few days ago when I traveled to Buriram to celebrate Sharon's 24th birthday. Frank, Ralph, Fred and Sharon were the sum total of my American contacts and all of us planned to be there for the party. Although we'd planned to only have a quiet get-together with snacks and beer, a couple of wandering Seabees pulled into town and decided this was no time to be quiet! They even chipped in to buy Sharon a gold-plated necklace and a silver bracelet. She looked quite embarrassed when they handed them to her. More beers were ordered along with buckets of ice and bottles of Mekhong. The soldiers seemed like basically nice guys and none of us envied whatever they had to endure on a daily basis.

During a break, Andy, one of the soldiers, went out back to take a leak, so I wandered out to join him and ask about their operations. He told me three health care para-professionals had recently been assassinated near the town of Baan Kruat and now the entire area was out of bounds to Peace Corps volunteers and Thai civil servants.

"Why'd they kill them?" I asked.

"The guerillas set up an ambush to knock out the local police chief who was supposed to pass through. Unfortunately, they spotted a jeep with three medical people on their way to administer cholera shots at a local school and thought it was the chief. Machine gunned the jeep into oblivion."

He casually gave his dick a fast shake, tucked it inside and turned to go. I heard the klack-klack whirring of a military helicopter pass overhead. Walking back to the party I determined I was not going to wander too far from downtown.

Inside, Andy waved me over and I sat next to him and Sharon.

"So, who's the asshole with blond hair that works with you guys?" Andy asked.

"You mean Thom?"

"I don't know. Whatever. I was on the train to Korat with my translator and saw this American kid sitting by himself, so we walked over to say hello and he gives us the big freeze. I said what the fuck? Oh, Excuse me, Sharon! So, I said, what's up with you and he walks away to another seat."

"We're really not supposed to hang around with soldiers or police," Sharon explained. "Local people would make the wrong assumptions."

"Hey, I wasn't even in uniform," he said. "What? Do I have the word 'military' stamped on my forehead?"

I laughed.

"What's so fuckin' funny?"

"Nothing. Not funny," I said. "You just don't look like a Peace Corps volunteer. I'm sure Thom knew right away who you were."

"Okay. Whatever. Hey, could we have another beer over here!"

I felt like a total hypocrite sitting there talking it up with Andy and the others, hiding the fact I knew perfectly well Thom's reasons for not speaking with Andy had nothing to do with forming wrong assumptions. Thom was adamantly opposed to the war and just as opposed to associating with anyone who was involved. My sympathies were all with Thom, but I got so lonely in Nang Rong I looked forward to just speaking English with American soldiers. I wished I were as strong in my convictions as Thom. It would be easier to look at my reflection in the mirror when I shaved.

Meanwhile, Frank, who was working as a volunteer civil engineer in Buriram, was scheduled to return to the States soon. Every volunteer who left increased my sense of isolation.

I managed to stumble back to Fred's apartment after the party and fell asleep to the sound of rain falling outside. A rooster's crowing got me up in time to dress and run over to the front of the Buriram Girls School for my return taxi ride. My regular taxi driver, Mr. Go (as it translates from Thai) wasn't there, but I spotted another taxi creeping along a block away. I waved frantically and he eventually made it to my corner where he explained he couldn't go to Nang Rong until he filled his cab. He introduced himself as Mr. Knife. Great! By the time he found several other riders, a few hours had passed and I knew I was going to be hopelessly late. My stomach growled and gurgled. I probably should not have had coffee at Fred's. I swallowed about 10 antacid pills and hoped for the best. The driver tried to make small talk, but the other passengers had all fallen asleep. Suddenly, he pulled over to the side of the road and asked me if I could drive. Several of the other riders looked at each other in alarm.

"Sure," I said.

"Good," he nodded, got out, motioned for me to get behind the wheel and he sat on the other seat. "I've been up all night and I'm too tired to drive," he said. "It's a straight road back to Nang Rong, so you can't get lost."

He fell asleep before I managed to familiarize myself with the shift mechanism on the side of the steering column. Thai traffic flows in the same direction as it does in England, so the steering wheel and pedals are on the right side of the car. Luckily, there was no traffic and I managed to lurch my way into the Nang Rong market safely, but too late for the start of the Chulalongkorn party. All the fine speeches and presentation of wreaths.... over! Off in the distance I heard a few drums rattling. The parade was about to start. I ran to my house, threw some water on my face, combed down my hair and zoomed out to join the festivities.

After all the speeches and drinks, I went home and gobbled a huge plate of fried rice. Even by early evening it was around 105 degrees with very high humidity. Someone knocked at the door. It was Wisut.

"Hello, my friend! Time to go. Time to go! Get up."

"What's going on?"

"Remember I told you before you went to Buriram that all the teachers and families and everyone would be going on a big picnic and party to the Ta-pec Village."

He noted my expression and said, "I *promised* everyone you would go."

And so, reluctantly, the good volunteer grabbed a few more antacid pills and left for the big party at Ta-pec.

....

October 25, 1967

I heard a voice behind me say in English, "I want 10 quarts of beer. Don't you understand? Ten quarts!"

Turning around in my seat at the Raxana Restaurant, I saw a slim, Thai man in the uniform of a teacher, standing beside a visibly upset elderly Asian, not Thai, gentleman. "I want 10 quarts of beer. Doesn't anybody here understand English?"

He spoke with a distinct French accent. Reluctantly, I stood up from my plate of fried beef in oyster sauce and walked over to them. The old man looked to be about 70. He had roughly trimmed, short white hair, wire-rimmed glasses, a torn t-shirt, faded jeans and sandals. A small girl of indeterminate age stood close by, her tiny left hand encased by his. The man stared at my approach, apparently shocked to see me, but quickly regained his composure.

"Can you make them understand I want 10 quart bottles of cold beer to take with me?" he asked.

I nodded, quickly told the owner of the restaurant what the man wanted and then nodded in the direction of my table. Seeing that beer bottles were being collected, the man gave me a perfunctory toss of his head and asked, "But, who are you? You sound like an American? How is it that you are here and able to speak this language?"

After I gave a brief explanation about the Peace Corps he introduced himself as Minoru Kida, a Japanese sociologist, who was in Nang Rong to research Thai village life. He had already written a number of critiques on the Japanese and Laotian village structure and he was anxious to carry on his work in Thailand. I told him I had to work at the school during the day, but that I would be glad to help out in any way I could in the evening or during weekends.

The following evening, a motorbike came by to pick up Wisut and me and drive us to where Kida was meeting with the village elders. He and his granddaughter were both sitting on mats, with Kida gesticulating wildly, trying to get some point across. He greeted us as long lost friends, inviting us to sit with him and have some beer. He seemed to be a little drunk on beer himself, but forged ahead in sign language and body English, much to the dismay of the Thais in the room.

"I can speak Japanese, French, English, Mandarin Chinese and I can understand Latin, but this Thai language is the most difficult I have ever encountered," he said. "I learned French while I was living and studying in Paris."

I guess that explained his Gallic-accented English which was thick enough to prevent his translator from understanding much of what he said. Several of the older men conferred among themselves in words spoken far too rapidly and softly for me to understand, but I sensed a certain animosity towards Kida.

"Is there something wrong?" I asked Wisut.

Looking extremely uncomfortable, he nodded.

"This foreigner is not polite."

Wisut used a Thai word that loosely translates as *polite* but also includes someone lacking a sense of decorum, protocol and taste.

"The elders ask him about his family, his home, his granddaughter and things like that, but the old man only wants to know right away about things the elders do not wish to discuss with him because he is a foreigner."

"What does he want to know about?"

"He asks them about ... how do you say it? The birds that fight?"

"Cock fighting?"

"Yes, that. Some people do that in Nang Rong, but it is illegal and not good Buddhism. And, he wants to know about *sato*!"

"The rice drink? How does he know about that?"

"He does not know the name, but he asks about what people drink that the government does not know about. He says in villages everywhere there is something like that and he wants to know what we have here, but he is not polite so they will never tell him anything."

"Is that why everyone is smiling so much?"

"Yes," he grinned. "Better to smile than say no."

"My translator is a fool," Kida said to me. "He is no help at all. Will you help me with my work here? I want to know about aspects of Thai village life that may not appear in the books. What kinds of things do they do for entertainment? What illegal beverages do they drink?"

With Wisut's reluctant help I forwarded several of his questions to the elders, but they always answered with questions such as: How is the weather in Japan? How many children do you have? Do you have brothers and sisters? How big is your house?

Kida waved his hands in annoyance as if trying to erase the answers he heard. He was on a futile quest and I was surprised that, as an anthropologist or sociologist, he seemed to be insensitive to the cultural nuances of a place like Nang Rong.

Then, silence. Kida sat there with his eyes closed, as if meditating. Then, abruptly, he turned to me.

"Too much beer. I need to urinate. Where do the men go?"

I smiled, looked up at the others and quickly translated his need.

Laughter! All the others slapped themselves on the back and rocked back and forth with good humor as if to say, 'Hey, he's human after all!'

We all got up and walked out into the soft night to a long stand of banana trees where we stood in a communal row. The sound of zippers moving down and cloth being pulled aside was followed by the noise of us all pissing on to the large, green fronds and thick grass. Kida kept peeing after the others had stopped and they laughed some more as they patted him on the back.

"He goes like a water buffalo," one of the men said.

Back inside, however, the wall of silence returned.

"I have a son-in-law in Bangkok," he said, "who told me that what I wanted to do here was impossible. That I would have to live here for months or years before people would share with me what I want to know. I told him I was too old. There was not time for that, but in my heart I knew he was right. And so (he gestured to the elders) he has been proven right."

Around us, Wisut and the elders whispered back and forth as Kida shared something of his life with me.

"My books and articles have been translated into many languages and I am asked by many universities to visit and lecture, but I have spent almost all my money in my travels and research. For the past few years I have taken Loki, my granddaughter, with me to act as a sort of *liaison* between myself and local children and eventually, their parents."

"Doesn't she have to go to school?"

"Oh, she is in school all the time," he chuckled. "No, no I understand what you are saying. Yes, she goes to regular school in Japan and sometimes to a Japanese school in Bangkok, but during school breaks she travels with me. She is a central figure in several of my publications. Loki is the light that illuminates small village secrets."

"Are these university publications?"

"Oh yes, some of them, but I have grown tired of the academic presses. All I wish to do now is write my own critiques of small village communities, but I am older now and starting to have health problems. Well, what do you think? Shall I try once more with these people?"

Through Wisut's help once more we asked the elders if the villagers voted by majority or unanimity.

"If the headman says to do something," Wisut replied, "you do it. If some villagers disagree they can go to the *nai amphur*, the mayor's office, who is the government. If the mayor agrees with the headman, that's the end of it."

Kida kept insisting that beneath the veneer of formal law there had to exist an undercurrent of social mores and customs, the *realpolitique* as he put it, that must, on occasion, conflict with official decrees.

I tried to convey this concept to Wisut as clearly as I could, but the answer still came back the same: there was no alternative structure and people either went along with the law or they became bandits, in which case they were ostracized by the other members of the community.

"What about making *sato*?" I asked Wisut on my own. "The local and the federal government have laws against making illegal alcoholic drinks, but I know everyone does it. How do you explain that?"

Wisut looked around uneasily as it became clear that even the elders picked up on my use of the word *sato*. In very slow and clear Thai he answered my question: Making *sato* is illegal and anyone who is caught making it is either fined or arrested or both.

I started to say something about all the *sato* parties we'd attended, when he leaned forward and gently touched my hand. It was an effective move.

"Do you know who the elder man is sitting behind Mr. Kida? He is the one who never talks. Do you know about him?"

"No, who is he?"

"He is the *khaman*, the headman of the village. This is his house. He has much honor. He will tell you that making *sato* is against the law. This Mr. Kida is his guest because he is a foreigner, like you, visiting Nang Rong. He must tell you what he must tell you. You must not ask him questions like that. No more talk about *sato*, okay?"

I nodded, dumbly. Kida had not heard what Wisut said to me, but guessed that something had happened. He started to ask me once more about Thai subcultures, but I cut him off by handing him another beer. He shook his head and looked down at his lap.

"I'm sorry," I said.

"I understand. Some things take time. I will return to Bangkok in the morning. Please thank everyone," he said, slowly getting up. "Ask them to forgive an impolite old man."

"But, I thought you couldn't…"

"Oh, I've been here long enough to pick up a few words."

The elders stood up with us and smiled when I relayed Kida's words. He returned to Bangkok in the morning and I never saw him again.

....

November 2, 1967

I found a new friend in town. He's only about a foot and a half tall and his name is Mek. When I first went into the market for a haircut, Mek was playing in the middle of the street. When my shadow covered him, he shrieked and ran straight into the barbershop, then peeked around to see if the strange foreigner was still there. When he saw me he screamed, i*Jah-eh*!ah-Thai for "Boo!"). I pretended at first not to see him, then suddenly whirled around and shouted "*Jah-eh*" back at him. He laughed and giggled so hard he fell over backwards. His mom, the barber's wife, began to keep an eye out for me and let him know when I was walking by their store.

He was a cute little boy with a tiny, perfect circle for a mouth and when he laughed his eyes crinkled shut.

Our get-togethers boiled down to Mek running out to meet me with him arms high until I rushed up, grabbed him, and tossed him high in the air. The townspeople became accustomed to our greeting and many of them would leave their shops when they saw or heard me approach. After Mek and I played around a bit, we would sit by the side of the road and exchange nonsense syllables. Lately, he rounded up a coterie of friends to lie in wait for me so when I went shopping after school I was often surrounded by half-a-dozen tiny boys screaming "*Jah-eh!*" and holding up their arms in the hope they, too, would be chosen by the ridiculously tall foreigner to be lifted high above the earth. If I pretended to ignore them, they wrapped themselves around my legs and held on tight as I pushed ahead, or else they tugged on my pants cuff. Mek's father refused to accept money from me when he cut my hair.

Ants once again invaded my house. This time they were big, black and slow-moving. I spotted a double line crawl through a crack in the living room wall then quickly fan out to cover the floor before regrouping into columns that headed for my bedroom. Wisut and I sprayed every corner and wall until the area was covered with thousands of curled-up, dried ant bodies. Although I didn't ask him, I wondered what Wisut was thinking in terms of reincarnation.

The Nang Rong Bank finally opened! It emerged from layers of rough scaffolding to be revealed as a gleaming white structure with delicate gold trim by the roof. Yesterday, the headmaster announced that any student who put money into the bank would be excused from classes that day. A deposit of $25 was worth a free lighter and $50 was good for a handbag. Most of the townspeople had never been to a bank and many of them dropped by just to watch the tellers make change or fiddle with their abacuses. In my case, it meant I no longer had to go to Buriram to cash my checks from Peace Corps.

November 13, 1967

This evening's temperature was actually cool. The Thais were all wearing sweaters. Maybe it was 65. Must be the wind chill.

Rolled out of my little cot, disentangled myself from my mosquito net and found I'd fallen in love with all my newly-acquired routines. Roosters always woke me up, but then I would lie there thinking about my parents back in Massachusetts also getting up early in the morning and going downstairs into the cellar to begin making sandwiches for the family business. I tried explaining to Wisut what my family did for a living, but the notion of Americans getting up before the sun to make several hundred sandwiches and then deliver them to drug stores, factories and barrooms made no sense at all. I later discovered the other teachers believed my family owned a large restaurant.

My house had no glass in the windows; just wooden shutters that were pinned back against the wall in the day and locked shut at night. First thing I did in the morning was open the shutters and peer out at a world of tropical greenery and listened to the chirping of strange birds and insects as the world woke up. Banana, guava and palm trees flourished nearby and the ground cover was thick enough to prevent me from ever seeing the actual soil. I turned on my short wave radio, slowly slipped on my crisp, brown teacher's uniform and peered out of each window. Smiling and chattering students skipped by on their way to school. Sometimes they glanced over in my direction and if they saw me in the window they quickly scurried away. I threw cold water on my face and head from the big, clay urn in the bathroom, doing my best to ignore wriggling mosquito larvae on the surface.

Wisut and I walked to the market area together, with him clutching the little finger of my left hand. Enormous banana fronds hung over our passage. In the market area we walked on powdered clay and sand, doing our best to avoid stiff ruts made by passing buffalo carts. A woman at the Raxana restaurant smiled at our approach and asked me if I wanted some fried duck eggs with my usual *patongo* and Ovaltine. Our regular table faced the street and we watched the morning market take shape with peasants coming in from the outer hamlets, to lay out their smoked fish, tiny dried crabs, bunches of onions and various herbs and spices, banana stalks and seasonal fruit. Then, at an unspoken signal, we got up and walked over to the school where students gathered in front of the flagpole for morning prayers, saluted the flag, sang the anthems, heard the bulletins of the day and, perhaps, watched a student or two thrashed with bamboo switches for some misconduct.

The teachers milled around after the students were dismissed on the field. We wanted them all to be in their rooms, at their desks and prepared to greet us by the time we got there ourselves. My lead student stood poised by my classroom door, waited for my nod as I approached. He stepped into the room ahead of me and yelled, "*Nakriene trong!*"(Students attention!"). By the time I entered they were all on their feet, staring at me. I looked them over, gave a stiff nod of approval and they seated themselves, waited quietly for whatever I had to say or present. I worked primarily on grammar and irregular verbs, so they were generally less happy than they'd been in the past. Obviously, if I was not carrying my guitar, then there would be no American folk songs.

Last week as I quietly nibbled a *patongo* at a restaurant in Buriram, waiting for Ralph and the other volunteers, when one of the customers looked over at me and asked, "Why do the American magazines say bad things about our king?" I had no idea what he was talking about. Several other people joined the conversation and eventually I understood that a recent issue of Newsweek Magazine asserted that the King of Thailand was a coward! Their reporter wrote that while on a tour of the southern provinces, King Bhumipol had been afraid to leave his helicopter because of rumored rebel activity in the area.

I told them all it was obviously a big mistake and that they would have to print a retraction. The small crowd around me smiled and someone offered to buy me another Ovaltine.

"Do you like Ronald Reagan?" someone asked.

I told him if by some chance Reagan became president while I was overseas I'd wait until his term was over before I returned. "He's an *actor*!" I said. "Why would anyone want an actor for president?"

"But, he is very handsome!"

"Bonsoon (a Thai movie star) is also very handsome, but do you want him to be president?"

They thought that was simply hysterical. Eventually, they left me alone to finish my *patongo* in peace. I was in Buriram because I received a telegram from Frank telling me that in honor of his years of service to the province, the owner of the local movie house (the only one with full A/C) offered a free screening of Dr. Zhivago for all Peace Corps volunteers. Our entire group assembled at Franks then walked over to the show. It had been so long since I'd been inside a movie theater the giant screen awed me almost as much as the velveteen curtain and the enormous speakers that hung on each wall. From the moment the theme music swept over us I was enthralled. Ironic that I had been living in Thailand, a place utterly lush with exotic vegetation, customs and language strange to my senses and people unique to all my past experiences; yet, I sat and stared at the Russian tundra as if *that* was the most bizarre sight I'd ever seen.

Did I get those goose bumps because I somehow sensed my own ancestors came from that area? Everything I ever heard from my grandparents enforced the notion that the average Russian was no friend to the Jews, yet as I watched the movie I was powerless to evade a sense of kinship with Pasternak's characters. Sentimental, romantic, the poet scribbled his verse on an elegant desk while a blizzard raged outside and wolves howled – I believed it all. King Bhumiphol's picture flashed on the screen at the end and as we rose to sing the King's Anthem, I was oblivious to everything around me. There was snow, snow all around me and the great steppes of central Asia were nearby. Abruptly, 100 degree heat slapped my face and ox carts creaked by on a dusty side street here in Buriram Province. I simply could not accept such an abrupt transition. The others chatted happily about the movie on their way across town for tea and dessert, but I fell behind, waiting to be alone, wanting to be alone, and think of Zhivago falling dead on a street in Moscow.

I eventually caught up with the others and had some delicious banana cream pie, but the images from the movie kept appearing in my head. Instead of walking away from the restaurant with Fred as I'd planned, I decided to leave with Thom, from the Boys School. His house is behind the school in the middle of a mud flat. The main reason I hadn't stayed with him before was because during the rainy season his house is an island in a small sea of mud. As usual, the two of us left our shoes outside, but during the night the rainy season returned and I found the remains of my shoes several yards downstream from his porch. And, just as I remembered it from before, Thom's house was surrounded by mud.

Still, it was a nice change to stay with Thom because he was much more politically articulate.

"The other teachers want to know why you aren't back in Nang Rong," Thom said.

"Why? Did I miss something?"

"They told me your village was having a celebration."

"Shit! I think Wisut did say something about a party, but I figured, you know, oh 'party' as if it was anything special."

"I guess it did mean something special, Burgess," he smiled knowingly. "That means you definitely must attend whatever comes up next as penance."

November 15, 1967

Thom was right about my absolutely having to attend the next event, which turned out to be a wedding between one of our teachers and a member of the border patrol. The bride and groom looked ridiculously young, somewhat dazed and resplendent in their wedding garb. I thought I caught the bride sneak a glance at her future husband, but he stared resolutely ahead. Wisut told me that the bride's family had consulted an astrologer to make sure this would be a lucky day for the couple. It also had to be on an even-numbered day of the month. I glanced around the room trying to get my mind off the pain in my knees and back from sitting in a semi-lotus position. All the teachers from our school were there in starched white shirts, creased slacks or modest dresses. Only the bride wore traditional Thai garb. Earlier that morning, the couple had visited the local temple to give food to the monks who gave them their blessings.

At the ceremony, a monk ran a white thread around the bride and groom and then circled them again to form a space that separated them from everyone else. After the eldest monk poured sacred water on their joined hands, everyone was invited to pass by, one by one, and poured water over therir hands. Wisut coached me on a good luck prayer called *rod nam sang* to recite as I bowed, briefly, before the newlyweds. That earned me a resplendent smile from the bride.

After all the ceremonial aspects of the wedding, the couple was whisked away and everyone reassembled at another house where food was served, Mekhong whiskey flowed and people danced. Wisut pointed to a large platter of food and said, "This is called *tum kha gai,* which means chicken soup with coconut that is spicy."

"It smells delicious. Do you know what's in it?"

After consulting the pocket Thai-English dictionary he always carried, he said it had kaffir leaves and lemon grass. I asked him what kaffir was, but he could not explain it any more than that.

"It also has *galanga* root," he said. "My dictionary says it is the Thai ginger, but not ginger like you know. Here, you watch me. Put rice on your dish, then put some *tum kha gai* over it. Very good."

Delicious and in a way that was a totally different delicious from anything else I had ever tasted. Experience had taught me to eat as much as I could before drinking. I danced with a few of the single teachers, but their hands shook and felt cold as ice. When I looked directly at them, they quickly looked away. My inability to make small talk didn't help. I retreated to a wall of other young men and after a few hours I followed them into a side room where a kind of bachelor party was going on. The groom sat smiling as the men began a round of drinking songs connected to weddings. I quickly realized that in between a catchy refrain, everyone there would sooner or later have to contribute his own verse. After listening closely to several of them I got the drift and focused on what I could sing when my turn came. Basically, all I sang was something like:

> *I'm the farang. I was there.*
> *Got so drunk, I sat on a chair.*
> *Some thought I was from Kampucha (Cambodia)*
> *But I was really from America!*

That earned major applause. The round of lyrics continued and became progressively less congratulatory and more bawdy. I couldn't believe what I *thought* I was hearing, until Wisut assured me that, yes, I was hearing it correctly. All the segments had to not only rhyme, but also fit the meter. Several lines that stood out for me went something like this (I'm forcing the rhyme into a very rough English equivalent):

> *Last night to the house because he had the hots*
> *But the bride shouldn't worry 'cause he's had his shots*
> *(chorus)*
> *Lady be good, on him you can rely*
> *He's tried it first on a butterfly (hooker).*

This being up-country Thailand, a bunch of guys began singing the lyrics to "I'm Saving My Money to Buy You a Rainbow" soon followed by "Clementine."

Around midnight the room began to spin and Wisut guided me outside to pour a bucket of freezing well water over my head.

Later, as we slowly stumbled back to the house under the dim light of a crescent moon, I asked Wisut if the couple had received many gifts.

"Yes, there are always many gifts for a marriage, but there is one gift the man must give the woman before the marriage."

"What's that?"

"It is called *thong mun*. Do you understand?"

"Gold?"

"Yes, gold! Not gold money, but jewelry made of gold. The man must give it to the woman."

"How much do they give?"

"If the man is a rich *farang* like you, then I think it must be a lot of gold!"

"You're joking, right?"

"Maybe," he smiled. "Maybe not."

The two of us crashed on to our beds and slept right through the crowing rooster. After I got up to take a leak and throw some water on my face, the whole world came into crisp focus and, looking around my house, all I could see was how filthy everything had become. Neither Wisut nor I ever seemed to empty the ash trays, sweep the floor, clean dishes or make beds. Wisut appeared, looked around, and shook his head.

"We need to clean up," I said.

"*Mai pen rai* (never mind)," he answered.

"No, seriously. We have to clean everything."

"Waiter!" Wisut called out, as if we were at a restaurant. "Bring this man some more whiskey!"

We both burst out laughing. I returned to the bathroom, threw some more water on my head, but when I tried to comb my hair I was horrified to see small tufts of hair in the comb. Jesus, what did that mean? What would my family say when they meet me at the airport and see a doddering, alcoholic, bald and tottering man come down the stairs, flicking imaginary geckos from his arms?

November 17, 1967

Yesterday evening it seemed as if all of Nang Rong was walking in the direction of *Nong Tamue*, the town's tiny lake, to celebrate the *Loy Krathong* Festival of Lights. Wisut told me that this festival began in ancient Thai history when the people gave thanks to the Goddess of Water, *Phra Mae Kongka*, for all her blessings. These days, he said, some people say prayers to the goddess and ask her to forgive everybody for polluting the rivers and lakes. He said that a *krathong* is a little banana leaf vessel, usually just large enough to hold a lit candle, a few flowers, a joss-stick and possibly even some money. I'm still not sure exactly how they picked the day for celebrating *Loy Krathong*, but apparently it's always on a clear night, under a full moon when all bodies of water ran high. People gathered by riverbanks or ponds and gently pushed their decorated floats away from shore. The idea was that the *krathongs* carried away accumulated bad luck and sins.

I was on my way to the water when an open truck came by with some teachers on board who signaled me to get aboard and join them on their journey to another village. Standing firm in the back, I coughed and sneezed as the red clay dust blew up from the road and into my nose. Someone handed me water. Someone else handed me a small bottle of Mekhong whiskey. It was a splendid ride. The women wore fine silk dresses and the men were resplendent in tight-fitting black trousers and glowing-white, starched shirts. The harvest moon was bright enough for the driver to keep his lights off and shadows of palm trees laced the road. I'd been taught the lyrics to the *Loy Krathong* song during training, so people on the truck were suitably impressed when I was able to join in when they held hands and sang:

Loy loy kra thong...loy loy kra thong...

136

A few giddy couples tried to make a dance moves as they sang, but there wasn't enough room and they cheerfully crashed against each other as the truck bounced along.

At Ta-pek Village, a number of saffron-robed monks sat near the water, chanted and waved feathered fans. A dance floor had been erected some distance from the water and local beauties were available as rentable partners for one *baht* (a nickel) a dance. The band (a drum, an accordion and a vocalist) did their best to wail out top Thai and American tunes. I wormed my way through the crowd to the dance floor, but it was so jammed with people all I did was stand still and smiled.

Eventually, enough people left or were gently pushed off the dance floor to allow for some dancing and even though the microphones crackled out a weird mixture of songs, the people danced traditional *Loy Krathong* steps. Suddenly, there was an abrupt silence as if everyone had heard the same disquieting sounds of screams and shouts from the woods around us.

"Bandits!" someone shouted, and people ran off in all directions.

A border patrolman I knew who spoke some English told me that some Cambodians had infiltrated the area from the nearby border and were going around with brass knuckles beating up men at random. Whether or not they were interested in working over emaciated American volunteers was a point I didn't care to test. I asked if there was a place to hide.

"Maybe these are communists or maybe just thieves trying to steal some water buffalo, but I do not think they want to hurt anyone too badly because then the army will come after them and it will all be very bad."

"But, they have guns!" I said.

"They know this is a popular celebration. They do not want to make everyone angry at them. If they have guns they will certainly shoot over the heads of the people."

I looked down at the top of his head and thought, "Over *your* head is between my eyes…" and began doing an excellent imitation of a Groucho Marx walk with my frame parallel to the ground.

People huddled in frightened groups until the Ta-pek community development director pulled himself up on to a table and in a running stream of profanity cursed the Cambodians, Laotians, Burmese, Vietnamese and whatever other nationalities the bandits might be. He never said anything about the possibility that poverty-stricken, local Thais might be the ones shooting. Several of his assistants tried to get him down, but when he felt a hand on his leg he became even more angry and kicked out at them. In the end, he only succeeded in losing his balance and fell backward to the ground.

Heavily armed Thai soldiers arrived and quickly fanned out, rifles pointed directly at the crowd. A man staggered out of the woods with ugly gashes on both cheeks and bloodstains up and down his shirt. Someone gave him a few baht worth of dance tickets and a tiny bandage that covered nothing. Several members of the group from my truck tugged me away and said it was time to return to Nang Rong. Surrounded by soldiers, everyone had to be frisked before being allowed on the truck. One of them suddenly realized I wasn't Thai and drew back.

"Hey, you GI?" he asked.

"No," I said in Thai. "I'm a teacher at Nang Rong School."

He stared at me, stunned, then turned to the driver and told him he was crazy to come here with a civilian *farang*. Did he want everyone to get arrested? This place was dangerous!

Everyone around me cheered and slapped my back. I climbed on board and squatted down behind the cab to give as low a profile as possible.

Most of the men, including the driver, carried bottles of Mekhong whiskey with them back on the truck, so the ride back was considerably less comfortable as the truck weaved its way home frightening the women, causing men to vomit and petrified one American. The driver passed out at the edge of the market and the truck rolled to a stop. I borrowed a bicycle from a student I recognized and pedaled back to my house. It was midnight.

All was black and empty. I saw a light shining in the teachers' lounge across the street, so I walked over to see if anyone knew where Wisut was. Sanguan and two of the janitors were keeping an eye on him. My poor roommate was on a thin, straw mat, his head lolled from side to side and he muttered deliriously. One of the janitors tried to force some boiled rice between his lips, but Wisut turned away and dry-heaved. The other janitor spotted me and leaped up to hand me a small bottle of whiskey. Not a good choice. I carefully picking Wisut aloft, carried him to a small cot and propped his head against a pillow. He protested that he wanted, "…to go to home sweet home…my family is here… now I go sleep…"

Sanguan gently urged him to stay on his back and take deep breaths.

"He made this for you," Sanguan told me, pointing to a small, but exquisitely decorated *krathong* float. "We stayed here with Wisut and waited for you to come home so we could all go to Nong Tamu together and put this in the water, but when you didn't come home they began to drink."

I looked unhappily at my poor roommate as he sweated on the cot and wished with all my heart I had ignored the men on the truck heading to Ta-pek. Then, somehow, Wisut managed to sit up and swing his legs over the side. He got to his feet. Sanguan and I swung his arms over our shoulders and half-carried him back to the house where he collapsed on a chair, gagged a few times, and clutched his stomach.

"Make some tea for me, please," he whispered.

I quickly boiled water and poured hot tea into the largest cup we had. He grabbed it, spilled some on his leg without a sound, then drank the entire scalding cup without a whimper.

"Thank you, my family," he said to me, then somehow managed to stumble into his own room and collapsed on his bed.

Next morning, he was up before me, but pale-faced. We walked to the market and although he tried his best to down some coffee and eat a soft-boiled egg, he just could not do it. On the way back to the house, the headmaster walked by us and gave us both a little smile and a wave. I don't think he heard Wisut's moan. Back at the house, Wisut admitted he just could not go to school and he asked me to deliver a note to the headmaster.

"What did you write?"

"I told him I felt too weak and sick to teach."

I made him another cup of tea, watched him fall quickly to sleep, then I went over to join in the flagpole salute and Pali prayer recited every morning in front of the main building. I left his note on the headmaster's desk and went to my first class. During lunch break, the headmaster took me aside and, as if he'd never seen the note, asked me where Wisut was. I told him he was in bed.

"Is he still too drunk to teach?"

"I don't know about that," I said, looking down, "but he was sleeping when I got back from Ta-pek and I found a note he'd written for me to give to you.

"Yes, I read the note," he scowled. "Return to your room and do your duty."

I thought I detected a slight grin as I turned to leave.

After school, I returned home to find Wisut reading in bed, alternately nibbling on crackers and taking sips from a bottle of orange Fanta.

"Hey, you, my family!" he said. "How is the headmaster?"

"Okay, but I don't think he believes the note."

"It's okay about that. He knows and I know and we all know, but I must write the note anyway, you know that?"

I admitted I did know that and wandered back to the living room that was beginning to smell of forgotten food fragments. I'd told Wisut last week we needed to clean the house, but he said it was too late because it had taken us months to locate a place for everything we owned and if we cleaned the house we would never be able to find a place again for every item.

··

November 20, 1967

I did not want to go to work today. I was afraid everyone would remember what happened in front of the flagpole last Friday. The headmaster was very angry with me because the results of a preliminary grammar test showed students in my classes did worse than any other class in the school's history. After he quizzed several students from my oldest group he discovered I had not strictly followed the work book that emphasized parts of speech.

"You taught them songs!" he almost yelled at me, "But no gerunds!"

We were standing in front of the flagpole, under one of Asia's bluest skies, when he lit into me and within seconds the air was hushed as students and teachers turned away from my public embarrassment.

"I asked Sompong, a student in your fifth division class, about prepositional phrases," the headmaster said. "He did not even understand my question. I asked Thiangthong, a student in your fourth division class, to recite for me the simple past tense of the verb 'to be.' He could not do it. The *simple* past! These are the elements of English upon which they are tested. You must stop singing songs and do your duty to this school."

"Yes, Adjan Suraporn, I understand," I said.

"Are you lonely here?"

"What?" I asked, looking up in surprise at the sudden change of topic.

"Are you lonely?" he repeated, smiling broadly. "You only have Mr. Wisut as a roommate. Perhaps you would be happier with another teacher? Is there room in your home for someone else, do you think?"

"No, thank you," I said. "And, I am not too lonely. Mr. Wisut is helping me a lot."

The headmaster drew himself up to his full height, his stomach and chest as hard and flat as a slab of granite, and gave a stiff nod.

"I think you will not go to Buriram this weekend," he said. "I think you will do new lesson plans about gerunds and participial phrases. Will you do that?"

"Yes," I said. "I will do that."

My walk from home to the school was slower than usual because I kept looking around to see if anyone was watching me approach on my march of shame. The banana tree fronds hung listlessly in the damp air as I kicked up small clouds of red clay dust. Mr. Chop, the janitor, saw me and gave me an enormous wave and a smile.

By the time I approached my room all the other classes were in session and my lead student, Sombat, stood waiting for me in the doorway. Just before I reached him, he turned, stepped into the room and cried, "*Nakhrien, drong*!" (Students, stand!) I nodded to him as I passed and stepped into the room. All their eyes were on me as I scanned their faces, and all I received in return were smiles. I nodded again to Sombat who in turn told everyone to sit and I began my lesson on prepositional phrases.

November 28, 1967

I'm writing this entry a few days after we all returned from a field trip to the city of Lopburi and the famous Monkey Temple. The trip took me completely by surprise, as most school announcements did that were not explained to me ahead of time by Wisut. Otherwise, I was clueless. My days have been filled with the green wonders surrounding my everyday life: banana trees in my back yard, guavas hanging by my bedroom window, coconut palms everywhere. For some reason, all that exotica mixed with the anxiety I felt in a strange geography and culture left me waking most mornings with a sense of dread. Quite a few of my students still seem petrified of me. I tried to be spontaneous speaking Thai, but truth was I feared making an ass of myself. I still screwed up with the tones enough to blurt out horrible curses or totally inappropriate statements. Even with Wisut's help and the friendly smiles of the other faculty members, I felt close to being a near mute alien in a verdant paradise.

I found out about the field trip when the headmaster walked into my room after class on Friday and told me I'd be leaving with the rest of the school on Sunday morning. There was no question about whether or not I wanted to go. I waited for the other shoe to drop. Finally, he said, "Khun Burgess, when you go with the other teachers you must wear your uniform. Understand?' I nodded.

All the teachers wore khaki uniforms a few times a week. Most of the country's schools were part of a national system and the uniforms teachers wore identified them as federal civil servants, complete with various decorations that identified rank that was linked to level of education, position and seniority. I was actually kind of excited when the time came for me to be measured for my own uniform, which was a new experience and within a surprisingly short period of time a local tailor presented me with the finished product. My trim, starched outfit turned out to be a badge of honor, earning me respect and more acceptance by the faculty and local villagers. More of the other single male teachers invited me out to drink Mekhong whiskey and soda water until we dropped. There wasn't much else to do except walk over to the municipal field at night and watch Japanese commercials projected on sheets hung between bamboo poles.

So it was that on Sunday, November 26th, a smiling headmaster took me aside with an arm over my shoulder and told me he this would be an educational trip for me as well as the students. He even addressed me by my Thai-given name, Pandit (as in the English word pundit) and said, "I know you will do your duty."

"I'm sure we will have a good time," I replied.

"Not me," he shook his head. "I stay here with Mr. Wisut and watch the school."

"Wisut's not going?"

"No, I have other work for him to do. Do not worry. Some other people will speak English and your Thai is getting better all the time."

So, that was that.

The ride was long and raucous. It was clear why the headmaster had not joined us. The other teachers exerted a lot less control on the bus than they did in their rooms. By the time we reached Lopburi I had a pounding headache from the uneven road and the shrieking of students. Young, novice monks greeted us. They were very calm, with smooth-shaven heads and saffron robes. The students immediately quieted down.

Once the kids were all safely off, I slipped away toward a promising sign in English that read: CHEESEBURGERS. Just what I needed to cheer me up and fix my stomach. When the owner cautiously handed me what I'd ordered I realized the sign must have been mere decoration because the rancid, fatty chopped piece of meat on a slice of white bread deserved its own title aside from that of *cheeseburger*. Sighing, I nibbled on a plate of warmed cashews and sipped from a bottle of chilled Thai beer. I considered the fact it was November and the time I usually sat down to an enormous Thanksgiving meal and my extended family. Cousin Max often made an appearance with his award-winning nose hair and bald, bullet head. He was a serious glutton, a bully and there was enough hair on his arms to weave a small blanket.

During one such meal, when I was just a kid, he deigned to notice me and asked, "What did you learn in school today?"

Shaking, I replied, "Columbus discovered America in 1492."

"Is that right?" he nodded. "Anything else of interest happen during that year?"

What could he possibly mean? I shook my head.

"Nothing about their royal majesties Queen Isabella and King Ferdinand of Spain eliminating all the Jews by death or deportation?" he asked, calmly.

"Max, for Christ's sakes leave the kid alone," my father spoke up.

Bang! Max's fist slammed the table and a small container of gravy spilled over on to my mother's white tablecloth.

"Why should I leave the kid alone?" he cried. "No one left the Jews alone! Why didn't his teacher tell him about that?"

He reached over and pinched my ear until I cried out in pain.

My father slowly got to his feet, the women pushed their chairs away from the table and Max released me and turned to my father.

"This is what they want. Jews against Jews," Max whispered. "I'm sorry. I am sorry everyone. Forgive me and return to this wonderful meal."

Then, not even waiting to gauge the response of his position, he began to randomly scoop massive amounts of food on to his plate and then stuff his mouth until sauce trickled down his chin and his cheeks bulged. All the while, he stared at me with his large eyes, the pupils of which seemed to shimmer and change from brown to green in a white sea surrounded by broken capillaries. I always avoided him after that, until at my bar mitzvah when he painfully squeezed my shoulder and said, "Welcome to the tribe!"

I hated him with the seething hatred a powerless child could only feel toward someone who was supposed to be a protector.

Back at the Thai restaurant, once the beer was gone and the nut plate empty, I left the entrée for the flies and walked back to the temple. A plaque on a nearby wall stated I had arrived at Prang Sam Yod, which translated as The Holy Three Prangs. Prangs, are cylindrical religious monuments made of sandstone. The structures were not of Thai origin. They dated back to the ancient Khmers who were Buddhists heavily influenced by Hindus. The largest central Khmer temple at Angkor Wat actually is Hindu, with the three central prangs representing the gods Siva, Vishnu and Brahma. The temple before me of Prang Sam Yod had a smaller version of the same three structures, but it turned out the main tourist attraction was an encampment of Macaque monkeys who had apparent control of the entire area and were untouchable because, legend had it, they were the descendants of Hindu gods.

Further along the wall was another plaque that explained Lopburi is even older than the Thai holy city of Ayutthaya, dating back to the Mon Kingdom that had links to India. I had trouble reading the rest of the plaque because it was stained with monkey feces.

Just before the entrance was a large colored billboard proclaiming the date of our arrival matched The Lopburi Monkey Festival.

"My teacher, do you have this in America?" Wirarat, one of my students asked.

His name had been Thiangthong, but he'd reached an age when he could select his own first name so he'd changed it to Wirarat. Yes, that was it, Wirarat.

"No," I said. "We do not have this in America. I think all the monkeys we have are in zoos."

"That is because your monkeys are not holy like here," he explained. "We have to hurry inside the gate because they are going to start the party."

"What party?"

"A party for the monkeys," he laughed. "Everyone can help putting out food they like such as bananas, cucumbers and eggs. Maybe even ice cream!"

"Ice cream? For monkey?"

"Yes, it is very fun. Come on. We must hurry. The more we can thank the monkeys, the more the monkeys will thank us and give us a good year ahead."

As I trailed after Wirarat through the gate I saw a small group of our students attack an obviously sick and mangy dog. The dog was too weak to put up much resistance and the boys poked and hit it mercilessly. I didn't pay much attention to where I was walking and ended up bumping into one of the other teachers, Mr. Somboon.

"This is very fun!" he cried, pointing at the monkeys ahead. "We must hurry and feed them. It will bring us good luck."

"Why are those boys hitting the dog?" I asked. "Doesn't the Buddha tell us to respect all life?"

He looked back at me, stricken.

"It is true that if you are a good person and gain merit and give food to the monks you will return to a higher station in life," he said. "Those who are mean and selfish and only think of themselves return to a lower station. I think the person who used to be that dog was very bad."

"Really?"

"No, not true!" he laughed. "Too simple. I tell you something maybe the way those boys think about that. They have not become monks yet. You know almost every Thai boy will become a monk. That is when they will truly learn about the teachings of the Buddha."

"Then they will know not to beat animals?"

"They will know to respect all life whether it is a sad dog or a beautiful butterfly."

I thought about what he said as I entered the temple and was immediately swarmed by a horde of monkeys, their skinny fingers digging into every crevice of clothing seeking food. One macaque larger than the rest paused to cock its head in my direction, grimaced and bared a set of frightening teeth. Rather than jump about waving his hands like the others, that beast stayed in place and focused his eyes on me with a thoughtful malevolence. Was that a glimmer of sadness, grief or pain within the depths of that feral gaze?

There was an enormous cheer then waves of laughter up ahead. I pushed my way though the crowd and stared at bananas, guavas, rambutans, cucumbers and lychee fruits beautiful presented in swirls and mounds. Hundreds of monkeys jumped up and down, screeching and pulling at each other's fur as they crammed pieces of food into their mouths, all the while urinating and defecating on the food and each other. High above them, in the background, the steep monuments of Siva, Vishnu and Brahma remained silent against a cerulean sky.

I felt something nudge me. It was the large monkey I'd seen earlier. He'd patted my back and when I turned, passed his paws up and down my front. My face was flushed and I could not tell if the water seeping from my eyes was salty from sweat or tears. The monkey's eyes held me in their gaze. I thought of Uncle Max who'd died many years earlier. He'd long been separated from his wife, my cousin Rachel, and I knew from family whispers those black and blue marks on her arms and neck were not there from bumping into furniture. She had not attended his memorial service and the other relatives who showed up seemed cowed and nervous as if they feared word of Max's death had been premature.

A smaller monkey tugged at my sleeve and the big one cuffed it away in one brutal slap to the face before returning to stare at me again, this time almost at eye level. He blinked, leaned forward and clutched my right arm. I was petrified and tried to peel away his fingers. The brilliant Thai sun beat down on the scene. Red dust rose all around putting an impressionist blur to the monkeys, food, students, teachers, monks and Buddhist statues. All was in slow motion. A butterfly gracefully moved its wings just to my left. The monkey gripped me even more tightly, its eyes ferocious and focused as if a malignant and intelligent force was trapped there that somehow knew me.

"Uncle Max!" I cried, and pulled free.

The monkey slapped me hard on my arm, jumped off to join the others at the food and left me to nurse black and blue bruises.

I thought of cousin Rachel.

By the time we'd herded all the students back on the bus it was twilight and we were all exhausted. Most of us had food stains and other unmentionable markings on our uniforms and shoes. Thank God, the driver didn't fall asleep on the return, but everyone else passed out long before we pulled into the bus station at Nang Rong. Nervous parents were waiting for us in the dark to hug their tired children and take them home. I managed to slip free and walk back to my house where Wisut was waiting with a fresh pot of tea.

The number of volunteers in Buriram is rapidly dwindling. Frank and Ralph are now gone and soon Sharon will join them. Some of Frank's colleagues threw a party for him and Sharon. When I arrived at the festivities with her, a pair of strong arms pushed the two of us toward the stage.

"What can we possibly sing together?" I whispered.

"There's a song on this paper," she said, as we shakily climbed up on to the stage. I peered down at the printing. There were the lyrics to "Exodus."

Somehow we managed to gargle through it and returned to our seats to muted applause.

By the time I returned to Nang Rong my stomach was gurgling. Polymagma tablets and lomotil barely helped. Wisut told me our local doctor was away at a medical conference in the south. Perhaps because I was feeling lousy I took it out on my morning classes. The first one really needed it. I picked up a small broom and slammed it against my desk a few times to get their attention and screamed at them to keep quiet and stay in their seats. The next class had three boys missing. I was told they'd skipped my class to go watch a basketball game. Orawan, one of my better scholars, confided to me that everyone knew the American teacher never hit the students; only the Thai teachers did that. What better logic? I had to figure out a way to tell them, "Don't push me too far!"

....

December 7, 1967

This date's significance was meaningless to the teachers; although, they were able to relate plenty of facts about Japanese aggression as it related to Thailand. When I spoke to Wisut about Pearl Harbor we were standing in front of a large map of Southeast Asia and once again I was struck by the way Thai map makers always painted their own country in bright red and alter the the map's perspective so that Thailand appears as a giant among nations.

December 5 was celebrated as the King's Birthday. Weeks before the holiday, most of the teachers and students were busy making displays, printing tickets and hammering together dance stands for a huge fair. Dozens of food stalls were set up by women from the entire district to sell hot coconuts, fried bananas, grilled chicken, *patongos*, stir-fried vegetables, a variety of different salads, tubes of bamboo filled with sticky (glutinous) rice, many types of curry made with everything from chicken to frogs and desserts such as sticky rice with mango and bananas in coconut milk. Several portable restaurants were also erected to sell more substantial meals, although they seemed to make most of their money on Mekhong whiskey and soda water. Money from the fair was allocated to help subsidize the displays and presentations in honor of the king on the celebration of his birthday.

Three large white sheets were stretched between three sets of bamboo poles in a triangle pattern, so whatever movies were shown could be viewed from any angle. The first evening, I drifted by to see what they offered, hoping at least for cartoons, but they played old Vietnam newsreels, a travelogue of the king and queen, ancient Thai romances and Japanese toothpaste ads. Near the Nang Rong District Office they'd set up a dance stage and tiny theater for a traveling Chinese troupe from Buriram. A few farmers laid out straw mats to sell mounds of rice. Hundreds of children ran from stall to stall buying plastic bags of colored, sweetened water and cheap candies. Several motorcyclists strutted about wearing heavy leather jackets and studded belts; they were also the only ones wearing fur-lined gloves. A steady wind arose and the cool evening breeze turned into a cold front that sent me close to a bonfire for warmth. A dozen women climbed on to the stage and began selling dance tickets. As the men became progressively drunker, they bought more buy tickets and danced unsteadily on the stage. A bus arrived with students from the Buriram Agricultural College. Wearing tight bell-bottoms, blue sweaters with white turtle-neck tops, high-heeled boots, long, slicked back hair, and a general air of insouciance, they leaped up on the stage and showed the locals what it was all about by performing the latest American dances and confused the women with their moves. More people wandered out to the field. I saw the headmaster zooming in and out of the crowd on his black Honda 500 making sure the teachers were all on the job. Then, I spotted Wisut.

"My job will be the best of all," he said. "The headmaster told me he knew how hard I worked on the design and the displays, so he promised me something good."

At that instant the headmaster screeched to a halt in front of us and directed Wisut to help collect tickets at the main gate. Not exactly a plush detail. He looked glum, so I followed him to his post for half an hour, helped him sell tickets and joked around a bit before heading home.

That evening, lying in bed, I heard the band play "Hang on Snoopy." If Thailand is this Americanized all the way in the hinterland, I found it frightening to imagine what things would be like here by the year 2000. The Thais have always hedged their bets in foreign policy, usually leaving at least one avenue open for realignment. They managed that during World War II by recognizing Japanese authority, declaring war on the allies, but maintaining an autonomous army in the hills which suddenly declared themselves the Free Thai as American forces advanced. The country has never actually been occupied by another country and after World War II they even gained some land by slicing off a bit of Cambodia. As the brief history lesson went through my mind the band played "Wooly Bully." How many more nights of this could I handle?

The fair went on forever. Peace Corps should have given me more lessons on how to socialize. I think I've averaged about five hours of sleep a night since this celebration began. For the first time in years my face erupted in an explosion of acne.

Eventually, the fair's band stopped playing. The King's birthday celebration was an awesome display of three-dimensional placards, displays and flower arrangements, full-dress parades and monks who chanted blessings for the monarch.

A care package arrived from my family just in time. The ants managed to get into everything again and I had to toss a kilo of sugar, vanilla pudding and some cocoa. Most of the cookies in the package were reduced to crumbs, but delicious crumbs. Someone included a can of sliced pineapples, which were available here in much fresher form, but I ate it all anyway. Maybe I missed the tinny aftertaste of canned fruit. I could not imagine who thought of adding a can of Spam, but when I cooked it up with some chili peppers it tasted pretty good. Packages of dried soup mix were also a tasty surprise.

When I thought of what I was eating, all this imported meat and fruit, when so much fresh food was growing before my eyes it reminds me of Gaugin's sojourn in Tahiti. He painted the natives and nibbled on canned French food. I remembered his work from the Boston Museum of Art: exotic and lush landscapes and women of Tahiti. Where were *my* accomplishments?

The big soccer game I'd heard so much about finally took place: a tough match between the border patrol and a team of teachers. I asked Wisut what the teachers' team was called and he said they were the Harbor Patrol. I couldn't tell if he was joking. The game should have lasted for two 45-minute sessions. At the end of the first half it was tied one to one; although the border patrol seemed to be much more skillful and in better physical shape. After the intermission, I waited patiently for the second half to begin, but eventually realized that the crowds were thinning out and the teams seemed to be packing up their equipment. I asked Wisut what had happened and he told me that, "The Harbor Patrol had some injuries and they wanted to send in other people, but the border patrol said no!" The Nai Amphur (mayor) was on hand, but when asked to adjudicate the conflict he said it was all too complicated for him and he didn't want to be the one to judge. So, that was the end of the game. Nobody seemed to be upset or perplexed about this decision, yet they were all cheering like wild men while the game was in progress. Maybe I just don't recognize civilized behavior when I see it.

December 21, 1967

I felt at once disoriented, comfortable and familiar to be back in little Nang Rong after several weeks of traveling. Wisut promised me he'd keep the house clean while I was gone and even pointed out a few points of interest I needed to visit on my holiday. The ancient city of Ayutthaya, just north of Bangkok, was the one place he said I absolutely had to visit and explore. He told me it had hundreds of Buddha statues from every important stage of Thai history. When I asked for a fast review of its history, he told me that from the middle of the 13th century until roughly the middle of the 17th century, in an area north of what is now Bangkok, existed the kingdom of Ayutthaya. By the 1760s the kingdom had grown into what later became known as Siam, which more or less corresponds to modern Thailand. Ayutthaya did quite a bit of trading with other Southeast Asian entities, as well as with interested Western nations, such as the British and the Spanish. He said that the name *Ayutthaya* comes from the Indian city of *Ayodhya* which figures prominently in the Ramayana. I promised him I would visit.

After I waved goodbye to Wisut, I took the spine-rattling bus ride to Buriram then I settled back on my second-class seat on a railway car that huffed and puffed its way south.

I had more of a sense of what I always imagined the capital of Thailand to be like when the train pulled into Ayutthaya. The graceful, ancient temples and slightly shabby monasteries struck me as far more exotic than the gaudy splendor of Bangkok. I teamed up with a few local Peace Corps volunteers who cheerfully took me on tours of the city. They showed me one bustling temple after another. Ayutthaya was, indeed, living history.

As the train approached Bangkok I saw skyscrapers and for the first time in many months witnessed traffic jams and hordes of people going about their daily business dressed in Western-style clothing. Wandering out of the station, I delighted in inhaling clouds of carbon monoxide that brought back memories of Boston and New York. If I squinted enough to keep humans out of the picture and just allowed hazy images of traffic into my vision, it was almost like being in America. Bangkok's unique smell, however, was always intrusive enough to keep me rooted in reality. No matter how dense the auto exhaust, there was a constant undercurrent of curry pots boiling, rice steaming, charcoal burning, backed up sewers stinking and occasional mounds of elephant dung reminding me of Boston's Franklin Park Zoo. Since I was there one day earlier than planned I decided to splurge on a taxi.

After cheerfully bargaining a taxi-driver down from 40 to 20 baht, I soon found myself in front of the Viengthai Hotel. Two plump Chinese businessmen emerged from a Mercedes at the same time and we eyed each other suspiciously all the way through the main lobby to an elevator that didn't work. We merged with several overly made-up women who didn't seem to have an immediate goal in sight and headed for the stairs. One of the women kept blinking her eyes at me, but all I could think of was getting into an air-conditioned room. Of course, the A/C did not work. My room had only a small television, a monstrous fan over the bed and running alongside it was a horizontal mirror. I quickly stripped, turned the fan to full power and stood under a cold shower.

Later, lying on the bed, I allowed the remains of the shower to slowly drip off my body on to a layer of towels. The windows were open, but screened. Good. Bangkok was famous for its voracious mosquitoes that bred on the canals. For a moment, I felt as if I was still up in my little village and my *tokay* lizard was scrambling across the ceiling, snatching insects on the run and waking me up with its strange gurgling cry. The fan didn't seem bothered by being on high and I luxuriated in the breeze.

I don't know how much time had passed, but I suddenly woke up to see alien shadows on the walls. A setting Asian sun was dying through yellow shades. I stretched, reached for a joint, lit it and looked around for the phone. After three good tokes, I dialed room service.

A greeting in Thai: *Sawadti, khrawp!*

Not wishing to chance a misunderstanding I replied in English.

Shortly, another voice came on the line.

"Yes? May we help you?"

"I'd like a massage."

"Yes sir. Someone will be up shortly."

The knock came *very* shortly which irritated me. I wanted to be in a situation where someone else would have to take my clothes off. She was about 5'2" with long, black hair and a typically mixed Thai-Cambodian turned-up nose. Depressingly aware of the fact that she resembled many of the young women in Nang Rong, I pushed the thought away. I knew there were hundreds of thousands of young Thai women in the city who'd drifted down from poor rural areas in search of work. This one had a pleasant enough smile. I wasn't sure what to do next.

"Do you speak Thai?" she asked, in Thai.

"Yes, I speak Thai," I said.

"Oh, you speak Thai very well," she said is reasonably clear English.

I walked over to the bed, sat down and raised my eyebrows. She reached behind her and released her *pasin*, allowing it to fall about her feet. Naked, at ease, she didn't even place a hand over a scant patch of pubic hair.

I lay back on the bed and felt myself getting excited. She curled up alongside me, stroked my body with one hand and began to loosen the towel with the other. The room was a giant sauna. The fan no longer helped. I glanced at her glistening face as she massaged my chest, belly, tentatively skirting my groin and down my thighs. I loved it when she reached my feet and expertly popped each toe with a satisfying release of tension. Her fingers traced the edges of my pubic hair. Instead of becoming more aroused, I felt myself becoming restless, irritated and angry. Why wasn't it working? I guessed the closeness of it all bothered me. I felt myself get soft. The girl continued to touch me, aware that something had happened. She was careful not to look in my face.

My pillow was drenched. I must have dozed off just after turning it over to feel the cool dryness on the other side.

How long had I been lying there, sleeping, before coming back into focus to find her tan-colored face staring down? I reached up and brushed away a strand of hair from her eyes. I felt like crying and stamping my feet. Why did I feel so weird? As if I wanted to be mothered and punished and turned-on all at once. Did she have a clue what I needed?

Suddenly, she reached down and squeezed my penis. I touched her breasts. She smiled. I patted her right cheek. She yanked her face away as if I'd slapped her. I smiled, leaned over and stroked her shoulder. This time, she merely tilted her head back and examined me through half-closed eyes.

"Do you have any idea what to do next?" I asked in English.

"*Mai khoawdjai*," she said.

"You don't *need* to understand," I whispered.

She leaned closer, cautiously. I kept my hands by my side and held my face out for her inspection. Slap! Right on the side of my face. Slap! She hit me again. I didn't blink. Slap. Slap. My eyes watered.

"Oho!" she exclaimed, looking down at my erection.

"Ouch!" I cried after receiving a stiff punch right on my nose, which began to bleed. "Jesus, isn't that a little over the top!"

This was ridiculous. Blood was everywhere and she was still swinging.

I fell backward onto the bed, laughing hysterically and stained the pillow red. Whoa! Suddenly, she was all over me, licking my blood for God's sakes! Before I knew what was happening she'd guided my hard-on inside her and abruptly I came. She relaxed slightly when she realized what happened and moved closer, allowing my head to be cradled against her small breasts. Her fingers brushed my eyes as tears poured out. God, what was happening to me? I heard her catch her breath. She began to rock me back and forth. I sighed deeply and fell asleep.

Something cold touched my face and I opened my eyes to see that she'd brought crushed ice up to the room She'd wrapped it in a towel and was brushing it against my skin. She wore a loose housecoat, probably what she put on to go to the lobby for the ice machine. A glimpse of her breasts with erect nipples got me hard all over again. I pushed the ice pack away and rolled up against her. This time it lasted for several minutes and we rubbed noses the way the Thai do in these situations.

"I told her that my Thai name was Pbandit and she laughed."

"*Chan che Lek*," she said ("My name is Lek.")

I knew it was a common nickname that actually meant "Little."

I didn't have the heart to bargain with her asking price.

By the time I woke up the morning was mostly shot and I stumbled down to the lobby restaurant for some fried rice and a cup of tea. From across the lobby I could see my reflection in the lobby's main mirror. I looked emaciated, pale and sick. I decided to walk around the city for a bit and for the next several hours I stumbled from food stall to jewelry booth until it was time to return to the Viengthai.

Even though it was only mid-afternoon I discovered that a few other volunteers had already left their hotel room for a restaurant across town. I took a deep breath and decided to join them; however, not before showering again with plenty of lather between my legs. When I stepped off the sidewalk to hail a cab, I was immediately surrounded by taxi drivers demanding to be my guide. I chose an older man who seemed unable to work his way in close to me and settled back in his cab to argue the fare. He quoted some ridiculous figure, but when I responded in Thai he looked at me more closely and asked if I worked for the government. I told him I worked for both the Thai and American governments and I was a teacher.

"Oh ho, then you must make a lot of money. Why do you bother to bargain with me over a few baht?"

"Because I'm a volunteer," I explained. "I *wanted* to come to Thailand (a little white lie, since I'd actually applied for the Trust Territories) and I'm only making $75 a month."

"That cannot be true," he said. "I myself make almost $300 a month just driving this taxi. You must be crazy to have a degree and work for so little."

I shrugged.

"You really only make $75 a month?"

"Yes, that's what some of the other teachers in Nang Rong make I get the same salary as they do."

"Nang Rong? You mean near the famous waterfall at Nakhorn Nyok?"

"No, the *other* Nang Rong in Buriram Province near Cambodia."

"Oh ho, then you really are crazy. There are communists up there. They will try to kill you."

"I know. I keep hearing that."

"Why do you risk your life for Thai students? What do you teach them? These are the children of rice farmers, aren't they?"

"Some of them have parents who work in the market."

"But, what can you teach them?"

"English."

"English? Is it a special class for those who will work with tourists?"

"No, they're regular classes. Regular students."

He regarded me skeptically. Maybe I really was crazy. The more questions he asked me the crazier I sounded to myself. He eventually agreed to half his asking price and dropped me off near the restaurant in Bangkok's Chinese section.

My friends, Roger and Sharon, stood on the sidewalk and when I approached Sharon's eyes moved back and forth from Roger to me.

"Did anyone ever tell you guys you look like skeletons?" she said.

'But, you look just as beautiful as I remember,' I thought to myself.

And so, together, we set out to explore the city. Wandering through various embassies, we ogled the travel posters that were posted to entice curious visitors. A fairy-tale painting of Istanbul's Blue Mosque looked exotic even from the vantage point of Bangkok. The embassy of the Soviet Union lured us close, but Sharon reminded us that we'd been warned that our own CIA scanned the front door 24 hours a day and tailed any American nationals who went in. We had a delicious dinner of steak and potatoes with cherry pie for dessert, but we'd no sooner finished than my stomach signaled that it had not been the wisest food to ingest. I took my leave, headed back to the hotel and sat in the bathroom for a few hours with cramps.

Around the pool of the Viengthai Hotel I struck up a conversation with a few self-described American "insurance agents, one of whom said he was an ethnologist working on his own with Thai hill tribes to determine what sorts of non-verbal communication the different tribes used to communicate with each other. I asked him for an example and he thrust his thumb in the air and said, "This sign means everything is okay." Did they think I was a complete moron? They probably worked for Air America or some other CIA financed entity. I stayed with them a few more minutes to be polite then left.

My volunteer group boarded buses for a trip to the Thai resort town of Hua Hin on the gulf for a conference. Thanks to a survey taken by Peace Corps Thailand, we were served local Thai food the whole time: superb curries and endless pyramids of fresh, local fruit. For the first time in months my nose quivered at the sensation of salt water and sea breezes. The mornings were cool and foggy, but the sun quickly dissipated the mist to reveal small herds of horses being led up and down the beach. They were for rent! I fulfilled an old dream by riding an enormous roan along the pounding surf. As I pulled myself up on to the saddle, I turned to the young man holding the reins and asked,

"What's his name?" He replied with a Thai word I didn't know, but as he handed me the reins he looked up, smiled, and said, "It means Tornado!" and I was off!

The conference itself was the usual potpourri of meetings and hassles about local issues: too many of the small, local schools insisted their volunteers stop focusing so much on verbal skills and teach grammar. What else is new?

Several of our Thai language instructors from our training in Hilo, Hawaii, were also at the conference and for many of us it was an emotional reunion with teachers we'd studied with during an intense three months. A few of the instructors zeroed in on my friend Roger and me obviously to see if our language skills had improved any after all our months in Thailand. I found myself tongue-tied and answering in primitive, short sentences, while Roger rambled on, holding their attention even with his mumbled speech to eventually earn their effusive praise. No comment for me. They were all so polite.

Alan, a volunteer who'd been sent to the distant outpost of That Phanom near the Laotian border close-by the Mekhong River, appeared to have lost the most weight, grown a dangling Dali mustache and developed a new, introspective personality. He spoke disinterestedly of his contacts with high Laotian officials due to his fluency in French and a rapidly developing skill in Lao. Where was the guy who'd offered to give free karate lessons? He was so calm and at ease with himself, so different from the guy I knew during training.

Many of the female volunteers seemed to have gained weight and lost some of their hairline. I never heard any explanation about the hair loss, other than a theory that it had something to do with missing trace elements in our diet. The weight differential between the sexes was explained as a cultural phenomenon. Men were freer to roam about town in Thai society, drink and smoke in public and urged to accompany their co-workers on long bike rides. So, the guys generally lived a more out-of-the house life-style than the women, who were usually dissuaded from too many adventures and seduced into sampling offerings of home-made pastries. Generalities, of course, since a fraction of all the volunteers looked remarkably the same.

One of the results of our changed dietary habits involved the digestive enzyme responsible for breaking down lactose. As one of the Peace Corps doctors explained it to me, the problem began when our systems, on a typical Thai diet, took in far less dairy. Our bodies responded with a diminished production of the necessary enzyme to break down the sugar molecule. Case in point: after having lived on a diet of rice and curry, a typical volunteers traveled to Bangkok and ate at a restaurant that served western food (including butter, cheese and milk), much of the lactose in his gut will not be absorbed. This results in painful episodes of gas and diarrhea for the volunteer.

On the other hand, I heard of Thai students who traveled to the U.S., had some initial problems with their new diets, but, in the end, became enamored with cheese-laden pizza with no ill-effects.

That first evening, one of the women took a walk with friends by the surf and was accosted by three men with knives who took her purse. Before the conference was over, the police had recovered the purse, but all her money and her passport were missing. We were told that the going rate for an American passport in Laos was $2,000.

In the midst of presentations, dinners and futures being planned, Peace Corps managed to give us all rather hasty physical exams that checked us out from nails to neurons to navels. After hearing other volunteers talk about food at their sites I came away with the impression I wasn't exactly situated on the pinnacle of Thai cuisine. Teachers from the North spoke of their spicy delicacies and those from the central plains raved about the fresh fruits. Not many from my group found themselves in the South, where the country's Muslims were the majority, but the ones I spoke with referred glibly to fresh seafood dishes and soups that put poor Nang Rong's tiny smoked and dried minnows to shame.

Thinner or heavier, just about everyone seemed pleased with their experiences except, possibly, for Miss C. whose mother flew in on a Pan Am jet, took one look at the local conditions and whisked her daughter on to her plane and back to American soil.

Tim Adams, Thailand's Peace Corps director, started to make disparaging remarks about the group's high attrition rate, but around that time someone wheeled out an enormous punch bowl loaded with very high octane punch. His speech eventually stopped and we all started drinking, then dancing then couples began to peel off to the corners.

George Papagiannis, the regional representative from the North, stared out at the dance through blood-shot eyes, then raised his punch glass to the ceiling and shouted something that sounded like, "May intimacy develop hope for tomorrow. May she never grow old!"

We all applauded.

"There is a somber cloud over the White House," he continued, "as one man, caught up in the grim realities of a war-torn nation, clutches his telephone, scratches his head and racks his brain as he wonders how the hell he's ever going to get out of this mess while all around him the crowds are shouting...he motioned for us to speak up and we all yelled: Resign! Resign!" At that point the party began to break up.

Several of us spotted the Russian ambassador and his assistant quietly drinking in a corner, so we invited them over to our table as we warbled our way through "Midnight in Moscow," quickly followed by the assistant singing a quavery version of "I'm Going to Alabama With A Banjo On My Knee."

More drinks arrived. The ambassador left, but not before his wife arrived to help ease the assistant back to his room.

My bus ride from Hua Hin back to Bangkok was a harrowing journey that involved burning brakes and a driver who genuflected every time we passed a Buddhist shrine. He had no qualms about playing chicken with logging trucks that swayed from lane to lane. Once the brakes began to burn, he kept his foot firmly on the gas. Finding ourselves alive and in Bangkok, a bunch of us checked in to the Viengthai Hotel, took long, hot showers and headed out for a final epicurean fling before returning to our frontiers. I think it was my friend Doug Buchwalter who recommended the Carleton Restaurant, amous not only for its rich American menu, but also for its white linen tablecloths and complimentary cigars after dinner.

Roger, Doug, Sharon and I cautiously entered the restaurant's air-conditioned interior and wavered for a moment at the sight of all those white cloth tables and attentive waiters. I had a sharp image in my head of Nang Rong School's so-called teacher's cafeteria: the long, wooden table, ancient metal and wooden folding chairs, open to the elements on three sides with a corrugated roof overhead. The janitor's wife would come slowly through the field hauling her little wagon of curries and soups for us. The teaching staff, in heavily-starched uniforms, patiently waited for the white metal plates to be filled and we joked about the morning's enterprises. All of that was waiting for me as I inhaled the scent of steaks grilling within 20 feet of where I stood at the Carleton's entrance. And then, we were inside and seated.

We were all drooling by the time food appeared.: roast chicken with tossed salad, noodle soup, small loaves of black bread, baked potato, sour cream and chives. Doug had something called the special steak sizzling before him with mushrooms and chopped onions while Sharon rewarded herself with a large t-bone and assorted vegetables. I opted for the steak platter, salad, Russian borscht, black bread, cheeses and whipped potatoes. No Mekhong with soda for our table! We split a bottle of red wine. After a while, they cleared the table and we launched into various desserts that included apple and peach ice cream over Dutch apple pie, peach melba with rum topping and cherry pie with vanilla ice cream. The conversation slowed to a halt as our bellies filled. Sipping fresh coffee with cream, sugar and a dash of Gran Marnier, we broke eye contact with each other and simply allowed ourselves to slide, gently into gluttony's warm embrace. A waiter appeared with a select choice of Havana cigars. Only Doug took advantage and lit up clouds of aromatic bliss. It had taken four and a half hours and totaled 386 baht – just a bit under 20 bucks!

Next morning we all managed to get up by 5:30, taxied to the train station, and took separate trains for different routes. The last thing we discussed was Christmas dinner: Doug planned to head to Chiengmai in the North and sample the Polish hams cooked by a local volunteer; Roger had a notion for Khon Kaen's regional feast of roast duck, while Sharon and I decided to stay in Buriram to taste Ralph's stuffed turkey.

December 23, 1967

I actually felt relieved, relaxed and reassured when my bus pulled to a stop next to Nang Rong's market. I was home! Vendors looked up and waved in my directions, female students covered their mouths as they giggled at my presence and, as I walked the short distance to my house I felt safe and happy.

Wisut greeted me at the door with tinsel hanging from his clothes and a big smile on his face. He couldn't wait to drag me inside and show me Charlotte's Christmas tree propped up in the middle of the room twinkling with decorations.

With a wave of his arm, he motioned to the tree and cried, "For my family!" What a wonderful homecoming.

The next morning was not so wonderful when I showed up at school to find a grim-faced headmaster waiting for me. No tinsel in sight. While I was gone, he'd administered one of my own comprehension test to one of my classes and was totally pissed when they finished everything in half the allotted time. He let me know in no uncertain terms that tests ought to take the entire period and mine must have been far too easy.

He thrust the finished tests in my hands and stormed off. I laid the papers out on my desk and began grading. Oh shit! The average score was 40 percent. I stuffed them away and hoped Adjan Suraporn would never ask to see them. Meanwhile, I told myself to buckle down and make my students work harder. The biggest problem was too many of the kids didn't really care about learning English and probably hoped the headmaster would release them early if they finished early.

One of the official pieces of mail waiting for me came from the Peace Corps office in Bangkok with a warning to all volunteers that smoking marijuana in Thailand was strictly illegal and that the government was cracking down on abusers. The director noted that a number of volunteers were languishing in various jails around the world because they were caught trying to smuggle dope back to the States. Something about the matter-of-fact tone of the letter made it all the more frightening. The world burns, we're dropping bombs like there's no tomorrow and bureaucrats are more excited by a whiff of grass than a cloud of napalm.

December 26, 1967

Sitting on the second story porch of the newer school building, I stared out at the close waters of Nong Tamue and the seemingly endless horizon of palm trees. I was content to be back instructing my classes, having curry with the other teachers for lunch and strolling through the market in the early morning haze and dust. Had all of this become so familiar I no longer saw the culture or experienced the different sensory impressions around me. One way for me to gauge my degree of excitement over my surroundings in Nang Rong is to count the number of photographs I took during the first three months of living here with the number I took during the second three months. Uh oh! Half as many! I resolved to more reverently savor each meal, party and trip.

My students were certainly happy to have me back and I realized I no longer had that familiar knot in my stomach when I woke up knowing I had to teach. This morning I presented a lesson plan from one of the school's workbooks about how the days of the week got their names. I never knew Wednesday was named after the Norse God Wodin. Isn't it sufficient to simply make sure the students know the names of the week in English without going into Norse mythology?

The second night I was back, Wisut and I got drunk sitting on the floor near the Christmas tree. After a while, the decorations and tinsel seemed more magnificent than ever and I thanked him again for putting together such a wonderful surprise.

"You are my family," he kept repeating, a bit glassy-eyed, as he poured me another drink.

"I'm sorry I missed your holiday," I said.

"What?" he looked puzzled. "What holiday did you miss?"

"Buddhist Lent. I went away during your important holiday."

"Oh, *mai pen rai* (never mind)," he cried. "Not worry about that now!"

"I'm just thinking about the *next* time we have that holiday. I promise I will be here and help you build the largest candle for the parade."

"My family?"

"Yes?"

"You are very good. Thank you. Now, we must go to sleep."

"Wisut… I forgot to tell you. I'll be going away again in a few days to Buriram to be with some other volunteers. Someone is going to cook a big turkey and a lot of their Thai friends from Buriram will be there with presents and lots of other food and drinks. Do you think you might be able to go there with me?"

He shook his head as if trying to fully absorb everything I'd just said.

"No. I cannot. When you leave here the headmaster tells me to take your classes. You just came back. Now you are going away again?"

"Yes, I'm sorry. I should have told you before."

"*Mai pen rai.* Go to sleep."

Although I felt badly about leaving Wisut behind to cover my classes, the pull of a big turkey dinner was too much to resist.

No one at the bus station seemed to be paying much attention as their local *farang* once again left town. In the provincial capital, I quickly went over to Ralph's house, but there was bad news. While he'd been away on a business trip to the Swine Raisers Combine in the nearby village of Krisam, someone broke through the chicken wire surrounding his yard and stole the turkey. By the time several other volunteers arrived, Ralph had embellished his story enough to make it sound like a major bank heist. We all extended our heartfelt sympathy to Ralph. For some reason we'd assumed that since the bird was stolen on his property it was his responsibility. As things turned out we were all billed for two turkeys: the stolen one and the replacement.

We spent most of Saturday baking cookies and cakes; the cookies were later fed to the dogs who whined as their teeth cracked on the hard-as-steel goodies. On Sunday, two other volunteers were supposed to buy potatoes, but both came down with the runs and were reluctant to leave home. Then, out of the blue Ralph received a call from the post office that a large package with his name on it had just arrived from the States. Turned out some forgotten aunt had sent him a CARE package filled with delicious foodstuffs like instant mashed potatoes and dried soups. After pulling out one goody after another,

Ralph invited me to join him on a short trek to find another turkey. The surrealistic image of me on the back of Ralph's motorcycle squeezing a terrified turkey under my left arm will stay with me forever. Finally, we were all together again standing close to the now-trussed-up bird, playing one-potato, two-potato to decide who would be the one to kill it. No matter how the game worked out, no one would do it. Ralph left for a hurried consultation with another neighbor who finally agreed to come over and slit the bird's throat and prepare it for the oven. The neighbor was no surgeon and I kept swallowing bile as he sawed his way across the bird's wiry neck. Underneath, a battered rice tin caught the precious blood. Old ladies from across the street drifted over.

"Who is getting the neck?"

I shrugged. Probably the ants.

"Who is getting the feet?"

What is this, a butcher shop?

Ralph kindly dispersed the goodies and gave the tin of blood to the executioner. I stared at the ragged, bleeding corpse and seriously wondered about my future appetite. Judy came out with a large pot of boiling water and we dumped the bird in until the feathers loosened enough for it to be plucked. Finally, trimmed and glossy, the bird was brought into Ralph's house and gently slipped into an oven after being rammed full of Judy's homemade stuffing and Sharon's spices.

Thom worked away at a monstrous salad, I put out the instant potatoes for a quick mix and by late afternoon we brought out a beautifully-browned turkey to be carefully placed on the middle of the table. The final napkins were being folded just as our Thai friends arrived: Ralph's boss from Provincial Agricultural Cooperative and his wife, Sharon's headmistress from the Buriram Girls School, teachers from Thom's school and a few close neighbors. We all stepped proudly aside to give them a clear view.

The Thais were stunned. Maybe the word was horrified. They looked askance at the bird and one by one politely took out handkerchiefs and covered their mouths before turning away.

"I think we should have cut the bird up into smaller pieces," Judy whispered. "This must appear utterly barbaric to them. I'm sure if we'd minced the meat into small enough pieces for a curry they'd be all over it, but this is obviously too gross."

I began to cut away some white meat, thinking it would somehow break the ice, but Sharon's headmistress broke away from the group and began to lean over the balcony. I glanced at Ralph who motioned me to the doorway. I put down the knife, lifted up the whole turkey tray and carried it inside where we cut it into very small pieces. Sharon and Judy served drinks as we re-distributed the meat. By the time we came back out, everyone had had a few beers or Mekhong with soda and applauded the now disguised turkey as a wonderful creation. We all sat down and ate heartily.

When we were finished with the main course, it turned out our Thai guests had brought over something for dessert: an enormous watermelon cut into neatly proportioned segments. Each portion had a tiny flag stuck into it with a different volunteer's name attached with suitable wishes for their futures: SHARON – To be rich, THOM –To be clever, BURGESS – To be smart, JUDY – To be beautiful and RALPH – To have a wife. After giving our own thanks and applause, there was a moment to reflect and wonder if these pithy messages were meant to describe what the Thai assumed *we* most wanted.

The next morning Judy took the early train for Lamplaimart and Sharon and Thom took off to teach. I stayed with Ralph and had a wonderful breakfast of fried duck eggs, home fried potatoes, re-heated stuffing, banana bread and three cups of coffee. Later, Sharon returned and made turkey sandwiches, which we finished off with cold beer and chips from the care package. In the afternoon, Ralph made the final tally, which came to 350 baht. That's when we realized our combined expenses included the cost of the stolen bird. Since Judy was already gone, she ended up being the only one to owe Ralph money and I left convinced that Ralph should have gone into banking and investments, rather than poultry and swine raising.

Bloated and happy, I splurged and took a taxi back to serene Nang Rong. The ride should have been more comfortable and enjoyable than usual since there were three teachers from Prakonchai School with me who spoke fairly fluent English. Unfortunately, they all crowded into the front seat and I was left to share the rear quarters with an obese farmer who allowed his pet white rat to cling to his left shoulder for the duration. Its beady eyes never left my jugular vein.

Back home, I found Wisut and the other male teachers waiting for me with a Christmas feast of fried beef in oyster sauce. They also had a big tub of freshly brewed *sato*. I sang "Jingle Bells." It was the least I could do. More *sato* was smuggled in under a basket of lettuce leaves. We drank through the night, singing ourselves hoarse, until Wisut gleefully cried, "Wait until New Year's eve when we really get drunk!"

The last thing I remembered was thinking a crushed piece of tissue paper tossed in the corner looked a lot like a white rabbit.

....

January 6, 1968

Wisut and I spent the day scrubbing the floors, dusting away cobwebs and oiling the hinges of the wooden shutters so when a high wind picked up we wouldn't hear constant squeaks. Later, we walked past the large guava trees near the path that led to the market. Shopkeepers stood languidly on the wooden sidewalks in front of their stores and waved. We strolled into the Raxana Restaurant and had a blazing chicken curry along with a chilled bottle of Singha beer. By the time we got back the electricity was flickering and Wisut started tinkering with a kerosene lantern to read by in case the power went out altogether. I could barely get my clothes off before I fell asleep.

Most of my students gave me New Years cards with various messages on them like : Be Healthy or Be Happy. Traditional Thai New Years is in April, but the January idea seems to have caught on here. For some strange reason the headmaster's son, Sa-thit, gave me a present of a sling-shot. Wisut made a face when he saw it and muttered something about not using it to kill anything. Hard to believe that I arrived here in the year 1967 and it was now 1968. Seemed as if a lot had happened.

....

January 12, 1968

I just returned from Bangkok where I had my first Peace Corps physical exam. The capital was just as exotic and prosaic as I remembered: bus fumes and flower stalls, obscure Indian movies and "The Graduate" (playing in a beautiful air-conditioned theater!), graceful pagodas dotting the landscape outside of the old capital of Ayuthya and grime-encrusted shrines in the capital itself. Air pollution mixed with high humidity made it difficult to breathe. Then I saw a sign that read: BARBER SHOP. Just like that. In English! I popped inside and was immediately hit with waves of cologne and hair spray. There were about a dozen barber chairs, but only a few of them were occupied. I guessed the other men leaning against the wall smoking or sitting on soft chairs thumbing through magazines were the other barbers. The only items that kept moving after I entered were the huge wooden fans that kept the hair on the floor drifting. Otherwise, it was perfectly still. All eyes were on me. Speaking in Thai, I asked:

"Can a *farang* get a haircut here?"

They all burst out laughing. One of the men gestured to an empty chair and deftly snapped out a fresh, white sheet. Just as I sat down, the questions flew at me:

"How come you speak Thai?

"Are you in the army?"

"Have you ever had a Thai haircut before?"

"Do you like hot, Thai food?"

"Do you eat rice?"

"How long have you been here?"

"Are you home sick?"

"Do you have a Thai girl friend?"

I finally waved my arms and started to give a few answers, which only led to more questions. Deciding it was time for me to throw out a few of my own, I asked them:

"How much is a haircut?"

My own barber pointed to a sign to my right that said: Facial – shampoo – razor cut – manicure – ears cleaned: Only 36 baht. "Give me everything!" I cried, and sank back for a truly sybaritic experience.

"Where do Thai people go for fun?" I asked.

"Have you ever been to Lumpini Park?"

"No. Can I take a bus?"

After they'd finished blow-drying my hair and hit my neck with one more splash of cologne, they directed me to the Lumpini bus stop and I was soon on my way. The park's vegetation was lush and the animals and I took turns to see who could stare at who the longest without blinking. I leisurely chewed a delicious taffy apple from a strolling vendor and wandered over to a small pond with ducks and a few benches. After I tossed the apple stick out in the water and watched the ducks fight over it, I lit up a Falling Rain cigarette and happily exhaled at the water.

Two young guys cautiously walked over and one of them asked me, "Hey you! Wanna buy fucky-fuck pictures?"

I frowned and told them they were very impolite. Stunned, they almost fell to their knees and *wai*'d me for forgiveness.

"I'm just joking," I said (the expression in Thai translates something like "talking handsome").

They laughed in relief and sat down next to me. We exchanged names and chatted about Thai food.

"How much do you sell the pictures for?" I asked.

"Americans pay five baht for each photograph," one answered.

"May I see them?"

They handed over a stack of black and white, blurry Japanese pornographic cards. Unbelievable.

"I have better pictures than these in my head," I told them.

"He's a philosopher," one said. "Let's go."

"Wait a minute. Maybe he can help us. How *should* we ask Americans if they want to buy fucky-fuck pictures?"

"First of all," I said, "it's better if you just call them... ah, 'dirty pictures.' "

"*Dirty*?" one of them repeated. "*Dirty*? Like that?"

"Yes, that's good. More polite than fucky-fuck."

They stood up, thanked me for the quick English lesson and walked off in search of customers.

The second Saturday of January is celebrated in Thailand as Children's Day. All the students, wore their boy scout and girl scout uniforms, were directed into our school's large woodshop area and gently seated by class. Facing the students were all the teachers, the headmaster, the mayor and various district educational officers. Everyone was decked out in tightly starched uniforms with appropriate medals and ribbons. Speeches were given extolling the virtues of our wonderful children who manifested our hopes for a prosperous future.

The students began to look a bit glassy-eyed after the first few hours and I was glad I had a seat, with Wisut, behind all the dignitaries. Suddenly, someone yanked my right hand and startled me into consciousness.

"You must go to the microphone," Wisut whispered to me. "They want you to sing a song for the students!"

I was glad they hadn't prepared me. Better that I just got to my feet and walk in a kind of stupor to the microphone where I stared down at the hundreds of little faces. I sang the tried and true hit: *500 miles.* After the first few lines they began to sing along with me! Even though I was sure they knew all the verses, I stopped after the first three, bowed to applause and took my seat. Wisut patted me on the back.

A week later Wisut told me we would celebrate something called Teacher's Day.

"Will it be like Children's Day?" I asked him.

"Almost the same," he smiled. "But, there is one big difference. The children have to go to Children's Day, but we do not have to attend Teacher's Day."

"Good," I sighed. "That means I don't have to get ready with another song."

"Too bad for you if you stay home," he said.

"Why?"

"The Buriram Education Office is going to have a special lottery for all teachers who attend the ceremony. They will give everyone a ticket when they go inside and then they will draw many of them for different prizes to be awarded."

"I thought you wanted to go fishing at Lake Tamue on that day."

"That was before I found out about the lottery."

And so, the two of us joined almost all the other teachers back at the newly-decorated wood shop. Surprise! The lottery tickets cost 10 baht each! Sensing the crowd's surliness, one of the MCs announced that prizes to be awarded were to be worth up to 100 baht. I happened to be sitting next to the headmaster, in the back, as the speeches rolled on.

"Do you think you will win a prize, Mr. Burgess?" he asked me.

"I hope I will win the first prize of 100 square feet of installed linoleum."

"No, I think you will win one of those," he said, pointing to a stack of neatly ribbed packages stacked at the back.

I nodded, mildly happy at the thought, and asked, "Do you know what's in those packages?"

"Yes," he grinned. "Kotex!"

I slumped back, depressed. Finally, the lottery drum was wheeled out and numbers were called. Everyone who walked up for a prize cracked jokes or did comic pantomime routines. It was like old-fashioned burlesque. The only thing missing was a stage hand running out, slapping the MC in the face with a powder-puff and yelling "MAKE UP!"

In the end, I was awarded a 5 baht lunch pail. Wisut got a pair of sox. The headmaster, much to the crowd's amusement, won a petticoat.

Notes from a few days later

Wisut waddled into the house carrying the remains of a gigantic watermelon, and announced, "This is for you. Very sweet juice."

"Hey, that's great. Thank you."

"Only one problem," he said.

What's that?"

"I all the time have to take a leak," he said, quickly putting the watermelon on the floor and ran to the bathroom.

Apparently, he remembered the slang I teach him much better than the formal sentence patterns.

Fred, the malaria eradication volunteer who operates out of Buriram, occasionally has to check in with the local director and when he does, he visits me, too. This time, he told me, there actually was a reason for his visit. The latest vector graphs for malaria cases in the district were showing eruption of cases where they'd already sprayed DDT. He dropped by my house on the rebound from a field survey. His eyeballs were red, dotted with grains of red clay dust, and his expression was grim.

"There's something fishy going on with George," he said.

I knew "George" was the name he used for his Thai sector chief.

I invited him in for a warm beer.

"The last few times I've come out here I've asked George for the statistics of the Lahansai region and each time he told me they'd been misplaced. This morning I dropped by the malaria office early and looked around myself for the charts and tables and, guess what?"

"They never did them?" I ventured.

"They did them all right," he said, with disgust. "I found them this morning tucked behind a desk in the lounge. You want to know what else? They've got a damn malaria epidemic going on out there!"

"Are you sure? Why didn't they say anything?"

"I'm not sure. All I know is that three weeks ago a team went out there to take blood slides and ask a few questions, you know the usual routines, checking to see if anyone had a fever or the shakes recently, and they came back with 23 cases of fever and chills and 18 slides, of which 12 proved positive for malaria. What do you make of that?"

"Sounds like an epidemic to me."

"Yeah. You know, it doesn't figure. Buriram has been pretty much free of malaria for years. They've already sprayed *tons* of DDT for so long it's a fucking miracle they still have any flies! And all of a sudden there are all these cases and George doesn't even say anything. He's a hard-working guy and he's always been really conscientious. As long as I've been here I know his team's been involved in reinforced spraying, gathering data and capturing mosquitoes now and then to see if they spot any malaria vectors. Once in a blue moon some drifter from Cambodia will carry a strain across with him and a vector will be spotted in some out-of-the-way village, but never anything like this."

"When was the last time they did any spraying in Lahansai?"

"Five months ago. According to the charts."

"Five months! That's ridiculous. What about the team that went out there a few weeks ago?"

"They went in for an afternoon then zipped back."

Fred hung around outside my house while I threw some water on my face, combed my hair, shaved and got myself ready for a meeting with local health officials. When we got to the offices, "George" was there sitting around with a few assistants as they stuck pins in a map of Nang Rong District. They all got to their feet when we walked in and Milo quickly mumbled in a Thai dialect that made everyone laugh and get comfortable.

"Have you met Mr. Duangchai?" Fred asked me, pointing to "George."

"No, I haven't. I'm happy to meet you, Mr. Duangchai," I said in Thai and *wai'd*.

He gave me a big smile and *wai'd* back.

"Why'd you say he had such a hard name to pronounce?" I whispered to Fred. "What's so hard about Duangchai?"

"Nothing. It's a little joke. Jesus, don't say his name again. He knows we're talking about him!"

I continued to smile and walked over to a window and stared out. Fred walked over to Dunagchai then around him to the space behind the desk where several rolls of large tracing paper leaned against the wall.

"What are these?" he asked Duangchai.

"Lahansai charts," he sighed.

Fred opened them up and spread them across the desk.

"It says here there haven't been spraymen in this region for five months even though there are a lot of malaria cases reported. Why?"

Duangchai spun around and threw his hands into the air, let them drop, and then turned to face us. Listening closely, I managed to more or less make out what he said to Fred.

"The chart is not finished. Only random sample show more than 50 cases of malaria."

"Fifty!" Fred exploded. "Why didn't you say anything?"

"Cannot! Cannot!" he paced back and forth. "If I show you the chart, then you will want to go to that place. No one can go to that place! Spraymen all tell me they will not go there. They say all the roads have bombs placed underneath and they will explode if a jeep goes over them. They told me that three bombs in the last six months have gone off. They all say if they go to that place they are afraid they will die. Too many Communists!"

"Communists!" Fred and I both echoed the word.

"Yes, Communists! Or, maybe some bad Cambodians or somebody like that. Very dangerous. I did not know what to say to you. I thought that if I showed you the charts you would want to go there, but I am afraid for you and I am afraid what will happen to me if anything happens to you. And I also think (this was where he gave a cautious smile) if you go to that place you will want me to go with you. What do you think about that?"

Dunagchai signaled his men to go outside. For a fraction of a second the three of us stood in a triangle smiling at each other, then Duangchai broke down and slapped his side.

"I was right, wasn't I?" he cried. "Now, you want to go to that place! Only crazy people go there."

Fred laughed. Apparently the wrong response. Duangchai's discomfort turned to rage. He half-turned and kicked his own desk. I looked away. His men's voices could easily be heard just outside the door as they furiously whispered to each other.

"Come on," Fred said. "Is it really that dangerous?"

Duangchai nodded.

"Okay, so how about if we take one jeep out there today just to look around, you understand, and then come back? If we find some people who have fevers I'll write a report for the regional office and tell them about our problem. Maybe Burgess here will keep us company. What do you say, Burgess?"

"Ah, Fred..." I stuttered and shuffled, "what if everything George, I mean Duangchai, told us is true? We could get our asses blown off from a landmine."

"Knock it off! Those things were probably planted a decade ago. There's nothing going on out there. You can take my word on it. It's actually very quiet. What do you say? I'll drop by the mayor's office and ask them if they can spare an armed guard if it'll make you feel any better."

"Oh, yeah, right, an armed guard would be perfect. Why don't we invite the police chief along just in case the bandits want a really worth while target?"

"I will go if Mr. Burgess will go," Duangchai said.

So, that was that. Fred went out and shanghaied a few members of the team to take some slides and drive the jeep.

The folks at the mayor's office weren't too keen about our plan, but they donated a guard, a member of the border patrol, to go along. He sat up front with an enormous automatic rifle and a few clips of ammo by his side. I was happy he didn't have the customary grenades bouncing on his belt.

We filled the jeep with fresh fruit, glass slides and other equipment for the technician, a dozen bags of DDT powder and several canteens of drinking water. The ride to Lahansai was uneventful and only the guard seemed talkative as the jeep bumped and gurgled over the rutted road. Lahansai is a desolate region where the people often do not have enough rice to last the year and often subsist on ground corn, which they do not particularly relish, for several months during the dry season. The town itself was a pig-pen, literally, with dozens of squealing black pigs here, there, across the road and under the few houses resting on stilts. Rains last year tore out the center of the road in the market section. There was a gulley running through three-quarters of the bleak center. No one was visible. The homes looked deserted. There was a mid-size army encampment several miles outside of town and an MDU (mobile development unit) on the very edge. No soldiers were seen outside the tents.

We stopped at an empty restaurant for warm Cokes. The driver then took us to the north quadrant of town where some local citizens were sitting around. The technician took some slides of their blood. We asked a few questions about who had fevers recently, left behind some medicine for them to take in case it came back, and then broke out the fruit. Afterwards, we piled back into the jeep, but discovered the radiator was still boiling and the engine wouldn't turn over. One of the locals wandered over and invited us to his house for some watermelon. It sounded like a good idea. We left the jeep in the shade of a leaning house and followed the kindly Samaritan home. From his porch we had a clear view of his neighbors who crept out of their houses to get a glimpse of us. The children seemed to be half-starved, with swollen bellies indicative of protein deficiency. The women, all wearing simple, *pasins* wrapped around their bodies from shoulder to ankle, stood around squinting at us. Many of them had eye infections. Several younger women breast fed their babies while standing in the shade of the porch. The few young men in sight appeared quite muscular, although a few had open sores on their legs and feet. The surrounding houses mostly had three solid walls with a partial fourth wall facing the street. In the sun's blinding heat, even the scrawny chickens seemed too lethargic to peck for food. Several children played nearby without any clothes, except for a few babies that had tiny loin cloths. When I dropped an empty cigarette pack several children ran for it to feel the cellophane and to sniff inside.

We chatted with the watermelon man for half an hour to calm him down a bit, then Duangchai asked him about Communists in the area. It was probably an idiotic topic to bring up, but the man simply shrugged and said he thought there weren't any Communists in Lahansai because no one cared about the people of Lahansai. Not even the Communists. The area was just too poor for anyone to be interested in them: Thai government or Communists.

Duangchai appeared disconcerted by the turn of the conversation and asked if any government people helped out. The man shrugged again and said they needed many things. When the rains came there was always water, but they had no place to store it and so when the dry season came they never had enough to drink. Growing anything was out of the question. The roads were too bad for communication or trade with Nang Rong, the nearest town of any size. Duangchai nodded and stood up.

The man got to his feet and clasped his hand warmly. We all thanked him for the watermelon and walked back to the jeep. As we drove out of town, children on either side of the gutted road got to their feet and stood at attention until we passed. It was as if we'd all been transported back to the Middle Ages where chattel stood rigid while power rode past.

Hard to believe we'd been in Lahansai a total of three hours. What a difference to pull into Nang Rong only a few kilometers away and see healthy, well-dressed people preparing for a party at the meeting hall.

As we walked back to my house, Fred explained that the malaria outbreaks must have been caused by groups of infected Cambodians crossing over into Thailand. Only one infected person was enough to start an epidemic. He alone could be bitten by dozens of female *Anopheles* mosquitoes. Fred explained to me that the symptoms of malaria – fever, chills and anemia – are caused by the malarial parasites that breed in red blood cells. Even something as simple as netting and a few cents worth of DDT was enough to prevent the spread of malaria. But, for whatever reasons, the disease continued unabated in every country bordering on Thailand. Each *Anopheles* sucked in a droplet of human blood, then sat quietly on a wall or tree while that blood is digested. The next time the mosquito bit somebody it deposited a tiny glob filled with malarial parasites into clean blood, sucked up what it needed, then flew off to rest again. Meanwhile, another human being has been infected. The only way to break the chain was by massive spraying of all standing water and killing the mosquito larvae. Of course, that much spraying might also drift over to where silk worms are breeding and that would be a catastrophe. Meanwhile, until Cambodia, Laos and Burma launch their own malaria eradication programs, Thailand will continue to be plagued with the disease.

Sitting along back in my own house I thought about Lahansai and how tragic it was that the federal government only seemed to respond to threats of 'communists' with armed guards, while for the same amount of money the people of Lahansai would have been proud supporters of the government for simply potable water storage, fertilizers, simple farming equipment and better roads.

....

January 25, 1968

My plastic shortwave radio picked up fairly objective news from the Armed Forces Broadcasting Network in Pleikou, Vietnam. They report events not directly connected with the war: rock music, interviews with local and visiting talent and zany public service commercials. Between songs, there were humorous skits. The early evening music programming is best, with programs that feature rock and roll with narrative asides from the Age of Aquarious and cautionary warnings to be sure and check with your quartermaster regularly. Then, "… and now, your fellow soul brother takes you to Central Stadium in Philly, with Little Steve Wonder."

Where is Kafka when we needed him? Yes, I think Franz would feel right at home in a culturally surrealistic Bangkok where elephants and Esso trucks battle for the right of way, bar girls sing out to passing soldiers and orange-robed monks glide by picking up merit where they can. As I re-wrote the notes I took during my last visit to the capital, I remembered hearing rock and roll blaring out between traditional Thai songs. Movies with titles like "Operation Bangkok" play bubble-gum rock while Thai heroes kick box the bad guys. Coffee houses in the capital were filled as much with mini-skirted temp-wives (with their GI husbands) and floating hookers as they are with regular trade. The social lines had blurred. These days, money alone seemed sufficient to gain entrance to most enclaves of Thai society (with the exception of the royal court).

When a foreigner, like myself, approached a Western-dressed Thai woman and speaks Thai she usually gets quite upset and won't speak at all. It's as if the roles and languages have already been assigned, the woman has already chosen her clothing and speech, so why should a passing American screw it up by speaking *her* language? I remember jotting down these notes in Bangkok's newly-opened first Kentucky Fried Chicken. The background music was "…I can see for miles and miles and miles…" I guess if I manage to make a visit every few months I'll be able to stay on top of the top ten hits. I wish I had a copy of Butterfield's East –West album with me now. That's what was playing the first time I got stoned in my high-rise dorm at the University of Massachusetts. *That* sure seemed like a long time ago.

My radio is now broadcasting warnings to all American servicemen that the Chinese New Year is approaching and it's time to be prepared for firecrackers!

"Hear that, guys? If there's suddenly a loud BANG behind you, please do not reflexively spin around and shoot. It's only a holiday!"

Within a few hours it became apparent that American forces *were* under attack and in the next few days I began hearing the phrase *Tet Offensive*. What a mess. The Thais don't seem to know what to make of it, except I got the impression they really feared the Vietnamese (unlike their public posture regarding Cambodians, Laotians and Burmese). My shortwave radio kept sending bulletins about the attacks and notification about all R & R leaves being cancelled. Could this be the end of it all? I got letters from family and friends asking me what's going on, I guess because I happen to be *here* instead of with them. I kept telling them. I knew almost nothing.

....

January 29, 1968

The *Ngeu* is coming to town! I think that's a word in some Chinese dialect. Wisut tells me a *Ngeu* (the word is pronounced in a high tone) is a Chinese fair. Every six months or so a carnival of one variety or another drops into Nang Rong and this time it's the Chinese.

During the day, Chinese carnival workers strained and sweated to set up tents and concession booths in the large public field in front of the government buildings. Under the sun's unremitting glare, the show appeared to be made up of shoddy, well-worn costumes, cracked and uneven sets, ancient tents laced with stains and miles of electrical wires and duct tape. Even as the show was taking shape, local people set up their own concession stands of bananas, dried fish, coconuts and candy.

Local Thai-Chinese merchants put up the guarantee for the main stage show that ran all day and night. Whatever the *Ngeu's* own concession stands took in is extra profit. I wandered away after awhile because the enterprise appeared so scraggly and run down.

By the time I returned, under a clear evening sky, a magical transformation had taken place. Incredibly beautiful women dressed in the finest silks strutted about gaudy and elaborate stage sets. Elaborately painted clowns juggled and did acrobatics. In the background, a wonderful Ferris wheel slowly turned the calm night into a carnival of moving colored lights so magnificent the stars themselves seemed obscure and uninteresting.

Wisut, being of Chinese ancestry, was prevailed upon by some of the locals to run a concession stand of his own (using his skills and friendships and their money). At the last minute he decided to go in with two other men who wanted to bring dancing girls from the provincial capital. Each man put up a third of the money and the women came as promised. One of the partners worked in the mayor's office and the other was leader of a local civil engineering crew. The women, electricity and rent cost about 800 baht ($40) per night and anything they collected over that was profit. The first night they cleared 800 baht even. The second night they had 800 baht by 11:00 and, as I wrote this entry, the last I heard was that they expected to do very well.

Playing it all back in my head, I realized that $40 paid for a night of 10 women shaking their booties off until two in the morning, all the electricity they needed and the use of a large, portable stage. Comparing that to the $70 a month Peace Corps paid me as a living allowance made me aware of how solidly middle-class I was.

A few nights ago, while watching the stage show, I spotted an old Chinese performer behind a tent putting on his make-up. In the dim light, he looked forlorn in his baggy outfit. I waved at him and smiled. He returned an enormous, toothless grin. Only a few hours later, while I was standing in front watching the show, I was astonished to see the same old man reappear as a Manchu warrior with a furious temper. As the other actors ventured on stage, mouthing their lines in sing-song Chinese dialect, they saw me standing like a thin, white giant in the midst of the audience and noticeably paused at my appearance. My friend, the Manchu warrior, had no problem staring right at me from the stage, stopping the play's action, and elicited a roar of laughter from the crowd. He made a funny face at me and the audience laughed hysterically. He worked me into his routine and at several crucial moments he did an about-face, stared at me until the crowd realized what he was doing, and only then he would contort either his face or his body. When I raised my camera he stuck out his tongue and everyone applauded. Hours later, when I was having a snack in the market, I saw him again, once more having reverted back to a lonely, small figure waiting in line at a food stall. He saw me eating and rushed over to ask when my photograph would be ready. When I told him it would take three weeks for color slides to come back to me from Australia he looked sad enough to cry. I asked him if he had an address I could send to, but he shrugged and replied he had no address, that he went wherever the boss decided they would go. He said the boss only shared that knowledge with his mistress. He stared at my camera and asked if I'd like to take another picture. When I raised it up, he puffed out his cheeks and made all the kids around us laugh.

Later, back at the show, wandering with Wisut through the food stalls and between tents, we passed a partly-opened tent where a bald, fat man was lounging on a rug, being fed something, spoon by spoon, by an absolutely beautiful woman dressed in a pale blue, silk tunic.

"That must be the boss," Wisut whispered, and I nodded, thinking to myself, "Only *she* share's the knowledge of the *Ngeu*'s destination."

We walked over to the dance concession where Wisut took his post selling tickets. Wisut gave away almost as many tickets as he sold. He even handed me a handful of tickets and told me to enjoy myself. Though the weather was a humid version of Hell, I

168

hopped up on to the dance stage and pretended to know what I was doing with several very pretty young women. Off stage, life continued as usual once you mixed in a lot of alcohol. One man attacked another for no discernible reason, trying to brain him with a flashlight. Luckily, it was a cheap flashlight that fell apart after a few blows.

I bumped into a young man who said he graduated from Nang Rong School 10 years ago. He said he worked as a translator for American MPs. I asked him to say a few words in English. He launched into a monotone delivery of ever obscenity I'd ever heard of and a few that were new. He said at 35 cents an hour he was getting rich. So rich, in fact, he could afford to hand me several dance tickets. Before I could turn around several young men approached whom I recognized as clerks from the bank. I only knew them as reserved men in sharply ironed shirts. Here, they were drunk, voluble and friendly. They insisted I meet their wives and have a few drinks until we all ended up on the ground. The wives left in disgust. The next time I opened my eyes I was in the shade and it was not quite so hot.

A few of my older students found me and dragged me away to see the freak show: several dried "mystery" fish and a man languidly smoking a cigarette with a white bandage over one eye and two knives stuck into his neck and right bicep. The blood looked suspiciously like iodine, but my students were scared witless. One of them spotted a vendor with fresh coconuts so they ran off, allowing me to drift back to the main stage where seven tiny Chinese waifs were waiting their signal to go on stage. They looked like they were straight out of a Tolkien story. One of them looked up at me and in a clear tenor said, "Thank you!" I smiled and said "Thank you!" She replied, "I love you very, very much." I thought about that for a moment, then asked, "Can you speak English?" She said, "Thank you!" I felt better.

Around 10:30 I found my bike and went home. As I wrote this account at 11:30, off in the distance I heard the fair still picking up steam.

Prayun, one of the teachers I admired most (for his classroom skills, kindness toward everyone and the absolute immaculate state of his everyday uniform) dropped by to offer me a drink of diluted Mekhong whiskey. After a couple of nips he said he was happy to see me home so early from the fair. I nodded, cautiously wondering what was coming. After a few more hits of whiskey he muttered something about how *that* show (with a contemptuous nod of his head) was not really for Thai people. It was for Chinese people! He understood I wanted to help my friend and roommate, but I should always remember I worked for the school ahead of Wisut and that I worked for the Thai government ahead of the school. I nodded, but he didn't say anything else, just looked down and for a second I thought he was going to be sick.

"I very drunk man," he said.

"Yeah," I agreed. "I'm drunk, too."

"Not drunk like me," he said. "Now, I must tell you that I say the bad thing about Mr. Wisut and he my friend." He looked ready to cry. "But I must tell you this because somebody tell me it is my duty to tell you. Do you know about that?"

I understood immediately. The headmaster was the only one I'd ever heard use the word *duty*.

"I don't know who is making you say that," I lied, "but I know you are my friend."

He smiled, sadly.

"I am your friend and Wisut is your friend and we are both your friend and, my friend, I must go. Goodbye."

I helped him down the stairs and watched him stumble through the banana trees in the direction of his house.

I'd heard about the many restrictions the Thai government has against Chinese business ventures, but most of them were ineffectual. Thai straw-men front for the Chinese owners. Still, I was saddened to know the headmaster felt obliged to have Prayun warn me about Wisut just because his father was Chinese.

February 2, 1968

Wisut never found out about Prayun's civic warnings to me and when I saw the two of them in the teachers' lounge laughing together I walked over and told them this date was a holiday called Ground Hog's Day. They thought that was hilarious. Of course, I had to start by explaining to them what a ground hog was and it was downhill from there.

Prayun invited me to join Wisut and a few other teachers over to the janitor's house for some home cooking and a few glasses of *sato*. Even properly manufactured, the ivory-colored liquid that's basically fermented rice, tastes horrible; however, when its made out in the wild, I've often seen dead bugs, pieces of twigs and roots floating on the surface. Since my stomach was still recovering from all the food and drink I'd had at the fair, I politely declined.

Turned out I was wise not to go to the janitor's house. The *sato* turned out to be poisonous and everyone at the party was up into the following morning vomiting under the guava tree. Mr. Chop, the janitor, insisted it must have been the food. Wisut agreed it could have been the food, so the following afternoon he and Chop took a few more swigs of *sato* and within a few hours were violently retching in the field. By then, even Chop was willing to admit there was a high degree of cause and effect and threw out the remaining *sato* to his pigs who didn't seem bothered.

Tim Adams, my Peace Corps regional director, sent a note to all volunteers in the northeast titled "Maryjane and her Friends." He wrote that he'd received too many reports of volunteers smoking so much dope and dropping acid that their job performance was suffering. So, this was official notice that anyone caught smoking dope would be shipped home immediately and it would be up to us to explain our premature arrival.

I hadn't heard about too many volunteers smoking dope and I certainly have never been aware of anyone's conduct or job performance being affected by it. The Thai like to drink and I think most of the American volunteers stick with whatever the locals are doing. As far as doing anything more dangerous than marijuana, I sure didn't know about that at all. The very idea of dropping acid here was enough to give me the chills. What would I suddenly hallucinate creeping out of the banana grove? Waiting for me under the house in the shadows? Squatting under my mosquito net?

Radio Pleiko was playing "Wooly Bully" when they broke into regular programming to announce that all leaves were cancelled, all R & Rs are off, a total curfew is being enforced, all military vehicles have been instructed to return to their bases, all soldiers must report in from wherever they are, all civilian aircraft is forbidden to land at Saigon Airport and all schools are closed. What the fuck? Did somebody drop a bomb on New York? The last issue of Time Magazine I received had a piece in it by our secretary of defense who said everything in Vietnam was well under control. Sure doesn't sound like it. I kept my ear to the radio for the next few evenings, but never heard details about what was going on.

The few Thais I've managed to have conversations with about the war seemed only concerned with the activities of Thai soldiers over there. Of course, being stationed so close to the Cambodian border, rumors run rampant all the time. The vaguest report of bandits, mines being placed or night-time strangers is enough to clear square miles of Thai citizens.

When I casually mentioned to some teachers that some of my friends around That Phanom further up in the northeast are volunteering to go into the mountains to teach Thai and English to the hill people, they assumed I was joking. They cannot conceive of anyone living up there in the first place, but the thought of volunteering one's services up there is viewed as out and out lunacy. One of the tribes, the Meo, are also involved in the fighting around Laos. Last time I was in Bangkok I bumped into one of the volunteers. Down to 125 pounds from 170, he already looked so thin to me I was afraid the trip alone would do him in.

Wow! Which is also the Thai word for "kite." It is a crystal clear day. The temperature suddenly dipped down to the low 60s this morning and everyone is walking around wearing heavy jackets and gloves. As far as the Thais are concerned we are now living in a walk-in freezer.

Last night I took my broken tape recorder to the radio repair shop. I'd already tried cleaning the recording heads and only ended up scoring them. The shop guy looked it over skeptically, and said he wasn't sure. He stepped behind a counter and plugged it in. All the lights in town went out! What did the Japanese pack into my little Aiwa? The shop guy just whistled and looked around with a flashlight for a portable generator. He yanked the start-up rope, let it run for a minute, then switched over all the store's circuits to the generator outlet and his lights went back on. My poor recorder gave one final high-pitched buzz and died forever.

I walked across the street to the Raxana Restaurant and found Wisut with a few friends drinking Mekhong and soda. The place glowed with kerosene lanterns because of the outage. I said something to him about the nice light they gave off and everyone oohed and ahhed. Guess they hadn't noticed.

Sitting with Wisut was a short, fat man and a tall thin one. The heavier man turned out to be the forest commissioner of Korat Province and the other guy was his assistant. As was typical in Thai civil service, the assistant had a degree in forestry and agriculture, but his boss had good will, family connections and no degree. The assistant only knew technical English he'd picked up at Khon Kaen University, but his boss knew GI slang he'd acquired at American air bases. It was a strangely invigorating dialogue.

Assistant: "You have the teak tree in America?"

Boss: "Thai whiskey number 10. Johnny Walker number one."

That sort of thing. We all quaffed good old number 10 and nibbled on salted watermelon seeds, sweetened vegetables and pork rinds. The boss called over one of the local kids and ordered some food. The kid kept shaking his head as each dish was named and, although our host appeared barely perturbed, his assistant grew more and more exasperated. He finally called out to the owner who was playing Chinese checkers a few tables away:

"*Mi arai bung?*" (What *do* you have?)

Mr. Pichate, the owner, sadly glanced down at his crumbling defense, slowly arose and walked over. He was about 5'4" with a stocky build and a large round face usually fixed in a smile. Wearing a simple, cotton *phakoma* (waistcloth), blue t-shirt and flip-flops, he did not seem prepared for a banquet. After listening quietly to everything his guests requested, he placated brought forth pots of steaming white rice, roasted leg of pig, sweet and sour duck in thick sauce and a light soup. Pan-stirred morning glory leaves in oyster sauce along with heated cashews completed the feast. To show my appreciation I ordered several quarts of freezing Thai beer and everyone dug in as if we'd just been released from prison.

Afterwards, we called out for toothpicks and the intricate delving for food scraps began. Tooth picking as an art had reached its peak in Thailand. One hand must be politely held over the wooden sliver while the picking and scraping commenced. No conversation was allowed. Neither is eye-contact. This was personal. Silence for several minutes, then sighs of relief, final licks of tongues and eye-contact was re-established.

Wisut yawned, stretched, settled back with a self-satisfied grin, gave me a big wink and began to cast a delicate line in the direction of the forest boss. Did Elder Brother Director know that there was a poker game in progress and would the kind host be amenable to joining Wisut and a few select friends in a friendly game? Of course, this big time Korat official wouldn't mind fleecing these up-country bumpkins. And where was this game taking place? At the electric generating plant, naturally, where it had been in progress for several hours. Hmmm, maybe my dainty Aiwa recorder was *not* to blame for the power outage after all. A consensus was reached. They stood up and headed toward the door and the game in progress.

Wisut switched to English and told me that unless I wanted to lose several days pay it would be better if I just went home. He, on the other hand, sensed great personal fortune coming his way and would probably not see me again until morning. His final words to me involved how to secure the house. Some time ago the knobs on both doors had broken off and we kept them shut by tying the doors to the frame of the house with wires. This time, he told me to bolt both doors from the inside, since he planned to return by way of my bedroom window. I reminded him not to step on my head like he did last time and he laughed as he waved goodbye.

I took off on my bicycle for home where I heated water for tea and nibbled on a crust of bread. I woke up around 7:00 to the sound of roosters and no Wisut. Then, I heard a scuffling on the outer ledge by my window followed by scraping of fingers prying open the wooden shutters. I sat bolt upright just in time to see Wisut, grinning maniacally, poke his head through my window.

"How did you do?" I asked.

"Hah! Good game. I thought not to stay, but they played very bad so I stayed after all. One hundred fifty baht for me! Aiii, now to school …. *chayo*!"

He crawled in off the ledge, singing snatches of "These Boots are Made For Walking." I blocked my ears as he wandered into the living room and turned on the record player. Soon the rafters were shaking with Sam the Sham and the Pharaohs singing back up to Wisut screaming in the bathroom as he poured cold water over his head. The drum beat was contrapuntal to Thai teeth chattering in the crisp morning air.

By the time I was dressed, he was radiant, flush with wealth and dapper in a fresh teacher's uniform. We strode off to school, Wisut clutching the little finger of my right hand. The students were already assembled before the flagpole and the headmaster with staff were at attention as we took our proper places in line. First came the pledge of allegiance, a formal bow to the flag and then a Buddhist incantation.

"… *alahansama sonkon tupawa* …"

Before we were dismissed, three boys were called out front for a bamboo thrashing on their legs and then sent out to pick up trash on the school ground for the rest of the day. They'd been caught with the smell of whiskey on their breath. One of the teachers discovered they'd stolen it from a wedding celebration. I wasn't sure if the more serious offense was the theft or the drinking, but there they were raking weeds with plenty of opportunity to repent for their sins.

I finally finished composing, typing and mimeographing my tests for next week's exams and was waiting to receive all the other tests from the English teachers. None of them could manage more than three words a minute on an English language typewriter, so I volunteered to type up the exams. There is such a thing as a Thai language typewriter and even the Thais have a very hard time with it. It must truly be one of the mechanical marvels of the modern world. The keyboard has to have room for a dozen vowels, more than 30 consonants, endless tonal notations that fit to the left, right, top and bottom of every syllable.

I wonder how much it would cost me to board up my bedroom window. It's one thing not to have glass panes and the use of simple wooden shutter; but the path into my house via my bedroom window by way of my pillow is getting out of hand. Last week, around 3:00 AM I heard scratching on the shutters loud enough to give me heart palpitations, but that was only a prelude to what happened next. Bursting through the opening, almost stepping on my head, was my friend Sanguan who worked at the private elementary school, just returned from Korat on the midnight train.

"Do not tell! I come with my gift for my wedding. Look!"

Before my weary eyes he popped open a small, velvet red box to reveal an astonishing diamond-studded engagement ring.

"Four thousand baht … I have no more money! Do not tell. Not even to Wisut. I will let you know when it is okay."

After vowing my lips were sealed, I bid him goodnight and fell back asleep. I swear, if one more Thai comes through that window I'll have a stroke.

....

Some notes on my teaching material:

In the old days, most Thai public schools through junior high school used a series of readers called simply Gatenby. This series was generally regarded as the bane and *bete noire* of every TEFL (teaching English as a foreign language) volunteer in Thailand. This series of cheaply produced paperbacks presented an almost infinite array of poorly written and pointless stories. Although these story/lessons were supposed to be the foundation for teaching grammar, vocabulary and syntax, only the most creative teacher imaginable might be able to figure out how to scoop actual pedagogic tools from them. Every Gatenby text threw out a few questions strictly related to the plot and left the creation of sentence patterns and word usage up to the teachers. During Peace Corps training our instructors gave examples of how to cull lesson plans from a typical Gatenby story. Most of us also smarted over British archaisms, obscure colloquial phrases and convoluted sentences that had impossible stress and inflection patterns. After several years of using Gatenby, Thailand's Peace Corps teachers implored the Ministry of Education to come up with something better. That something turned out to be the Southeast Asian Regional English Program, commonly referred to as SEAREP. These books were jammed with vignettes of historical significance along with science and geography plans. I heard it said the series was written with a scientifically selected vocabulary, no slang and tight, declarative sentences. Although SEAREP was light years better than Gatenby, I was still bored by the staid presentations and the repetitive queries at the start of each chapter. On the bright side, I continued to be surprised at the quirky subject matter. Who decided it was important for Thai students to know the basic tales of Norse mythology?

I created many of my own lesson plans that dealt with timelines and tenses. I almost lost my sanity trying to express the future conditional or the subjunctive to students who only knew the present continuous.

The Thai language has what are known as tense particle which can be plopped down in various spots in a sentence and that particle says immediately if everything stated is happening, has happened or is about to happen. Quite simple and quite sane. No wonder both the students and I went a bit nuts when I drew the inevitable timeline on the board and tried to explain why English verbs change appearance with tense.

"Where you go?" is still the most common greeting I get in the market from my students.

"I'm going to the market. Where are you going?" I reply.

"I go market," is the inevitable response. "You go market with me?"

I go crazy.

My youngest class finally finished their text lesson and as a treat I told them they could ask me any question they wanted as long as it was in English.

"Have you ever ridden an elephant?"

"Have you ever eaten *loti* (a local pastry)?"

"Do you have a girl friend?" (Lots of laughter.)

My brightest student, Supachi, held up a picture of something and asked me if they had that in America. I looked closer and saw it was a barely-clad movie star. Very smart kid, although the other teachers tell me he's impudent (their word!). I think he's great and I often call him Superchai.

Another class wanted to know more about America' space program. That session didn't last very long. Are we on the third or the fourth planet from the sun?

My latest challenge in the market concerned a shopkeeper named Somboon. He once offered to trade me a kilo of Thai sticks for my guitar. I actually gave the idea some thought, but I couldn't remember which shopkeeper he was. Then, after that warning telegraph I received from Peace Corps, I decided to just forget the whole thing.

February 10, 1968

There were movies at the municipal field last night. A very large sheet was stretched tight between two bamboo poles and the audience (children from town, drifters and one bored Peace Corp volunteer) sat on both sides of the screen to watch Thai cartoons with very poor quality animation and innumerable Japanese commercials, mostly about toothpaste and soap.

Then, a commercial for Fab! The opening scene showed two elderly peasants dressed in raggedy shorts, ancient t-shirts and white pith helmets lurching down some rural road.

Both of them had long poles they used to casually tap the ground, making it hard to figure out if they were supposed to be blind or simply in poor health. Suddenly, a white knight on a white horse appeared. The sputtering sound track hammered out an unsynchronized rhythm of hoof beats as the knight approaches the peasants. A voice cut in, hysterically screaming in northeast dialect:

"Nee sokhabroke….sahat lao!"(Here it is dirty….now, clean!)

As the last word was spoken the knight's lance touched the pair as if to impale them and they momentarily disappeared in a cloud of smoke, only to reappear not only cleaned-up, but dressed in formal, ancient traditional clothing of silk and silver. Actually, they didn't even look like the same two peasants. As the smoke cleared, the word FAB appeared superimposed on the screen. Seeing that familiar brand shimmering on a white sheet on a field in northeast Thailand was an almost hallucinatory experience. Briefly, a warm flashback of family memories washed over me.

··

February 25, 1968

Three more students were caught drinking whiskey. Sadly for them, it was the headmaster who spotted the deed. Wisut told me on our walk to the school that they would be punished today. On a fairly crisp morning, all the students gathered as usual in formation in front of the school and the flag pole. After we finished saluting, chanting a Buddhist incantation, singing the national anthem and the king's anthem, the headmaster walked around to face the student body and call out the names of those to be punished. Mr. Chop, the janitor, squatted on the ground whittling several bamboo thin enough so they could be whipped through the air. The students stepped forward and bowed to the headmaster who, in turn, nodded to Prayun. Of course, someone further down the chain of command got the dirty work. Chop handed him the bamboo and he swung them through the air so rapidly they made a hissing noise. The front row of girls squealed and retreated. There was an undercurrent of laughter.

One of the other teachers leaned over in my direction and asked if this was the way they punished students in America. I said I thought corporal punishment had long since been stopped, but maybe not in all of the states. He looked shocked.

The first student stood with his arms folded across his chest and was told to lean slightly forward, exposing more of the tender flesh behind his knees. Prayun slashed away five times right at that tender spot. From my vantage point I easily saw red welts appear. The student did not even wince. After the fifth stroke, Prayun dismissed him and he walked directly to the headmaster who clasped his shoulder and whispered something in the kid's ear that made him smile. The same scene was repeated with the others. In the end, they all bowed to Prayun, the headmaster, and us, then went smiling back to their places.

I asked Wisut what the headmaster said to the students who'd been whipped to make them smile.

He said, "He told them to smile!"

When I returned home there was a small package waiting for me that someone from the post office had kindly dropped off. I don't know what my mother was thinking, but it must have been connected with a fear that her oldest son was in danger of losing his cultural heritage. This time she sent me a fairly large can of gefilte fish and a small packet if instant horseradish (just add water). I opened the can, scooped a few spoonfuls out onto a plate and offered it to Wisut, who squinted at it and exclaimed, "Looks like fish dead a long time."

"Yes," I told him. "It is fish, but just ground up. Would my own mother send me something bad?"

"Not bad, just dead."

"Will you stop this dead thing, please?'

I mixed the horseradish with water and after it plumped up a bit I gingerly tapped a small spoonful on to the plate with the fish.

"Eat it with this," I said. "It's very hot, but makes the fish taste good."

He delicately raised a morsel of fish mixed with the horseradish to his mouth then ran to the window to spit it out.

"Is it too hot?" I asked.

"Not too hot," he said wiping his mouth. "Just not Thai hot. *Farang* hot is different hot. Not good."

I finished off the fish by myself.

The next several days were fairly uneventful at school, almost as if all the students were on their best possible behavior after having witnessed the punishment in front of the flagpole. I worked long and hard trying to make my SEAREP chapters more interesting and at the same time more relevant to the national test all Thai students have to take. Merely doing verb substitution drills didn't cut it. I'm focusing almost all class time now on parts of speech, recognizing prepositional phrases and verb conjugations. All of my students have extraordinary memories, so they're able to parrot back anything I ask, but when I move on to having them apply what they've learned on the written page, it's a disaster.

FOR THE RECORD: I'm taking a trip to Korat, one of the largest cities in the northeast, and a mecca of American food places. I don't plan on keeping a diary while I'm traveling, so whatever is added here will be on reflection, looking back.

Feb. 27, 1968
Dateline: Korat

Since our regional director had arranged a kind of teacher training program between PCVs and Thai teachers, I decided I'd be virtuous and join Fred (malaria eradication) and Sharon (teacher) to be part of this get-together in the bustling city of Korat. The minute our train stopped the three of us headed for a restaurant with American food.

We found what we were looking for at the Foremost Dairy Bar where they served up cheeseburgers, French fries, onion rings and milk shakes. I felt rice and fish sauce make room for American-style calories. Reluctantly, we left Foremost and strolled through the city. Because Sharon is Chinese-American the Thais all assumed she was Chinese-Thai and since she was walking with two Americans she was probably a hooker. Sharon said that when she first arrived the Thais in her city immediately assumed she could speak Thai because she looked Chinese (i.e. Chinese-Thai) and even after she'd gained some fluency they still treated her as perhaps not the sharpest tack in the box.

After eating, we found the high school where the training was to take place and discovered the program was actually to mix, mingle and test the fluency of students at the high school.

On the way, we stopped off at an American-style restaurant to thoroughly wash and clean the dust from our hair. There were hundreds of students more than eager to test their English with us and they were all quite fluent. The sponsors placed one American at each of several tables so everyone would have equal time with us. My first conversation was with a stunningly beautiful, raven-haired woman who spoke English as fluently and casually as I did. Her first question to me was why on earth I'd chosen to live and teach in such a low-life area as Nang Rong? I explained I hadn't actually chosen Nang Rong, but after having spent some months adjusting to the food, language and culture of the town I had to say I really liked it. She explained she spoke English so well because after gaining basic skills in a specialized school for foreign language study, she'd earned an American Field scholarship to Indiana. Our time was up and I moved on to a young man who wanted to know if I helped the students in my school learn to play American baseball. Short answer. No!

All that chatter stimulated our appetites so we were delighted when several enormous platters were brought out with mounds of fresh-steamed rice and small bowls of fish sauce along with *Massaman* beef curry. I think I'd had a version of this back in Nang Rong, but not this good. The chunks of steak were tender mixed with coconut cream, curry paste, roast peanuts, cinnamon (and, according to several students, fish sauce, concentrated tamarind, brown sugar, cardamom and bay leaves). Unbelievably delicious.

Several students politely told me I spoke Thai like a country bumpkin and I really should practice more with people, like themselves, who came from areas closer to Bangkok. In a way, I took that as a compliment.

Soon after the food was demolished, requests were made to have the Americans get on stage and sing some songs. Sharon and the others politely demurred, but Fred and I walked up on stage where Fred took the initiative and, speaking with intensity to the crowd, pleaded, in Thai to "Please forgive me for not being able to speak Thai very well…"

Crowd: "No, no, you speak Thai very well!"

Fred: "Thank you. You are all very polite. But, it's true. I know I can't speak well and I certainly cannot sing, but my friend (nodding at me) not only sings well, he sings THAI songs!"

And, with that, he turned on his heel and left me alone on stage.

Fred knew that Wisut had tutored me with endless patience in learning the words and music to a couple of popular Thai songs and when I managed to somehow croak my way through them, the applause was deafening. But, and that's a big BUT, when they quieted down, questions were thrown at me from the crowd, asking (I think)Where had I been teaching? What did I do for a living? Was I married? Did I have a Thai girl friend? And that's when they discovered although I had an okay gift of mimicry, I really did not know their language. I felt like a fraud.

I slipped off stage and allowed others with a shade more talent to take over. The raven-haired, beautiful student from Korat was still around, but I soon had the feeling she had not been overwhelmed by my performance and, in fact, seemed to not want anyone else to see she was next to me. I wanted a drink. One of the Thai teachers gave a signal announcing a finale. All the Thai students formed several concentric circles and softly began singing Auld Lang Syne, first in English, then in Thai. Hearing that familiar music coming from those smiling, Thai faces made me remember those maxim about how music brings people together.

The students went quietly to their rooms, Sharon was shown where she'd be sleeping and I joined Fred as we followed a Thai teacher to a larger room with three beds. As silence settled on the rest of the campus, our room remained lit and noisy as Fred and I exclaimed over the teacher's two prized possessions: a rifle with a telescope sight and a German Luger. He laughed and said he liked using the Luger to shoot away branches that obstructed his view. We all laughed again as if that was the funniest thing we'd ever heard. I picked up the Luger, pointed it out the open window and pretended to blast away. The teacher looked a little nervous and said something like I should look more carefully before I actually shoot. I tossed the gun over to Fred, who deftly caught it and pointed it between his eyes and smiled. The teacher snatched the gun from him and adjusted something on the handle.

"What's that?" I asked. "What'd you just do?"

"I make sure the…ah…the safety is on."

"The safety?" Fred echoed him, turning white. "You mean…?"

"Sure," he said, beaming. "This baby is loaded!"

And with that he unlocked the safety, pointed it out the window and Klaaablooeyy! My eyes watered at the explosion as several large twigs were turned into splinters. Fred remained, quite pale, on the edge of his bed.

Someone yelled something from another room and the teacher quickly began fanning the air toward the window. Then he stuck his head out and yelled something in Thai.

"I tell them I blow up fireworks!"

"Yeah," I nodded. "That's the ticket."

With my ears still ringing, I asked which bed was mine and not turning to even see what Fred was doing, I peeled off my clothes, slipped under the sheet and fell asleep almost instantly.

Morning wake up came with sunlight streaming on to my face. Sounds of students talking and passing the room got the three of us up and out to the central patio where Sharon was sipping fresh juice. We joined her in thanking everyone for their hospitality, politely declined their offer of a Thai breakfast (fried rice and fish sauce) and after packing up we moved off down the street where we found a western restaurant and surreptitiously feasted on cheeseburgers, fries and coffee. Finally, sated and happy, talking with each other a mile-a-minute about our time together, joking about our sun burns from all that walking around, we were back at Chira Railroad Station where we were told a northeast train would leave at noon.

As we walked around waiting for the train, we bought some bananas then walked around looking for a place to ditch the peels. Dozens of people appeared to live in the station, sitting on the filthy floor, casually following us with their eyes. Several very old women crouched against a wall chewed betel nut leaves, red juice dribbled down their chins. An old scent of kerosene lanterns hung in the air and many children offered us fried chicken wings, fried banana slices, juice in little baggies, chunks of a variety of fresh fruit on wooden slivers and lottery tickets.

By the time we got on board we were exhausted and it was all I could do to stay awake for the right stop. Buriram greeted us in a haze of red dust and screams from samlaw drivers. Several taxis screeched to a halt in front of us hoping to get a good fare with three farangs. Ignoring them all, we parted company. Sharon walked on to her house and I walked with Fred to his place where we stripped, threw cold water on ourselves, wrapped relatively clean sheets around ourselves and fell asleep on straw mats. When I woke up, somewhat refreshed, I saw Fred hunched over his desk reading.

"Hey, what's up?" I asked. "Mail from home?"

He shielded the papers with his body.

Uh, yeah," he said. "These are just some letters I've put off answering. One of the teachers from a school I went to in Philadelphia told his students to drop me a line and I guess they *all* did!"

I got up, stretched and looked over his shoulder to scan dozens of envelopes.

"Look at all this mail! What kind of questions did they ask you?"

"Oh, it's nothing worth looking at. I went to a Catholic school, you know, and so these kids, well, I don't know what he told them about what I'm doing, but, uh, they seem to have some weird ideas."

"Oh yeah? Let me see a few?"

I scanned a few lines in astonishment from one letter to another, put them down and stared at him.

"What the hell are they talking about?" I asked.

"Well, like I said…they don't…"

"This kid hopes you do well with the lepers! Another one hopes you find a cure for the plague! My God, what did your friend tell them about you?"

On weekends, students often dropped by my house and we played games.

Local fisherman casts net on outskirts of Nang Rong.

Standing with nang rong school faculty. Wisut is directly in front of me holding a cigarette. Sanguan is wearing a watch.

Nang Rong School female faculty.

Lunch with the Nang Rong School faculty.

Nang Rong early morning market, 1967.

Nang Rong morning market.

The bus to Buriram (and back!)

In the midst of banana stand with my student, Wisai.

Girl and her sister who delivered water to my house.

"Well, he didn't know, I guess, ah hell, Burge, I have no idea what this means. One of them wanted to know if working for the Peace Corps was a good way to get into the CIA. Most of them see me as a brother in Christ…"

"A brother in what?"

"I'm Catholic, remember?"

"Fred, yeah, I understand, but the thing is, it's just that, I mean, they seem to think you're not only working in medical research, but that you're *pious*."

'I'm not sure what you mean by pious, but I am a practicing Catholic. And, don't forget, we're talking about a school I went to in my neighborhood. I knew a lot of those kids. Those girls who wrote those letters to me are knock-outs!"

"They're what?"

He grinned, making enormous jerk-off motions.

"Ass-hole!" we both screamed.

I went to sleep and Fred continued reading his fan mail.

Later that evening, just as we were discussing where to eat and whether or not to go to the water tower (a euphemism for the red light district), Sharon's voice broke through asking us if we were decent. After Fred yelled we were *always* decent, she walked in and said she was going to join Judy, another volunteer for dinner over another teacher's house and we were welcome to join them. The two of us simultaneously mumbled something about going out to get a few beers and maybe we'd meet them later in the open market.

"I know what you're going to do," Sharon said in her teacher's voice. "You're really going over to the water tower, aren't you?"

"No, honestly," Fred said. "We really are only going out for beer. Or, at least we really were going out for beer, but now that you've put that tempting possibility into our heads we are only men. But, who knows? The evening's open to change."

Sharon glanced over at his stack of mail.

"Aren't you going to write to those students back home about visiting the ladies who live near the water tower?"

Fred rolled his eyes.

"If any more people find out about these letters, I'm going to begin initiating really strong security in this house! Really, Sharon, Burgess and I are only going out for a drink, right Burge?"

I smiled and shrugged.

"Asshole!"

Sharon left and we finished grooming ourselves before walking out into the humid night air. The city was steamy with heat and the smells coming from the hundreds of venders who had their stands set up everywhere: chicken, fried bananas, curry, soup, candies, segments of sugar cane…bicycle chains hissed as riders appeared out of the night from all directions. The regular shops were closed, but the restaurants were open and Pensee's place, run by a cute Chinese-Thai woman who'd taken it over after her husband died, served what most of us considered to be the best Western food in northeast Thailand. Catering to the fairly well-to-do merchants, visiting foreigners, an occasional Peace Corps volunteer and provincial officials, she always served orders that included plump roast chicken, or pleasantly seasoned beef, crisp pork pieces, elaborate vegetable and salad plates, savory rice and onion dishes and best of all, she baked delicious breads and pies. Pies! What unknown hero in the past had shown her how to make pies none of us knew, but the grapevine from district to district always included what Pensee had cooling on her pie rack.

We waved hello, ordered a few quarts of freezing Singh Beer, a plate of roasted cashews to nibble on while the main dishes were prepared, and settled back in utter and complete happiness. Outside, passing samlaw lights gave a carnival air to the streets. Dark all around us, but inside we were bathed n a warm, yellow light and cooled by the magic in our glasses. I raised my bottle and held it against my forehead.

"Don't do anything exceptionally weird, Burge, but an American family just walked in," Fred whispered.

I put the bottle down and turned. It *was* an entire American family. Swarthy father, pale and anemic-looking wife, and two small girls. Pensee had already led them to a table and all four of them were staring at us.

"Who are they?" one of the little girls called out.

"Quiet!" her father said. "They're soldiers from Korat. Remember, we saw them at the station. Now don't stare. It's not polite to stare."

I felt a strange ripple of machismo run through me. They took me for a soldier!

Fred and I looked at each other, nodded, and we walked over to their table and introduced ourselves as Peace Corps volunteers.

"Oh, my," the father said. "That means one of you must be Fred!"

Fred nodded, anxiously.

"A recently admitted member of my parish, a young man named Lek, says he often stays with you and does chores around your house, isn't that right?"

"Ah, Lek! Sure, that's right. He helps me out a lot. So, he's in your parish? Does that mean he's converted to Christianity?"

"I don't know if this is the place to discuss it, but, yes, Lek did converted to Christianity. I do hope his conversion eventually will have effect on *you*, Fred."

I tried not to smile.

"What's that supposed to mean?" Fred asked, not smiling

"Well, as I said, this isn't the place to be talking about such things, but as a Christian, as a *true* Christian, I have explained to Lek the duties and obligations of faith. Eternal salvation is not granted on a whim. It has been difficult for Lek to observe you drinking alcohol and entertaining in an unsuitable manner and still hear you refer to yourself as a Christian."

"What has being a Christian got to do with drinking alcohol?"

"Young man, I was afraid this would happen. My hope is not to confuse Lek with false interpretations of being Christian means. As a member of the Evangelical Baptist Church, we offer high reward for observance of…"

"Excuse me, but you are right, sir," Fred interrupted. "We better drop this."

"Of course, of course, please do not let us interrupt you any further with your [he paused to stare at the empty beer bottles] dinner!"

We walked back to our own table, sat down facing away from the holy table, and picked up our beers. Fred downed half a bottle, then, between biting his nails, said, "Amazing! Absolutely amazing. Doesn't that jerk *realize* Lek's just hedging his bets the way most Thais do. Christians! Hah! Why doesn't he visit Lek's parents so he can see the Hindu spirit house and the joss sticks and the Kennedy half dollar on a string and the little wooden figures representing God knows what? Christian! Where's our food? I don't even want to think about this."

After saying goodbye to Fred, I checked my calendar and realized I had a fairly long vacation coming up. On top of that, Bob Charles our regional rep had invited all the PCVs from the northeast to a get-together in the university town of Khon Kaen to have a little party, reconnect with members of our training group and make friends with other PCVs who lived in the area. He also strongly suggested some of us volunteer for something called Camp-Thai Am in Udorn-Thani Province just north of Khon Kaen. Maybe after I finish helping out with Camp Thai-Am in Udon Thani Province, I'll be able to keep on going and make it to Vientiane. Bob Charles explained to me that the camp would be a joint Thai/American venture involving Thai students from several northeast provinces, a dozen or so Peace Corps Volunteers and an equal number of Thai teachers. Volunteers would give crash courses in English to the kids and maybe model lesson plans to the teachers. There also promises to be the usual camp activities like games, arts and crafts and sports.

That sounded good to me. If I took part, I'd be close to the Laotian border and that'd be my chance to have a few adventures. Of course, I didn't have a visa, but I'd heard the border between Laos and Thailand was so porous it'd be easy to find a small motor launch and be carried across the Mekhong.

I hoped the Laotian border was open when I arrived at Nong Khai (a Thai border town on the Mekhong River). My plan was to reach the camp around March 19th, followed by a train or bus ride to Nong Khai, somehow figure out how to get across the Mekhong, get into Vientienne and find a place of ill-repute I've heard of called the White Rose. After that, I'd swing back into Thailand, take a bus to Pitsanaloke, get a ride to Chiengmai up north in time for the Water Festival and maybe even buy some new clothes (a volunteer in Bangkok told me it's a great area for hand-made clothing). Finally, take a train straight down to Bangkok, pick up my living allowance for April and May and a 1,000 baht ($50) clothing allowance and with my new wealth, take a mad dash to Malaysia and the free port of Penang. I might even be able to get a 3rd class ticket for a trip to Singapore and drink a gin fizz at Raffles (reading something by Somerset Maugham as I do so). Lot of plans, but who knew the future?

Wisut walked with me to the station and we had a farewell cup of tea waiting for the bus. It arrived with the usual screech of brakes and cloud of red dust and I got on board. It was only the second time I'd seen Nang Rong spread out before me from the vantage point of a bus's height. Did it seem any different to me? The people languidly going about their business, sounds of the Thai language that now, on occasion, made some sense to me, those crazy-looking buses all bedecked with banners and pennants and colorful bits of hand-made pictures along the wooden sides, the dogs scratching and pissing in the dirt, the wandering ice-cream man dragging his steel box on wheels loaded down with blocks of ice and treats made of frozen coconut milk and coloring, the elderly people eyeing it all as they chewed betel-nut leaves, a thin line of juice running down their chins, the swaying palms, the stink of old garbage from the canal behind the bus stop attracting flies and mosquitoes, the ubiquitous smiles from the oldest woman leaning against a fence post to the smallest child running naked except for a tiny loin cloth, they all smiled and smiled and smiled. Time for the bus to take off and carry me to the next adventure: first, Khon Kaen, then Camp Thai-Am and then on to Laos and who knew what?

March 5th 1968

I'm jotting these notes down in utter exhaustion following my participation in a morning softball game and an afternoon soccer game.

The back-story is that I'd heard from a Volunteer named Steve Landau who asked me to help him out with a fund-raiser. He has a number of students who would love to take part in Camp Thai-Am in Udorn, but they did not have the means to get to the site or spare cash for food and clothing. His idea was to have as many Volunteers as he could muster to travel to his town and play what would probably be the first game of softball in the area. Initially, the idea was to have the American Volunteers (from malaria eradication medical techs, community development workers and teachers) play against some sort of local Thai team. Later, he let me know that he'd managed a contact with New Zealand volunteers, an American group of seabeas and a small contingent of Japanese doctors. The fund raising could take place on a number of levels: sell tickets to the game, ask some of the locals to show some support by just contributing money and, finally, have students pass back and forth through the audience with little collection pails. I shared this with Ralph (CD), Thom (teacher) and Fred (malaria eradication) who all offered to join in (although in the end Fred had to bail because his help was needed with DDT spraying).

We purchased 3rd class tickets on the fast train to Srisiket Province and pretty much stayed on our feet during the entire three hour ride, trying not to step on stray roosters, loose fruit or slide on puddles of betel nut juice. Steve met us at the train station and took us all by taxi to his home in Khukhan Village. After meeting his host family we had a delicious meal of local goodies and bedded down for the night. Thom, Ralph and myself collapsed on a large bed and proceeded to toss and turn and break wind throughout the night. Apparently the fine meal we'd had must've contained bacteria strange to all our systems and we took turns making a path to the squat john throughout the night.

I should mention here that Peace Corps-Thailand gives every Volunteer a little medical kit upon arrival and among other items it contains: thick, pink polymagma tablets to be chewed and taken with water; tiny, white lomotil pills to basically cork you up until a better solution can be found; and, a compound of some sort of opiate or codeine packed with some other soothing medication that's supposed to ease up our poor digestive tracts, but could be habit-forming and only to be taken if the first two do not work. The three of us took all of the above.

Up at dawn, we had Ovaltine and dried rolls, our stomachs rebelling at the mere idea of anything more, threw water on our faces and hair and set out for the practice field. A fairly large crowd had already formed and various players were strolling in from every point on the compass. A Thai P.E. teacher, rule book in hand, directed students where to drop white lime to guide the running lines, and then ordered in a sprinkling truck to wet the dusty area. A battery-powered microphone was set up by the chairs where officials would be seated and the Nai Amphur came forward to meet us. It was at that point a half-track filled with Japanese doctors arrived, smiling and showing lots of teeth and fairly new Bermuda shorts, waving their arms, shouting out stuff in Japanese and making tiny fists as if to frighten whomever their opponents happened to be. Right behind them were the New Zealand community development volunteers, most of average height and all appearing to be totally emaciated, red-faced with blond hair, who hopped off their vehicle and stared rather incredulously at the playing field and the stacks of bats and balls and people. Finally, with a blaring of horns and squealing of brakes, the American team arrived in a couple of jeeps. They looked enormous. I've already spent so much time with only Thais or very thin Americans, that these guys with their massive biceps, great height and enormous mass were positively frightening. One of them, a double for Hercules, looked down at me, laughed, rubbed my head with a mighty paw and ran out in to the field.

Steve established the make-up of the teams: Americans and Japanese doctors vs. the Peace Corps Volunteers and the New Zealanders. Ralph was the pitcher and I was the catcher and everyone else faded back. The Americanss were up first. At the microphone, a Thai teacher welcomed everyone to the game with kind words and told the assembled multitudes that "…people here have come to play from all over the world here in Srisiket. They have come from Japan, from America, from New Zealand to play the first softball game in this province…athletes from everywhere will play softball this morning and in the afternoon they will play soccer against the Thai teachers team…" This last announcement was certainly news to me!

The first pitch was thrown and a Japanese doctor hit a low fly to center field. It was immediately dropped by a New Zealander, who, upon gathering his faculties, threw the ball into the bushes outside the field and the doctor was home free. Going to be an interesting game. Ralph called a conference at the mound and there the New Zealanders stated they'd never even heard of softball never mind actually play a game, but they were willing to help us chaps out for this worthy cause. Ralph chewed his spittle, I put back on the ill-fitting catcher's mask (severely restricting my field of vision) and the game continued. The next two Japanese doctors popped out and an X-Ray technician was stopped at second base as he tried a suicide dive to the plate. Score: 0–0. Three peace corps volunteers up. Three peace corps volunteers out. CBs at bat. Ralph pitched it in right over the plate, there was a sound of Thor's hammer, the crackle of air as it was split asunder, the barely audible woooooshing sound of the ball as it climbed and climbed and climbed to finally flicker out of vision, then dropping out of orbit down on to the hapless form of a New Zealander who ran in zig-zag fashion beneath the approaching shadow (to catch it? to avoid it?) and another run was scored. Strangely enough, the following fours Americans all did the same thing and before long the score was 12–0. Ralph held another conference. I became the new pitcher, a New Zealander became catcher and Ralph joined the hapless (helpless?) outfield. The game continued from one unmitigated disaster to another. We only planned on playing 7 innings, but by the 6th inning the score was 19–2 against us and something had to be done.

Then, Thom came through in the clinch with by batting in a three run homer, giving an X-Ray tech a mild concussion in the process. With our loins girded to make a last ditch come-back, we sacked the ball again and again until the score stood at 20–9. Finally, accumulating three short outs, the Americans came to bat again and amazingly we held them to one home run and the game ended in the next inning with a final score of 21–9. The crowd cheered, the loudspeakers crackled, and photographs are taken of all participants. The crowd retired and we went off to eat (what?) and drink bottles of fairly cold beer and soon after that fall into deep slumber.

We got up around four in the afternoon and trudged back to the field for soccer. The Thais were all in uniforms. The Americanss were red-faced and dizzy from too much beer. In the first half the Thais led without too much energy on their part by 6–1 and the Americans, Japanese and New Zealanders swayed from the heat and shortness of breath. I stumbled over the sidelines holding my sides, panting. Thom took my place. The New Zealanders saved the day for our side by suddenly arousing themselves into action and scored four goals in quick succession, managing to hold the Thais on to our side of the field. Again, applause by a refreshed crowd, more pictures all around and the mayor came forward tp place flowered wreaths around the necks of all players. One of the Americans was so tall he had to kneel down in order for the mayor to get the flowers over his head. We slowly retreated from the field and the heat and dust out to whatever bathrooms we could find. Was it that previous meal still wreaking vengeance on us? Finally, I joined the other volunteers to whatever beds or mats we could find and slept into early evening when we joined the New Zealanders in their Land Rover to downtown Srisiket for showers, delicious local food and Thai beer. The games were over, new friendships formed and enough money raised to send Steve's students to Camp Thai-Am.

March 10, 1968

When I arrived in the large, northeast city of Khon Kaen there were a fair number of American servicemen wandering about on R & R from Vietnam. I explored several side streets just to get a feel for the place and invariably ended up in front of a massage parlor. Although I'd never been there before, I had the impression this was a city undergoing major changes.

I soon bumped into several volunteers I sort of knew from training seminars and was immediately depressed by their fluency in Thai. In fact, the minute I arrived in town I heard a radio program hosted by Harriet Greenfest, one of the volunteers in the area. Now that's what I call fluent! Interesting to meet people from my own training group and see how they've changed: the men all much skinnier and the women somewhat heavier. A few people have a new, sort of distant look in their eyes as if they've seen things that have deeply affected their vision of the world. Formerly talkative volunteers now seem almost taciturn. Two of the women returned home early because of pregnancies: one from a local Thai villager and the other from another American Volunteer. The males all seem to be sick with one ailment or another, mostly GI diseases. I've heard speculation that American female PCVs get absorbed into the same protective milieu as Thai women and thus are not as affected by heavy drinking or venereal diseases. One thing we all had in common: stories. The regional rep was true to his word and the party he threw was loud and loud with plenty of dancing and excellent local food.

March 14, 1968

After all the meeting, greeting and partying it was time to move on to take the train to Udorn Thani Province and get the scoop on Camp Thai-Am, the organization we'd raised all that money for in Srisiket. Once in the city, I walked around trying to get a feel for the place. Udorn is located between the provinces of Khon Kaen to the south and Nong Khai to the north. This area has been occupied for so long they have bronze age archeological sites. Recently, there's been construction of the Udorn Royal Thai Air Force Base. Built primarily by Americans, it's one of the many take-off sites for U.S. war planes that fly out to bomb Vietnam. I also heard there's a lot of CIA Air America types floating around here.

The official seal of the province shows a Hindu giant who's referred to as The Giant of the North. That's the interesting aspect of Thai religious history. Udorn as well as my own little Nang Rong, has many ruins built to Hindu Gods. Buddhism and Hinduism and a pantheon of minor deities all rolled through this place, so America's impact with a mere air base is minor in the context of the region's history.

With all of that in mind, I found it sad to see so many sections of the original Udorn with square, wooden and stucco houses juxtaposed to sterile office buildings, grotesque municipal centers, crummy night clubs, strip bars and massage parlors. Along the base are tailor shops, motels, bar-b-que pits and cheap 'bungalos.' Shell trucks roar past in seemingly infinite lines. B-52s, like black pterodactyls, fly overhead shaking foundations.

I had to get away from all that for a while, so walked down a side street with no American presence and a few noodle shops. The first place I stopped at had a scent of fresh vegetables and spices hanging around. I ordered a feast of noodles in a bowl, *kuai-tiao*, that had fresh sprouts, chopped up local vegetables, pieces of pork and right on top a fried egg. One of the first Thai words I learned during training: *Khai dhow*. It literally translates as *egg like a star*, but really just means *fried egg*.

For the first time in their variegated history the Thai people have no back door to politely exit if things get sticky and the war goes the wrong way. With all their chips on the line, it has abruptly come to their attention that their American ally may be developing a mild case of scruples. I have yet to meet one Thai who approves of the anti-war movement in the States because (I sense) they have become one with us and they fear whatever happens to us will happen to them. Only three years ago, Udon did not have one stretch of paved road, now it's a vital link of the Friendship Highway that runs from Bangkok, like a giant skipping stone, connecting all the American air bases: Bangkok to Rayong to Korat to Udorn. Massive GI hotels have sprung up financed by the war, mostly Chinese business interests with cash, and growing as the war grows. PX goods are for sale everywhere.

··

March 16, 1968
Camp Thai-Am, Udorn
City Udorn Province

Udorn Thani School, where Camp-Thai-Am is held, is made of wood, masonry and stucco. It was apparently built before the infusion of war money. It follows a quasi-classic Thai style of straight lines, heavily ornamental cornices and fixed awnings for the rainy season. Bathrooms are, unfortunately, also classic Thai; but I am pretty much resigned to squat johns by now. The students' showers and bathrooms are little more than wooden shacks over holes in the ground. The girls have running water, but the boys have to haul up water from a deep well. The brackish water would probably kills normal mosquitoes, but the Udon variety have mutated into a particularly vicious strain that could probably live on human blood alone. I swear I saw one deep a deep breath when I sprayed it with DDT.

The first day of camp is well under way in extremely hot and humid conditions. PCVs gave tests to gauge student language ability. Each volunteer has their own group to teach, play with, lad in calisthenics and generally make friends with for the duration of the camp's existence. Just for fun, every student group has been named after an animal. I am leading the mighty PANDAS! There are twelve students from all over northeast Thailand and few of them know more than a few other children in the whole camp. One of our first projects will be to make sure boys and girls from Loey and Korat or wherever don't cling together, but make new friends with other students and, hopefully, with the Peace Corps volunteers, too! The typical student at camp has never left his own province and in many cases not even his own district.

Initially, I was in charge of theater productions, then to 2nd place and finally dropped before I had a chance to spot a new star in the Thai heavens. Now I have the distinction of being in charge of *special programs* i.e. field trips.

My old friend, Thom, whose blond hair still fell over his forehead, was in charge of much of the camp's structure. My first thought when I saw him approach me from the front of the school was, "My God, I thought he was thin *before!*" I quickly learned why Thom is running so many things: his temperament seems suited to paying attention to all the small details that make organizations work! He's also very good at delegating authority. I'm so much more easily distracted. Within a few hours of reconnecting with him, I realized although Thom arrived in Thailand after I did, he was already speaking Thai much better. Why did Peace Corps send me a book locker filled with so many books written in English. Such a temptation! Thom obviously read a lot of books from the locker and *still* learned a lot more Thai. I guess if I was honest with myself I'd recognize the irritation as envy. I remember his telling me a few weeks before camp that he was so excited because he'd overheard two of the female teachers telling an off-color joke within his presence, thinking he'd never get the slang, but he did! When he burst laughing, they loked away embarrassed. I thought that was a great story, but it depressed me all the same because I couldn't imagine reaching the point where I'd get Thai humor in Thai! Maybe Thom's language skills have something to do with the way he pays so much attention to the way people speak, pronounce words and articulate what they want to say. He quickly picked up on my Boston accent and I, in turn, poked fun at him for his little language quirks he said are common in his part of the country, such as statements like, "Come here once."

Here at Camp Thom and I seem to have a little more distance between us than we've had in the past: getting together to talk about books, give each other hints we'd picked up about Thai language or culture and share experiences from back in the states. But, ever since I began hanging out with Fred, I felt as if Thom was distancing himself from me. Might have something to do with the fact that neither Fred nor myself is shy about talking with American soldiers and because Thom is so deeply philosophically and personally opposed to the war he disapproves of such conduct. Of course, the more closely Thom articulated his position, the more ashamed I was of my own casual allegiances and stayed away myself. So, here I am about to work with Thom, and hopefully our initial friendship will re-forge itself.

Thom's sense of place and order and my proclivity toward chaos have already clashed. He's often after the kids to pick up after themselves and I have the sense he wished I'd pick up after myself, too! Although I was often upset over the constant turmoil of my parents' household, they actually did keep a lid on things in a loose sort of way. With all the shouting and yelling, the rooms were littered with books and the meals always involved politically discussions. I fought it and yet managed to assimilate it. Thom's background of real neatness, order and strong moral code makes me attracted to him and put off at the same time. If nothing else, I certainly look forward to the two of us having time to discuss novels and poetry we've read and liked and maybe even have a political discussion or two, because we're really much more alike than not.

On another aside, the students have had a veritable plague of upset stomachs, fevers and headaches. I imagine after they find out about the types of classroom activities, plays, songfests and outings we have planned, they'll come around. I also have a horrible feeling that after two weeks of plays, songfests and outings I'll be more than ready for another kind of vacation. The initial schedule: days start at 5:30 with exercises, then a run around the school field. I get a military deferment and escape basic training so I can take part in the equivalent of basic training in Udon Thani.

My Mighty Pandas look as sad as I do at 5:30. Then, comes bathing, breakfast (boiled rice and fish sauce), laundry cleaning and four hours of classes. English is spoken at all times with signs everywhere to remind the students of their new language obligations. The Thai teachers who were volunteered were at first bemused then taken aback by the prospect at what was ahead. The women were pretty much trapped on campus, but the men seemed quite capable and willing to simply disappear into the lounges of Udon if we continued to insist on this camp madness. I gathered most of them viewed the camp as a free trip to Udon. There may have been a few volunteers who felt the same way.

The Thai kids didn't want to go to bed on schedule. This morning they were up at 4:00 AM and raring to go. I thought at first I was sympatico with my Pandas. I can see now I was wrong. It's going to take a lot of work to wear them down. Maybe we can force them to make little baskets and wicker furniture until they drop. What an idea! Hand-crafted artifacts from Thailand should be worth a bundle in NYC. Maybe I'll bring up this brilliant idea at the next staff meeting.

Everyone slept on cheap, thin straw mats in the classrooms. I picked up a used mosquito net for two bucks, then discovered it was only long enough to cover a Thai dwarf. The first morning I discovered my ankles had been bitten by a googol of fleas, gnats and mosquitoes. My back was killing me. The mats were about one-eighth of an inch thick and the floors were made of teak. Other problems: there's an enormous American airbase nearby; immense jets are overhead day and night on missions I didn't even want to imagine: Laos, Cambodia, Vietnam; the city of Udon Thani is stuffed with soldiers, dope dealers, pimps and prostitutes. How very, very sad this felt to me. When there's discussions of body counts and wounded, there should also be time to discuss the maiming of another culture.

My Pandas just had a contest against the Porcupines and beat them handily. Also, my Glorious Pandas took first place in the "Picture-Puzzle" contest. I wrote them a team song:

> *Here come the Pandas marching down the street*
> *All the Pandas are out to eat*

When you see them coming
You better step aside
All the Pandas coming
Side by side
Side by side!
(cheer: MIGHTY PANDAS!)

This morning everyone was up at 5:30. The moon was still in the sky as we all did our push-ups over dew-moistened grass. By the time I'd finished a few laps around the field I was ready for bed.

I have to admit the food's been okay. Typical northeast Thai peasant breakfast. But from now on I'll be having breakfast across the street from the camp. Boiled rice and fish sauce at 7:00 AM just doesn't do it for me. We all paid 200 baht ($10) for the privilege of eating with the kids, but I'm going to view my payment as a contribution to the camp and eat out as often as I can. All this physical activity demanded more than chicken soup and curry.

Yesterday, as I was walking outside the school grounds, a samlaw driver stopped near me and the driver, assuming I was from the nearby American air force base, asked me "Hey, GI, where you go?"

I replied, in Thai, that I was out for a walk.

"Hey," he persisted in English. "You want massage?"

"No, thank you."

"Hey, you want some good food?"

That stopped me. I hopped in and he drove me to a clean, well-lit place, but Hemingway had just left. Filled with air force personnel. The waitresses were more reminiscent of massage parlor women than waitresses in a noodle shop. I ended up getting a delicious order of ravioli, hot garlic rolls and coffee.

Back at camp, the variety show we put on for the students was a smashing success. A few of us rigged up a parody of Snow White and the Seven Dwarves. One guy played Snow White in a mini-skirt and blouse stuffed with old newspapers (for profile). I was one of the dwarves, Dopey. The kids rolled on the floor laughing.

The next morning we went on an outing to the temple of Phra Phuttabat Lang Tao to see an enormous footprint of the Buddha.

After lunch, we visited ancient cave sites dating back to the stone age. The students were quite respectful and quiet. On the bus ride back we sang *…if you miss the train I'm on, then you'll know that I am gone…*over and over again.

....

March 23, 1968

When the morning whistle blew for calisthenics no one paid any attention. The whistle blower eventually gave up in disgust. Everyone was simply exhausted. Last night, following a student performance of Snow White, the students paired off and performed little skits that *they'd* created for our benefit. When they all joined hands and sang their version of Home On the Range, we applauded wildly. Someone wheeled out the portable cooler and we handed out Cokes to everyone. Finally, when it seemed as if everything that could be performed had been performed, we all joined hands in one circle and sang popular songs in English and Thai.

I was so hyped after all that, not to mention all the Cokes I consumed, I stayed up until two in the morning working on the script and directions for a puppet show. The students will pull the strings and the teachers will help with costumes and staging.

This Sunday, our field trip has been expanded to include a visit to Khon Kaen University, the gigantic Ubonratana Hydro-electirc dam and a trip to a local television studio. One problem that's emerged during camp hours is that the Thai male teachers slip out a side door, go into town and carouse around. The women end up doing almost all the actual work. I've heard some of the female volunteers giving pep talks to the other women, telling them they should stand up for their rights and balance the work. Most of the time all they get in response are a bunch of Thai women covering their mouths and giggling.

Dave, a volunteer form New Jersey, worked with his group in the cafeteria on dance routines for the Peter Pan production coming up. Harriet and Kathy, two volunteers from New England, are in the art room helping with puppet construction. The best part of all this is that the kids think we know what we're doing.

My shins and ankles are covered with bites. The mosquitoes don't seem to care about blood types or Rh factor. Blood is blood. How come the Thais aren't bothered? No, I should re-phrase that. How come the Thais don't seem to get bitten?!!!

The camp statistics have been compiled: there are 100 students, twelve PCVs and fifteen Thai teachers. The English language instruction aspect of the camp seems to be going well. The students are already speaking much more fluently and we have to be on our linguistic toes. We used to be able to speak to one another, rapidly, without any fear of being understood; but, that's no longer true. The Thai teachers, on the other hand, don't really seem much interested in English language development. I wonder if all this was reversed and the camp was located in the United States would I be that disciplined about learning Thai?

A few days later

It's late in the afternoon and I've just finished doing my laundry. Standing hunched over a galvanized bucket for two hours ringing detergent out of my clothes is no picnic. My shirts are finally done, but wrinkled beyond belief. Is there an iron here? How do the kids manage to stay so spotless? Some of them must be hiding irons or secretly sending their clothes out for dry cleaning. Another thing. The PCVs sweat like pigs and the Thais always seem to serenely deal with the heat in such a way that the most strenuous exercise leaves them with a slight sheen to their skins. Back in Nang Rong, I recall playing badminton with Wisut and Sanguan for hours at a time, sweat pouring down my face and into my eyes and they'd seem to be practically cool! It didn't help that they always killed me in every game. I feel like such an un-evolved sloth compared to the Thais. Finally, how come the kids keep appearing in starched white shirts. Does someone have a secret can of spray starch they aren't sharing?

All the plays are now in rehearsal and the puppet shows will be ready to be performed in a few days. Weather remains hot and sticky.

....

March 26, 1968

Oh, my God, this is exhausting! The kids are up at all hours then get up hours earlier than they have to, just to talk, bathe, wash clothes and then run around the field. I think 99% of them are having the adventure of their lives. We recently showed them how to play softball. The equipment came from the American airbase. Thom called some community relations person, explained what we were up to and was told to drop by any time and pick up donated sports equipment. He later told us that when he arrived, he was immediately ushered into a colonel's office, introduced to the leader himself, then a few captains and was told to prepare for photographs. Thom told us the colonel seemed a bit disappointed to see only one representative showed up from Camp Thai-Am, but he forged ahead for the benefit of his secretary's tape recorder and the base photographer. Thom received bats, leather gloves, and pure white Wilson softballs. The entire ceremony was later released through U.S. Air force News. Thom told the colonel we were thinking of having an American-style picnic for the Thai students and wondered whether the base could spare any food. Could they, indeed! Why hadn't he asked before the ceremony? In any case, he was given some papers to show the guys at the commissary for 226 hot dogs, two cauldrons of baked beans, six cases of Coke and all the necessary condiments. They promised the food would be delivered in an air force truck and guaranteed whatever was cooked hot, stayed hot and whatever was supposed to be chilled, would be chilled. He also said that a tour of the base would be arranged for all the kids and teachers, promising there would be an enormous Huey Helicopter available for inspection and some special fire-fighting equipment on display. The colonel closed by reminding everyone this base was, after all, on Thai territory and that the students, as citizens of an allied nation, had every right to see at least a piece of what was happening on their turf. Thom told me he was tempted to ask what our own country was really involved in, since most of us didn't actually know the complete story, but decided discretion was the better part of valor.

Before we made the trip to the air base I spoke with a few of the Thai teachers about their feelings regarding this enormous base being on their soil. I'm not sure what I expected to hear, but I was totally taken aback by what really seemed to be a sense of indifference. I've been around Thais enough by now to know if they're being polite, evasive or honest (I think). One of the women showed some emotion when she mentioned all the orphaned

GI babies (in Vietnam, Cambodia and Thailand) and I'm pretty sure I detected a passing wave of anger. A few of the men joined in and agreed that American soldiers seemed to take their relationships with Thai women too casually. Just as the conversation was heating up, the Thais suddenly all looked at each other and went silent.

On the day of the visitation, large, modern buses took us to the base. We passed through three security stops operated by Thai soldiers and the final two by Americans who seemed prepared to blast us for the smallest mistake. Once inside, all was cordial and welcoming. First stop was the Huey. If it's possible for green paint to glow, then the Huey glowed. We were all in awe, but the kids got over it first and raced to be the first inside. The two airmen assigned to us were very young and were gentle and playful with the students who loved, I mean loved, taking turns placing a pilot's helmet on and turning around to salute us. The fire fighting equipment spread out on a large tarp didn't seem very exciting until a large fire was lit nearby and we watched the power of foam extinguishers blast those flames out. Strangely, but perhaps not surprisingly, the low point of the visit was in the cafeteria where they had hot dogs, beans and lemonade ready for us to gobble down. The lemonade was apparently okay, but the kids just kept playing with their food until we realized they were not going to eat it and moved on to see parachutes packed and then watch a demonstration drop. By mid-afternoon we were all sun burned, tired and ready for the familiarity of the camp.

That evening, the Thai teachers performed a candle dance for us. Watching those graceful forms gracefully sway before us, holding candles to illuminate the dark gymnasium, I forgot how tired I was and stared, mesmerized, until the end.

March 27, 1968

When Mike Feder, one of the other volunteers in camp, passed me in the halls, we each nodded, said "Shalom!" burst out laughing, punched each other on the shoulder and moved on. It's a way for two wandering Jewish boys to crystallize the fact that somehow, a few generations after our grandparents escaped Hitler for the golden shores of the New World, we found ourselves in southeast Asia. Mike's group were the Cobras. I kept ragging him about the name. I mean, really, who wants to be a cobra? This morning, seven of my Panda girls challenged seven his Cobra girls to a soccer match. Mike bragged that the loser had to buy the winning team ice-cream at the city market. My girls easily trounced his, so we marched downtown where Mike got sundaes and popcorn for my kids and I did the same for his. We were both taken aback watching them sprinkle sugar on the popcorn. The local citizens stared at us as we marched by and I picked up very bad vibes. Mike dropped back to walk alongside side me and whispered, "They think we're GIs out for fun with small girls!" Just then two of the girls got close to us and asked, in Thai, if the ice-cream was really free. Some of the people on the sidewalk heard us talking and I guess a light bulb went off. "Oho, they're teachers!" someone called out and suddenly we were surrounded by smiles and waves.

After walking around for over an hour, the sun beat down mercilessly and we decided walking back was merely sadistic so we whistled for several screaming happy students. Back at the school, the drivers demanded three baht each (15 cents), which Mike and I thought was pretty reasonable since it'd been a long, hot ride with fully loaded vehicles. My Pandas were horrified. They screeched like viragos at the drivers, calling them names and told us not to give them more than one baht each. We looked at each other in shock. Each of us had casually paid four baht for much shorter rides ourselves. The drivers were furious and cried out as they pulled away, "American teacher number one! Thai students number ten!"

After we showered and changed, the kids, with their relentless energy wanted to play softball with the new equipment. While we were still setting up, several blond-haired American kids came over to watch and after a while asked if they could join in. It was so weird to be speaking English so fluently and casually with little kids. And, they're so white! I twitched whenever they touched me as if I were Thai and they were the foreigners. Anyway, I quickly began to think of them as pale-faced demons who got on my nerves when they began pushing the Thai students around. The Thai kids were petrified of them and the Americans, because they picked that up, became even more aggressive and pushy. By the time the game ended, I wanted to take each one of them aside and whack their butts. We did not offer a return match.

That evening, after a delicious meal of fried rice, fish sauce, pork curry and sweetened bananas in evaporated milk, we had the puppet show and even though there were slips and mishaps, the audience laughed and cheered.

March 30, 1968

Considering the reality of Udorn City being top-heavy with bars and prostitutes, primarily because of the influx of American air men, it's a fairly quiet place. The local air base does go out of its way to make a good impression, so every month a sizable donation is made to various municipal charities. Apparently that's enough to balance off the bar fights, cases of VD and traffic accidents and deaths. Fact is, there is rarely any trouble between townsfolk and base personnel, except for an isolated murder now and then, with most of these cases proven to have been based on trivial motives like sex or money.

Last night, I spotted a few volunteers slipped out the front door and walked in the direction of the market. It was so dark, I couldn't tell if they were men or women. I did my best to catch up, but my plastic flip-flops kept slipping off my feet. On the outside, I waved over a samlaw and told the driver to follow that samlaw ahead with the three Americans in it. He basically ignored me and continued to pedal at his own pace.

"Where are you going?" he finally asked me, in Thai.

I couldn't think of any place in particular, so I told him to just keep going.

He swiveled his head around.

"You speak Thai very well," he said.

The usual flattery, which by this time got on my nerves because I know I spoke Thai like an imbecilic first grader. But, I nodded my head politely sensing he had something else to say to me.

"Do you want girls, opium or dirty movie?" he asked.

I told him I just wanted to buy a little grass, thinking at that instant I said it I was asking for trouble. Peace Corps would kick me out on my skinny butt if it was ever proven I'd bought dope and smoked it. In a town like Udorn there were probably military spies everywhere.

The driver nodded and said he knew where he could get me half a kilo for less than one American dollar. Although I wondered what I could possibly do with that much grass, the possibility of acquiring so much so cheaply was more than I could resist. We traveled a very long distance into an area of the city I'd never seen, past shanty-town, beyond the perimeter of the actual city, to some ramshackle buildings that reminded me of the red light district in Buriram. Sure enough, just as a stray lamp illuminated my face I heard that familiar call:

"Hey, honey! Where you go?"

I was tempted to pause and teach her the correct verb form, but decided against it. We stopped on the edge of a field. The driver told me to sit while he went to meet someone. I felt very exposed. The night was completely black and when a pack of feral dogs sniffed around the samlaw I considered making a break for it. I was sure they'd tear me to shreds before I reached the road. I decided to stay put, prayed the dogs would eventually leave as I loudly hummed the Thai national anthem in hopes it would act as a verbal talisman. The driver returned to inform me his connection had been sound asleep and was not willing to get up for a measly half kilo sale. The two of us peered at each other through the dark. Finally, he said he knew of another place we could try, but it might be a bit more expensive. I shrugged. What were a few more baht? Besides, he'd driven me so far! I felt obligated, for his sake, to buy something from someone.

We drove back through the market, behind the bars and factories, off Posri Street to a small restaurant which had about a dozen samlaws parked out front. The driver pulled over and spoke with one of the other drivers and, after glancing in my direction a few times, they both turned back to the restaurant and eyed the hip-swinging hookers. I couldn't really blame them. Just then, two tall guys walked over to my samlaw and before I could say anything my driver was gone. The two guys wore tight slacks, American-style sweaters and lipstick! One of them said something to me, but I turned away hoping they'd just disappear. In all-too-clear English, he cried:

Hey, man, you in my country now! When I talk, you listen!"

Jesus, they had real muscles!

"I'm sorry," I said, "I didn't know you were talking to me."

"Oh, very polite," he said. "Now, you fucking American very polite. Hey, you really think you some handsome, huh?"

"No," I said. "Not too handsome."

His pal reached out and ran his hand alongside my cheek. I slid lower in my seat. Suddenly, my driver returned with the biggest, bad-ass Thai I'd ever seen. His rolled up t-shirt revealed enormous biceps. My two admirers quickly drifted away.

"You think you some hot ass, man, but you shit, you nothing…" their voices faded off into the dark night.

Mr. Big asked me how much money I wanted to spend on dope. I told him ten or fifteen baht. He turned to my driver, gave him a tight smile as if to say 'Why are you wasting my time with this?'

My driver shrugged, got back into his seat and Muscle wedged himself in beside me. We moved on to an even more disreputable part of the city. I began to deeply regret I'd started this adventure. We paused at a small shack where a wizened Chinese-Thai elder with a Ho Chi Minh beard sat rocking. He had no marijuana, but plenty of opium. Did the foreigner want some opium? I firmly shook my head. By this time I was flashing grenade explosions with visions of MPs hustling me off to an endless stay in some vast federal prison. What in God's name had I gotten myself into? We were off again, this time bumping along a narrow path behind the Foremost Dairy plant. Again, we stopped. My companion flexed his right muscle and asked me for 20 baht. I would've given him a 100 if I had it. My stomach started to act up and cramps hit me full force as my driver joined the other guy off into the dark. I desperately wanted to get out of the samlaw and take a shit behind some shrubbery, but I was more afraid of cobras, roving bandits and the fear that my pals might return while I was squatting. They eventually returned with a small package of grass and I sighed in relief as my stomach settled down. Mr. Muscle said a few fast words to the driver who made a fearful expression and cringed as if he'd been told he was about to lose his balls. As he wedged himself back into the seat with me, Mr. Bicep told me it'd taken a lot of time and trouble to get me what I wanted and he figured I owed him another 10 baht. Thinking only that I would've offered a kidney, I gladly gave him a 20 baht note and sighed in relief when he calmly pocketed it and called out for another samlaw. I stuck the dope inside my shirt and we took off. About halfway back to the camp my driver began talking to himself about policemen and how much he hated them. At least, I think that's what he was saying. I tapped him on the back and asked him what was going on? He said that policemen were all the same, always taking money from hard-working people, from innocent people and especially from poor people who had no power. I thought about all that for a minute then asked him how police were involved with what we'd just been through. He slammed to a stop.

"Don't you know?" he asked me in surprise.

"Know what?"

"That man was police! Who else could find marijuana at night?"

I was sick. Visions of a police raid at the school filled my imagination. I could see Thai narcs, all karate experts, smashing down doors. Looking for me. I'd actually told the cop who I was and what I was doing in Udorn. My real name! What a klotz!

"Why didn't you let me know?"

"I thought you already knew," the driver sneered.

"But, what if they come to the school?" I almost cried.

"You mean you really work at the school?" he looked at me, stunned.

"Yes. What can I do?"

He laughed. I hated him for his Buddhist acceptance of things. Nothing else was said for the rest of the trip. At the gates of the school, he said, "I think you are happy now. You are back at school and you have your thing to smoke. Please give me 20 baht."

"Twenty baht for a samlaw ride? This guy was dreaming. Still, I reached into my pocket and four crumpled five baht bills. In three more hours the whistle would sound for morning running, push-ups and jumping jacks. I rolled myself a join and inhaled deeply right there against the front metal gates of the school. I sucked in again. Whoops. My system was flooded with chaos, sense and time distortions and before I knew what hit me I was sitting on the cracked sidewalk, head lolling. Hmmm, forgot about the qualities of Thai grass. I suddenly had a sensation of being enshrouded by spider webs. Trying hard not to shriek, I somehow managed to find my way inside, then up the stairs to my little cubicle. Neither whistles, nor students, nor blood-sucking bugs got me up until after the formal classroom sessions were well under way. At noon, I tried to stand and saw my ankles had a million mosquito bites and were puffy, red and swollen. I threw some cold water on my face and stumbled down stairs where I bumped into Thom who stared at me in disgust.

"You could at least make an effort to keep up with the schedule and pull your own weight," he said.

"Why don't you…" I started to say, thought better of it, and ran around the field with my Pandas instead.

Almost the end of Camp

After sharing, eating, cooking and making new friends, it was time to clean up and get ready to move on. But, there was one more surprise to go! Someone came up with the idea of giving the students one final writing assignment entitled "Why I like Mr. (Miss)_____" with the space to be filled in with the name of a team teacher. Here's a sample of what I received from my Pandas.

Suriyan wrote, "Mr. Burgess is a Panda. He is in Panda Team. When his pupils make the ball game, his pupils are very smart. His pupils are never defeat. They are very smarter than other teams. Mr. Burgess is a man. He is very handsome. When he is talking he is handsome. His team is the best in Camp Thai-Am.

Prachum wrote: "Mr. Burgess is a good teacher. He teach well and he look at the boys and girls well. Mr. Burgess is not loathsome. He is a knowing teacher. He is industrious, so I love him.

Wittichai wrote: "Mr Burgess is a good-tempered man. He is very, very fun in Camp Thai-Am. He loves his students very much and he likes to play with us, too. If he has time, he will play with us and teach us in the classroom. He always speak a fun word that makes us laugh. He is in the Panda Team and he is my teacher so I love him very much.

Khian wrote: "Mr. Burgess come from Boston in the U.S. He is a Peace Corps and he has taught in Nang Rong School. But now he had to study at Camp Thai-Am, so he come to us. He have a good temper. He likes to teach a song, play games in the classroom. So everybody love him. Do you love him? And he is handsome and he always has the glasses on his eyes.

After reading the above, and more, I think the Pandas are the best. I think they are very smart. Also, I'm glad someone finally realized how handsome (as opposed to loathsome) I am. Pandas, I love you all.

....

April 4, 1968
Dateline: Vientiane, Laos

I stayed one more evening in Udon after the camp officially finished, had a few drinks with the other volunteers and back in my hotel room made plans for the next leg of my vacation. Early the next morning I was able to get a fifty cent taxi ride to the Thai river city of Nongkhai and then a samlaw ride to the banks of the Mekhong River. At that twilight zone of currency everything seemed to be acceptable: dollars, baht, francs, marks and something that sounded like a *geep* but was transliterated into English as *kip*. The ratio exchange at that time was every American penny was worth five kip. Once I had that part straightened out in my head, I joined the crowd that had gathered by the water's edge to haggle with the motor-launch skipper. There was no sign of the border patrol or a clerk with visa stamps. The boat guys had the panache of Venetian gondoliers, without the costume. I focused in on one and managed to bargain my price down from one American dollar to fifty cents, but just as I was congratulating myself, a Chinese kid calmly handed over the equivalent of twenty-five cents and was given his ticket, no questions asked. The brown water flowed fairly quickly and the distant bank seemed to be a haze of shrubbery. I was crossing the Mekhong River from Thailand to Laos and I wanted to suddenly find and fall in love with a lithe Laotian-French beauty and start our brief romance together when we reached the other side. No such luck. Our landing site was composed of a rickety flight of wooden stairs that led up to a large Pepsi sign and a small greeting in English, French and Laotian That read: WELCOME TO LAOS. I hauled my bag up the shaky steps to a white visa office where the merry Laotian custom men smiled and waved me through to a taxi stand. Seven of us jammed into a Datsun and, after shelling out about a dollar each, we were driven twenty kilometers over a hard and bumpy road to the administrative capital city: Vientiane. The royal capital, named Luanprabong, was further up the river and at that time not a safe venue for westerners.

With my chatty Thai vocabulary and a few irregular French verbs, I had a tough time explaining where I wanted to go. I'd heard the International Volunteer Service often allowed volunteers to stay over on their grounds, but I was unable to describe the organizations name or purpose to anyone. One guy offered to take me to where he thought I wanted to go, so I took a chance and ended up at the local United States Information Service building. Not much information for me there. I walked back to my samlaw driver and told him I just wanted a clean, inexpensive place to stay the night, assuming he'd take me to some relative's dive, but he took me to the Bis Hotel which appeared clean, airy and altogether satisfactory.

Out on the city streets hundreds of motor scooters and Japanese cars zoomed back and forth. It was so different from my quiet and soft Nang Rong I was momentarily dizzy from all the movement. Vientiane seemed like an extended village with real buildings here and there, but the underlying feel of rural Laos was never far beneath. I noticed many side streets with small shops that opened right on to dusty frontages where the pace seemed less hectic. French nationals were everywhere: tall, bearded men who strode ahead purposefully, dressed in European-style clothing that showed off their builds in a way the more casual and looser clothing of Americans never could. The shop windows had letter in Laotian (which looked a lot like Thai), French, English and Chinese. The few times I attempted to communicate with merchants in Thai they looked at me as if I were crazy. They'd inevitably break in with a polite "Parlez-vous francais?" The French influence was immediately seen in the layout of the city plan with its wide boulevards, tree-shaded sidewalks and *patisseries* at every corner. The architecture ranged from the straight, no nonsense lines of American buildings (USON, AID, USIS) and companies (Shell, Caltex, Esso) to the brocaded buildings, stucco-layered with personal touches in wooden carvings on doors and window frames from the days when Laos was one of the French Trust Territories. The older buildings were built back from the road to allow room for trees, while the newer ones impinged right to the edge of the sidewalk, greedily taking into shadow what they could not cover, thrusting themselves out at every passerby.

Vientiane is not a tax-free city, yet soft goods such as clothing, food and tobacco were extremely cheap. Signs advertised custom-made suits of fine broadcloth for $30.00 and fine-cotton, fitted shirts for $4.00. French wine was available everywhere, even in cans! Only after a long walk in the heat, past new construction and paved roads, did I come across buildings erected by Laotians: peasant shacks reminiscent of northeast Thailand built of hard-wood planks and corrugated roofs. Eventually, I found my way back to the city where I saw, looming over a main boulevard, a not-quite-finished immense arch. It had detailed statuary and carvings on its side and top. My initial thought was it had to be Laos' answer to the Arc de Triomphe. At its base I saw a plaque announcing it was called The Victory Monument. I could not for the life of me imagine a victory of such scope by the Laotian army, such as it was, worthy of such a structure. Later, some Kiwis from Auckland told me that most of the funding for the arch came from the United States and was supposedly destined for a new highway between Vientiane and Luangprabong. I guess that's why it's so difficult to get from one city to the other except by river boat. Big arch. No roads.

One of the reasons I headed for Vientiane was the rumor I'd heard of a hippie couple who'd opened a western-style coffee shop that served deep-dish apple pie with vanilla ice cream. I had no idea what it was called or even if it still existed. So, I raised my right hand and signaled a samlaw to pull over. The driver's name was Luk and before I could tell him where I wanted to go he started telling me stories about his family. Between his mix of Laotian and French I gathered he had an enormous mother-in-law who was eating him out of house and home and three huge daughters who seemed to spend their lives trying to be just as fat. Luk finally admitted he had no idea what I meant by apple pie or coffee shops, but he did know where a lot of interesting ladies lived who just loved foreigners like myself. Temporarily putting my dreams of pie on hold, I asked him how much they cost. He said their prices ranged from six hundred kip to several thousand. "What's the difference?" I asked. He told me it would be like comparing his wife when he married her to the way she is now. With that, he threw both hands in the air conveying a sense of girth and side-swiped a Honda. Neither stopped. Luk went on to tell me that good dope costs less than tobacco, but anyone with money wouldn't be caught dead smoking grass because it had no status. Five Star Hennessy was the way to go. I made a mental note that Wisut had asked me to bring him back a bottle. Bad news, Luk said, was as of midnight tonight, April 4, 1968, opium smoking was officially illegal. I admitted I was a poverty-striken traveler. Really! Reluctantly he dropped me off in front of a place called The White Rose.

Inside, a large dimly-lit room was cluttered with unmatched pieces of furniture and shadowy figures entwined on couches. Were they really…? Yes, they were! Pernod seemed to be the drink of choice. A short, tubby woman came bouncing over to me, wrapped her arms around my waist, and wiggled her nose back and forth against my shirt until it opened and I felt the tip of a hot tongue nuzzling my belly button. I could not resist. She led me to a back door and stairs that led up to a cubicle. In the middle of this tiny space was a ridiculously small, narrow bed. In fact, it looked like an ironing board. She shucked off her wrap and in a flash she was on the *bed* with legs akimbo, making cat-like noises for me to join her. I was too nervous to completely undress, so I just dropped my pants and shuffled over to her and tried to somehow join her and the bed. I felt the whole thing groan under my weight and suddenly things did not feel sexual, rather more creepy as I looked down at someone who seemed to be more like a little girl with breasts and pubic hair. Beneath her head was a filthy-stained pillow that gave off a rancid odor. I felt her trying to cross her legs over my back. I held my head away from her, arched my back, the bed shook and suddenly the two of us crashed to the floor with an enormous bang. Someone stuck his head in the door, but the woman urgently whispered something to him and he left. This was all too much for me to handle. We both dressed. The bed was ruined. I pulled out a bunch of hundred kip notes and handed them to her. It seemed to be enough, she gave me a slight bow of the head and I made a fast exit for my hotel room.

Bright sun woke me the next morning along with a few million mosquitoes, and I quickly dressed and found a place that served coffee and croissants. Ah, the joys of French civilization. Wandering around the city gave me even more a sense of being in a city that had no center. Various buildings had armed guards or soldiers keeping an eye out front; but, they all wore different uniforms with varying insignia. Some smiled and others frowned. No one knew what was going on in other parts of Laos, except there were plenty of rumors Americans were on the plains or in the hills or maybe even in the city somehow hidden in the shadows.

Once more, I signaled a samlaw driver and in infantile French asked about American clubs. He nodded and took me to a ramshackle building set far back from the street. It was painted red, blue and yellow and had dozens of banners and flags hanging outside. The sign out front said: THE THIRD EYE. Underneath was a crudely painted open eye. Looking up and down the street I saw a few dozen other joints with similar facades. I struck up a conversation with a few New Zealanders and they pointed out there were many shacks half-hidden behind palm trees and banana fronds.

"Those are very low rent," one of them said.

"Yes," the other said, "and you don't even have to rent them for the whole night."

"Indeed," his friend continued. "If you suddenly have the urge to study the Ramayana or have someone read tea leaves these places are for you."

Since I'd been walking around for hours I asked them if the Third Eye also served food.

"Not real food, mate," one said, "but the Americans seem to like the pie."

Oh, my God. I'd found the place I was looking for.

"Does it come with vanilla ice cream?"

"Can't say for sure, mate, but some kind of cold topping and they'll even throw in a banana, which seems like overkill, but there you have it."

The bartender's name was Digby and the pie he served me was still warm beneath a few scoops of real vanilla ice cream. I inhaled in satisfaction and looked around. The place was filled with travelers from everywhere and they all had great stories: Did I know I could buy a cheap used car in Germany and sell it for a fortune in Saudi Arabia? Joints were passed and time slowed to a crawl. Darjeeling was ready for harvesting in the Malaysian highlands. Khatmandu was the place to go for bricks of black, sticky hash. Of course, it was even cheaper in Afghanistan, but they had scary jails there and once in no one ever heard from you again. I sank back into the soft cushions, smoked some more and began to be fascinated by the designs of the rugs and the wall hangings. Dozens of parasols in paisley colors hung upside down on strings, turning beneath red, white and blue spotlights that bordered a distant light show. Someone pointed out the small rooms where one could relax for a day, a week or a lifetime smoking opium. I muttered something about it now being illegal and everyone had a good laugh. Colored slides flashed against a wall: race tracks, beaches, old houses on Martha's Vineyard. Everything blended in with shadows of the slow dancing patrons, weaving to an ensemble of two guitars, one mouth harp and a tambourine.

I'm gonna give you a sugar cube (3 times)
If you'll just give me some of your love…

This went on for more than a dozen stanzas. Was there a camera somewhere back in the dim light taking snapshots of me sitting lotus-legged, lapping up apple pie with no thought or interest to a country named Laos.

Some time during that blur of days I visited The El Morocco which offered Frank Sinatra-type crooners. Then, there was Marcel's Place for small talk with other travelers, neat shots of European brandy all served by Marcel himself, a visiting Frenchman who'd decided to stay.

La Maison des Amis turned out to be what for Vientiane constituted a high-class brothel. I don't even remember how I found it. There must've been a samlaw driver involved. I think I was looking for the White Rose, but, having absolutely no sense of direction I found The House of Friends. A tall, lithe Eurasian women walked over to me after I had a drink and started smoking a Thai Falling Rain cigarette. She had enormous brown, liquid eyes and a tight, red mouth that sent out clipped French inquiries that fell apart when she realized I spoke English.

"May I help you?"

"I think so."

"Do you find any of the women here attractive?"

"Yes."

"Excellent. I'll get you another drink and if you'll please tell me which one…"

"You!" I blurted out.

She seemed mildly surprised. I realized then she was at least several years older than the other women. I was suddenly aroused and stood up. She glanced down at my crotch, made a sound with her tongue and gave me a fast nod. I followed her to a back room, then through a wall of swinging colored beads into an even smaller room with a mattress on the floor and a desk covered with opened letter and a few photographs of children pasted to the wall. The envelopes all had French stamps. Her family? She slipped out of her loose dress and revealed a black, skimpy bra and red panties. Her surprise at being chosen had long worn off and I felt waves of utter boredom sweeping my way. I tried to reach her on the bed before she threw her body into the open-limbed posture. Not fast enough. She was prepared. Her breasts sagged on either side of her chest and I saw stretch marks from a pregnancy. As her fingers began to manipulate me, she arched up and I was suddenly inside her as she scratched my back hard enough to make me cry out and despite all my misgivings I quickly had an orgasm.

She made brief cooing sounds when she realized what had happened and for some reason even this minute expression of caring made me feel better, especially as she wiped the sweat off my forehead. I slowly rolled off and sat on the edge of the bed. She joined me. I smiled at her and she smiled back. I felt an almost overwhelming need to cry. She cautiously touched my side.

"You are quite thin. Most Americans are fat, no?"

"Yeah, I think most of them are fat. Pourquoi?"

"Ah, I knew there was more to you. Vous Parlez Francaise, n'est-ce pas?"

"Oui, Je parle un petite peu."

"De quoi pense-tu?"

"Comment s'appelle?"

"Madeleine. Y tu?"

"Monsieur Vie."

"Ah, Mr. Life. Very funny."

In a second the bra and panties were back on and she was, once again, an aloof hostess. "Please leave 1500 kip on the table."

I pulled out two 1000 kip notes and dropped them. She could tell how much it was by the color of the currency and gave me another polite nod, turned, and left the room.

Depressed, asking myself why I'd acted like such an ass-hole just as she was beginning to open up to me, I got dressed and walked back in the direction of the cash register. Madeleine was standing there, casually still and gave me a whispered, "Bon soir, monsieur" as I left the relatively cool room for the humid bell jar of a regular night in Vientiane.

Once outside, I broke into a cold sweat, suddenly convinced I'd contracted some horrible STD. I forced myself to calm down, took a long walk by shops selling woven mats, bolts of silk, bronze Buddhas and wooden carvings. Up ahead there was a large, smoky fire. Someone was burning a mass of weed. I stood there for a few minutes inhaling deeply. My old feeling passed away, I hailed a samlaw and went back to the Bis Hotel for a cold shower and a nap.

There's supposed to be a civil war going on here, but it's only sporadically apparent. The languid pace on the side streets reminded me a lot of any quiet Thai village. However, when I tried to negotiate a trip up the Mekhong to the royal capital of Luangprabong, all the skippers bowed out. They said the Pathet Lao fired on any boats carrying westerners. Meanwhile, the shops were full. The roads were busy with all sorts of traffic. Workers were out cutting the green grass in front of the various American compounds where blacktop driveways held Ford station wagons. Hurricane fencing kept all these areas off-limits to casual strangers.

Life in Laos continued while idiots like me dropped by for a sip of the bitter-sweet life of a doomed city and its subtle rhythms.

Riding back to the border in a decrepit bus I tried to remember all my recent adventures. Who will I ever be able to tell about Jean Bernard, the volunteer in Chiengkarn who had a background in circus arts and taught her students to juggle fruit and walk a tight rope? Would I have to wait until I was back in America before I could find anyone who cared about the fun I had in Sanakhan, the Laotian town across the Mekhong River from Chiengkarn, during the Sangkram Festival (Thai New Year). Could I properly describe the mad crowds that threw water at all by-standers from an open truck? Who would care to hear about Jean-Pierre and his wife, part of a French-sponsored United

Nations Geological Survey Team in Laos? My high school French teacher would have been horrified to hear my struggles with that language and ultimately resort, in vain, to Thai. The French threw a glittering party for New Years with Haig & Haig running like water and the French nationals decked out in clothes they must have pulled from steamer trunks. Sitting together under a pale Asian moon, Jean and I had our wrists entwined with pieces of knotted string as good luck tokens for the year ahead.

Rumor had it the French were looking for gold deposits. They insisted they were doing nothing more than taking soil samples for future archeological digs. What was that sparkling on the banks of the river? Mica, they said. Nothing but mica.

I felt exhilarated to awake on a muggy morning, drape a towel around my neck and slip into the fast-moving current of the Mekhong River for my daily shave. I held a mirror before my face and carefully skimmed a layer of suds from my cheek and chin before slowly moving the razor down across new stubble. Behind my reflection I saw slow-moving commerce on the Thai banks; in front of me, through a light haze, was Laos. As I shaved I tried to picture the Chinese warlords that swept through this part of Indo-China in search of armed caravans; Khmers, out on patrol from Angkor Wat, seeking likely sites for Hindu shrines; isolated Mao hill tribesmen who trekked from one poppy field to the next as they worked on their dream-inducing plants; Frenchmen with no visions yet of Dien Bien Phu yet to cloud their horizons, stretched the borders of a French empire; and the Americans, supplied arms to all sides in order to contain an undeclared war. Now, the Lao Royalists were fighting the Phathet Lao. Poor, desolate, peaceful Laos wanted only to be left alone.

....

April 6, 1968

I was on a bus headed for Chiegnmai, Thailand's main northern city and the summer residence of the royal family, when I spotted a portly Caucasian sitting by himself. He introduced himself as Ulrich Brennberger, a German tourist. He rarely looked up from a paper bag on his lap from which he periodically pulled pieces of French bread to stuff in his mouth. Then, I noticed a small pile of egg shells next to his seat. That turned out to be the other item in the bag: hard-boiled eggs. At the first stop, I trailed him over to a soft drink stand and caught his attention. He seemed astonished to find another westerner on a Thai bus, but quickly went into his story. Every six months he sent his wife and kids away on a trip and the other six months he traveled himself to different parts of the globe. He appeared to be about forty, with slightly fading red hair and generally in robust health. Turned out he spoke several languages and was part owner of some large corporation in Mannheim.

Ulrich's Story

In 1954 I journeyed to the United States to see what life was like over there. Friends told me it would be more convenient if I entered as a student, so I enrolled in a since class at Ohio State and managed to get a job driving new cars from the factory to owners all over the country. It was a wonderful opportunity to see a whole new world and meet interesting people. I took hundreds of slides and I kept a daily journal of all my activities. I was once stopped for speeding during one of the new car deliveries and I was quite worried what would happen to me in an American court since I had only visitors status from a foreign country. I had visions of formal German courts in my head when I made my appearance at a city court in Chicago. First, I was astonished at how many people were in the court room doing the court's business: typing, writing on forms and telling people where to stand or sit. It began to look familiar to me. I realized that all the people standing near me were also there for speeding tickets and that we were going to be charged en masse by an entire squad of civil servants whose sole job, it seemed, involved nothing more than filling out slips of paper connected in one way or another to all of us present in court. The judge, a man in black robes sitting up high above us, never spoke. Slips of paper were handing to all of us and at the same time we were all told that we were guilty as charged and we would all have to pay a $10.00 fine before being allowed to leave. Someone asked if there were any objections, but there were none. We all paid, we all had our slips stamped and we all left through the door to freedom. It was all very tidy, efficient and, in fact, quite appealing to my Prussian heart.

After we reached Chiengmai, Ulrich and I boarded a small bus to visit a tiny village known, in Hudson's Guide to Chiengmai, as The Umbrella Village. Everyone there was involed in the production of beautifully colored, wooden umbrellas. Ulrich was amazed to see how many well-made umbrellas could be turned out by hand, using only available materials, even down to the minuscule slits of bamboo used in the parasol portion of each umbrella. The two of us stared almost in a trance at the men, women and children who worked intently with primitive tools, whizzing off a complete umbrella every twenty minutes or so. Ulrich said he liked the cohesiveness of the operation that managed to encompass family ties within an otherwise production-line operation.

We wandered through town, I downed a bowl of noodle soup. While Ulrich ate another egg, I devoured my own egg that was included with pieces of shrimp, pork and vegetables. I kept stirring the whole thing up with more crushed peanuts and fish sauce with ground pepper. Eyeing my soup with great concern, Ulrich mentioned he thought the efficiency and division of labor in the umbrella village reminded him of that traffic court in Chicago.

Field trip with students to Temple of Buddha's footprint.

Posing with local fishermen on the road to Prakhonchai Village.

With Steve, Ralph, Thom and others at soccer match.

Arriving in buriram with two students who won a writing contest.

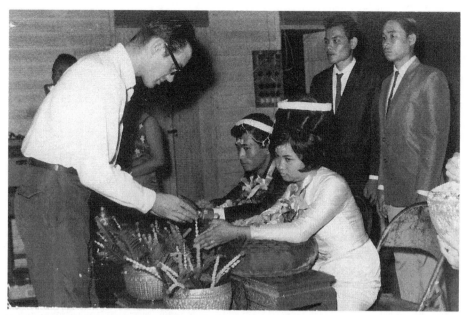

Pouring water to bless the newly-wed couple.

Wisut and I stand before his Loy Kratong creation.

Possibly the first marshmallow roast in Thailand.

Wisai, my student and friend,
near a stand of bananas.

Although Ulrich never did any research about Thailand before he began his journey, he an insatiable curiosity and boundless enthusiasm. On the climb up the steps of Doi Suthep to the king's summer palace near the famous temple of Wat Pradhat, he gave me some background about his company which manufactured various tools and machinery for export. He was one of three directors, having worked his way up from being a legal consultant to boss. He said he soon found himself making more money than he ever dreamed possible. This would seem to imply he was rich, but Ulrich was as tight with a baht as he apparently was with a Deutch mark.

I never got a thrill out of bargaining for goods, even in Thailand where it's a way of life. Ulrich, however, wanted to see some haggling and persuaded me to be his later ego at a Thai antique store. Several American tourists were leaving as we entered, carrying a pair of weather-worn Buddhas. I had a feeling their pitted appearance was acquired more through delicately applied acid than wind, storm and sun. The owners, husband and wife, stood up and smiled politely. Ulrich strode over to examine some wooden Buddhas, then asked me to get a price. I asked the man in English (Ulrich's German-accented English did not get through to the owner at all), how much it was. He explained it was part of a set that cost a total of $20.00. Ulrich frowned. I switched to Thai and said I thought that was kind of high. Both husband and wife beamed, threw a signal to each other, and the woman left to get us some tea and sweets. We chatted for a bit about Nang Rong. They were confused when I explained to them I was not from the famous Nang Rong with the waterfall in Nakhorn Nyok, but a small, town in Buriram. The Buddhas, it turned out were not that old and $20.00 was a bit high. We sipped tea as Ulrich wandered through the shop peering through glass cases at ivory chess sets.

Ulrich noticed the tea cups, walked over, downed his in one gulp and hunched forward as if at a high-stakes card game. Prices were discussed, abandoned, re-set, and finally established at $2.75 each or $5.00 for the pair. Ulrich was very happy, the owners seemed pleased and I was elated.

As we traveled from village to village, Ulrich still kept away from the local cuisine, but liked to watch me eat everything. I kept an eye out for buses or taxis, but Ulrich delighted in hitching rides and almost whooped out loud when we were picked up by a charcoal merchant in his dingy truck. He tipped freely at restaurants, always gave coins to beggars, and obliquely offered me money for my services, which I just as obliquely refused.

When it was time for him to board his bus for Bangkok, he grasped my hand and urged me to visit him in Mannheim.

"We shall take long walks in the Black Forest," he said. "It will be enormous fun to carry rucksacks filled with dark bread, cheese and knockwurst. We will walk and walk until we reach a beer garden where we shall eat everything we've carried, drink the local beer, and then take a pleasant nap in the shade. Afterwards, I'll telephone my house and have them send someone to pick us up. Yes, it will be quite nice."

"You call someone to pick you up?"

"Of course," he sighed." All the Americans think one must be a fanatic to hike. It is actually quite comfortable."

....

May 19, 1968

We parted company the next morning and I took a bus to the ancient capital of Sukhothai. I was stunned to discover that the newer part of the city had burned to the ground only days before. Only blackened foundations of buildings and temples remained along with vast swaths of ground in ash and debris and, strangely, a few clothing stalls that had managed to escape the fire. The grotesque image of a blackened, blank-faced Buddha stared out at me from an alter around which nothing remained standing.

After walking around and around the horrible, smoking ruins of what had once been a Thai city, I noticed a dozen or so people in the middle of the ashes and debris, bent over, appearing to be looking for something. That's when Mike, the local Volunteer, showed up and explained to me that there had been a fair amount of gold in the various temples and those people were trying to find whatever was left. Ironically, the oldest portions of the city had been saved and that's where Mike took me on a fast, informative tour. He told me that the name of the province, Sukhothai, meant The Dawn of Happiness. Sadly, not too many of its inhabitants will be waking up to a happy dawn any time soon.

I hadn't realized the significance of this area until Mike filled me in one some salient facts such as the founder of Sukhothai, which had once been a capital in its own right, was ruled by King Ramkhamhaeng the Great who was the one responsible for forging a Thai alphabet and pretty much set up the basis for a political system, recognized the importance of Buddhism in the lives of the people and established rules for the monarchy.

Mike and I went out for noodle soup that had delicate spices that added scents and tastes new to me. I asked him if his own house had been burned and that's when I found out he actually lived in Sawankhalok, located further north in the province. Our meeting had been pure chance because he'd only showed up to witness the aftermath of the fire. He had to tutor me for several minutes on the pronunciation of Sawankhalok, which I learned, is historically famous for its fine ceramics dating back to the 13th century. Mike told me that archeologists have discovered ceramics from this area scattered throughout Asia, probably as part of early international trade.

We took a taxi to Sawankhalok where he lived in a large, sort of ramshackle, comfortable house which we shared for the night. Next morning we were off to Pitsanalok, Taak, Uttaradit and finally Bangkok where the two of us were due to have our physical examinations. First, we treated ourselves to cheeseburgers then on to an air-conditioned viewing of Bonnie and Clyde. Seemed very well done, but incredibly violent. Both of us left the movie with heads ringing. Back at the Peace Corps office we had to take a strong purgative, wait, and then leave stool samples with the medical lab to examine for parasites. I went on to see a dentist, but had to leave Mike behind because for some reason the purgative had given him constipation! My dentist was Dr. Suwanne, absolutely gorgeous, who skillfully filled something like six cavities and told me that two molars were so bad they'd have to be pulled soon. While she was drilling away and pain started building, I looked into Suwanne's moist-black eyes, which in turn peered deeply into my own and I felt nothing but pleasure. No novocaine!

I spent the rest of the afternoon wandering the streets of Bangkok, nibbling occasionally from noodle stalls, making small talk with some merchants and realizing, to my own surprise, that I did not feel as isolated anymore.

Next morning I had fried rice with an egg on top for breakfast then off for more shots: typhus, typhoid, small pox vaccination, gamma globulin, cholera and a TB skin test. I met with the doctor for the results of my other tests and heard that I was the only one in my area who had neither worms nor intestinal parasites. He casually mentioned he'd diagnosed five cases of VD, several types of parasitic infestations, an almost ruptured appendix and a heart murmur.

Newly arrived volunteers were just arriving for their medical briefing. They looked so fat! How did I look to them?

I chatted with Oy, the front desk clerk, about what was happening with volunteers around the country. She told me that all community development programs had been temporarily suspended by the department of the Interior. That was run by General Prapas, a right wing power who obviously did not like the idea of Americans wandering his country and telling the farmers what a co-op was and how to organize themselves. Several days ago he'd cancelled an item in the legislature that would have *reviewed* the *possibility* of allowing labor unions to develop as they had existed before the military coup.

June 4, 1968

As June rolls in so do the birthdays: Thom was twenty-three on the 2nd and celebrated in Buriram. Wisut is nine days older than I am and the two of us will party right here in Nang Rong, together. He's my *elder brother*, as the Thais say, so his wish is my command. Following Thom's birthday bash, I followed a few of the community development volunteers along with malaria eradication workers out to plan a visit to the red light district. Buriram's is located in the shadow of the city's water tower, so the euphemism is we all went out to *the water tower* and had a good time. The local samlaw drivers told us a new house had opened up and the girls were so beautiful that rumor had it they'd moved here from Chiengmai where all the women are tall, lithe and pale-skinned. One of the volunteers laughed and asked the driver how much the house had paid him to spread such rumors. Since the driver just looked down, we took that to mean the women were probably short, unattractive imports from the Cambodian border. We all decided to walk and as we passed the recently shuttered stores and flickering lamps we joked about what the women would look like and I felt exhilarated, almost light-headed in anticipation. All the while, part of my was wondering about what I was about to do. I'd never done anything like this in the states. All of us had been introduced to these kinds of visits by fellow Thais who just presented the activity as part of local male culture. I remembered Thom telling me he was sure it wasn't part of *all* Thai male culture, but the truth was I felt so lonely so much of the time I just wanted to hold someone, intimately, and feel something other than a damp, sweat-soaked mattress for a change. I'd run all the other possibilities through my mind. Dating another Peace Corps volunteer? That seemed like asking for trouble and getting into something I'd have a hard time getting out of. Dating Thai women? Almost impossible considering my limited language ability and the fact that everyone in the village knew everyone else as family, so the gossip would start at once. It seemed the houses were the safest bet even if whatever happened was never more than a business transaction. I wondered if the other guys somehow fooled themselves into momentarily thinking these brief get-togethers were anything more than that? The several encounters I'd had so far certainly hadn't been wonderful sexual experiences, but they'd all involved some brief hugging and holding. One time, a fairly attractive woman began stroking my thigh in the darkness of the Nang Rong to Buriram bus and I almost came in my pants. An old crone sitting next to her cackled as she watched the show. When we reached Buriram, the old woman took me aside and said that for fifty baht I could go home with the other woman. I nodded without a thought and within minutes I stepped into a small room with her and flushed as she silently latched the door shut and blew out the kerosene lantern. That was one of the few times I felt as if more than a commercial transaction had taken place and not just because the sex itself wasn't the typical mechanical movements. When we were finished I held her close to me and almost cried at finding myself body-to-body with another person. Soon, though, she slipped away and stood in the middle of the floor. Puzzled, I sat up, swung my legs over the edge of the bed and peered out at her.

She was on her knees, head bowed almost to the floor saying *thank you* over and over and she shuffled across the floor to hug my legs. I felt goosebumps and waves of what? Love? Closeness? A kind of free-floating tenderness to her. I tried to make her stand, but she kept shaking her head. I began to feel upset with myself. Why was another human being doing this to me? For me? It was all too much. I got off the bed, dressed and walked out, making sure to leave a generous tip on the mat. The old lady who'd led me there was crouched by the door. She'd probably been watching the whole thing through a hole in the wall. Leaving the place behind me, I was sad and irritated at the woman for making me feel so badly about myself.

Weeks later, I was talking with a guy in charge of a surveying crew running a new highway into town and he asked me if I'd been to any of the local houses. I admitted I'd been to a few and we joked about the *water tower* jokes. He rolled his eyes and said, "You know, I was here a few weeks ago and some old crone hooked me up with an absolutely knockout woman. I couldn't believe she was a hooker. Most of the gals I've encountered here have been complete skags, but this woman was not only really attractive, but kind of subdued and quiet. Always looking down, if you know what I mean. I nodded, knowingly, but filled with growing apprehension. "Hey, I guess you must know about the one I'm talking about, right?" I nodded again. "You know the part I really liked," he said, grinning, " is right after you screw, she gets out of bed, gets down on her knees and bows. Man, made me feel like a million bucks. On top of that, she was a great lay, wasn't she? Really soft and…"

I was toying with a steak knife imagining slitting his throat, but somehow managed to keep a neutral expression and let the conversation run its course. I *hated* him. Really *hated* him. But, why? It was just business, wasn't it? Was it because he'd so easily shattered some illusion I'd accepted that I'd been a different man to her than any of the dozens of other she'd slept with? Was it some sort of possessiveness on my part, or did I actually care about her? I never returned to that house again. I later heard she'd married a government worker who'd been passing through on business.

One of the guys I was walking with suddenly looked up and said, "That must be it up ahead. That place with the pink light in the doorway."

We stumbled toward the light, all of us light-headed and drunk, joking with each other as guys do when they're about to do something they're not really proud of.

Suddenly, I remembered. The woman's name was Oraphim. No, no, I told myself. Don't think of her name.

Several Thai guys were standing on the front porch and a few were inside talking with the woman when we approached. The men all quickly got up and walked away. The women looked us over, definitely unhappy.

"Where did you soldiers come from?" One asked. "They said there weren't going to be any soldiers here," another chimed in.

"We're not soldiers," someone said.

"Not only are we not soldiers," said Richie, a guy who'd already re-enlisted for another year of community development work, "but we all speak Thai and we eat rice and we like hot food!"

All the women burst out laughing and began talking to us and to each a mile a minute. Several began to chatter in some Cambodian dialect, which Richie understood, and quickly interjected a few words of Cambodian slang, to the effect, *No use trying to be sneaky and speaking Cambodian, because I know that, too!*

At the sound of someone speaking Cambodian, several Thais came back inside. Richie delivered one of his standard community action talks in Khmer dialect, which, considering the situation, was pretty funny. Everyone applauded when he finished. Someone went out for beer, the women dropped their professional roles and went into a back kitchen to boil up some rice and create some really hot curry. We passed the camera around and everyone took photos of everyone else. There was no thought of business and we all stayed for an hour more drinking beer, talking and eating the volcanic curry. During a lull in the conversation I saw a few of the women giving each other a look that seemed to say, *Okay, fun's fun, but we're working girls and it's time to take the next step.* The Thai men laughed and pointed back and forth making jokes about who they thought would team up. But, it was just too much of a circus atmosphere and we told them we'd be back at a later, calmer evening and maybe, if they were good, even give them copies of the pictures.

The next morning Thom sarcastically asked if we'd had a good time. I described what had happened and how it'd turned into nothing more than a happy get-together, but he didn't believe me.

"You think I'm making this all up," I asked him, "so as not to let you think we're just a bunch of lust-driven pigs?"

"Well, yes, I do."

I stared back at him until he had to grin.

"Okay, I believe you. But, the whole idea of going to those places is just nauseating. Why do you do it, Burgess?"

Richie looked up in mock surprise.

"Why do *you* do it, Burgess? Oh, is Burgess the only one who has a soul worth saving? The rest of us are just unrepentant degenerates who will never be saved? Is that it?"

"Yes," Thom said. "That is it! I don't have anything to say to the rest of you, but Burgess knows better and he should be ashamed."

I felt my face turn red as Thom turned to leave under a barrage of heckles and groans.

June 6, 1968

Bored after correcting a stack of papers, I turned on the Armed Forces Network and heard the announcer say in a matter-of-fact tone that the long-awaited James Brown concert was canceled. In the same breath, he went on to say that later in the evening there would be a special program about the ASSASSINATION of Senator Robert Kennedy!

What is happening in my country? Are the Kennedys only being raised as rifle fodder? Is Ted Kennedy next? I remember waiting in a long line for hours to hear Teddy speak at the University of Massachusetts. I don't know how many hundreds they crammed into that auditorium. We all stared up at the microphone-studded podium, waiting for him to appear. There was a stir as the senator walked toward the stage from the back. A high-pitched buzzing followed him. As he turned on stage to look out at us, I felt (or heard) a sigh of relief as if to say, "He's safe with us. On this stage he must be safe." Problems with the microphone prompted him to make a disparaging remark about the Republican who'd installed the PA system. He moved into his speech from a wave of laughter, punctuating his message with that familiar chopping motion of his hands. Midway through his speech, while pausing to turn a page, there was the explicit sound of a *click* that reverberated through the hall. He stared up at the balcony with a stricken expression. At that instant, we all saw the dormant fear he must carry every day suddenly etched on his face. But it turned out to be nothing more than old wood settling, and the tension receded. He continued to speak.

So, what happened to Robert Kennedy?

Just yesterday I'd finished putting pictures of all the candidates on my bedroom wall, with some apt quote under each one, for any visiting student to read. Under Robert Kennedy's photo I had printed "The Once and Future King."

I knew deep inside I really wanted McCarthy to get the Democratic nomination.

Shit, the announcer just made the announcement again. It must be true.

Yes, so I was for McCarthy, but Kennedy was always so *real* to me. I rooted for McCarthy even though part of me felt he was a will-o-wisp candidate compared to the hard-driving Kennedy. McCarthy might come up with great legislation, but it would take a Kennedy to get anything through Congress. I'll bet the conservatives are all hugging each other now. I only hope McCarthy gets nominated and elected now if for no other reason than to strengthen the civil rights voting act.

Now the announcer is saying he was shot by a Palestinian! What? Who? Something about his being angry about a speech the senator had made in support of Israel. I just feel like crying. It's as if John Kennedy was just killed all over again and I'm standing in the parking lot of a school with my car radio turned up as the bad news reverberates across campus.

I cannot believe there's some inane commentary now about an up-coming beauty contest. Stupid small talk comparing Thai and American standards of beauty. How can they go so far off the real news? I keep feeling the news over and over again, blaming *them*, whoever *them* may be. What kind of maniacs do we have floating around the United States? I'll bet anything he was killed by some mail-order gun and the NRA will be right on message saying this is no reason to squelch small arms sales. I don't even know if Kennedy won the California primary. Recent news from the states never really touched me, but now I wish I was there. I wonder what the Thais will say. Will they care that much? Ah, but then, would I be mourning their Premier Kittikatchorn? Not much.

Some people take a piece of you when they die. Donne, of course, was right. Listen to the bell tolling.

Now, Dean Martin is singing. How can they maintain normal programming at a time like this? How sad are the Joint Chiefs?

I simply have to cope with the world I'm in and hope my country will continue to produce the energy people, the real people like Robert Kennedy, ones you don't have to touch to know they exist, live, pulsing with the will to be!

Damn   Damn   Damn

....

June 10, 1968

Bob Rice, a Peace Corps evaluator, came out to see how I was getting along. He arrived hours after his expected time, exhausted, with red-veined eyes, dripping white mustache and losing more sweat by the minute than I did in a day. I'd hoped to show him the early morning market, but there was nothing left by the time he appeared than tiny smoked fish and crustaceans from local ponds. He came on very friendly, apologizing for his late arrival and mentioned he'd already visited every other Volunteer in the country. I was his last. I was afraid whatever conclusions he may have expected to reach about PCVs must have already been realized or discarded. Poor, little, ragged Nang Rong and skinny Mr. Burgess could not possibly make any difference in his final summation.

Since the Boy Scout celebration had been the night before, my students were exhausted and could hardly sit straight, never mind perform. We ran through a few verb substitution drills, then I gave them a writing assignment while Mr. Rice looked through old compositions.

Whenever he looked away from then, the students all stared. They whispered among themselves how strange it was to see a man named *rice*. He looked up a few times and smiled. I suddenly realized he couldn't speak Thai. He was simply someone who roamed the world making these sorts of evaluations, but he'd undoubtedly heard plenty of jokes of his name after reviewing several hundred volunteers.

I pulled out stacks of student haikus my students had been working on. Now, that had been a difficult lesson explaining the structure of haikus: three lines having, respectively, 5, 7, 5 syllables per line. I didn't try to limit them to any topic, just have them write about whatever topic came to them. Miss Utsanee's was on top of the pile and Bob Rice smiled when he read it.

dog bit my father
My father was very sad
I shall bite the dog

Next, I showed him papers written by the MS-3 class on their outside activities. A girl named Imerb had handed in a dandy.

On Saturday I went to Buriram. I bought a piece of cloth. It was very beautiful, but it was very cheap. I like the color of light purple. It is my favorite color. In the afternoon, I went to my friend's house and we castrated roses.

Imerb's little gem made my day.

Mr. Rice, heavy-lidded and impatient, commandeered a taxi for himself and returned to the train station and waited for a connection to Bangkok. Hope he checked into a nice hotel with A/C and patted himself on the back for all his hard work.

After he left, I did some chores at school, bought a few odds and ends at the market and walked home through indescribable heat. Wisut must've been off on one of his own errands and all I wanted to do was throw a few plastic pails of cold water over my head and crash on my springy little cot. But the neighborhood dogs decided this was as good a time as any to serenade me with howls beneath my house. Maybe they were waiting for another batch of bad bread. Where were the cobras now that I needed them?

Preparations for the Wisut/Burgess birthday party: three quarts of Mekhong whiskey, a gallon of *sato*, a dozen bags of peanuts, several pounds of fried beef, half a dozen roasted pig legs and several large platters of fresh and fried vegetables. Wisut set up a table outside the house and strung colored lights in and out of the shrubbery. We even have a microphone and speaker in case, as Wisut phrased it "…people maybe want to say something…" Fred arrived last night and Thom arrives tomorrow with another American who is here courtesy of some pharmaceutical giant to do research on southeast Asian parasites.

Since I hadn't heard anything from John, a nearby malaria eradication worker who sometimes hung out with Fred, I decided to pay him a visit at his home in Surin Province. Standing in front of what I hoped was his house, I asked some young ladies if an American volunteer named *John* lived there. They stared at me, puzzled, and one finally said, "No one by that name live here." I explained the person I was looking for was six feet tall, thin, with blue eyes and brown hair and worked for the malaria office. "Oh!" they all chorused. "You mean *John*!" I felt my brain beginning to short out, then realized that the *John* I spoke out loud was said in a rising tone, because I'd been pronouncing it as part of a question. Their *John* was spoken in a low tone. Two completely different names as far as they were concerned. Once that was straightened out, I knocked on the door and said, "Hello *John* (low tone), how's it going?" He rolled his eyes and asked, "Okay, what's that all about?" I told him. Next time I saw him at my party I called out "Hi *John*! (falling tone" He said, "I'm sorry, you must have me confused with someone else. My name isn't *John* (falling tone). My name is *John* (low tone)." Guess you had to be there.

"How's the job going?" I asked him.

"Very low morale here. These guys were on a low pay scale and they'll do, or not do, whatever they need to in order to get by. I confronted one of my sector chiefs with 15 blank spaces where he was supposed to check in upon arrival. The guy laughed in my face, checked off 15 spaces and walked away."

"What's that mean?"

"It means he's got another job to make ends meet and because he's civil service he knows he'll never be fired."

"I've got a cousin like that back in Boston. He works for the post office. Same thing."

We hung out for a while, then I had to hurry back to Nang Rong to greet my regional rep and his wife who were passing through. I showed them around and that evening I treated them to an excellent meal at the Raxana Restaurant. Early next day we took a bus out to the 11th Century Khmer-style Hindu ruins at Phanom Rung dedicated to Shiva. Eerie feeling walking through the remains of palaces and temples built before Columbus took off from Spain. How did they manage to move those enormous stone blocks? And, what held it all together? There was no sign of mortar. All precise cutting and engineering.

We would have liked to stay and examine the workmanship, but it was so hot and humid our stay was brief.

After they left I asked Wisut to fill me in some more on the ruins we'd just visited. He said they were extremely old, even before the advent of Buddhism. He said most of the people at that time belong to something called *Pram*. Could he tell me more about it? He said this *Pram* had three major gods and to make it even more complicated these gods sometimes appeared in other forms. Our little talk took forever because both of us kept turning to dictionaries. I asked him what the names of the three gods were. He said the only one he remembered for sure was called Prasiwa. Within one of the smaller buildings there was a magic stone that represented Prasiwa's penis and was called a *siwalyngam*.

I remembered in one of Han Suyin's books there was a reference to a similar stone called simply a *lingam*. Sounded like the same thing. I was frustrated that Wisut and I talked at cross purposes. I asked if he'd ever heard of a God called Krishna. He said he hadn't but he would look some other words up. A few minutes later he totally surprised by asking me if I'd ever heard of something called Hindu. He said *Pram* was another word for Hindu. Then, he asked if I'd ever heard of a God named Krisna. I took a deep breath and said I'd just asked him that myself. He shook his head and said, no, I'd asked him about a God named Krishna, with an 'sh' sound. Keep calm, I told myself. We're almost at the end. After a few more minutes I decided my original idea had been correct. Phanom Rung, built by the ancient Khmers, was a center of Hinduism. So, this Prasiwa was actually Siva or Shiva! The guide book had been correct!

Another teacher, Mr. Prayun, came by and he knew enough English to explain that the footprint of Buddha located at the mountain top is an example of Buddhism's acceptance of other religions. The gold squares that I'd seen carefully pressed on to that stone could have been placed there by members of an early form of Hinduism or maybe even some earlier cults that still existed in India along with various types of animism still strong in remote Thai villages along with the tiny spirit houses seen in front of many homes. I sighed. Mr. Prayun told me I had to go to his house and he would tell me more about the history of Buddhism. After he left, Wisut dropped his dictionary and said we had to start making plans for our combined birthday party coming up. I agreed, but told him I had to first take a break and check out my developed slides from my trip to Chiengmai and surrounding villages. He nodded and left for the market.

I peered at the slides through a small viewer. There was a beautiful shot of a silk-worm farm that reminded me of my initial surprise at seeing how silk is made into fabric: very shallow straw baskets were filled with mulberry leaves that had the silkworms feeding on them that wove cocoons, the silk cocoons were taken from the baskets and hung on branches of nearby trees, after the pupas emerged they took the cocoons off the branches and put them in pots of boiling water making sure to pull free one strand of silk which is itself attached to a bobbin that winds that one strand with four others to make one final strand of silk thread which is deposited into a waiting basket. That's the raw material. After the thread is boiled and bleached, it is woven on hand-looms into yards or bolts of silk; all in all, a laborious, exacting process which doesn't yield much of a cash crop for the peasants, but realized large amounts for the final product overseas.

By the time I'd gone through all the slides, Wisut was back, pacing the living room. He dragged me out of the house to the scene of the future party. We began setting up tables and getting food and drinks ready. More people showed up than the two of us expected. All the teachers from the school appeared along with the entire local Peace Corps malaria program. There were also representatives there from the famed meteorology and electric generating departments. Tons of food and drink, dancing. Best of all, no one threw up. My American guests were surprised and entertained by Mr. Wasan, the weatherman, and his ability to sing every Elvis Presley song ever recorded. Strangely enough, the one song everyone knew and joined in to sing together was Hava Nagila. We surely live on a united planet.

Wandering around outside the following morning all I found were a few peanut shells and *sato* stains on the concrete pad beneath my house. Then, I discovered I was not alone. Fred, the malaria guy, had been the first one up this and he joined Thom in setting up a breakfast for me of tea and coconut pie (purchased at Pensee's restaurant in Buriram the day before and carefully packed in ice for my morning's pleasure). Wisut was gone by the time we'd finished the pie, so he was not on hand to see the stares that greeted us all as we trooped through Nang Rong. I waved goodbye to everyone at the bus depot, then turned to face the new day.

....

June 27, 1968

It took my stomach a long time to recover from the party and I've been subsisting on weak soup and boiled rice. I woke up today feeling better, maybe because it turned out to be only 85 in the shade. My classes have gone smoothly and I even pronounced all the names closely enough so that the students responded when I called them.

There's been loud banging and clanging for the past few days as a new green, metal roof is installed on the school. I imagined if any enemy aircraft flew overhead they wouldn't notice us because the roof blended us in to the rest of the greenery. From light breakfast through the school's lunch of frog curry my gut held up pretty well so I decided it was time for a treat and stuffed myself in one of the town's restaurants. Although I was looking forward to eating alone, a border patrol guy noticed me and, after grabbing a few of his friends, sauntered over to my table. He asked the owner what I was having, grunted, and quickly gave him orders before sitting down with his friends who all took turns telling me how handsome I was. The one I'd known from before, Manny (at his insistence), spoke fairly fluent English and I discovered he'd been tutored by the town's former volunteer. The table was quickly covered with bottles of freezing Thai beer, plates of *moo daeng* (roast red pork), fried morning glory leaves in oyster sauce and warm cashews. Manny filled me in on border incursions and how much he hated the Cambodians. Soon, the rest of the order arrived and we had to add on another table to hold it all: wide rice noodles in thick gravy with pork; gang *massaman* (Manny insisted and the chef explained the name of this dish came from the fact it was created by Muslims and contained: curry with coconut milk, pepper, tomatoes, brown sugar, fish sauce, tamarind, cardamon and other spices and chunks of beef—it was all too much to follow)); *mee krop* (crisp noodles over an incredibly delicious kind of sweet stew); *khao soi* (chicken curry made especially in the north). Manny told me it originated in Burma, and is another dish of crisp noodles served over red curry, coconut milk and chicken. I was told to squeeze a quarter of a lime over it just before eating. Fantastically delicious).

As the meal went on and more border patrol guys joined us, the restaurant heated up and we ordered more beer. Manny clutched my shoulders and told everyone how he used to think the previous volunteer, Charlotte, was the best American he'd ever met, but now….well, NOW, he'd found a new best friend. And, why didn't we all leave the restaurant together and go find some beautiful Thai woman. Everyone burst into laughter. Yes, yes, they insisted, I would go with them and have sex with some beautiful Thai women and they would be proud to have me with them because, after all, wasn't I handsome, intelligent, brave and very light skinned, strong, impossible to get drunk and most of all, wasn't my dick the biggest in the world? Wild laughter all around.

We began to spice our beer with shots of Mekhong whiskey. I remembered a character from Cheever's Wapshot Chronicle thinking 'whiskey on beer, never fear/ beer on whiskey, very risky.' So, I was safe. Okay, time to fake them all out! Smiling, I turned to Manny, clasped his hand and proclaimed *"Niang silang bong-tay?"* (which means "Do you love me?" in the same dialect). As it happens, that is all I know in that dialect, but it was enough to win over five drunk border patrol guys into believing I was a master linguist. The restaurant owner cautiously approached the table (probably because he was scared shitless of these young, drunk guys with automatic weapons) and asked politely we take our trade somewhere else. One of the guys, a teenager, growled something in his direction, but Manny quieted him and we all got unsteadily to our feet, threw piles of money o the table, and headed out for Manny's house. I whispered a few words of apology to the owner, who patted me on the back and said it was all okay. We ended up at the home of their sergeant who happily invited all of us inside where we drank even more whiskey and soda, danced the night away right out into the street until I was so dizzy someone had to carry me home.

Although Nang Rong School is relatively small by national standards, thanks to astute behind-the-scenes management by the headmaster, Adjan Komanchai, it is affluent. The headmaster has skillfully developed sources in Bangkok and Buriram, along with local fund-raising affairs to the point we have had a hefty operating surplus for many years. This extra cash was placed in an interest-bearing fund with district personnel administering its growth. Recently, with so many projects going on at once, the school, for the first time in a decade, had run out of operating capital and sent a request to the local Education

Office for a transfer of funds. After some delay, the headmaster became tired of filling out the same forms and walked over to their office in person. Not being one to quibble when many baht were at stake, he walked into the office of the highest official and demanded to know why the fund transfer had not been made. There was a brief silence, then he was told the official knew of no such request, but to please wait and he would call in his second-in-command. In a re-telling of the story, the headmaster said the man who came through the door and saw him, turned "whiter than the foreigner (me)." It turned out there was a small matter of 40,000 baht missing. At the moment, the local jail has a former highly-placed education in one of its cells. Long live Thai justice!

Speaking of justice, the new Thai Constitution has finally been presented to the king for his signature. It's been over ten years to get the wording sufficiently vague to be approved. General Phrapas, Head of the Department of the Interior, Inspector of the Port of Bangkok and director of several other plum assignments naturally had deep power over its final wording and approval.

While the Constitution was slowly prepared for presentation, word around Bangkok was that whole new vistas of civil liberties were opening up. Many of the more sophisticated members of society viewed the new Constitution as a kind of Bill of Rights that guaranteed new freedoms such as the right to petition and the right to congregate. Near the Parliament Building, a crowd gathered a few days ago to demonstrate against raising the bus fare. Many students from Thamasat University stood patiently to hear the speakers. A cordon of police arrived along with high-pressure hoses, tank trucks and a few riot squads. For the first time in recent Thai history the people did not instinctively disband and slink away at the first sign of government strength. As things turned out, the crowd turned on the troops, pushing them aside, and walked in a mass toward the central complex of government buildings, cheered on by several nearby Peace Corps volunteers. The police and soldiers were so taken aback by what happened, they were momentarily stunned into silence. General Phrapas immediately made an announcement that although Thailand now had a Constitution, it didn't mean that martial law had been lifted. Groups of more than five people were to be disbanded, more stringent measures were soon to be introduced to guarantee Thailand's independence from Communist influences! And, domestic tranquility would be maintained! One person who does not have to worry about tranquility is the general himself who is so loaded with titles, honors, interests and owed favors the only thing he needs to worry about is the safety of his personal hoard of gold. He is also in charge of all primary schools. His staff made the primary schools part of the Ministry of the Interior. I suppose there may come a time when students stand in front of their schools in the morning to salute the flag, honor their king, say a prayer to Buddha and promise to kiss you know who, where. Still, there is a piece of paper called the Constitution and many Thais have hope for the future.

June 29, 1968

A new nai amphur (mayor), Adjan Somchai, has been brought in to find the facts behind the embezzlement scandal that was discovered in the Office of Education. Wisut explained to me that everyone had some idea there was a shortage of funds, but everyone was also very much concerned with *graehng jai.*

The phrase means that you are reluctant to impose upon someone or simply being aware of someone's feelings or respecting someone's privacy. Whether there was general stealing going on or not, the person who points a finger becomes the one who has disturbed the status quo. *Graehng jai* always lets everyone know exactly where they are in relation to anyone else. If someone stands low in the grand scheme of things they tend not to say anything negative about the person who stands higher. I kept waiting to hear the result of the investigation, but I came away with the sense there were too many people involved, meaning too many people would be hurt, and it was better all around if the district somehow restored the funds and dropped the whole matter completely.

Out of the blue, Wisut asked me if I knew who Lord Baden-Powell was. He expressed astonishment when I admitted the name sounded only vaguely familiar.

"He started the Boy Scouts," Wisut exclaimed.

Meaning?

"Tomorrow is Boy Scout Day."

Meaning?

"All Thais celebrate Boy Scout day, including Nangong School's students."

Ah, that meant I had to get ready for some sort of celebration tomorrow. I was told it was very important for the students because this was a time they could more easily win some merit badges. There were going to be speeches and parties and everyone had to wear their scout uniforms and those uniforms had to be spotless with sharp creases. Wisut also mentioned it was a bad day for him because the headmaster reminded him that if he did not get himself a pair of boy scout shorts, he'd pay for them himself. I wondered if Wisut never wore shorts because he was so small that shorts would make him look like a student himself. I don't know how he got out of it, but I never saw him in shorts. Ever.

June 30, 1968

I bumped into Manny, the border patrol guy from the big dinner, and we had a small reunion of sorts an other restaurant. For the first time, a Thai asked me if he could pay for his half of the meal later because he was short of cash. I stammered that I barely had enough for my own half. He brushed away my protestations and told the owner to put the whole tab on his account. Then, in a low voice to me, said, "Tomorrow, you take me out, okay?"

I dumbly nodded. Later, I told Wisut about what had happened and he asked me, "You going out with him a lot?"

I said I didn't think it'd be that often, then asked why. He calmly told me that Manny had recently tracked down a few Cambodian peasants who's stolen a water buffalo and blew them away with his Smith & Wesson.

Then I remembered during the drunken scene at the Smile Restaurant Manny had whispered to me that if anyone ever gave me any trouble, to just let him know and he'd take care of it. Great. It was like a gift from the Mafia, and I knew they always came with strings.

Wonderful breakfast of fried rice, eggs and tea under dappled sunlight reading John Barth's *The Floating Opera*. Then, I forced myself to study Thai verbs and memorize vocabulary. Memories returned of that wonderful bakery/restaurant in Vientiane where they served cheese omelets, baked their own croissants and crusty tarts along with newly-ground coffee and real cream.

Meanwhile, times are very much changing right here in Nang Rong Village. For the first time, I noticed quite a few of the morning market vendors sold their wares in plastic baggies rather than banana leaves. I was reminded of that when a light breeze blew a used baggy right up to my feet as I enjoyed my fried rice. Probably won't be long now before they'll find plastic in the small streams and bobbing on the surface of *Nong Tamue*. Progress? Meanwhile, Mayor Somchai took it upon himself to have the local power plant renovated in order to start generating electricity twenty-four hours a day! Within a few days, a truck from Buriram arrived carrying a huge new generator and, suddenly, the lights no longer went out at 10:00 PM What will it all mean to the early morning market when people know they can buy refrigerators and have food fresh for days at a time?

July 5, 1968

Whether it was in honor of July 4th or just because he's a good guy, Thom telegraphed me from Buriram that he'd received a care package from home and, since all the other volunteers were out of town, would I share his goodies with him? Quicker than you could say George Washington is the father of our country I was on the bus from Nang Rong to Buriram where I oooh'd and ahhh'd as Thom unveiled the treats: instant soups with dried chemically preserved noodles; small, tins of beef stew made with shreds of beef and slivers of potatoes all bathed in chemical preservatives; potatoes chips (mostly whole); and most astoundingly, a large, plastic bag of marshmallows.

We each had the same idea at once. Share the marshmallows with students. Brilliant! Then I realized Thom was staring at the floor shaking his head.

"What's wrong?"

"What do you think?" he asked me. "I mean, really?!!"

"They'll eat them! I know they will."

"Oh, sure, maybe a little. You know these kids are not half as adventurous as we are when we're presented with something smelly on a plate. One of them will take a nibble, try not to make a face, and when I ask him if he liked it he'll say, 'Yes, my teacher' and that'll be the end of it."

"I don't know what else we could do except maybe serve it over rice."

"Yeah, maybe with some fish sauce (he grimaced)."

"And some *som dam*," I said, referring to a very hot side dish made with sliced papayas and chili peppers.

"Yes, well, the point is we've got a few dozen marshmallows here and I think that we…wait a minute. Here's Somchai, one of my students."

A short boy with a nervous smile warily stepped in holding an English workbook. He gave each of us a half bow.

"My teacher, you help me with the gerund?"

"Okay," Thom said. "But, first I want you to taste something."

Somechai looked around uneasily. Thom opened the bag and took out a marshmallow and handed it to him.

"Here. Taste that."

Somechai held it gingerly, raised it near his nose, sniffed it briefly then pressed it with his fingers.

"Is joke?" he laughed.

We looked at each other uncertain of his meaning.

"No," I assured him. "It's not a joke. It's food."

"Not true, my teacher. Is plastic."

"He may have something there," Thom sighed.

"No, really, Somchai." I said earnestly. It's a kind of candy. Take a bite."

"I sorry to bother you," he said. "You help me with gerund tomorrow?"

Somchai bowed once to each of us and left.

"We've got problems," I said.

"No problem," he said. "We're going to have a party."

That afternoon, we bought new batteries for Thom's portabe record player, cleaned the back yard, cooked a cauldron of rice, sent out for several different curries from the best restaurant in town and contacted as many students as we could to spread the word that a party was about to be held at Thom's house.

By six o'clock the temperature had dropped to the low 80s, the rapid train to Bangkok had just pulled in out of the station, samlaw drivers encircled the train station searching for fares, the last taxi to Nangong Village was off and away and students began to arrive at Thom's place. Neighbor's opened their shutters and peered out at the festivities. The students stood around in their casual, after-school clothes, trying hard to appear calm. When we began to hand out plates of rice and curry everyone began to talk at once and the record player blared out popular Thai songs and American rock and roll numbers.

The kids started singing along with the music and even danced a few tentative steps to gauge our reaction. We walked out to the center of the yard and joined them.

"My teacher, is party?" one asked.

Thom nodded.

"Is holiday?"

I shook my head.

"Birthday! Birthday for our teachers!" Somchai shouted.

"No," Thom said. "Just a party."

"How old are you?" a student asked me.

"It's not my birthday either," I said.

He looked puzzled. It was getting dark and most of the kids had finished eating and were standing around in small groups talking quietly.

"Listen everybody," Thom called out. "I want everyone to find a few small pieces of wood and make a pile in the middle of the yard."

Several boys ran quickly towards the edge of the house looking for wood while the others waited for Thom to repeat himself in Thai and then go on to explain that we wanted to start a fire. Excited, the joined the others and quickly raised an enormous pile of dead branches, dried leaves and wood scraps. Thom lit the pile and as the flames rose higher, we stood in a circle as people have done for thousands of years and stared at the flames, entranced by the mystery and beauty of fire. Night had fallen.

While I stayed behind to talk with a few students, Thom quietly slipped into his house and emerged with his bag of marshmallows. I noticed that Somchai recognized the bag. He whispered something to a friend who in turn covered his mouth, giggled, and passed what he knew to someone else.

Thom held up the bag. It was very quiet.

"This is some special dessert from America," he said in a quavery voice, and then repeated himself in Thai with more self-assurance.

There was an unintelligible babble from the crowd and then several voices were heard to murmur, "Not true. Plastic!"

The circle of students around the fire widened. Thom, exasperated, reached into the bag and pulled out a marshmallow which he held out for all to see in the flickering light.

"This is food!" he declared. "I want everyone to find a long piece of bamboo for themselves and then return here."

More babbling, and then the crowd dispersed.

"Do you think this will go over?" I asked.

"This could be the beginning of a legend," he whispered.

Soon, all the students had returned with bamboo sticks. Thom reached out for Somchai's piece, jammed the marshmallow on the tip and held it over the fire. It immediately burst into flames, flared then began to turn black. He pulled it back. Somchai regarded the black, wrinkled mass with open distaste.

"This is a present for Somchai," Thom said.

Everyone laughed. Somchai made a face. Thom held it closer to Somchai's mouth, but its appearance made him retreat.

I walked over and peered closely at the marshmallow remains.

"It looks like coal," I said in Thai.

A fresh wave of laughter erupted mingled with shouts of "Plastic! Plastic!"

"Thank you, Burgess," Thom muttered. "Now I know what friends are for."

Carefully tugging at the crisp nugget, Thom managed to get most of it off the bamboo, trailing strands of white ooze on the ground. Raising it to his lips, he daintily nibbled the outer layer, then, with a sigh of rapture, gobbled the whole piece. The crowd moaned and some of the future clowns pretended to throw up or else turned in frantic circles holding their stomachs in mock agony. Acting as if he were totally unaware of these shenanigans, Thom deftly lodged another marshmallow on to the bamboo and again held it over the fire. This time the students watched more closely as he let it turn black, cool, and then pop it into his mouth. Somchai appeared more dismayed than anyone else.

"And now," Thom said. "It is Somchai's turn."

After being slapped on the back by several friends, Somchai ventured forth and burned his own marshmallow. When it cooled, he shut his eyes and then as if his toe-nails were slowly being removed, he raised it to his mouth and took a small bite, then a larger one, and finally jammed the entire piece inside and chewed it with gusto.

"What do you think?" Thom asked.

"My teacher…."

"Yes?"

"May I have another one?"

And then came the flood. A dozen bodies wedged in around us and the bag of marshmallows. Hands reached out to yank away globs of the oft, white irregular cubes. Within a very short time there were over a dozen bamboo sticks held over the fire and other students were yelling at them to step aside. Somchai was allowed his own space, perhaps in honor of having been so brave.

Later, when the fire began to die, we sat on the ground and sang songs. One by one, the students got up to leave, but before doing so they all stopped by Thom and thanked him. As the last group left, they playfully punched Somchai and kidded him about the delicious *plastic*. The great marshmallow party had come to an end.

Since it was still fairly early, Thom and I decided to walk into town and celebrate the Great Marshmallow Roast by indulging in a fine meal of Thai food. Thom's fluency seemed to have increased exponentially and the instant we sat at a table the owner came over for some conversation. I gathered Thom asked for something really delicious and then, unlike restaurant meals with my other friends, we sipped iced tea. The meal that eventually arrived was fried red curry pork (*mu pad gang dang*). Served with coconut milk and plenty of rice to soften the spiciness, the curry was absolutely superb. It was as if so many meals of Thai food I'd had before only prepared me for this one. We each lit up a cigarette when the last of the curry was gone and Thom started throwing out some possible desserts. We settled on Mango and Sticky Rice and Coconut Sauce (*Kao niew moon mamuang*). This turned out to be the absolutely perfect dessert for the occasion, with a mixture of sweetness and saltiness all melded together with the sticky rice. I felt full and wonderful and even virtuous at not having had even a sip of Mekhong.

I left for Nang Rong early the next morning in a taxi, but arrived to find the whole village totally silent. The taxi driver started mumbling to himself as if he couldn't quite figure out what was happening. All the stores were shuttered. No one was walking around. The morning market was deserted. It was like a scene out of the Twilight Zone. I told the driver to let me off at the school. I spotted Wisut standing close to the flagpole, hands in his pockets, staring down at the ground. He looked up as I got out and walked toward him. I'd never seen the expression on his face before: sadness beyond grief.

"What's the matter?" I asked him.

"Little girl ran in street very early this morning and taxi from Buriram just hit her very hard and she fly into air and she die."

"Oh my God, I am so sorry to hear that."

"Yes, that is why everything stop now. Everyone wonder what to do."

"What do you mean?"

He looked at me incredulously.

"Little girl was killed by car. This never happen before. No one knows what to do now? Maybe stop taxis from coming."

"You mean, this was the first time a child was killed by a taxi?"

"First time. Yes, first time," he repeated.

It took me a while to process what he was saying because I was coming from a country where tens of thousands of people were killed every year by cars and now I was hearing about a town treating a traffic fatality as if it were the end of the world. The enormity of the tragedy overwhelmed me. No wonder the shops were closed. I was in the middle of great changes: plastic baggies to replace banana leaves, electricity now available all day, a new paved road to the provincial capital, taxis available now for a much faster ride out of town and the town's first traffic fatality. The silence was deafening.

July 27, 1968

Since my last entry, I visited Bangkok for an annual physical exam and there I met the Peace Corps physician, Dr. Copley. As I stood before him in his office, he stared at me intently and then back at a picture in my medical folder.

"You don't look like the picture in here at all," he said.

"That's me all right," I said, looking at the snapshot.

"But, your chin in real life is much larger than it appears here."

"I photograph well," I said. "What can I say?"

"Hmmmm, let me ask you a few questions. Have you noticed any problems putting on gloves?"

"Gloves?" I asked in dismay.

Both of us were sweating even under the fan in his office.

"Oh, of course not, what am I thinking? You wouldn't be wearing gloves here, now would you? How about shoes? Any trouble getting your shoes on?"

"No," I said, fearing the worst. "My pants are feeling a little loose. Maybe that's because I've lost so much weight. The collar of my shirt is loose."

"That's not relevant. Do you wear a hat?"

"Yes, but it's a big, old straw hat that was always too big."

"Too big!" he exclaimed. "Now, that doesn't fit."

By this time I was really worried.

"What do you think is wrong with me?"

"Frankly," he said, "You have a classic profile for someone with acromegaly."

I collapsed back in my chair.

"How do you know?"

"One is never sure at the early stages," he said. "Let me tell you about it."

I tried to relax but my hand kept straying to my chin.

"The condition of acromegaly is caused by a malfunction of the pituitary gland. When you're young, this gland is responsible for sending out growth hormones and when you reach maturity this activity stops and the bones begin to calcify. With acromegaly, the pituitary gland, for reasons yet unknown, wakes up, ceases being dormant and begins to send growth hormones to the head, hands and feet. Did I ask if you have trouble getting your shoes on?"

"No," I whispered. "No trouble at all."

"Well, there are still some other tests to be made. You know, if this condition, this secretion of the pituitary, increases beyond normal rates during early life a condition known as gigantism occurs."

I suddenly had a sharp image: a photo from a biology test of an enormous man with his arms draped over the shoulders of his normal parents. Was that it?"

"But, that's not *your* condition," he said. "We need to check and see if there have been changes in your skeletal profile. I'll write a prescription for you to get some new X-rays and we'll compare with the ones we have on file. See if they're congruent."

"And, if they're not?"

"That'd be a good indication you have acromegaly and we would need to take steps to treat it."

"Did I catch this in Thailand?" I asked.

"You don't *catch* acromegaly," he said, smiling. "Did I ask you about your shoes?"

"Yes, they fit fine."

"Yes, well, we'll need to have some X-rays taken, you understand?"

"Uh huh, what happens if whatever I have isn't treated?"

"The bones in your head, hands and feet will continue to grow until your brain is crushed and you'll die."

I realized I'd developed a pounding headache, my shoes no longer fit, my hands enlarged before my eyes and I sensed my chin jutted out before me."

"Acromegaly is a rather esoteric condition," he said. "It's so statistically rare I should never see even one case here during my tenure. The fact is, I've already diagnosed one case and you may be my second."

"If by some horrible chance I do have acromegaly, is there treatment?"

He immediately broke eye contact.

"I mean, it's not experimental, is it?"

"Oh no, nothing like that. Peace Corps will fly you to the Walter Reed Army hospital and treat you with cobalt radiation."

"What's the percentage rate of success of all those who had the treatment?"

"Oh, I think they all made out okay."

"How many is *all*?"

"Maybe half a dozen or so," he said, looking over my shoulder out through the window at passing traffic.

"Half a dozen? You mean like six? This has only been done on six people?"

"Well, as I said, it is a rare condition. There haven't been many opportunities to work on a treatment."

All of a sudden I was no longer merely a patient, I was an *opportunity*. In any case, the interview was over and he told me I could return to my teaching duties at Nang Rong. Then, almost as an afterthought, he said," I forgot to mention another sidelight of this condition is diabetes. We'll also have to test you for tunnel vision."

Dr. Copley made an appointment for me at Bangkok's Seventh Day Adventist Hospital. I left his office in a daze. Acromegaly! What could I have possibly done in a previous life to deserve such a diagnosis?

Later, at the hospital, they x-rayed my entire body and told me my negatives would be sent to a radiologist in the states for study. The good doctor gave me a couple hundred baht to go out and each rich food, raise my metabolic levels to stateside average, and then take a glucose and phosphorus tolerance test. The ordinary up-country Thai diet had apparently changed my insides so much, I needed to be jolted back to normal.

Later, back at the hospital, I was given a pint of glucose to chug down then they told me to urinate. I did that and then they took some blood and told me to wait. About thirty minutes later I was called back in where they sucked up more blood and told me to urinate. I couldn't go. They said to wait some more. Thirty minutes later they took more blood and again I couldn't urinate. This lasted all morning. The minute I left the hospital I had to pee so badly I ran into a hotel and used their restroom.

Then I went to see an ophthalmologist who tested me for tunnel vision. Vision – yes. Tunnel – no. Then, I returned to Nang Rong, gave Wisut a hug, shared a few drinks at the Smile Restaurant and I told him of my medical adventures.

Eventually, I received the following letter:

Dear Burgess:

The results of your x-rays have come back and indicate to me that you ought to get some more studies done. The tests so far do not show you actually have acromegaly, but there are slight changes in your x-rays. Slight as they are, they're still abnormal. The best thing would be for you to come to Bangkok sometime next month and plan on staying for a few days so we may get some additional tests completed. It may even be possible for you to have these tests done in Khon Kaen. I will notify Dr. Harris, my replacement, what these tests are for, and then I will expect you to write either to him or to myself notify one of us what your plans will be.

I don't think there will be any problem, but I feel it is safer to learn everything we can to rule out any possibility of acromegaly.

Hoping you are fine, be seeing you before long.

Cordially,
Sherman Copley
Peace Corps Medical

He *did* say he hoped I was feeling fine, didn't he? Eventually, I contacted a Dr. Harris who reviewed my records and confided to me that perhaps Dr. Copley was a little acromegaly-happy. He had previously diagnosed a case among Thailand volunteers, and that was after everyone disagreed with his diagnosis. Now, it appeared he was going out of his way, seeking acromegaly where it really didn't exist. My x-rays, as far as he could see, were fine and I had nothing to worry about. In any case, Dr. Copley had finished his tour and he was back in the states. But, Dr. Harris cautioned, if I ever had trouble getting my feet into my shoes, to get in touch with him at once!

July 28, 1968

Dozens of boy scouts camped along the side of the school. They started small camp fires, gathered wood and told stories. I had a vague memory of scouts in America unpeeling hot dogs from Saranwrap to singe over their fires. Thai kids each had a kilo of uncooked rice and a few dried fish from the nearby lake. More bonfires were lit and local government officials arrived for the festivities. There was a madcap parade through town with dancing, cavorting students, several musicians and a street filled with laughing and cheering townspeople. Off in the distance, coconut palms stood stiff against an animated horizon that swiftly passed from delicate shades of pink and violet to the blank darkness of night. Several scouts fainted from heat and excitement. I happened to be close-by when the first students collapsed and helped carry him into a medical tent that had been set up for just such emergencies. A doctor passed some ammonia under his nose. His eyes flickered, opened, saw me and promptly fainted again. The doctor motioned me away. Poor kid must've thought he was hallucinating.

237

Thirteen school sent cadres to perform funny skits. I managed to follow about 20% of the dialogue. Between skits, the teachers danced the classical candle dance. Beneath a full, yellow moon against a wall of palm fronds, the swaying dancers appeared unworldly.

I thought the best skit concerned a shopkeeper who sold magical dolls. After telling the audience how clever his dolls are, the shopkeeper turned to a young couple that entered his store to make a purchase. They tell him they want to see the dolls perform. The shopkeeper obliged by 'winding up' several student-dolls, making a *gak….gak…gak* sound as he pretend to turn some mechanism on their backs. Each doll did a brief dance, sang a song, and then chatted with the couple in the language of its nationality. The Chinese dolls jabbered away in what to Thai language speakers sounded like a fast-talking parrot. The audience roared at the singsong patter; but, I noticed the Thai-Chinese members of the audience weren't laughing. The final doll to perform was dressed as an American cowboy and even before was wound up to perform all eyes turned to me. I just shrugged and smiled. This doll moved much more awkwardly than the others, seemed to trip on its own feet, pulled a wooden gun from a holster and waved it around, all the while yelling what sounded to me like: Whoa! Hey! Come here! Howdy! More faces stared my way.

The mayor, who sat next to me, kept asking his aid where his motorcycle was and the aid kept telling him to just sit through one more act. They cornered him when it was time to give awards. He was still presenting plaques when I left.

Several nights ago there'd been another celebration; a going a way party for the local tax accessor. Wisut told me he was one of the most hated men in town because of his unwillingness to accept any gifts in lieu of favors, extensions or showing some flexibility in his judgments. After hearing all this, I asked Wisut why there were so many people celebrating at his farewell party. "Because they are happy to see him go," he replied. They called me up on the stage to sing a song. I made something up called "We hate to see you go … we hate to see you go … heigh ho the derry-O, we hate to see you go!" Only Wisut got the point and kept slapped me on the back once I was off stage.

July 30, 1968

The school term ends in four weeks and most of the teachers are making travel plans. I'm planning on a trip to Rayong on the southern coast to see the Viskochils, a couple I was friends with during training. I was intrigued by their letters to me explaining a writing project they'd started with their students called 'Picture Composition.' I remembered when that lesson plan was introduced to us during training. I think it was one of the linguists who explained that most Thai lessons involved a great deal of memorization, but Picture composition was an approach to teach Thai students to be creative in their writing. Basically, the first lesson started with a picture of an interesting looking person. The teacher told the students to talk about what they knew about this person. At first, the students shook their heads and said they know nothing. The teacher then postulated a few ideas. Did this man come from Bangkok or some small village in the northeast? The students were urged to guess. Did the man have a family? Was he a farmer? A teacher? A mayor? The students began to get the idea. The blackboard was soon filled with background material about the now not-so-mysterious man. After that, picture composition became a favorite part of every writing lesson. That's what Sally and David Viskochil were doing with their students and I was eager to visit Rayong, see them teach PC and, most of all, I eagerly looked forward to reading their students work. The writing samples they'd sent amazed me with their creativity.

But, four weeks was still a long time off and I heard from Wisut we'd been invited to the home of the town's meteorologist, Mr. Wasan, who spoke quite a bit of English if the topic included cloud formations, barometric pressure readings and wind currents; but, the area in which Mr. Wasan was really outstanding was in the area I'd call "Preslomania." After a few hours of eating and drinking, Mr. Wasan announced he knew the lyrics to every song Elvis Presley had ever recorded. By the time the other guests departed, Mr. Wasan stood up and sang every song from the movie KING CREOLE.

Looking back over the past few entries I realized I'd skipped an adventure in the capital with Fred, the malaria eradication volunteer. I'd been in the area for a two day training session with local Thai teachers who taught English and went over model lesson plans. By the time it was all over I was exhausted and looked up Fred. Surprisingly enough he was home instead of out with ddt spray teams or measuring the square footage of homes in the boonies so they'd know how much material to carry next time they were in the area. Turned out he had a third year medical school students with him from Florida named Wendell who specialized in infectious diseases in southeast Asia. After crunching a few bowls of fried pork rinds and downing a few beers, we deduced it was time to help Wendell break his vow of chastity and took him to the most famous local house of ill repute, known by all as The Pink House because of its exterior stucco coloring. We explained to Wendy, as Fred insisted on calling him, that there was a certain decorum in visiting such a place. As we pulled up in a government-supplied jeep, the front area was populated with samlaw drivers, civil servants sipping beer, women from the house draped over the front porch and clusters of customers who sat on the graveled yard waiting their turn. The entire region had only one movie a week, an occasional fair, lots of drinking and the red light district. Technically, prostitution was illegal. There was a lookout posted who checked with other customers to make sure new arrivals were okay to let in. The pink house had a central room with an unfinished wood floor, a few cracked wooden chairs and an overhead fan that sometimes worked. Cigarettes butts were piled up alongside empty beer and Mekhong whiskey bottles. The woman who ran the place was a former student of a previous Peace Corps Volunteer, so she spoke fairly good English. Decked out in colorful Chinese nylon pajamas, she initially looked a bit scared at our arrival. One American was okay for business, but three at a time was enough to make the other customers leave. Then she recognized Fred from a previous visit and all was well with the world. Fred introduced me as a visiting teacher and she grimaced. No money in teaching. Everyone knew that. Then, he introduced Wendell as a doctor and everyone looked up. Women poured out of the woodwork with aches, pains, rashes and discharges we didn't want to hear about. Fred tried to bluff his way on to the welcome wagon by claiming he was also a medical technician, but they laughed and made jokes about how he made his living killing mosquitoes, which was okay as far as it went, but wasn't at all like being a doctor like Adjan Wendell. Wendell patted himself down and muttered sadly he'd forgotten his stethoscope. No worries. One of the ladies produced one of her own and Wendy was in business listening to heart palpitations, tapping chests and placing his ear against perky breasts whenever the opportunity presented itself. Then it was crunch time. How much did we have to pay? Wendell got a freebie for giving medical advice. The going rate was 30 baht (about a buck and a half), but they asked us for 60 because we were hairy and probably had diseases they'd never dealt with before. We settled on 40. All the girls wanted Wendell. Once we were all in our little cubicles I heard crazy laughter coming from Wendell's area. He later told me it was because his girl wanted him to put on a condom and he'd laughed when he felt it. The brand name was 'Buffalo' and he said it had the texture of burlap and sandpaper. Willing to take a chance, he said he rode bareback.

A guy would really be courting disaster in a Thai whore house without at least a balloon for protection. Peace Corps gave us plenty of instructions and warnings about that, not that they'd actually chastise anyone for getting the clap, but they promised they'd be miffed if we didn't take elementary precautions.

All that talk of VD reminded me of an interesting experience I'd had in Buriram some time ago when they prescribed antibiotics for my own infection and the doctor also gave me some additional med that he said would cut down on the acidity of my urine so it wouldn't be so painful when I urinated. One of the side-effects of this treatment was that it turned my urine a brilliant red. On the second day of treatment, I went to the mens' room in a local movie and when I started to pee, a Thai customer who was standing downstream from me, looked up horrified at the red tide headed his way. He stopped in mid-stream and left.

··

August 13, 1968

Just when I think I've mastered a small bit of the Thai language, something happens to shred my self-confidence. Yesterday, walking back to my house from school for a quick break, I passed one of the teachers who looked a little harassed and upset and I asked her:

"Are you okay? You look tired…"

"Meat?" she asked with a strange look in her eye. "No, you have to go to the market to get meat."

We passed each other by a wide margin.

My mother asked in one of her letters if I would like her to send me any clothes. I quickly wrote back to tell her NOT to send anything except sox. All the ones I've purchased here seem to be made from some strange, artificial fiber that resists fitting no matter what size and felt like steel wool. That's also a pretty good description of locally made condoms, but I didn't go there.

Sally Stonberg, a former English teachers from a community college I attended, told me she and her husband were traveling to Thailand and said they'd love to take me out for dinner and, of course, I could bring a friend. I went with Wisut, who waited deep inside the terminal as I stood on the tarmac scanning to passengers. I spotted Sally right away and waited as she approached…and, walked right by me! "Sally!" I cried, and turned, to see her look over her shoulder at me.

"Oh, my God, is it you?" she said, hugging me tightly. "Don't worry," she whispered in my ear, "I won't tell your mother!"

It eventually dawned on me that she was talking about how thin I appeared. They sailed through customs, picked up luggage, checked into the Siam Intercontinental Hotel and decided we'd have dinner right there. Wisut was pretty tongue-tied and Sally didn't get much out of him. The menu was enormous and Wisut pored over it intently.

"Look," he pointed. "Fried rice here cost eight times as much as in Nang Rong!"

We laughed, then Sally and I each ordered big steaks and her husband and Wisut had Thai food. During breaks in the service we all smoked and ordered mixed drinks on the side. Eventually, we walked them up to their room. Wisut and I were both in awe of the room and its accoutrements: incredibly soft, enormous beds, chrome and enamel bathroom fixtures and views of downtown Bangkok. We made plans to meet mid-morning the following day and I left with Wisut to stay with him at his sister's house in far different part of the capital. His sister and her kids were up watching television when we arrived.

"I kept telling my children that students in America don't watch television all the time and that's why America is so strong," she said, nodding at her kids.

I didn't have the heart to correct her. We made our way up to our beds on the second floor and I was up all night running to the bathroom. Obviously, my digestive system had not been prepared for the sudden influx of steak, potatoes and apple pie.

The following morning I had to call Sally to apologize and tell her I had some sort of stomach virus and wouldn't be able to join them for sightseeing. By the time my stomach returned to normal, a few days later, we caught the train to Buriram and then a bus to Nang Rong where school would be in session the day after we returned.

August 28, 1968

Quite a few Thai educators have gone to the states for advanced graduate degrees. The doctor in my village told me he'd gone to study pre-med in Indianapolis and from there to Ohio for his M.D. Here in the northeast Thai province of Udorn, where I am now, I had an opportunity to meet and work with Dr. Prateep who received an M.Ed from Ball State University. He had the idea of establishing a working seminar for Thai grammar school teachers who want to specialize in teaching English. So, here in an old Boy Scout camp, I've joined Dr. Prateep, some other Volunteers and a large contingent of Thai teachers to practice just such a seminar. Typically, Thai teachers obtain a diploma from a secondary school then attend a teacher training school for two or three years. At that point they are qualified to teach at the *prathom* level (similar to elementary school). English language instruction begins at the *Prathom* 4 level. Following *prathom*, students enter the *matayom* level. My school in Nang Rong, for example, is at the matayom level. Most of the participants at this seminar are young, recent graduates, have taught for two or three years and have limited fluency in English, but a wide grasp of English grammar. The Ministry of Education directed specialists in lesson-planning, methodology, verb and noun substitution drills and some pronunciation. Although the ministry asked for as many Volunteers as Peace Corps could provide, the seminar only ended up with myself, Thom and Heidi who works in the north but heard about the project and decided to attend on her own. Although Thom and and I have some limited background in teaching and we're slightly more familiar with the Thai dialect spoken here, we never would have succeeded without Heidi's help. Regardless of dialect, he Thai fluency was far above ours and she arrived with an infinite supply of games, lesson plans, songs, dances and energy!

Fifty-six teachers were involved, two-thirds of them men. Initially, there wasn't too much contact between the Americans and the Thais. The volunteers weren't sure of their roles and the Thais weren't sure about us. I discovered there were some teachers in the group from Nang Rong who knew me (or, of me) even though I'd never met them. Apparently, they spread the word that I wasn't a total evil monster. That said, and Heidi's vivaciousness, interactions between us picked up. Dr. Prateep was a catalyst for everything that happened. He was simply so bright, gentle and sensitive everyone was draw into his orbit. He showed us photographs of him taken in Munci wearing an enormous coat standing stiffly with a big smile as snow flakes fell all around him. The Thais couldn't get over the photos and asked him questions about what he ate, how did he stand the cold and what was it like living in close contact with so many Americans? He never said one negative word.

Most of the lectures presented by the specialists were in Thai with specific examples suddenly popping up in English words and phrases. I could not possibly keep up, but Heidi seemed to be doing okay. There was even some friction between her and a teacher from Surin Province who apparently believed he was the expert not only in comparative grammar, but also in mastery of how to present the material. Following Heidi's explanation of a rather arcane element of English syntax, this teacher re-iterated what she'd said in Thai to make sure no one missed it. Heidi listened intently, then stood up to say, again, in Thai what had just been said, but in even more clearly articulated Thai (according to my sources) that brought a round of applause. Right after that, she looked stricken and spent the rest of the day apologizing to the other teacher for her rude behavior and threw out more than a few self-deprecating remarks about how not cool she had been.

Most of the teachers had a chance to present a model lesson plan. Mine was a modified verb-substitution drill that I presented on a blackboard out in beautiful weather, lush trees and hanging flowers all around. I think I was inattentive during my own presentation.

Every evening we did Thai and American dances and sang songs. Heidi delved into her limitless supply and kept every session lively. My favorite song/pantomime she taught was called "In a Cottage in the Woods" involving singing the same song over with accompanying hand mimes, each time dropping a stanza of lyrics until at the very last choses the singer is left making hand mimes only. A the sight of 56 teachers straight-faced, standing in a circle singing and acting out the song, I only wished someone had a movie camera to record it for posterity. Classes began at six and usually didn't end until close to ten. During one evening session a Thai teacher brought out a bamboo rattan ball and started a game of *takraw*. Soon everyone was part of the circle, trying to keep the ball in the air, using anything but their hands, laughing when Thom and I ineffectually kicked and elbowed our way into bruises, but no points.

Dr. Prateep was always on the alert for potential problems. He told the kitchen and commissary staff simply to give us anything we requested. One day I asked for Falling Rain cigarettes and couldn't understand why the man behind the counter looked as if he was about to cry. I told not to worry about it, but he apparently went to Dr. Prateep and the next morning I found a carton of Falling Rains on my bed.

Toward the end, we sang popular songs for the Thais and they then showed us some local dance steps such as the *chalerng* (crocodile). The teachers from Nang Rong called out my name and asked me to sing the title song from a James Bond-type Thai film called Operation Bangkok. The song was titled *Pet dat pet* and although I'm sure I dropped more than a few words, that song earned me the only sustained applause I'd received. I reminded myself to buy some super present for Wisut who struggled for days to teach me the song. The final evening concluded with the three volunteers singing the *Loy Kratong* song, usually sung during the harvest festival when people all over the country launch small boats with lit candles with a forgiveness of past sins and hopes for a good future harvest, together on stage and then took turns dancing with everyone else on the main floor. The teachers were, without exception, kind and gracious, exemplifying all that's serene and sensitive about the Thai people and their culture. The last meeting of the last day was presentation time and we gave small gifts to the Thais who, in turn, overwhelmed us with bolts of Thai silk.

After we all thanked each another for our gifts we drifted outside among the trees and share a few last words with those we'd become closest to. Several of the Thais asked us what motivated us to become volunteers in the first place and why we'd selected Thailand as our country of choice. I knew all of us had simply been told we were going to Thailand, but our answers implied we'd always heard about the beauty of the country and the gentleness of the people. Ironically, our made-up stories were all true. They were simply after the fact.

During this final meeting some of the teachers asked us questions on a more personal and political level.

"Some people say that Thailand has become an American colony. Would you care to comment on that?"

"Why is the Negro problem as yet unresolved in your country?"

"Could you please tell us the difference between the moral codes of the Average American woman compared to the moral code (as you have experienced it) of the average Thai woman — also, with respect to basic dating behavior?"

The volunteers agreed that the enormous influx of American arms, men and money into Thailand had exerted a large influence on Thai foreign policy, and the fact that Thailand for once did not seem to have an alternative back-up foreign policy in case we abandoned them was probably the most dangerous aspect of their bonds with America. Thom smiled, but Heidi looked upset. Other questions were bandied back and forth, leaving the three of us sweating, defensive and ill-at-ease. *That* seminar brought home to us behind their serene smiles, the Thais were quite aware of the difficult predicament their country was in and given the opportunity were more than willing to voice their concerns.

September 1, 1968

For the past few hours I corrected the first term exams and pulling at my hair and bit my lips. Hanging on a knob of the desk is a small bag of cookies. On the floor, rested half a loaf of bread. I listened to the radio in the background, nibbled some bread, had a cookie and graded a few more papers. I had only two more sets to go and then I'd be able to make notations in my grade book and then I'll officially be finished for the term. I think finished in more ways than one. Once my headmasters saw my grades and the sheer lack of grammatical knowledge my students have displayed, he may call Peace Corps and ask that I receive early termination.

I've talked myself hoarse in class, tried to make the lessons interesting and still I ended up with students scoring five out of thirty. The finally proof comes when they all will have to take the government test at year's end. How can any of them pass? I've seen those tests and quickly estimated I'd be lucky to get more than 60% correct. The grammar questions seemed to be deliberately constructed to fail as many students as possible.

So, why was I here? I was given to understand the Thai government made a decision to have English become the third language of the country, after Thai and Chinese, for purposes of international tourism and understanding of another culture through language. Could it be that the whole Peace Corps Teaching of English program had been forced on the government by America? I know Chinese businesses that control so much commerce here weren't exactly ecstatic about Volunteers sent out to form farm cooperatives. Perhaps looking back, analysts will say the US benefitted by having so many of its citizens absorbed other cultures and brought back with them an appreciation of these foreign worlds to American shores and help dissolved the isolationist tendencies so common in the states.

September 9, 1968

I woke up this morning to the roosters crowing, feeling rested and even cool with the first light of the sun on my window frame. Half a dozen dogs started a ruckus under my house and I leaned forward from my bed to watch them fight. I think there was one female in heat being fought over by the others. Wisut screamed something from his room. I think he came home very late from a party. His small feet slapped across the wooden floor to the kitchen where I heard water splash from a larger container into a smaller one, footsteps again, wooden shutters opened and then another scream accompanied by the sound of water falling and dogs yelping and whining as they scuttled off for cover. Silence. I stared up at the cobwebs through my mosquito net, rolled over, checked the time and I decided to get up. Wearing a loose shirt, jeans and sandals, I hopped on my bike and pedaled off to the morning market, swerved away from errant chickens, dogs, kids and a few water buffalo to stop in front of a stand and bought a few tiny pancakes, a banana and then went across the street to the Raxana Restaurant for a cup of Ovaltine. I've started to pick up more than a few bits and pieces of Cambodian slang, so when a dog suddenly ran into the restaurant and began biting its own tail as it ran in circles, I called out, "*Dja geh, dja gud!*..." which is supposed to mean 'mad dog.' Everyone in the place burst out laughing and an old farmer hobbled over to my table crying, "*Dee maak!*" (Very good!) and tried to buy me a glass of whiskey. Small victories.

Back home, Wisut told me there was news about a new schedule. The headmaster had decided the students were not improving enough so from now on there would be Saturday classes in the morning and I would have three of them.

Speaking of classes, all mine have been smooth and easy, almost as if the students didn't want to break my good mood. The lessons I'd worked out in minimal pair drills, verb substitution drills and use of prepositional phrases were calmly digested. Now, at noon, I cheerfully walked out to the extended galvanized steel overhang in back of the school and joined the other teachers for lunch of rice, spicy meat sauce, chili peppers and lemons. I've learned to love *gluey buachee* ("banana like a nun's robe) with its ultra-sweetened evaporated milk, coconut milk and sugar. All of the above goes down nicely with very sweet iced-coffee. Not bad for about 18 cents.

This past weekend my friends Fred and John visited with students for a field trip up to the ancient Cambodian ruins at *PhanomRung*. Soon after we arrived it rained and we unwrapped our banana-leaf lunches of fried rice under a stone arch and eagerly scooped up every grain as the soft rain pattered before us on to giant stone blocks. The carved cobras soon dripped water from their mouths and with ugly, dark clouds further on the horizon, a time of uneasiness fell over the party. As soon as the rain stopped I took out my camera and snapped a few photos.

We played around for about in hour, ran through and on top of the ruins, climbed some of the towers and gazed out at the farmland off in the distance. The students from Buriram were uneasy and they definitely didn't like it when we explored some of the small chapels. We decided it was time to return and slowly walked back down the mountain in a quiet procession. In town, I joined them at the bus depot and waved them off, then walked into the market area where I stopped for some *guayteo* (a kind of noodle soup) which I liberally laced with crushed peanuts, peppers and sugar. By seven that evening when I returned to my village I passed late work crews and farmers beginning their daily trudge to their own homes, God alone knew how many kilometers away. A few carts drawn by water buffalo slowly sank into the soft clay ruts through the center of town, swayed from side to side passed the market and on out to the distant farms. The early-evening coconut stands and dessert concessions started to appear which meant there might be a movie tonight, maybe even a real feature film and not the usual Japanese toothpaste commercials flashed on to stretched sheets in the middle of some field. Motorcycles, like angry bees, zoomed by me; as I headed out they passed me on the way into the night's possibilities.

I stood briefly, turned at the top of my stairs and stared out at the monastery under construction They've worked on it since I first arrived. In the last falling rays of sunlight the gold paint and encrusted glass baubles on the newest portion of the temple glistened like some massive jewel above the dusty courtyard. The year 2502 stood clearly in bright colors from the roof. The year was now 2511 B.E. I'm sure they'll srtill be working on that temple long after I have gone from Nang Rong village and this exotic, wonderful world.

September 22, 1968

Pity I haven't won the national lottery. If I had, I'd have flown my family over here, introduced them to my friends, taken them out to eat at the Smile-Smile Restaurant, strolled with them through the grounds of the nearby monastery and toured the ruins at Phanom Rung mountain.

This has been a quiet Sunday. I've finished washing my dirty socks. Although I now have a laundry lady, Thais have an aversion to touching socks, so here I am doing my own. I know Thais regard the bottom of feet especially dirty. If one is sitting in a chair it is definitely very impolite to point your toes at another person.

Saturday morning I did my three hour teaching stint, mostly reviewing the week's lessons, then had spelling games. I don't know why, but the most common problem word is *bread*. They always spell it *brad*. The students wanted to keep on playing after noon, but I was too tired because of Friday night's activities. That day started off with the headmaster approaching me between lessons and telling me it was time to begin a lesson on the pluperfect-conditional tense. My God, if he isn't badgering me about gerunds its about the pluperfect. The day was hot even for this area and I wasn't too excited when a teacher from one of the private schools came by in the afternoon to ask me to present a model lesson plans to his students and faculty. Although I was afraid I didn't have the energy to give my usual dynamic presentation, I ended up going and after class their headmaster invited me up to the teachers' lounge for a drink or two. He looked about sixty, but by the afternoon he could have passed for a hundred and seven. Like many older Thais he chewed betel nut leaves and his teeth were corroded and stained almost purple by the juice. He had the same jaundiced eyes as my own headmaster making me wonder if they both had liver problems. One of his sons was a teacher at his own school and the other son had a master's degree from some university in the States. He teaches at Mahasarakhan University (a highly respected school in Thailand). I asked him whether I would ever have the opportunity to meet the university son, but he said something in Thai, some sort of aphorism, I couldn't understand. He repeated it for me several times so I could write it down phonetically. Later, at home, Wisut helped me look it up in my Mary Haas Thai-English dictionary and found out the most common translation of what he told me was, "He comes to visit me once in a blue moon."

Okay, back to the private school. There were four other teachers in the lounge with us while we sipped Mekhong whiskey. Rain lashed against the weather-gray sides of the building for hours. We drank and talked and talked and drank until the wind died down and there seemed to be barely enough light in the sky for me to find my way home. When we first started drinking there were three quarts of whiskey on display and by the time I left they were all empty. How could that be? And, we're talking quarts based on a imperial gallon. Even more! Somehow I found my way home, Wisut was sound asleep, I crashed on to my little cot still dressed, half-heartedly pulled the mosquito net around me and slept the sleep of the dead.

That's why I was so easily tired during Saturday morning classes. All I could think of was returning home, stripping off my sweat-stained teacher's uniform and pour buckets of warm water over my head. I'd prefer ice water, but there was none to be had. Then, disaster struck. I'd no sooner entered the house then Mr. Sanguan, my old buddy from one of the private schools, was back. He'd been instructed to take me to visit the home of the other headmaster's local son. Naturally, he lived out in the scrublands far beyond the perimeter of Nang Rong Village. Poor Sanguan. Everyone tells him how to live his life. He tries to always follow the political winds. He seems to be afraid of everyone, but his libido keeps getting him into occasional romances with local women. I have the feeling he usually wants something more, but the minute the woman's family find out who he is, he's dropped. He was also dropped from the private school because he'd already taught English two years and they were on a rotating schedule. Didn't make any different if he had the most knowledge of English. What did matter, he explained, was that if he had been allowed to teach it one more year then the school would have to give him a kind of tenure, and that was something they were never going to do for him. Now, he teaches Thai literature and is not happy. Consequently, he's always currying favor and that's why when the headmaster said to get me, he got me, and drove me several miles on the back of his tinny motorcycle to the local son's home.

The headmaster's son is named Pinisuk. He's married to a lovely, intelligent woman and has two, tiny, round-faced children. By the time we reached his house, Pinisuk's wife had a hot meal prepared and ready to eat on a beautifully colored mat. At that moment, I noticed Pinisuk whispering something intently to Sanguan, who, crestfallen, left the house. Poor Sanguan, always pushed away from the action.

Pinisuk told me that in honor of my visit he wanted me to sample different kinds of meat, but until that very afternoon he had managed only to track down pork and chicken. Smiling up at me, he pointed to a tree and said that on a branch of that tree he'd found the third variety of meat. There on a small plate, between a platter of grilled chicken and a large dish of pork slivers mixed in a curry, rested a scorched lump that appeared to be the corpse of a small bird. His wife asked me to give it a try and I worked a minuscule wing free and sucked off the meat. It tasted a bit gamey, but otherwise edible. She told me it was baby owl!

I stayed on for about four more hours, spending half that time going over various English language grammar drills with my host. In exchange, he drilled me on some simple sentence patterns in Cambodian. I expected to visit Angkor Wat some day, so Cambodian would come in handy. I was surprised to discover Cambodian is not a tonal language like Thai and is similar to English in its sentence structures and basic sounds. The word usage is also closer to English. e.g. adjectives precede nouns, whereas in Thai, nouns precede adjectives. Our language lessons over we drifted outside and watched the pigs and chickens cavort. The house was totally isolated and surrounded by thin woods and vast scrublands. There's no electricity or plumbing, but it was immaculately kept. The floor had the same sheen as that of my school. Its a glow that comes from daily polishing with coconut husks, typically a job for students or children.

From the infrequent contacts I had with Pinisuk at school I assumed he would be as dictatorial a father as he was a teacher; however, in the company of his family he was quiet, gentle with his wife and children, soft-spoken and even-tempered. It was easy for me to forget the often gruff, surly and arrogant behavior he displayed around other teachers, especially Sanguan who has a fear of authority figures. Before I left I had one final drill in Cambodian, then took notes from his wife on how to cook a particularly delicious dessert of mangos and coconut milk.

As if on cue, Sanguan appeared and drove me, silently, back to my house. Wisut was there waiting with Mr. Wasan, the town's meteorologist. Even though it was still blindingly hot, Wisut, Wasan, Sanguan and I played badminton. Wisut and Sanguan defeated myself and Wasan 21 to 19. I was soaked in sweat while the other three seemed to have a slight patina of moisture on their skins. Then we all went into my bathroom room where we threw cool water from a large clay pot over our heads. Wasan soon left to gather some weather data for the district office, Sanguan had to return to his village of Sweet Vegetable to help his mother, so I joined Wisut for a snack in town. While there I helped a woman in one of the shops reads the label on a can of paint and explained to her that since it was latex she could not use paint thinner with it. Wisut seemed impressed.

Then, we dressed up for a going-away party for a local police lieutenant. I sang "If You're Going to San Francisco" to cheers and applause and then the "Loy Kratong" song for even wilder applause. Have to remind myself to take this all in. Back in the States nothing like this will ever happen again to me. Following my numbers, an attractive local women sang a Laotian love song which was absolutely enchanting. I've started thinking of my own big party, my going away party, looming on the horizon, and wonder what will happen then. How will I ever manage to give a speech to the faculty in formal Thai? Could Wisut possibly help me enough for that? Drank some Mekhong whiskey and pushed it all out of my mind.

The entire municipal hall that held the festivities was jammed and I had trouble breathing. I started edging toward a side door when a beefy hand fell on my shoulder and turned me around. It was the Nai Amphur (mayor) who said in a loud whisper, "…if you try to leave early I will shoot you…" (laughter). I finally slipped away at eleven made sure a police assassin wasn't behind me, and made a beeline for home and sleep.

Not pleased at all to have Wisut shake me awake at six in the morning to go with him to help the lieutenant load furniture on to a truck and ride with him to his new home in Korat and help him unpack! Wisut told me all this so matter-of-factly I didn't even question it, but inside I kept praying "Please, please have a full truck!!!" My prayers were granted. By the time we arrived the truck was full and so the lieutenant pulled out of Nang Rong with family, friends and furniture and waved to me as I stood at the side of the road waving back with a big smile.

We trudged back to the house, slept until noon, then got up, threw water over our heads and strolled into the market where we had roast piglet, fried beef in oyster sauce, two quarts of chilled beer and fried tender green leaves of some kind on the side. Just as I was thinking, 'Take me now, Lord, I'll never be happier!' Thom from the Buriram Boys School appeared. Nervous, that he might want me to do something, I cautiously chatted with me for a few minutes. Turned out all he wanted to do was touch base with me before he left for Lahansai Village to renew a friendship he had formed with a Thai teacher during a recent seminar. Although he promised he'd stop by on his way back to work, he never did – probably because they made him drink too much in Lahansai! Every time I heard anything about that place it involved an attack on a government official. They sure don't get many visitors in there, so when someone like Thom showed its pretty much a guarantee they'd hold him as long as they could.

Next Sunday I'm supposed to visit the elementary school teacher, Mr. Pinisuk, again and travel with him deeper into the forest where he promised he'd instruct me on how to use his rifle for shooting game birds. He also told me that an old man I spoke with near his home wanted me to return so he could teach me how to prepare Thai desserts. His name was Somsak and he also promised to show me how to throw a Thai fishing net.

My subscription to the New Yorker ran out and I'm not going to renew. Nothing in there seems relevant or funny anymore. When the mayor dropped by to look through my old magazines, he only wanted to look at Time.

I bought four fighting fish from one of Thom's students in Buriram. Gave me something to watch when I'm looking up from Thai grammar lessons. I left them in a large jar, but a day later there were only two and this morning there was only one with a few wisps of fins lying on the bottom. I continued to feed the surviving fish mosquito larvae I found in my bathroom water barrel.

Wendell, the med student who visited here a while back, wrote to tell me he's back in Mississippi. He said the state seemed to be filled with maniacs who all planned to vote for George Wallace. He went on to say that the first thing he did back on his home turf was to burn a Wallace poster in front of the state police barracks. Then, he joined the local chapter of the NAACP. At the very end he said upon receipt of his MD he plans on moving to New England and practice medicine with sane people.

September 23, 1968

I made a new friend at the Raxana Restaurant this morning. His name is *Sii* (rising tone). He's a West Indian who operates a clothing store in Korat with his father. They were in Nang Rong attempting to sell cloth to local merchants, but with no success. Both of them spoke fluent Thai and English. Very enjoyable talk with them about our experiences here and memories of our respective homelands. Sii's father asked me what I thought about the riots in Chicago and which party did I want to win the election. Was I thinking in terms of personalities or abilities? I told him I loathed Nixon and had a hard time liking Humphrey because of his unswerving loyalty to Johnson and his Vietnam policies. I also told him I had strong doubts about Nixon's ability to run the country democratically, and had little faith in him as a human being with feelings for minorities. I was blown away when the father said, "Yes, for myself, I think McCarthy is the best man." American students had to run their asses off in New Hampshire to bring McCarthy's existence to the electorate and here was this Indian merchant in Thailand not only aware of the candidate but actually knew a lot about him. Then, sadly, he asked me why America didn't just end the war by dropping an H bomb on Hanoi? Time for a drink.

I recently heard a helicopter hover over the village. Since all government aircraft is banned from night flights, the teachers were sure it belonged to either the Free Thai or to Cambodians. The Free Thai claimed to be a force composed of indigenous Thais who were dissatisfied with the present regime and wanted to bring in a new government through revolution. The helicopter did not appear again until ten that evening. The next morning I heard a search light that had been set up on top of Phanom Rung Mountain, near the ancient ruins, briefly silhouetted the aircraft before being blown out by rifle fire from above. The radar station near the mountain alerted the Royal Thai Airforce to send a plane from Buriram, but by the time it arrived, the helicopter was gone.

....

September 26, 1968

I'm in trouble. It started when I presented model lesson plans at the private elementary school due to my friend Sanguan's urgings. After all, I figured, I'd already met the private school's headmaster and his son, Pinisuk, so I figured if any quarrel erupted over my behavior they'd keep it in the family. I never considered that Mr. Sanguan could be using me himself until he approached me one morning and said I should not continue with my lessons at his school. The more he talked, the more I realized that there was an estrangement between Sanguan, Pinisuk and the headmaster. Father and son had been at odds for a while over teaching assignments, but joined forces when it came time to chastise Mr. Sanguan, who wanted to remain in the English department. The headmaster told him to stick strictly with Thai literature. That was when I realized Sanguan had lured me over to do presentations at his school in order to give himself some leverage to get back to teaching English. Since the headmaster resisted any change in assignments, Sanguan's argument to me was that if I followed the headmaster's orders it would be a personal affront to him and show weakness on my part. Looking back, I think I had sort of realized Sanguan had been using me, but I still wanted to help him because he always seemed to be such an underdog and in the end the students might have benefitted a little from my lessons.

I shared all this with Wisut, and he told me that the private school's headmaster was known to have a temper, that his son Pinisuk was probably not to be trusted and Sanguan was the kind of person who not only suffered from an overdose of bad luck, but he had a remarkable ability to pass that bad luck on to others. His advice to me was to disassociate myself from all three of them. I hated the idea of just suddenly dropping my assistance at the school and also dropping Sanguan. I'll have to decide soon whether or not to continue my lessons at the school. Sanguan has been driving me over there on his motorcycle. If I just bicycle myself over to the school it would appear to be a slap in his face. Then I remembered that Sanguan was also the one who is supposed to drive me over to meet Pinisuk's friend, the old man, who wanted to talk with me. What a mess. Would it ever be possible for me to maintain Sanguan's friendship, my contact with the primary school and maintain a professional relationship with the private school's headmaster?

September 27, 1968

Following Wisut's suggestion, I wrote a letter to the headmaster and told him I was sick and would not be able to present my once-a-week lessons at his school. This gave events another week to work themselves out. Classic Thai resolution to an apparently insoluble problem: postponement. Keep doing that until there's a tacit understanding I'm not returning. No one is at fault. No one can be blamed.

Today, I went to eat at the Raxana Restaurant without Wisut. He was out riding his bike with his friend, Chalerm. I ate a small plate of fried rice with an egg on top and some fish sauce on the side. The Nang Rong police chief was with an aide at a nearby table. When I got up to leave, he motioned me over. Because most Thais in town have only ever heard me speak Thai by way of lyrics of popular songs I'd memorized, they assumed I was fluent. Most of the time, I responded to conversations the same way I would if guys were talking about working on their cars: Oh yeah? Really? Cool? But, actually had no idea what the conversation was about.

I saw Wisut and Chalerm pedal by, glance in at me, and quickly sped away. If anyone had a choice to speak with the chief or disappear around a corner, most would opt for the corner. Typically, once you sit to drink with the chief, you don't leave until everyone else at the table has slipped on to the floor. After the chief, his aide and I finished off a pint of Mekhong the Nai Amphur (Mayor) showed up. Adjan Somchai, as he liked to be addressed, had attended college in the states and was fluent not just in English, but American English. He'd replaced an elderly gentleman who'd been mayor as far back as anyone could remember. Suddenly, the town had a hip mayor who often appeared wearing commando-ranger-camoflage uniforms, an enormous .45 holstered on his right side and a bandolier of cartridges strung about his ample waist. An Australian bush hat rested on his head. He and a contingent of border patrol police had just returned from a foray up Phanom Rung mountain, probably peering around sandstone cobras looking for Cambodian irregulars. That noisy helicopter had been getting on peoples' nerves. The mayor had do be seen doing something about it. He also had fluorescent lights installed on new poles all the way from the primary school to the meeting hall. Workmen had protested the installation could not possibly be done in the time allotted, but after the mayor explained to them where they could end up if it wasn't finished, they managed to do everything he asked in record time. More lights have been strung to the edge of town. He also had the road to Buriram paved. Now, for the first time, taxis have started to compete with buses for passengers.

Back at the restaurant, the three of us began drinking from a quart bottle of whiskey along with a bucket of ice and several bottles of soda water. The aide disappeared for the mens room, never to return. A jeep rattled by. It was the village doctor, Adjan Boonsok, the Ball State graduate. This was the first time I'd sat a table with the chief, the mayor and the doctor: Nang Rong's triumvirate of power. Most of the conversation took place in English with the chief complaining that although he knew English, he hadn't had an opportunity to practice it. The mayor turned to me and, in English, said, "The chief keeps two women in his house to make love to, while his poor wife slaves in the kitchen."

He turned to the chief and asked, "What did I just say to Adjan Burgess?"

The chief hemmed and hawed and finally said, "You tell him I have the fine house and my wife work hard."

The doctor laughed so hard he almost fell off his chair. The chief asked me if I knew the Thai word *galee*.

When I told him I didn't, he said it meant *prostitute* and giggled to himself, before holding up his hands and began ticking off every synonym in Thai for prostitute. Adjan Boonsok looked around uneasily and urged him to lower his voice. From the kitchen came sounds of hysterical laughter. The mayor then asked me if I thought any women in Nang Rong were beautiful. I told him I thought there were a few. They leaned over the table and asked, "Who?" I was in a bind. God help any woman whose name I brought up. I tried to weasel out of it by saying I couldn't remember any names, but Nang Rong certainly had its share of lovelies.

"I am the mayor," he said. "You must tell me what I ask. Where do they live? What do they do? And what are their names?"

"There was one teacher I met in another district during a training seminar who was quite beautiful," I lied.

"Aha!" he cried. "What district does she live in? I will have her transferred to Nang Rong so you may be close to her."

I tried to think of the most out-of-the-way place I'd ever heard of in Buriram so as not to incriminate anyone.

"I believe she lives in Phuttaisong," I said, naming a remote district in the north of the province.

The Nai Amphur looked very uneasy. The doctor laughed again, even harder, slapping the table all the time. Tears came to his eyes. The police chief's face was locked in a grimace as if he was expressing some sort of empathy with the mayor.

"You…you…you…"the doctor kept trying to say something, but could not get it out.

The chief got to his feet, mumbled something about not understanding what was going on and said he had to take a leak.

"You understand plenty!" the doctor shouted at his back. He turned to me and said, "The mayor has a, what shall I say, girlfriend who is a teacher at Putthaisong Girls School. Perhaps it is the same one, eh?"

The mayor ground out a smile, but muttered something under his breath to the doctor in rapid Thai I couldn't follow. The doctor gave a polite cough and started sipping his whiskey in silence.

"Well, never mind about her," the mayor said. "No, no, don't tell me anymore. I don't want to know hear any names. People should have their privacy."

And, that was the end of that.

....

Even later

Forgot to mention about how hard I pedaled against the wind in a violent rainstorm yesterday. Thoroughly drenched, I wheeled into the post office grounds and tried to dry off inside the rear building. The office was closed, but a kind watchman let me inside. That was when I experienced an eerie sensation that I had been there before. The building was relatively new and I was positive I had never been inside, yet I was overcome with a sense of deja-vu. I took a deep breath, try to orient where I really was, and that feeling swept over me again! What was happening to me? Suddenly, it hit me. When I was a small child my father used to take me to a friend's business office and the smell in that office was exactly the same as that mailroom in Nang Rong. It was the odor of stale tobacco! My father's friend, Jimmy Gordon, smoked cigars, and his office was always redolent of their stale smoke. There I was seventeen years later, twelve thousand miles away, feeling as if I was once more sprawled on Jimmy's office rug reading comic strips, while the two men smoked and talked. The post-office was covered with ground-out, small cigar butts. I looked around, dazed, for my distant father.

The rain eventually stopped and I bicycled back to my house for a fast change of clothes, then on to the school just in time for lunch out back with the other teachers before my afternoon classes. In the past, the curry had always been composed of either pork, chicken or beef with a hodgepodge of onions, spices and chopped vegetables. That day's serving appeared to be the same brownish curry and I saw with the other dishes sprinkling on a bit of fish sauce, when I suddenly realized everyone was staring at me. My first thought was my hair must still be sticking up in the air from the rain and I tried to pat it down. Still, they stared. I picked up my spoon and placed some of the curry in my mouth. The assistant headmaster waited until I'd finished the dish before volunteering that he always thought there were certain Thai foods that foreigners didn't eat. Now, he smiled, he could see he was wrong.

"What," I asked, "did I just eat?"

No one knew the word in English.

"*Gop!*" a teacher said with a dazzling smile. "You ate *gop*. We are surprised."

Everyone burst out laughing.

"*Gop...gop...gop...*" the assistant said, making small hopping motions with his cupped hand across the table.

"Frog!" I exclaimed.

"Chai," he said, "*Frok* (sic)."

I chuckled nervously. Peristaltic waves began to break against the back of my throat.

"Of course," I shrugged. "I knew what it was all the time."

A few days later

Fred arrived from Buriram and joined me for a beer and some roasted nuts at the Raxana Restaurant before we took off for a holiday at a bustling city near a major American airbase called Korat. The road was in terrible condition from the rains. Most of the homes we saw along the way were half under water. Our bus driver had to pull over several times to let the engine cool and that allowed us a chance to look over what small children sold by the side of the road: spicy ears of corn, grilled chicken parts on sticks, watermelon slices and coconuts. Without warning, we were suddenly in the middle of the city. Construction projects were everywhere as was the dust. We stumbled off the bus and walked over to a restaurant named The Wolverine where we had ham steak, fried vegetables, delicious small breads, mashed potato and Cokes. John, another malaria eradication volunteer and the captain, found us while we were absorbed in the food. John ate some of my ham, asked me to forgive him and we saluted each other. By that time the additional orders for John and Thian (the captain) arrive and we watched them eat. Outside, we leaned against the building, smoked cigarettes, inhaled some dust and just laughed at nothing in particular. Then, we walked over to a Dairy Queen and had banana splits. Time to walk around the city, stare at the rickety scaffolding of emerging buildings and throw a softball back and forth in the middle of the street. By dusk, we ended up in front of the Wolverine Restaurant again and decided it was time to try their roast beef sandwiches. We topped them off with mustard and horse radish. Perfect!

Since we had no idea where to stay, John suggested we drop in on Bill, another volunteer, who turned out to be a very hospitable and extremely funny guy who regaled us with stories about getting lost in the forest seeking malaria vectors with a team of med technicians, accidentally bumping into camps of homeless people who seemed to be literally living off the land, and experiences with local missionaries. Under a full moon, we walked over to the C. Lon Massage Parlor. We each left a five baht tip to a fat woman at the front door and walked through to a room that was divided by glass wall behind which stood, stretched, sauntered, entreated, smoked and yawned about a dozen young women in tiny dresses all wearing numbers. The deal was you picked a number, spoke it into a microphone and the woman met you in a hallway, haggled about the price and what the two of you planned to accomplish and eventually ended up in a cubicle barely large enough for a massage table. On closer examination most of the women did not look all that attractive, but we were full of youth and roast beef and didn't care. I chose #5 because she stood way from the others. In the hallway she wai'd me deeply, dabbed at her eyes, told me her name was Noy and she really wasn't a Suzy Wong (!) and that she was only doing this because her family was starving. I immediately thought of the wandering people we'd met in the woods and tried not to allow myself to believe it was all part of a scam. Her massage was perfunctory as if she couldn't wait to get to the part where she pulled out a tube of Brylcream to finish me off. I felt better after a hot, soapy shower where Noy scrubbed me all over. As we were leaving, drunken American soldiers were arriving. We went from there to a garish nightclub where small boys, with cigarettes dangling from their lips asked us for lights and tried to pick our pockets then swore at us in fluent English when we pushed them away. Bill grabbed a kid's hand halfway into his left pocket tugging at his wallet, and later discovered he was missing two hundred baht from his right pocket. The club was filled with Black American soldiers who also played wildly improvisational blues on stage. Thai women danced with the men on the floor, others carried trays of cheap beer. We sat at a rear table and an enormous waiter took our orders with a cryptic smile. All the guys on the floor wore peace symbols or buttons for a sane nuclear policy. Because there was a one o'clock curfew for military personal the place emptied by 12:30 and we joined them, only to be stopped by MPs who politely asked us "…are you gentlemen members of the military establishment…?" We showed them our Peace Corps IDs and they waved us on to Bill's place where we broke out his cache of whiskey, smoked some dope and read his back issues of Playboy. Finally, one by one, we fell asleep. During the night I heard someone violently retch outside. I woke to the sound of roosters crowing with a moss-mouth and stiff neck from the hard floor.

After dousing our heads on Bill's large water jug and brushing our teeth with bottled water we went to a nearby breakfast place to rejoin the captain who'd stayed in an air-conditioned room by himself (he said). At the restaurant, he was back in immaculate uniform and was almost unrecognizable as the guy we'd just partied with. Ignoring the menu, we ordered fried eggs, bacon, home fries, toast with marmalade and endless cups of coffee with sugar and real cream. Then, we realized we hadn't had any juice, so downed glass after glass of fresh orange juice. The captain kindly offered us all a ride back in his jeep, but the bumpy road made us all sick along the way and we vomited into puddles of muddy water. We stopped briefly at Nonki Village for Cokes. They dropped me and Fred off in Nang Rong while John and the Captain continued on to Surin. Fred and I took turns dipping our heads in my enormous ceramic bathroom container, trying not to accidentally swallow the mosquito larvae that floated on top, then played badminton until we collapsed, napped, had fried rice and Thai tea at the Raxana, then Fred left for Buriram.

I had no idea where my roommate had gone, so, alone in my house, I stared at the black and white prints I'd just gotten back from a long ago trip to Phaom Rung ruins. They brought the whole experience back. Dropped back on to my cot and finished reading Hersey's TOO FAR TO WALK. Disappointed. Twentieth Century Faust was boring. Started reading Barrett's IRRATIONAL MAN: STUDY IN EXISTENTIAL PHILOSOPHY. Switched over to a list of Thai adjectives and fell asleep.

The following morning Mr. Sanguan showed up to tell me all his problems with the private school had been resolved. There'd been a rivalry between himself and the headmaster's son. He said the headmaster became like a wind-up toy when his son was around, but when his son was gone he merely looked tired. His actual words. Maybe there's more to Mr. Sanguan than I thought. He also told me there were no longer any plans for me to meet Pinisuk's friend, the old man, or learn how to cast a Thai fishing net. Have to say I was relieved by everything he said and even more relieved when he just left. Just as I was about to take a nap, Wisut appeared with a member of the border patrol and a short-wave radio. At the same time, the mysterious helicopter hovered over the town. They asked me to listen to voices over the radio they said were coming from the helicopter. They were in French! I figured they'd be very excited about that, but they were disappointed they weren't speaking English. What did it mean? The border patrol guy said he was hungry, so we walked over to the market for fried rice, roast nuts and beer.

Dateless mind ramble

The last of the female volunteers from my province have left: Melinda from distant and hard to reach Styyk Village; Judy of Lamplaimart; and, Sharon from Buriram girls school. My pal Fred comes by occasionally to gossip and Thom is always up for a visit, but I'm no longer feeling a need to constantly make contact with Americans. I'm sick of hearing weeks old news. Old issues of Time Magazine might as well be arriving from Pluto. After a day's work, I collapsed back on my cot and begin to wrestle with newly-emerging fears: what will I do back home? should I apply to graduate school? what about my school loans? I feel totally detached from student protests, minority repression and news flashes about world pollution. I needed to get a graduate degree in something useful, but the thought of school felt like sticking pins into myself to stay awake during monotonous lectures. It was deadly calm outside, as if Nang Rong Village were in the eye of a hurricane, but there are no clouds, no harbingers at all of things to come.

October 7, 1968

A visiting soccer team from Lamplaimart Village came into town and looked pretty bedraggled getting off the bus. I asked several of my student how they thought we'd do in the game and they all replied, "No way!" No way, what? No way we're going to beat them. Oh. Their pessimism was not without foundation. We lost the big game five to one. Then, in the afternoon, we switched to basketball. When the two teams lined up along the foul lines to be greeted by the Nai Amphur, the crowd laughed. Wisut explained to me (as if I were blind) that the joke was in the color contrast of the two teams. Nang Rong kids all had lots of healthy Cambodian genes and appeared quite dark in comparison. The Lampaimart visitors, mostly sons of Chinese-Thai businessmen, appeared almost lily-white beside them. The first half was pretty close, but in the end the visitors had to win because they played as a team and we played for individual glory. Nang Rong's students appeared stockier and stronger than the willowy Lamplaimart guys, but while the local kept taking chances, the visitors played cozy, neatly structured games. Every time there was a jump shot one of the visitors came down injured, but Nang Rong couldn't disable the entire team, so we lost. After the game here was a big party in front of the school, with lost of food, drinks and games to play, but a sudden downpour drove everyone inside where the kids sang songs together and the teachers danced with one another. When I asked Wisut why the kids didn't dance, he looked at me in horror and said that students did not dance—if they knew what was good for them. Before departure, both headmasters shook hands, said a few kind words about each other's schools and took a few rounds of applause.

The following morning, as if there had never been any disagreements, the other headmaster's son, Mr. Pinisuk, showed up very early on his motorcycle and kept revving it under my window until I woke up. He reminded me that I still hadn't met the old man who was going to show me how to throw a fishing net and his wife wanted to meet me again and treat me to more desserts. Soon, we were off to *Tunnunhuk* (Broken Road) Village and then to *Nong Cheer Mai* (*Swampy Woods*). After much slipping and sliding we finally arrived at Swampy Woods and met the old man, who had the same Thai name as I did, Mr. Pandit. We sat around and smoked, talked and sipped Mekhong whiskey, waiting for Pinisuck's wife. She arrived with a few other women who all joined the old man's wife and preparedbowls of *laap*. As Pinisuk raised one finger after another, he listed the ingredients: fish sauce, mint, onion, ground chili, lime juice and uncooked rice that had been roasted to a brown color. He said it could be made with beef or poultry and could be cooked or served raw, but either way it is diced up finely and mixed with whatever other vegetables are handy. He said the roughly ground toasted rice is called *khao khua*. Shrugging, he apologized for not having any sticky rice (glutinous) which is usually served with *laap*. I forgot to mention, there were also some fried frog with sweet cakes on the side. After we'd finished, the women cleaned up and we strolled outside to have a look at the nets.

Mr. Pandit told me there was a fine art to throwing this type of net that local fishermen had been using for many years. The net thrower has to be careful so that once the net is thrown it blossoms out, into a full circle, and then settle evenly upon the water, trapping everything beneath it. The lead weights not only helped keep the net extended when thrown, but also kept the net in place under water. Pinisuk said that just knowing how to hold the net was important. Pandit agreed and added that the thrower must be able to master the wind-up leading to the throw itself. Finally, he said, the thrower had to develop a knack for knowing when to yank back a bit while the net still had forward momentum so that the net's full circumference was utilized. Pandit demonstrated several smooth casts, choosing exactly the right second to yank back and allow the net to settle slowly over the ground in a clear arc. By the time he handed me the bunched-up net, I was feeling pretty pessimistic. It seemed to me as if the lead weights were already entangled. Only when I held it in both hands did I realized how heavy it was. I envisioned tangling my entire arm before the release, sort of like getting my thumb stuck in a bowling ball hole. I tried my first cast, over dry land, which resulted in a mass of net and lead weights falling with a clank, crushing a dozen or so fragile flowers. Pandit laughed and assured me that if any fish had been beneath that net I certainly would have killed and captured it.

Several women who'd come out to cheer me on joined in the laughter. After eight throws I caught on and they allowed me to try it over a small stream. I captured three tiny crabs. The women went back to prepare more food and the men opened a bottle of Mekhong whiskey.

I had the feeling Pinisuk wanted to be even more of a friend with me, but he was nervous about losing face by hanging out with a foreigner too much. After Mr. Pandit left for home, I was left with Pinisuk on his back porch, sipping Mekhong highballs and staring off in silence at the moonlit rice paddies. Suddenly, there was a sound of gun fire. Pinisuk looked up tensely at the sky. The women came out and looked up over our heads. A dark shadow slowly began to cover the moon. More guns fired, some of them sounding like ancient artillery pieces stuffed with grapeshot. Pinisuk said that in Thai mythology a sleeping giant named Rahoo occasionally woke up and tried to eat the moon. The shadow that passed over the moon was his mouth devouring it. He said that if it was a smooth swallow, with some edges showing, it will be an average year; however, a total passing with no edges showing heralded a good year. If, however, a total shadow passed over, backed up, then finished crossing, it will be a very bad year. We were all silent when it appeared that the total shadow backed up twice. The guns kept firing sporadically throughout the rest of the night. Were they goading Rahoo to try again?

Pinisuk left his wife at the house and drove me along shimmering-white rice paddies to my door. Beneath my mosquito net, I stared up into blackness wondering if the very bad year ahead would affect me.

....

October 16, 1968

Fred and John, unexpectedly showed up for a visit and decided to stay over night. At school, I raced through a few minimal-pair drills, slipped into prepositional phrases and finally, ended exhausted with a crudely drawn timeline on a chalkboard purportedly showing future tense of the verb *to be*. My buddies scooted around town during the day, peered into Nang Rong's nooks and crannies and reported back to me at the end of school that the town was dead. As I changed from my school uniform into a garish Hawaiian shirt from training days on the big island, dark clouds rolled over the town. Rain fell and my roommate was nowhere to be seen. We hunkered down in my house and looked over the remains of some dried dope still moldering on my desk. The steel roof magnified falling rain drops and we stared out at a few students running madly for shelter. John produced a half pint of Mekhong whiskey which the three of us seized upon and sucked dry. A monsoon hit the roof and we would hardly hear ourselves think. Fred ran into the rain screaming, "It's warm! Its a warm rain!" John and I joined him, and the three of us skidding on the mud and old banana fronds, from mangro tree shade back to rutted road all the way into the market area like a band of screaming loonies. My shoes were waterlogged. Since I'd lost one along the way, I balanced myself by kicking the remaining shoe free into a puddle. Fred and John, in sandals, jumped over and over into rain-soaked ruts. All this after we shared a mere half pint. At the Smile-Smile Restaurant we ordered fried beef in oyster sauce, fried morning glory leaves in oil, spiced chicken breast, onion and pepper slices, three bottles of cold soda and a quart of Mekhong, management was happy to oblige. For the first time, everything I thought I ordered actually was placed on the table; however, instead of a quart bottle, he delivered a pint! The problem was that the Thai word for bottle could be construed as a pint or a quart. We corrected him, but said we'd keep the pint anyway and bought him a Sprite as a tip. Our food lingered about five minutes, the soda and ice about ten and by then we were well on our way to swigging warm whiskey straight from the bottle. The owner came by and cautiously whispered a number in my ear. Turned out it was the bill. We laughed and threw a bunch of bills on the table, then ordered more whiskey. I realized John was silent, staring glumly at the floor, Fred stared straight ahead at oblivion. The kid returned and gingerly felt the hair on my right arm. I was never thought of as being very hairy back home, but in Thailand I was a gorilla.

"My friends! What have we here?"

It was the mayor, smiling, half-drunk himself, heading our way. John shook his head as if to say, what better thing could possibly happen than to have the mayor show up.

"You I think I know," the mayor said to Fred. "I have seen you before, haven't I?"

Fred squinted, stared back wide-eyed and exclaimed, "You, I know! I have seen you before!"

The mayor looked around uneasily, too late aware he was trapped in the company of madmen. Luckily for him he had not yet seated himself, so there was still a chance he could make a break for it. We sensed his intent to spring for the door. He shrugged, backed away, and took the stance of one who has just dropped by to borrow a cup of rice.

"I do not believe I know your other friend, Mr. Burgess," he said to me, hopefully.

John, grinning madly, stared down at the dust patterns on the table.

I tried standing, but slowly as if I was at the bottom of an ocean, and motioned with my hand.

"This is my friend, John."

"And, this is my friend, Fred," Fred said, pointing to himself.

I tried to impart a knowing glance. We were all men of the world, were we not? I mean, just look at all the empty bottle.

"Ah, Fred and John. I see," the mayor smiled tightly. "But, you are not teachers like Mr. Burgess."

"No," said Fred. "We do not diddle like Mr. Burgess. We are the knights of Malaria. You may salute."

"I am very glad to have this opportunity to meet your friends," the mayor said, softly, retreating in the direction of a more known universe. "You must come and visit me sometime."

"You must come and visit *me* sometime," Fred declared, somehow managing to stand up.

"Yes, of course. Please, I know my way out. No need to move from the table. It has been a pleasure."

As he walked out the door Fred declared, "Jesus, what a fat ass."

It was late. No other customers had braved the rain that lashed the road and soaked a row of pork strips that had been carefully arranged to dry in the sun. Fred lifted the remains of the last pint.

"Bitter gall in a foreign prison," he muttered in a strange accent. "Anyway, I like your mayor. He's a keeper."

"He's okay," I said. "He got the main road to Buriram paved, didn't he?"

"Was that him? I completely forgot about that. Hey, let's drink to the road. Where's the kid?"

"Oh no you don't," said John lurching erect. "I'm already seeing purple anopheles and I'm no mood to see anything bigger. Let's get the hell out of here."

We pushed the chairs aside and dug into our pockets for money. Bills of every color fell on to the table. The kid stood and stared. The owner started to say something about the bill, but Fred shooed him away.

"Last of the big time Farangs," John said, morosely, dropping his last green twenty baht note. Let's go."

The owner scratched his belly and looked back and forth between something he'd written on a piece of paper and the loose pile of bills. As we left I turned to wave, but he was happily counting money. The three of us stood, looked at the fat, warm drops that fell on to the cracked wooden sidewalk, then Fred pushed John forward and we ran after him hooting and screaming. My feet skidded on mud and gravel. Fred made it to the middle of the street and raised his arms high and called out to some patron saint for sun. I shivered. We ran off toward a field, past an enormous truck that was being unloaded. John and I were already well past it when we realized Fred was behind, screaming into the wind.

"It's a jute truck! Help me get that jute unloaded!"

The Cambodian team that was struggling to empty the truck stared at us in horror, or terror or astonishment. We grabbed Fred and tried to drag him away. He'd picked up some Cambodian during his trips to the border and he began to harangue them in their own language. They stared, amazed, then laughed. Fred pulled free, jumped on to the truck and began throwing bags off on to the mud. The work crew kept laughing, waving their arms as we again managed to get Fred back to earth, only to fall over backwards into a huge puddle of thick mud.

"Come home with us!" Fred called to them. "We have good Mekhong whiskey for our friends."

By then they were back at work unloading the truck. The rain began to diminish and we walked over to the district parade ground and up to the police station. Totally covered in mud, we needed a place to pass for warmth and breath. Fred bounded up the stairs to the main entrance. I'd been in Nang Rong for many months, but I'd never been that close to the jail or even considered going up those stairs. Fred stood by the front door waving his arms saying something intently to a worried-looking guard who held his rifle between himself and this crazy foreigner.

"I….want….to….borrow….your….rifle…" Fred repeated the words slowly.

The poor man stared at us in wide-eyed terror, clutching his rifle across his chest, and screamed at us to take our crazy friend away. The other police were sleeping inside and they might not be very happy to see the foreigner. The captain himself might return at any moment. The prisoners had been nervous because of the storm and he didn't want them aroused.

We followed Fred inside and realized we were surrounded by men in steel cages stretching their hands out to us through the bars pleading for cigarettes, which Fred was managing to dole out from a soggy pack. We tried to close in on him, but he threw the remains of the pack into a cage and ran to a back room.

It was the captain's office. Fred skidded across the floor close-by a policeman who'd been sleeping beneath a mosquito net near the desk. The poor man peered out at us for an instant then pulled the covered over his head. Obviously he was having a very bad dream. Fred picked up a pile of papers from the desk and let them fall like confetti. I grabbed his shoulder and yanked him out of the office. John was in the hall calming a guard as we made our exit. We managed to stumble down the stairs to the field and back to the house where Wisut, looking upset about something, let us inside and quickly retreated to his own room. Fred and John took all my blankets and crashed on the living room floor. I fell on my cot, wet clothes and all, pulled my mosquito net loose from its moorings, and fell at once into nightmares, horrors and unconsciousness.

The following morning, the roosters crowed and we banged into each other all holding our heads. Wisut was gone. Fred ran to an open window and vomited down on to the cement below.

"What did I say to the mayor in the restaurant?" he asked, after heaving himself dry.

"You kept repeating back whatever he said to us and then you said he had a fat ass."

"Shit, well I better hang on to whatever memories I have of Nang Rong, because I don't think I am ever returning here again. Hey, Burge, you got anything to eat in that room you keep calling a kitchen?"

"Maybe some left over friend rice, if the ants haven't found it. Let's take a look."

The kitchen was filled with foul smelling dishes, ant-laced bags of sugar and a few rock hard *patongos*. Nothing even worth considering. Fred looked around, gagged and walked outside. We stumbled and tripped all the way to the market for cups of Ovaltine and waited for the bus to Buriram. We kept an eye out for the mayor, but he remained hidden. The bus suddenly made the turn into town and my friends got on board and left. I stood alone in the clear, clean morning air waving goodbye and wondered about the day ahead.

October 29, 1968

Mr. Wasan, the local meteorologist, managed to borrow a boat from his office last weekend and we spent the day floating on a nearby pond called Nong Tamue. Since it was an aluminum rowboat it floated high on the water even with Wisut along for the ride. He remembered I didn't swim and brought along a life jacket in case we capsized. The sun burned down, a light breeze crossed the water and coconut palms all around finished the scene. We started off with some Mekhong whiskey, a case of soda water, some canned smoked shrimp, fried morning glory salad wrapped in banana leaves and chunks of roast pork. I don't know what King Bhumipol did on his yacht, but he couldn't have had more fun than we did on Nong Tamue. Several of the teachers had homes located on the edge of the water. We paddled near shore and sang out for them to join us. A few ran from their homes to see what the noise was, then seeing us waving empty soda bottles in the air, splashing water and erratically rowing, they howled and went back inside to drag their wives out to see the entertainment on the water. Gradually, twilight arrived and we quieted down as the silence of the pond grew. Slower and slower, we paddled, finally we drifted alongside the lotus-jammed shore. Softly, the sun descended, and was filtered through thunderheads and rising moisture broke the sun's rays into splashing violets, pinks and greens. The final, lingering hue was sea-green and Van Gogh-blue, with wisps of pink. It seemed as if a fine haze hushed the world. The dark green coconuts trees turned black and the first stars emerged. We fell back and stared up at the sky, at falling stars, the dimensions of vast space, and finally a great pumpkin moon that ponderously swung out into the sky's middle.

We continued to drift and drank, paddled in the direction of a road that ran parallel to the water where a passing motorcyclist paused to see if we were okay. We asked him to go to the market and bring us back more whiskey. Strangely enough, for he was a complete stranger to us, he returned with a bottle, which we opened and offered him the first swallow. But, he merely nodded and peeled away in a spray of gravel. We paddled back to the middle where we finished off the bottle and passed out. There was no moon when we regained consciousness and aimed once more for land. Three candles burned on the prow of the boat to guide us in, but each mooring we attempted was the wrong one. All the houses that had been lit up on shore suddenly went black. Somewhere in the darkness there was a rickety pier waiting for us to arrive. After almost capsizing a few times, Wisut cried out we were going to be trapped on Nong Tamue for the rest of our lives. Enormous flying beetles zoomed in on the candles and smashed against our faces. I began to fear there was a giant serpent lurking beneath the dark water waiting for us to make a wrong move. Then, out of sheer blind luck we found the right pier and docked the boat. Mr. Wasan headed for home, wife and children, but Wisut and I were too manic to adjust easily to a quiet evening so we headed across town toward the mayor's office and even from a distance we could hear there was a party going on. I remembered it had been advertised as a dry party, but the two of us were so juiced we were ready to accept whatever they offered. The music faded out for a few seconds when we made our entrance, then gentle hands reached out and drew me to the danced floor where everyone was doing the foxtrot. Just as I was thinking of making a break for the door, someone tugged me up on to the stage where a microphone was thrust in my face and I sang "If you miss the train I'm on, you will know that I am gone, you can hear the whistle blow a hundred miles…"

....

November 3, 1968

Wisut told me that since feet are considered the dirtiest part of the body, no one wants to clean someone else's sox. So, while my new laundry lady is cleaning the rest of my clothes, I'm about to wash my own sox. Tomorrow I leave with Wisut for Ban Thanon Hak to celebrate Loy Kratong Day.

The Peace Corps Newsletter had a classified ad that gave me goosebumps: *NEPAL TRIP—I am interested in hiking through the Himalayas sometime around February. The hike I have in mind would involve flying from Khatmandu to Pokhara, then hiking up a river valley between Annapurna and Deligher to the Tibetan Plateau and, if possible, getting close to the ancient Eternal Flame shrine. Roundtrip hiking time would be 11-12 days including travel to and from Thailand, total time being 20 days. Contact Dan c/o Provincial Health Office: Trang, Thailand.*

Me! I wanted to shout it out. Even vicariously, I was thrilled at the idea. Meanwhile, back in the real world, I have tests to correct.

I gave a quiz recently to one of my classes about the legend of Rip Van Winkle. How this ancient Dutch story found its way into a Thai manual of study is beyond my ken, but I presented it the best way I could. Here are the results:

Who was Rip Van Winkle?
>   *He was the king.*
What did he see in the forest?
>   *He see in the forest bird.*
What did the game sound like?
>   *The game sound like bananas.*
What did Rip Van Winkle take a drink from?
>   *He drink from home.*
How long did he sleep?
>   *He sleep a long bed.*

Guess my teaching contract will not be renewed, at least if my headmaster has anything to say about it.

An article in the Peace Corps Newsletter by a teacher from Bangkok said that Thai students hear only the tone and inflection of new vocabulary words before they actually hear vowels and consonants. He suggested a simply experiment to test his theory. Stand before a class and say the words *elephant* and *alphabet* using the same tone and inflection with each word. Then, ask the class if you've just said the same word three times. I tried it with two of my classes and everyone enthusiastically agreed that I had, indeed, repeated the same word three times. *Elephant*....*alphabet*....yes, exactly the same!

....

November 5, 1968

Election night in America and I sat in my small room listening to the Armed Forced Radio Network broadcasting from Pleiku, South Vietnam. I sipped sweet tea and nibbled on a piece of cake I made several days ago (trying to ignore the dead ant bodies). I voted for Humphrey and hoped for the best.

Thailand recently celebrated the Loy Kratong Festival. This was the second time around for me to join in the festivities honoring the harvest moon. Knowing I'm celebrating a holiday a second time around gives me the feeling I've really been here for a while.

The entire area between the school and my house was filled with students and teachers making colorful flower arrangements. Some stood in the shade of guava trees waiting to be fitted for costumes. The headmaster beamed big smile at everyone. When he spotted me, he shouted out that I, the foreigner, would also be dressed in a traditional Thai outfit. Everyone cheered. I walked faster. This was news to me. A traditional Thai outfit would not lok well on me.

When I got back to my house it was deserted except for the gecko lizard that scurried across the ceiling as I entered. Practically every night around two in the morning that damn gecko screamed: DOOKEH...DOOKEH....DOOKEH....DOOKEH...repeated itself many more times before it faded out as if running out of breath. I remembered that if the gecko lizard managed to reach seven cries it was good luck.

A few minutes later a student arrived and told me that Wisut had gone to the market to buy some food. How was I supposed to know that the message *meant* he was buying food for a trip that had nothing to do with me. Even though I assumed he'd arrive eventually with food, I was hungry, so I slipped out the door, got on my bicycle and pedaled through the banana trees. I managed to even circumvent the crowd and made it safely to the Smile-Smile Restaurant where I had a huge helping of fried rice, pork strips on the side, a heap of fried morning glory leaves and a freezing quart of Thai beer. All was well with my world as I inhaled from a second Falling Rain cigarette. Someone was calling me!It was Wisut waving at me from the sidewalk. Why was I sitting there, he asked, when I was supposed to be back at the house being fitted by a tailor for my traditional Thai costume? Wisut peeled off on his bike, I paid my bill, gave one last lingering look at the possible desserts and returned home.

Several faculty members had already killed a quart of Mekhong whiskey and admired each other's costumes. I had a few quick drinks myself in honor of the moon God and then it was time to try on some pantaloons, several layers of cummerbunds and a pull-over shirt. Everything was made of Thai silk. I was afraid to sweat. Wisut arrived resplendent in primary colors, held his arms out when he saw me, rushed over for a big hug, spotted the bottle and also toasted the Harvest moon. Our students greeted us outside with screams and cheers. As I bent forward to take a bow, I felt my pantaloons begin to slip away, so I returned inside to have a nylon cord tied more tightly around me to keep everything up. Another band of silk was wrapped around me to hide the cord, and another length of silk was passed between my legs and fastened front and back with hidden safety pins. How did they do it back in the old days?

By the time I was properly outfitted the kids outside joined as on a merry march to the front of the school and from there into a long processional leading to town. Somehow Wisut and I ended up in front, singing the Loy Kratong song, dancing the *Ramwong* right up to a waiting line of buses. Once inside, we cheered and waved as we started our journey to Ban Thanon Hak which is located between Nang Rong and Buriram.

The bus rolled slowly through town with me on the left and Wisut on the right, hanging on to the doors with our fingernails (hard for me, since mine are bitten). Inside, students screamed and drunk teachers teetered down the aisle as the bus weaved and bucked its way over rutted roads into a kind of never-never.

Happiness evaporated when my stomach began sending warning signals that all was not well. Fried rice, pork strips and beer not having a harmonious relationship with three recently chewed oranges, two bags of peanuts and a half pint or so of whiskey consumed so far en route. Luckily, I always carried a small container for emergencies just like this one: polymagma tablets (causes nausea, dizziness and constipation) and lomotil (primarily just plugs up one's gastrointestinal system).

The bus wheezed through Paal Waan (Sweet Vegetable) where we picked up a few more passengers who were hoisted in through windows, and on we bounced along a tedious path through immense throngs of celebrants, all carrying their own *kratongs* (floats), everyone covered in layers of flowers, all mostly drunk, singing and laughing down the road. The harvest moon was strong enough to cast shadows across the dusty road. More whiskey was thrown aboard. Policemen smiled and waved us through crossroads, their pistols prominent by their side, their automatic rifles leaned against palm trees alongside stacks of banana-clips of ammo. We were very close to the Cambodian border. On the far horizon, colored threads streaked across a star-strewn sky and a red cloud hovered over everything. At Tununhak Lake we stopped, surrounded by crowds, and passengers erupted from every door to fall on those standing close-by.

Near the lake, more people stood holding candles. Extended loops of fireworks continually exploded. Incendiary devices flew threw the air. Rockets were launched, fell, picked up and re-launched, until they finally exploded in spirals of sparks only a few feet above the milling throng.

Mekhong whiskey was literally splashed in my face along with compliments about my beautiful clothing. Wisut beamed with pride as the Nang Rong School float, an immense boat constructed of styrofoam from bomb-casings, wire, plastic and nerve, was lifted by our students to the judges' stand. Prizes were to be awarded for: Best Idea; Best Executed

Idea; Best traditional Costume; and a Grand Prize for Miss Loy Kratong of Nang Rong District. After our float was gently settled on to water, Wisut and I clapped and sang the Loy Kratong song again and again. Voices called out for us to dance. We circled each other, doing an impromptu *Ramwong*. Faster and faster, the tempo increased, until we were twisting and shouted more than were dancing. Students shrieked our names and *Wa-too-see… Wa-too-see!* Dripping and exhausted, we finally stopped. The students broke rank in search of fresh talent. Cartwheels, sparklers and rockets hummed into the sky and exploded or hissed and whirred into oblivion. Hissing fragments fell near me, were picked up and thrown into the air. Several costumes burst into flames when rockets became entangled in the loose sleeves and baggy pantaloons of traditional costumes. Three large floats dissolved in flames before they had to touch water. I kept turning around and around trying to keep tabs on falling rockets and caressed the Buddhist medallion Wisut had given me the week before.

"If you wear this when the bullets come," he said, solemnly, pointing to the heavy, plastic encased medal, "It will not hurt you."

I nodded, feeling tears welling up.

"Yes," he went on, "if the bullet hits this you will not die! BUT…(he laughed and pointed to his head, neck and stomach)…if bullet hit here…or here…or here…, then, too bad, you must die!"

It all came back as hellfire and brimstone exploded around me. I was cautiously worming my way free of the densest part of the crowd when I heard my name called. My students shouted my name and demanded I get in the middle and dance for them.

Then, it happened. A wrenching pain in my side quickly followed by minor explosions in my abdomen. I recognized that weak-legged feeling and knew I had to find a bathroom, fast! I spotted Wisut and explained what was happening. He quickly led me toward a group of women on the periphery who were dispensing water bottles, and from one of them he captured a key to one of the few available toilets. Walking with one hand under my silk vestments clutching my belly, I followed a wavering flashlight along a worn path to a padlocked, minuscule hut. We quickly opened it up and Wsiut helped me unwind my finery before I stumbled into a dark space, reached with my foot for the edge of the squat john and lowered myself over the hole. I was drenched in sweat, finished my business and finally emerged to find Wisut waiting for me with the costume. Somehow I managed to return to the center where my students were still screaming my name and urging me to dance. I suddenly conceived of Hell as a place of perpetual celebration linked with diarrhea. I no sooner started dancing than the cramping hit again and unable to stifle a cry of pain, I dove through the crowd, found the hut, but it was locked and no ladies around with a key. My costume clung to me like steel webbing. I kicked, hammered and scratched. Nothing. I bent over double in pain. I scuttled behind the hut, willing to choke cobras for my own plot of ground, and tried to remove bolts of cloth, safety pins and nylon rope. The sound of women talking and laughing drifted over to me from even deeper shadows. I heard water falling on grass. More laughter. Somehow I managed to extricate myself and hung my butt over a clear patch of grass until the camps stopped.

Back at the party, this time looking more like Emmett Kelly than a prince from the court of Siam. Wisut ran up to me with s silver trophy. He told me that I had won second prize for best traditional costume. Then, he took a second look at my clothes.

"You not get second prize for *that*!" he laughed. "You not even get 100th prize, I think!"

Then, all the kratongs were lit and set afloat, dotting the water's surface with flickering candles. An immense float with a live woman inside was hauled out to the lake's center by some poor, mud-spattered soul using a rope clutched between his teeth. Certainly worth first prize for fortitude.

After the last candle died, the moon was over the horizon and everyone was exhausted, the students were herded back into the buses and driven back to Nang Rong. The girls all had to be personally escorted to their doors. Dawn's first light hovered on the highest tip of coconut palms when the last girl was dropped off. Wisut and I joined the others at a restaurant for boiled rice porridge. A certain cure for head and stomach. As the market erupted around me, we waved goodbye to each other and walked slowly home, kicked the heavily, dew-covered grass and sucked in the clean, cool morning air.

At the house, Wisut stumbled to his room and passed out. I peered into the kitchen and saw the ants had managed to crawl into my sugar bag that hung from the ceiling. In my own room, the mosquito net had collapsed on to the bed. Enormous, black beetles flew through the air, smashed themselves in kama-kazi attacks against the walls. The dookeh lizard flicked its tongue down at me from above. I ignored it all and fell into bed, drained of energy, emotion and solid matter, but before settling into dreams, I reached out to turn Armed Forces Radio Network on low. Falling asleep to the English language was soothing.

The bright light of mid-afternoon brought consciousness and the horrible broadcast nightmare that Richard Milhous Nixon had just been elected President of the United States.

···

November 13, 1968

I just received official papers from Peace Corps regarding my up-coming termination on April 1, 1969. Although I have no desire to extend, I do expect to spend two more weeks with friends who live further south. They asked me to join them in a fourteen day series of lesson plans using the Picture-Composition theory of creative writing. A polite note with my paperwork mentioned that Peace Corps has an agreement with the State Department to make maximum use of U.S. carriers in order to minimize our balance of payments with other countries. They also suggested a list of countries to pass through on the way home. In the end, we'll have received the cash equivalent of the cost of a one-way ticket from the capital of our host country to the capital of our home state. Since it's 12,000 miles either way between Boston and Bangkok, I'm able to fly east or west.

Local news flash: A pharmacy in town owned by a Vietnamese couple was visited by a late-night taxi drop-off. An unknown male, of indeterminate national origin, left the cab, pounded on the store's metal grating until the owner came out to see what was going on. The stranger shot him through the heart, killed him instantly. The taxi left and no one's been able to track back to see who'd been the passenger. All shops are shut tight now by 10:00 PM and no one was willing to talk with me about what happened. Finally, a police friend told me he'd heard the man's wife had recently left him for a lover in another town and it was the lover who'd returned to kill the husband and apparently make sure he'd never get his wife back. Nothing to do with agents of the Viet Cong or Cambodian Secret Police, as later rumors implied.

On another note, most of the Thais I spoke with about the election back in the states were rabid Nixon fans, but a few were swayed by me to root for Humphrey. When Humphrey lost they all looked at me as if I'd given them a tip on a really slow horse.

I saw *Bridge on the River Kwai* in downtown Nang Rong and enjoyed it in a special way few other Americans will. As I reported earlier, all major films arrive here without a sound track, because the movie theaters have no sound, they plug microphones high up in a stand behind the audience where a Thai male reads all the male passages from a printed script, and a woman does all the women and children. Alec Guinness was given a high, squeaky voice, while Bill Holden had a deep bass. All the Japanese simply seemed to cackle when they spoke.

Radio Armed Forces Network continues to extoll the virtues of our presence south of the DMZ, very little news of stateside politics, but a lot of rock and roll chatter, local talent shows and station breaks with phony commercials that are supposed to be funny. The Grand Ole Oprey gets a lot of air time. There must be lots of southerners in the army, because that's what they love. A friend of mine from Wisconsin has a brother who's been station in the big airbase at Korat, but when he came by for a visit he had a drawl that sure did not come from Madison. I guess when you're linguistically surrounded you succumb to the local dialect.

....

December 12, 1968

I feel slightly off-kilter to be back in Nang Rong after having gone to Korat for Thanksgiving with Fred, John, Bill and other malaria eradication volunteers. I stayed at Bill's place where we had a real feast of turkey, smoked ham and noodles. Then, Fred and John left on a slow boat to China, literally. They traveled to Hong Kong and Macao by boat and plan to fly back. Following all the Thanksgiving parties, it was time for me to travel south to the resort town of Hua Hin to meet up with someone I'd become friendly with during training.

As usual, it was a wild bus ride to Hua Hin, amidst bundles of produce, cackling chickens and old people who chewed beetle-nut leaves. The driver hurled that bus down a two lane road as if a tidal wave was on our tail. Hua Hin, sizzled under the Siam sun. Deserted beautiful beaches and enough salt spray and fine sand in the air to remind me of Cape Cod. I reconnected with my friend and after a few minutes of hugs and catching up, we wandered into the touristville part of town and signed in at a run-down hotel. There were no other American tourists and, happily, no other volunteers. Even though we hadn't shared much during training, we quickly fell into a rhythm together as we walked along the beach at night, went for a swim in the cold surf, horse back riding along the shore, shopped for cheap trinkets and finally, delicious meals of local seafood. We were red-faced and permanently sandy when we trudged back to the hotel for hastily improvised showers and sweet cuddling. Late evening was the best, when we sat up reading in bed, small mounds of paperbacks all around, pillows fluffed behind us, conscious of being in Thailand, yet secure in our tiny oasis. Early each morning, we walked over to the Grand Hotel that overlooked the gulf. A phalanx of waters awaited our every desire, eyes on alert for tourists who never appeared while we were there. The first time we propped open the menu we exhaled in delight and surprise before ordering bacon, eggs, hash brown potatoes, toast with butter and marmalade and a small pot of coffee that tasted like really good coffee as we remembered it could taste. Within our time frame and small space it was like an all-too-brief honeymoon, and when it ended, we said our goodbyes at the train station in Bangkok. Falling into one of my fantasies, I imagined we were being filmed by some Italian director making an on-the-scene shot of lovers reluctantly parting. Bangkok Train Station: Take one!

....

December 24, 1968

On Friday, I took a bus from Buriram to Korat, and then the train to Khong Kaen, a large city in the northeast to attend a gathering at my regional rep's for a Christmas dinner and party. I was on the bus for over seven hours. Finally, the driver paused by the side of the road and asked me again where I was going. When I told him, he said it would be best if I disembarked right there and rent a samlaw who'd take me right to my destination. After cross-crossing a mile or so of terrain I saw another volunteer, named Dick Treverio, who gave directions to my driver. I found out later that Dick had re-enlisted and was almost through his third year. He rented two houses and he was the sole provider for many students. As I heard the story, it seems Dick began by helping one of two children, but every time he moved he took his old helpers with him to join the new helpers he acquired with new digs. Currently, most of his living allowance is spent on at least ten Thai students in each house. I had the impression he was going to live here forever and end up as the grand patriarch of several hundred Thais.

Khon Kaen struck me as a large and growing city with peripheral commerce associated with Thailand's involvement in the Vietnam War. I heard there were only about 100 Americans living here full time, but not the sort of big American influence as it appeared in Korat. The city had sixteen banks, many farmers co-ops and a fine university. Somewhere in the midst of this bustling metropolis I found the home of my rep, Bob Charles, who greeted me from his front lawn ladling out a punch composed of: 6 quarts of orange juice (fresh), 6 quarts of Mekhong whiskey, 5 limes and some sweetener. Over a few ice cubes it tasted like chilled ambrosia with a kick. Lots of socializing, hugging and drinking and then the food was served: 6 baked hams on wooden platters, two enormous pots of baked beans, a large platter of potato salad and about 18 loves of fresh bread. I inhaled, I ate and I was happy.

Hillary, an attractive and caustically witty volunteer from England was on hand to add a dash of panache. After hearing her speak the King's English for a few moments I realized all the more clearly why Thais insist that people from America and citizens of England do not speak the same language. Hillary mentioned problems she'd had as an English teacher while serving in a large school that also had a few American Peace Corps volunteers. I politely guessed they were mostly differences in pronunciation, but she vehemently shook her head. "How about questions of syntax, diction and word usage?" she replied. I started to back away. "In fact," she continued, "I think England should send Language volunteers to the United States!"

Later that evening, Bob walked over to the tall front gates and slowly opened them wide enough to allow a large number of Thai students to enter. They all carried lit candles and sang Christmas hymns. I noticed a few tears around me as they passed. "Oh, my God, what comes next…a presentation of *A Christmas Carol*?" I heard Hillary mutter. I couldn't help turning to her with raised eyebrows. "What?" I whispered. "You don't like it?" "It is all quite hideous. You Americans never cease to insert your own cultural baggage wherever you go. Besides, most of these hymns are of German origin. Sorry, can't help myself. Just not in the spirit." After she turned and started to walk away, I felt this ecstatic rush of arousal run through and I wanted to follow that stiff-shouldered back of hers, wrap my arms around her waist and whisper unAmerican remarks in her ear. But then, I pulled back at the thought of all that uneaten ham still piled high.

December 24, 1968
back in Nang Rong

I felt quite chilly this morning. Wisut used a formula to change the number from Centigrade to something I understood which was 45 degrees F. Our meteorology friend, Mr. Wasan dropped by and he assured me it couldn't possibly be below 60 F. Maybe I felt more susceptible to a change in temperature because my Hua Hin sun burn is still with me. I'm peeling skin from both calves. Ironic to be suffering from chills and sunburn at once.

Later, I heard in the teachers lounge that the headmaster was away on medical leave. He had to have sections of his intestines removed. Hard for me to imagine that tall, ramrod erect figure in a hospital bed.

Wisut wanted to give me a Christmas party. I told him over and over he did not to have to do that, but he's convinced it's a must for every American regardless of creed, color or religion. "Besides," he gave me a big smile, "it will be a holiday. Don't you want a holiday?" What could I say to that? Right now he's searching all over town for an artificial tree the previous volunteer lit up during *her* Christmas holiday.

December 30, 1968

There have been too many holidays and my tidy schedule linked to lesson plans and grammar goals was blown to bits. Who knew about the King's Day; The Queen's Day; the Moon's Day and maybe High Tide Day?. Last month we had Malaria Day and soon there will be Teachers' Day followed by Childrens' Day not to mention King Chulalungkorn Day. Sometimes my students appear in the morning only to march in some afternoon parade. When that happens they are excused to join in the fun and games by the market. Every now and then, there's a whole day to teach. I would have appreciated a calendar ahead of time, but Wisut insisted that until each holiday came around no one knew for sure. It was always up to the headmaster. Today, for example, I just found out that New Years Day will be celebrated on Tuesday as a prelude to the real thing on Wednesday. Thursday will be basically a shell because everyone will be recuperation from Thursday and Friday will be thrown to the four winds because, well, it's Friday. My school is supposed to offer remedial classes on Saturday morning, but that hasn't happened for a while. One of the grades I taught will have their big exam on March 3rd and I must have them finish their work book and still leave time for review. To top it all off, school officially ends on March 15th, but after the big exam I doubt much will be expected or accomplished. Teachers will have their students doodle in work books while they grade piles of papers all before the end-of-the-year parties!

Big soccer game yesterday in the government field between local schools quickly followed by the Nang Rong School alumnae played basketball against Ban Thanon Hak alumnae. Although my knowledge of basketball rules were slim, I did think it strange that a player had to practically walk the length of the court with the ball in his hands before a penalty was called. Or, they took after Thai boxing where quite a bit can happen on the court before a call was made.

That night, after the athletes had a chance to bath, rest and change clothes, they invited me to join them for a party at the science teacher's house. A few of them were a little nervous because they had to catch the lone bus out of town for Prakhonchai Village at 9:00 PM, even so, we sipped Mekhong all the way to the house. Mats were already on the floor and food was being placed as we arrived. They had a great drinking song going for a while and I wish I could write it down, but, after all, it *was* a drinking song and I was drunk along with everyone else. Suddenly, someone called out the time! The Prakonchai group leaped out and made a mad dash to the bus stop, only to realize at the last second that *the driver was running with them!* I think they left a few hours late.

After the bus left, I tried to bicycle home and had the distinction of being the first of three men to fall into a rice paddy. The gym teacher flew off the road behind me on his Honda and broke one of his fingers.

Next morning I walked over to the post office and got my mail. Money. I was able to pay off a tailor who'd made four shirts for me. I also owed money at The Raxana Restaurant where I'd picked up the tab on a few parties. Finally, on the last turn before reaching the school I stopped off at the photography shop where I still owed a few baht for developing and printing.

Later that afternoon

School ended and the students put on their white pith helmets, hopped on their bikes and headed home. Most of them returned home after a hard day's work at school, only to work some more for their parents. They'll have to carry water buckets for their drinking water, work in the family garden, prepare portions of the evening meal after walking or biking more than five kilometers. The girls had to get up at five to sell produce in the early morning market and then rushed home to get dessert trays from their mothers who had been trying to sell Thai desserts throughout the day. In the evening the girls will sit in the field near the free movie and try to unload leftover desserts and other food portions they were not sold in the market. My students who live on farms have never known a meal composed primarily of meat. Typically, all their meals were some kind of rice curry with minuscule portions of chicken or frog along with a few vegetables.

Last week I had a spelling contest for all my classes and the first prize was a trip with me to the provincial capital, an overnight stay in a hotel and all their meals in a restaurant. Wisut thought this was much too exorbitant for a mere contest. "And, what if a girl wins?" he asked. Hmmm, I hadn't thought of that. "You must offer separate prizes. The boy winners go on a trip and the girls…" he looked puzzled. "I don't know about the girls. You must ask the women teachers what would be acceptable as a prize for them."

As it turned out, all three prizes were won by boys and we had a wonderful time taking the bus together to the capital, then getting two rooms at a hotel (one for me and another for them), and eating out at a few restaurants. I quickly discovered it was the first time any of them had ever eaten at a restaurant (never mind stay at a hotel!). I ordered my usual meal away from home: beef in oyster sauce, fried morning glory leaves and white rice. The kids kept reading the menu over and over, but they simply could not bring themselves to order anything but bowls of rice with a very thin sauce poured over it, and tea. They thought it was all wonderful and I was vicariously excited by how important it was to them. I realized how fortunate I was in my role as a foreign teacher who made slightly more money than the other teachers and lived in a house rent-free without having

Nang Rong woman drawing water from well.

The author stands at a beautiful beach in southern Thailand.

Chinese fair play with Manchu king.

Most Buriram farmers still plowed their fields with water buffalo in 1968..

Farewell photo with Sanguan and local students.

Regular torture. Singing before a crowd.

The mayor speaks at my farewell dinner.

My farewell speech.

a family to support. The four of us sang songs all the way back to Nang Rong where their parents waited for them at the bus stop.

....

January 1, 1969

When I walked over to the market this morning with Wisut to give food to the monks, everyone was saluting everyone else with *Sawadtii, bee mai...choke dee, bee mai*. [Hello...Happy New Year...Good luck for the New Year]. Merit in Buddhism may be achieved by giving something to the monks, but if you do it on New Year's Day, it is especially meaningful. In the past, when monks were totally dependent on daily contributions, this custom meant more than it does now. I have heard that monks in Bangkok still walk the line for food, but back at their temples they contribute much of it to the poor or even feed portions to stray animals. Historically, the quality and quantity of food given to monks has been indicative of well the harvests have been. Nang Rong must have had a bumper crop this year. I was quite moved by the sight of all the monks from local temples wend their way across fields towards the meeting hall in their saffron robes. They each held gleaming rice bowls. In front of the town hall, townspeople stood in their best clothing and chatted about each other's businesses. Each monk had his bowl filled before he passed more than a dozen people. Helpers with large enamel basins followed the monks down the line and as each rice bowl filled the monk turned and carefully emptied his portion into a basin and presented his now empty bowl to the next person in line. There was more food to donate than there were monks to receive it. At the end of the line walked a very small monk whose rice bowl was not only filled, but was overflowing with rice, meat cakes and pastries. The ground around his feet was coated with a layer of freshly steamed white rice.

The big basketball game today was between Nang Rong District and the Blue Team. I never did learn who they are, where they are from or why they were called the Blue Team. Especially curious since their uniforms were yellow. Nang Rong beat them in an all-elbows game that injured more fans on the sidelines than on the court.

Because I'm six feet tall everyone here assumed I was a fantastic basketball player. No matter how I phrased it, no matter how I swore I was a total klutz at all sports, they refused to believe me. I had been willing to sing on stage (even though I can't carry a tune); willing to dance in public (even though I have two left feet); however, I refused to show how totally uncoordinated I truly was. Besides, I've seen enough basketball games where the neck, groin and eyes were popular targets while jumping at the net.

In that vein, the Great Annual Football Game between government workers and the shopkeepers took place this afternoon. Mr. Anan, one of the teachers, asked me to play on the government team, but when I told him I was twenty-seven he sadly kept me off the court. Players had to be at least thirty-five to participate. Funny thing was most Thais my age look about eighteen; on the other hand, many of the locals who were in their mid-forties looked like they're ready for social security.

I did not think anyone knew what the score was by game's end, but everyone agreed it was a lot of fun. Everyone played with great élan. The crowd gave them all a standing ovation.

Back at my house, I decided to type up the day's impressions while one of my students, Wiboonchai, looks over my shoulder. He's jumping up and down in excitement because he just read his name on the page.

....

January 2, 1969

Even though it's pretty hot early in the morning, I can hear students cheering at the footraces taking place on school grounds. Groggy, lying in bed, I see several small birds flit madly inside my room from wall to wall, then, by random flight, make it into the kitchen where they peck at old rice grains on the floor. Well, that's today and considering what I went through yesterday I deserve a longer stay in bed.

Hmmm, what about yesterday? Wisut told me that when the games ended and all the prizes awarded, both sides would join forces and run to the meeting hall for a party.

The game went on forever. I slipped away to change clothes and maybe wash up a bit. On my way back I noticed there was some commotion at the janitor's house (just behind mine) so I strolled on over. Turns out the janitor and the groundskeeper had just finished brewing a fresh batch of *sato* and they invited me to sample it. Sitting on woven mats under a canopy of Asian stars, we sampled the sato and nibbled some freshly broiled fish heavily spiced with hot seasoning. More of the school's workforce showed up. None of these men had been invited to the party, so they decided to have one of their own. After a while we were all singing songs and beating out rhythms on the floor and walls. When the sato was gone, the janitor produced a quart of Mekhong. That was when I learned something new. It was perfectly okay to mix the remains of the sato batch with fresh whiskey. From a distant land someone asked me something about Wisut and I suddenly remembered I had another party to attend. After apologizing for leaving early, I stumbled on over to the big meeting hall.

Turns out that while the men were playing at sports, the women had cooked an enormous meal and thoroughly cleaned the entire building in anticipation of a celebration. By the time I arrived, the Nai Amphur was on stage standing before a drunk and dazed band, waving the crowd on and calling out the names of anyone he spotted in the crowd. Glass after glass of whiskey was handed to me, diluted only with tiny ice cubes. Apparently, all the sane people had been locked out, and the lunatics were in charge. Staid and sedate officials I only knew from formal government ceremonies, were on the stage beating on drums as if they were tom-toms. My friends from the post office, arm in arm, sang team songs, folk songs, popular songs and even a few patriotic songs. Men ran around goosing each other, then walked into walls. The women, off by themselves, giggled at the transformation of men they once knew. Only one man was able to walk over to the women's side, groping his way as if he didn't want to hit any oxygen molecules, and actually asked one of them to dance. Seeing a couple on the floor, the band struggled to its feet and managed to put out a long, dissonant wail, before collapsed into silence. Various personalities managed to get up on stage and call out the names of various other personalities to get up on stage, say a few words, accept some praise, take a hefty pull at an engraved silver cup filled with some unnamed alcoholic beverage…then all would scramble off stage and mingle on the floor. Only a trumpet player and a drummer remained on stage. People formed long lines as if forming bunny hops, wiggled from side to side, wall to wall, all the time laughed hysterically.

Suddenly, the double doors were flung open and the border patrol appeared. They wore olive-gray uniforms and carried M-14s over their shoulders. Immediately behind them came the district police in snappy brown and white uniforms with .32s by their sides. Several men had what appeared to be grenades dangling from cartridge belts and I tried had not to think about *that* too much. The ice was gone. The soda water finished. Whoever was still drinking, took only shots of pure Mekhong whiskey.

Around 10:00 o'clock a few dozen men managed to get on stage and were singing. I was somewhere near the middle of the floor, one arm over the shoulders of an elementary school teacher, the other over a bank clerk. There was a minor explosion on stage as the Nai Amphur pushed his way to the microphone and half a dozen bodies fell off stage. He raised his arms for silence and in the hush that followed, the drummer, who'd managed to remain upright, began a slow beat that harbingered the singing of the King's Anthem. All laughing sopped and in an astounding display of instant sobriety, everyone present gravely joined in singing. When they finished, the drummer beat out several more slow tat-gums and then exploded into a furious riff that laste for a good five minutes. The Nai Amphur stood in stiff attention, then raised his arms and shouted CHAI-YO! The party was over.

Outside, a truck revved its engine, people who'd arrived from surrounding villages drifted out and quietly boarded for a long ride home. The driver stuck his head out the cab window just before pulling away and I recognized him as the leader of one of the snakes dances.

How did he get into the hall? No matter, the Nang Rong crowd cheered as the truck pulled away. The riders, all standing in the back, waved and screamed out the names of friends, cheers from the game and invitations for all of us to visit them soon. The truck wove unevenly down the road and finally disappeared behind a stand of banana trees easily visible beneath the light of an enormous moon.

A mass of policemen and border patrol soldiers gathered in the center of the field and fired their guns at the sky. A few die-hards from the party stumbled out on to the grass with pint bottles in search of young women from the city of Korat who'd been paid to dance with the locals. None of the few women present were willing to dance with these drunks who shouted angry words at them as they walked away toward friends in the village who would take them in. Fights broke out between police and border patrol men. Wisut gave a tremendous sigh, clapped my back and nodded in he direction of the house. I smiled at him as he made a jab with his fist as if to hit my stomach, but stopped an inch away. I pretended to vomit, and, laughing to ourselves, we walked the familiar road back to our house and sleep.

January 26, 1969

This Sunday morning my alarm clock was bright sun. Flinging wide the wooden shutters, I blinked out at the greenery and listened to the sound of students playing ping-pong. Reverberations reached me from the big drum at the temple, wheels from the water girl's cart creaked by and leaves from the mango trees rustled softly. I strolled into town around ten and bought eight baht worth of rice cakes and ate half of them at my usual morning restaurant with two eggs, some pork strips and a steaming cup of Ovaltine. A very old man sat at the next table. At first I thought he was falling over in my direction, then realized he was leaning over to talk. I could barely understand a word because he spoke with a strong northeast accent and many of the tones sounded unfamiliar to me. Gradually, I understood him to say he was a friend to the former volunteer and that he'd taught her how to play the *saw-oo*. He said she was quite fluent in Thai and very polite. I was very proud of the way I managed to grasp the meaning of entire paragraphs from a word here and there. Of course, I was never sure of my conclusions. In fact, I was like Shakespeare's Moth who said,"Methinks I have attended a feast of words and come away with the scraps…" As I got up to leave, the old man said his house was not too far away and I was welcome to visit any time. Why not? I asked myself. How the hell was I spending my time anyway? Making cakes? Come on, Needle! Meet the people! I sat back down and told him I was free to visit right now. His watery eyes peered back at me and his right hand began to shake.

"Excuse me," I said. "I did not mean to be impolite."

"You want to come to my house?" he asked.

"Yes, if it is not too much trouble."

With surprising strength, he quickly got to his feet and began shaking my hand. The two of us laughed aloud in the quiet restaurant. The lady at the charcoal grill peeked over at us to see what was going on. Shaking his head from side to side, the old man said the other volunteer may have been okay in her own right, but I was really fine. We walked, small fingers linked, to the door. At the edge of sunlight I had an idea and asked the owner if he had a small bottle of Mekhong for my new friend. "For him?" he asked. When I nodded, he reached out for a small bottle of *Lau Khaow* and whispered to me he preferred that to whiskey. Wisut offered that stuff to me once with a warning I ignored and almost burned my throat swallowing. Could they actually have distilled alcohol from rice? My memory told me it was the nearest thing the village had to a universal solvent. Cheaper than Mekhong, too.

We slowly walked, little fingers still linked, through the remains of the morning market, down a side alley, past a one man charcoal-oven facility, to the tottering building he called his home. Small children stared out at us as we scrambled up the broken steps to the first room of the house. The old man sat down at a bench surrounded by carpentry tools, reached up and took down a partially carved deer's head, and motioned for me to sit beside him. As he carefully whittled a right ear, he told me of his early life as a soldier in some long ago completed campaign and then how he had found his way to Nang Rong and began his small business of making animal heads from discarded blocks of wood. Soon, other members of the household presented themselves: a consumptive young man and his screaming wife along with a dozen or so children. The kids were very quiet, but kept their eyes on me the whole time. The young man coughed up blood casually into a dirty cloth and occasionally rubbed his chest. His wife kept taking down her hair and replacing it atop her head. There was something about her eyelids that struck me as different. Then, I realized the old man was talking about her. He explained she was the only child of a Nang Rong man and a wandering Japanese soldier who somehow found his way to the area during WWII. She seemed unconcerned that the old man was talking about her and paid attention only to her hair. He uncorked the bottle I'd bought and we passed it back and forth as I pretended to drink and he spoke of his war memories. Long ago and far away, he had been part of a labor force that worked for a long time on an enormous bridge near the Burmese border and of how many American and English soldiers were forced by the Japanese to work on the bridge even though they were sick and weak from old wounds, poor food and heat. I asked him if he could remember the bridge's name. He shook his head. It was a short name, he said, but he thought it might have been Burmese. As he spoke, the children crept closer to my side until the woman abruptly started screaming at them and they retreated. When the bottle was empty the old man lolled back against a post and fell asleep. I wanted to shake him awake and say, "They made a movie about that bridge you worked on, old man, and it stared William Holden and Alec Guiness…" but I left him to his dreams, the woman to her hair, the kids to themselves and the young man, who had remained silent throughout the conversation, well, I left him to the short time he had left. I walked slowly out to the alley and back to the main street. The sun was very bright and dust stirred up by a passing buffalo cart made my eyes water.

January 29, 1969

I lived through this month in a series of shivering mornings. My students never changed the type of clothes they wore and in rooms that had neither heating nor cooling, many of them shivered right along with me. I tried to keep my classroom atmosphere fast-moving and as interesting as possible by interspersing games with lessons. The students loved giving me what we in the west would call tongue-twisters, except they were tone-twisters: a series of multi-syllabic words with a myriad of different tones falling on top of one another. They never ceased to find my attempts hysterically funny. Finally, I told them it was my turn and on the blackboard I wrote: How much wood could a woodchuck chuck if a woodchuck could chuck wood? They stared at it in silence. I slowly read it aloud. They looked at me in wonder. "Now, you say it," I told them. One by one, they stood up and said, "chuck…chuck…chuck…" and collapsed in laughter.

The assistant-headmaster has sat in on my classes a few times and although he seems to be a friend of mine socially, in the class he never stopped scowling. He eventually approached me and said, "You have too much fun all the time. You must teach gerunds." I don't know why sooner or later everything comes back to gerunds. His concerns seemed justified because all the standardized tests taken by my students show very low scores.

No good news from the outside world either. One of the teachers old me that the mayor of Lahansai Village and several of his men were ambushed on the Lahansai-Buriram road at night. The driver was shot in both thighs, two border patrol policemen were killed outright and the mayor was seriously wounded. I have a black and white photograph of myself standing with the Lahansai mayor, Suwin, in front of the local malaria eradication office. Naturally, I thought back to Fred's co-workers who were so reluctant to travel in that area to take blood samples. Fred does not yet know about the attack because the convoy only recently passed through Nang Rong first on its way to Buriram with the wounded and the dead bodies.

February 1, 1969

I woke up this morning with an after-taste of too many cigarettes and too many shots of Mekhong. Luckily, I still had a small amount of toothpaste and after cleaning my teeth and rinsing my mouth over and over again I decided I was fit for work. My lead student, Somboon, spotted me walking toward the room. He quickly stepped inside, stood at rigid attention and called out: *Nakrian! Trong!* [Students! At attention!]. The boys in their white shirts and blue shorts and the girls in their white blouses and blue skirts, stared up at me and waited. I started off with a minimal pair drill. Simply cannot work on spoken English too much because there are so many sounds we make in our language that do not exist in theirs. The words this day were RYE and RICE. Since Thai does not have any words that end in an S or sibilant sound after a vowel, words such as RICE are especially difficult for them to pronounce. That's certainly ironic in a country where rice is omnipresent, but, I suppose, only ironic to a westerner. I managed to teeter from one class to another, flipping through my lesson plan book, maneuvering from minimal pairs to verb substitution drills.

I am going to the market.
will
I will go to the market
went
I went to the market
shall
I shall go to the market

Finally, the last class was over and I headed back to the house to clean up a bit. I hadn't shaved and black stubble was especially prominent on my chin. I don't know what happened to my hair, but in my dusty mirror no two hairs seemed to be in partnership. My clothes looked pretty wrinkled. Too much to deal with. I threw water on my head, tried to pat down my hair and headed for the Raxana Restaurant where the owner, for the 8th time, asked me when I was going to return to America. What would I do without rice? How would I be able to live without spicy food? I nodded back as I had done many times before and wandered to the back where he kept artifacts of western food. There was a rusty can of navy beans that looked leftover from WWII and I told the owner to cook it with pork strips and onion slices. I also ordered a pot of rice and a quart of really cold Thai beer. I propped up the latest Time Magazine with a Nixon medallion on the cover, turned to the People section, and thought to myself, "Needle, you are such a middle-class boob!" Everything arrived just as I'd ordered it. Even the beans came out okay when I scooped them up with white rice and a touch of peppery fish oil. Then, sated and happy, I lit my fifteenth *Sai Fon* cigarette of the day and began to dream of desserts I could not possibly order. Then, reality! Wisut charged through the front of the restaurant with Chalerm, another teacher. They were both neatly combed, wearing Hawaiian shirts, black slack and sox to match. They gave off a powerful cloud of cologne.

"You must come with us to a party for Mr. Manu, the Nai Amphur' assistant. He will celebrate his fortieth birthday," Wisut declared.

"If I went there I'd have to go home and shower and change and…everything," I finished on a plaintive note.

"Go fast!" he insisted.

Eventually I was spiffed up enough and the three of us walked quickly to a large hall located next to the new $13,000 home of the district education officer. He must have done well in land speculation. There was an enormous sign up declaring that Manu was forty years old and that everyone wished him long life and happiness. Wisut arrived with Chalerm on his motorcycle. I came up behind them on my bicycle. I prayed that somehow I could circumvent the entire affair. My stomach was stretched tight with navy beans and beer. I didn't want to eat any local treats and I certainly did not want to drink any Mekhong. They loaded me with both and I found myself sipping whiskey and nibbling on pepper-fried fish salad. Someone from the band approached and asked me if I'd be willing to sing Happy Birthday after the second instrumental number. This was a band that specialized in instrumentals because any ordinary singer would have a really hard time keeping pace with the band's constantly changing tempo. There were two trumpets (one strong and one weak), an immense bass (played by the tallest man in Nang Rong), a tambourine man (who did not actually have a tambourine, but shook anything that rattled (generally in 2/4 time if the band is playing 1/2 or in 1/2 if the band is playing 2/4), a drummer (who tried very hard to maintain a steady beat, but who was often a substitute for the weak trumpet player if the weak trumpet player played poorly), a bongo player (who seemed to have had professional training (but, here too, something was amiss because his training was in classical Thai music—pretty far off the beaten path of western tunes). At times, the bongo player approached the rhythm of the drummer, but then one or the other pulled ahead. Finally, there was an accordion player. My ears followed the accordion when I sang. That evening I found myself starting to sing Happy Birthday at bass profundo and worked my way down from there. Since the microphone stops functioning at anything lower than middle 'C' the audience was gratefully excluded from hearing my voice amplified. The band continued playing long after I stopped singing because, after all, how many words were there in the song? They just wanted more and I had no more to give.

I returned to my seat, next to Wisut and drank more whiskey because Pinisuk, who promised to take me rabbit hunting but never did, was sitting nearby and swore it would be impolite if I didn't share his enthusiasm for the party by drinking. He also told me that his name was no longer Pinisuck. He had changed it to Grip. That's what it sounded like to me. Reminded me of my student Sangiap who changed his name to Wirirat. I usually got hung up in the middle and called him Wirrrriiii…Anyway, I was nibbling on an orange when the hostess of the party, Manu's wife, approached and offered me a long skewer holding a tomato, a potato, a piece of meat, an onion and a piece of pineapple. I tried the pineapple first only to discover it had been dipped in really hot chili pepper powder before braising. Yikes! People on stage chanted the praises of Manu. Manu went on stage and sang his own praises. Then the band lurched into a beguine and Manu told me to dance. I told him I didn't beguine which upset him because he'd asked the band to play a beguine especially for me. Finally, the band played a ramwong, which I sort've knew, and I asked one of the teachers to join me, but she resisted, saying she didn't know how to do it, which is ridiculous. I kept standing on one foot and another until she gave in. It turned out she really didn't know how to do the ramwong.

There was a commotion outside as a military jeep screeched to a stop by the door and four armed guards got out. They stood at attention with automatic rifles in place and saluted as a man of enormous girth emerged from the back to huff and puff his way to the dance floor. It was the provincial police chief. He shook everyone's hand then he danced with the most beautiful woman. The shishkabab tasted better after more whiskey. Mr. Grip (formerly Mr. Pinisuck) left my side to take the place of the weak trumpet player who in turn went to the drums. Chalerm walked over to join me and as he sat down his chair collapsed and he fell forward, unable to stop his momentum, into the table before us which held glasses of whiskey, soda bottles and a bucket of ice. Laughter all around. The Nai Amphur arrived wearing his favorite combat fatigue, ranger-commando suit with a double loop of cartridges about his waist and a .45 on his hip. He looked like a Thai John Wayne and never stopped smiling, talking or eating. He settled back with the chief until someone shouted for him to sing something. Manu, drunk, started tugging at me to dance every time the band played. I began to enjoy the party less. Then, Manu took his wife's hand and they did a tango, alone on the floor. They were magnificent. Even with Manu drunk and his wife more than a little top-heavy, they actually moved with grace as Manu controlled the situation with a marvelous combination of wrist power, finger signals and whispers. Manu appeared like a wraith beside his wife's bulk, but he guided her like a tug boat tweaking the Queen Elizabeth into port. After the dance Manu collapsed and his wife went to check the food supplies.

The chief and his guardians left and the Nai Amphur, glowing, got to his feet, walked over to Wisut and asked, "Are those sixty pieces ready?"

Wisut nodded.

"Make sure they're all smoothed down."

Wisut nodded again.

"You're sure they're ready?" the Nai Amphur asked.

"Yes," Wisut said

The Nai Amphur made it out to his jeep, revved it up, stalled, ground gears, backed into a tree, swerved on to the road, slid off on to a soft shoulder, stalled again and finally puttered away. I asked Wisut where he was keeping those sixty pieces of whatever it was the mayor asked him about.

"I do not know what he was talking about," he told me.

"But, you seemed so sure!"

"He's the mayor," Wisut said. "If the mayor wants to talk about sixty pieces of anything, then I say okay. Do you think I will say the sixty pieces are *not* ready? Never mind. He is drunk. Tomorrow he will not remember."

Then, the band in a final shot at immortality, stood up and played The King's Anthem before it collapsed in exhaustion. Several young men and women who must have been waiting for the end, appeared and started collecting bottles, clearing tables and cleaning the floor. The last of the female guests slipped out a side door. The house just behind the hall was opened, a mat placed on the floor and the remaining guests began to play cards. Wisut joined them, so I figured it was a good time for me to leave. Scooping up a handful of peanuts to act as a binder to the mass in my gut, I looked around for my bike. It was still there against a tree. I peddled home.

All quiet at the house. I hauled the bike up the steps, propped it against a wall, tied two rubber bands from the broken doorknob to a nail on the wall to keep the door shut, gave myself a hasty, freezing few buckets of water over my head, wrapped a towel around my waist, parted my mosquito net, half turned to click on Radio Pleikou, fell back atop the inch thick mattress that rests on a bamboo frame, and fell asleep listening to Dust Springfield singing "…the only one who could ever love me was the son of a preacher man…"

The giant tokay lizard hanging upside down above me tried his best to wake me with an imitation of a man being tortured, but I ignored it and dreamed of Manu's wife.

February 3, 1969

The headmaster left for a four day sojourn to parts unknown. Adjan Azwai, the assistant headmaster, bumped into me this afternoon, looked me up and down and said,"I am not teaching on Saturday. You do not have to teach on Saturday. I think no one should teach on Saturday. Will you teach on Saturday? "No," I shook my head. "I will not teach on Saturday." He smiled and we parted friends.

A student ran up and handed me a telegram. It was from Fred, telling me to leave immediately and meet him in Buriram for an adventure. At least that's what I gleaned from the jumble of letter on the page. I was on my way to the bus depot when Wisut stopped me and implored me to stay. He said there was going to be a big celebration of the first election in many years. I shook my head and told him I had to leave on an emergency. The minute I teamed up with Fred we trotted to Pensee's Restaurant where we dined on tender fried beef in oyster sauce, steamed rice and a few quarts of chilled Thai beer. After telling each other a few short catch-up stories, we fell fast asleep. Around eight the next morning, acclimated as we were to Thailand typical temperature, we felt absolutely freezing in the 56 F. degree Saturday morning chill.

While devouring some hot Ovaltine and a few fried *pathongos* Fred told me we were going to team up with Jennifer, a community development volunteer from the area. He explained he'd been in contact with a school in Fairfield, Connecticut eager to raise some money for a worthy project in Thailand and he needed the CD volunteer to help introduce him to the locals. Fred decided we'd scout the more rural villages, even going so far as to drop in on the always-difficult-to-reach Styyk. Fred snagged one of the office jeeps, a driver and dropped by Pensee's on the way out of town to pick up some of her delicious chicken salad sandwiches (which we kept on ice in a medical supply box). We bounced our way out of town, doing okay, until we reached the turn-off for Styyk and hit an almost impassable road that was being built by local farmers on their own. Four-wheeling it, we hung dearly to the jeep's roll bars and didn't stop until we spotted an ancient woman who seemed to lean in our direction as we approached, so we picked her up, along with her bag of betel nut leaves and her red teeth and red drool. Although she spoke Thai with a strange mixture of tones and occasional Cambodian vocabulary, we managed to follow the story she told us about how beautiful she was as a young woman and of her *farang* boy friend. *Farang* in this neck of the woods usually means an American, and we smiled at her fantasy. Fred asked her when this all happened and she said it was during the time the Americans were fighting the Japanese. Turned out the boy friend *foreigner* had been one of the many Japanese soldiers who'd been stationed in Thailand during WWII. Eventually, we had to stop and give our wounded bodies a break from the bad road. When the old lady indicated this was where we parted company, we offered her half a chicken salad sandwich. She sniffed it suspiciously, shook her head, wished us good luck and walked away. Jennifer had a Swiss army knife she used to cut the sandwiches. Our driver brought his own fried rice wrapped in a banana leaf. Jennifer continued to impress me with her fluency in Thai and by the many people she knew by the side of the road. Although she'd never been to Styyk, she'd obviously been in this area more than a few times. When we stopped to stock up on watermelons at a roadside stand, Jennifer chatted easily with local men and women about crops and the weather predictions. I couldn't help but admire her language skills and ability to bond instantly with everyone she met. She was only a few years older than me, but I felt very immature in her company.

Back in the jeep, Fred took out a camera and told us he wanted to take as many colorful and interesting slides as he could, so the faculty and students back in Connecticut could see what the area looked like before and after construction of the project. The goal was to raise enough money to build two small school buildings in the villages that were remote even by Styyk standards. We were in heavy woods and unable to see much of the road ahead. The driver stopped and said he had to take a leak. We looked at each other and as the driver pee'd in front, Jennifer ran to the left side and Fred and I hosed down vegetation on the right. Back inside, we hadn't gone over more than a dozen or so more bumps when we came to a small clearing in the middle of which stood a small temple and monastery. Fred told us that according to reports he'd heard this village educated all its students in the prayer hall of the temple, but the people loved the idea of having their own school building.

Looking around, we could see a few dozen small homes, all high off the ground on reinforced bamboo stilts. The students had been in the temple's study hall, but upon our arrival everyone rushed out to greet us. The headmaster shouted to his second in command who shouted at the students who giggled and pointed at us. Other teachers appeared briefly, took one look and raced home to change their clothes. A few monks lit cigarettes and posed, frozen into that aloof posture only monks seemed to handle well. Eventually everyone encircled us: students, teachers, school administration and city officials. As one, they all bowed slightly in our direction and pressed their palms together in traditional greeting which, we in turn, reciprocated. Dozens of questions were thrown at us all at once, but only Jennifer seemed capable of responding.

After our mission was made clear and introductions back and forth had finished, we were directed to the road leading out of town and a small, slightly cleared area where they indicated a school could be built. We took photos of the road, the clearing, monks, buffalos, teachers and students. I sat astride an enormous gray water buffalo that tried to brush me off with its horns. Fred and Jennifer told everyone present about the funding process and what could be expected. More pictures taken. I slid off the beast and joined the others at the headmaster's home where we were served chicken curry and a cloudy, fermented rice drink that I knew was illegal. Nobody seemed to care. A few of the teachers brought in watermelons from the jeep. They were perfectly green and round on the outside and bright red and deliciously sweet inside. The Thais called them *luke namtan*, which literally translates as *sugar babies*.

Our driver appeared and by the expression on his face we figured it was time to return. Jennifer said she alone had taken over one hundred slides. Back in the jeep, we *wai'd* our new friends, and bumped our way home. We dropped off Jennifer at a friend's house and the driver dropped us off at Fred's place where we nibbled on fried eggs and curry wrapped in banana leaves the people had given us on the way out. We finished it off with watermelon wedges. Fred looked up at me and burst out laughing. His face was covered in red clay dust with a smattering of watermelon juice hanging from his chin. I must've looked the same. We took turned using Fred's bathroom where we scooped up really cold water from an enormous clay pot and washed ourselves off. Finally, wearing relatively clean clothes with combed hair, looking more or less respectable, we went out for a walk in the warm evening air. By the railroad station, samlaw drivers smoked and gossiped. Shops were all open, but not many customers were around. Taxis drove aimlessly from corner to corner, their drivers calling out their destinations, searching for customers. We reached the red light district.

There was a new sign, in English, posted in front of one of the houses: WELCOME TO THE PINK HOUSE. The insides had deteriorated considerably since our last visit. There were a few lethargic women who stared at us, but didn't speak.

"I think this crew is on the rebound from one of the American airbases," Fred whispered.

"I don't think you need to lower your voice. No one else speaks English."

Outside again, I couldn't help think about the plight of the women who worked at these places and for a fleeting moment tried to imagine myself in their place, opening up for anyone with cash, feigning affection, knowing with certainly that for whatever reasons I'd become ensnared, I would only inevitably find freedom when customers no longer found me attractive. I turned to Fred.

"Let's go see a movie. Doesn't the theater here have air conditioning?"

We bought two tickets for four baht each and sat through *They Died With Their Boots On* starring Errol Flynn, Olivia de Haviland, Anthony Quinn (as Chief Crazy Horse), Sydney Greenstreet and featuring Hattie McDaniel. We chewed salted sunflower seeds, laughed at the outrageous dialogue the Thai *readers* chose to create from the written script in front of them and, in the end, stood with the crowd as a picture of King Bhumipol flashed on to the screen and the king's anthem was played.

Back at the house, Fred wrapped himself in a bed sheet and slept in all his clothes. Wrapped in two discarded blankets and all my clothes, I also slept until it was time to catch the 7:00 AM bus out of town to Nang Rong in time to change my clothes and prepare lesson plans for my first class: advanced composition with an introduction to gerunds.

February 5, 1969

Wisut was eager to tell me about the party I missed, but I could hardly keep my eyes focused. There'd been a Thai boxing match and an all-night movie in the main field that honored Adjan Tam (rising tone) who is one of the leading candidates of the government party running as a representative from Buriram Province. Wisut explained to me that since the first Constitution was finally approved after a ten year study session, Bangkok set up a date for candidates to file for office. They also gave a tabulation of population centers that showed how many representatives could run in that area. Chances of a morning market merchant running was pretty slim since one mandate was each candidate had to post a 10,000 baht bond. Any candidate who didn't garner a minimum number of votes would have his money taken by Bangkok. I rubbed my eyes and tried to pay attention. I was told Buriram was given five openings and the government had five candidates for each slot. Wisut took out a torn campaign poster with Adjan Tam's face. It had the same effect on me as Nixon's jowls. I loathed him on sight.

Suddenly I heard loudspeakers blaring from the parade grounds. I turned to Wisut, who shrugged, and said Adjan Tam would be speaking.

I stepped outside and heard sounds of a band playing an introduction for something big. It was Tam, whose voice even as far away as my house, sounded staccato and reminiscent of a 1930's Bavarian harangue.

Too much for my poor head. Wisut told me that Tam was very big in the concrete industry and owned several rice mills. A distant crowd roared their approval.

"What do you want to do?" I asked Wisut.

"I will take a nap," he said, and left me.

I wandered into the market area, saw the District's medical officer and sat down at his table. He had a degree from Ball State University. After my conversation with him I walked back to the house and tried my best to remember everything we'd discussed. The following dialogue is more or less what I remembered; but, not exactly what we each actually said.

"Is this really a democratic election?" I asked him.

"I think most of local people who know anything at all dislike anything to do with the government."

"Where do the candidates come from?"

"Bangkok finds wealthy citizens who promise not to embarrass the government by voting independently. For their loyalty they receive government contracts for their businesses. I think your country is not very different."

We both laughed.

"Mr. Tam is closely associated with an important military man named General Praphat," the medical officer said, "who made his reputation destroying farming cooperatives, unions and spreading lies about anyone he disliked."

"This is beginning to sound more and more like my own country."

"The last time they had an election, the government's candidates were always surrounded by bodyguards, who not only guarded, but often coerced the voters. Still sound familiar to you?"

"No, this is sounding pretty grim."

"The last election resulted in a military junta that ruled with an iron fist. Newspapers reported that men with yellow badges (a symbol of the government party) often hung around polling places making sure votes went their way."

"Doesn't the public get fed up with this?"

"Oh yes," he nodded. "the last time there was a rally for government party candidates in Bangkok, many of them were booed off stage and some had things thrown at them."

"Do you think the same thing will happen again?"

"The people of Bangkok are more educated. They may actually manage to vote in independent candidates, but out here, if you go to the field, you will see many men wandering around wearing yellow badges."

....

Several days later

I was taking a late afternoon nap the other day when Thom and his students rolled into town to visit the Cambodian ruins at Panom Rung. Turned out most of the Nang Rong teaching staff had been waiting for them. They arrived in two buses filled with students and a Land Rover jammed with teachers and government officials. Not many Land Rovers in this neck of the woods, since they go for $15,000, but that doesn't seem to stop the Chief Education Officer of Buriram Province from owning one. I'd met this guy earlier and remember he had a kind face. He also tod me that he would not correct my Thai if I didn't correct his English.

They swept right by me in a cloud of red dust and by the time I caught up they were on the front porch of the school drinking what appeared to be coconut milk. They called out for me to join them and have a drink. Since my stomach had, as usual, been out of sorts, I raised a glass to my lips and even before I tasted realized it was *sato*. Gagging, I placed it back on the table. The Ed Officer winked at me and asked, "You know what people say when they drink?"

"Good luck?"

He shook his head.

"Cheers?"

No go.

"*Lechaim?*"

He thought that over for a second, shook his head again and cried out, "Yo ho ho and a bottle of rum!"

While the others at the table discussed administrative problems, Thom walked with me over to my house to look at slides I'd just had processed in Australia. But, he didn't seem remotely interested in slides. I asked him what was wrong. He told me that right after news of the shooting was heard in Buriram, school was closed and a military helicopter landed in the city from Lahansai with the Nai Amphur on board, bleeding and half-hysterical. Then, another helicopter arrived from Nangong with the bodies of dead policemen. The earlier story I'd heard turned out to be only partially true. The attack at Lahansai, in which two border patrol police were killed and another four severely wounded, turned out be only the beginning. As the funerals were being planned in Buriram, the bodies were prepared for shipment to the local monastery. The Nai Ampur and four of his assistants left Lahansai in a jeep in order to attend the ceremonies and cremations. As they passed over a small, wooden bridge halfway between Buriram and Lahansai, a man waiting beneath the bridge fired up and riddled the vehicle with bullets. Although the driver was wounded in both legs, he managed to keep his foot on the gas, sped over the bridge and picked up speed, going at a fast clip when they were hit again by men who stood on either side of the road and raked the jeep with automatic rifle fire. Somehow they managed to keep going even though by this time everyone inside was bleeding.

Thom said he was at the municipal field when the helicopters landed. The doctor asked Thom to join him in the medical tent for an examination of the bodies before they were cremated. Shuddering, he described seeing two covered forms brought out on stretchers, stiff arms dangling out from under white sheets. He followed the doctor inside and stood as far away as he could while a perfunctory autopsy was performed.

"My God, why did he want you there?" I asked.

"I really don't know. Excuse me, I have to go to the bathroom, again."

My own cramps started while he was doing his business. The rainy season has been over for a long time, and the stale water from local wells is probably contaminated. The instant he returned, I quickly went in myself.

"Sorry, there's nothing but an old Sears Roebuck catalog with stiff, shiny paper," he called after me.

I decided to stay over, drink green tea and see if my stomach recovered enough for me to take the bus back to Nang Rong. The two of us had no sooner sat down in the middle of his sparse living room then he lurched to his feet with his hand over his mouth and ran again to the bathroom. I began to consider the possibility that Thom's entire house was somehow poisoned with parasites. The thought would not go away.

"Thom, I have to go," I called out, but there was no answer.

At that instant Fred pulled up in a government jeep, looking dashing as usual in his creased brown uniform and sharp black mustache.

"Hop in," he said. "There's a small fair going on just a few miles in the countryside. I hear they've brought dancing girls in from as far away as Uttaradit."

"Fred, don't you know they've been hauling in dead bodies from the countryside?"

"Too true! Then again, we've all only got one life. We better live it," he said, and patted the seat.

"Against my better judgment and my stomach's growl, I joined him as he roared over to a restaurant called the *RanGun Eng* (which means *Togetherness Shop*, or, possibly, *The Shop Where we Do It Ourselves Together*). Fred sipped some Mekhong and I nursed a bottle of soda water. He looked up expectantly when I finished my drink.

"So, you feeling better?"

Off we drove to the fair. Only two baht admission fee. A few of the young women waved at Fred and called out to him by his Thai name: Deerek. He'd told me sometimes they called him *The Indian* because of his mustache. Someone handed us a bunch of dance tickets so we jumped up on to the stage and danced with a few of the women. Faint applause reached us. I was dying in the heat. Wheezing and coughing I managed to jump off the stage. Fred joined me and stared.

"What's your problem, man? You look wrecked," he said

"Come on, Fred. I'm older than you. I'm twenty-seven!"

"What's that mean?"

"It's three years older than twenty four."

"Deep. Didn't know you were a heavy thinker. Okay, let's get a cool drink."

"No more drinks!"

"I'm talking about an orange Fanta, okay?"

One of the young dancers walked over and began whispering in Fred's ear. I tactfully walked away to pee behind some trees. By the time I returned he'd negotiated a weekend tryst with her in Korat.

February 6, 1969

A high wind blew all night and cold air drifted into my room. I didn't have any more blankets, so I put on some old clothes and wrapped my mosquito net around me. By morning, I expected to see ice crystals. Wisut peeked in on me, shivering, and said.

"The cold season is here."

"Do you know the temperature?"

"In your language, I think maybe 60 degrees F."

How will I ever be able to deal with a New England winter?

Wisut left this morning for Nongki Village with his friend, Chalerm, to help out at one of schools to be used as a voting station. Both schools in Nang Rong and two of the temples are also being utilized. I wandered down to some of the local polling stations with my camera to record the first voting here in over a decade. Nothing. No one. Along the way back to my house I pedaled by some polling stands near the school and although the area was filled with teachers and aids to help out, there are virtually no people voting. I went out for tea, read an old copy of a magazine and looked up and down the street to see if anyone was on their way to vote. I walked back to the restaurant and asked the only customer there if he'd voted. He stared back at me as if I was crazy. I do not understand what's happening.

Almost midnight

Wisut returned to fill me in on election returns. He told me when he arrived at Nongki, along the Korat Road, about half an hour's drive from Nang Rong, he found utter confusion. The election officials were old men who'd been given the job through political patronage. Since Wisut only received 35 baht for helping and it cost him 80 baht in expenses, he wondered why anyone was doing it at all. He said he thought maybe there was some other kind of payment he wasn't aware of.

"What did you do while you were there?" I asked.

"I talked with some people and smoked two packs of Gold City cigarettes. I didn't even include that as expense."

He said he went from table to table reading instructions, organizing lists of the last census, and relaying collated information to other teachers who seemed to be indifferent to the whole operation.

The two major parties who were running candidates were:

1.) The Government Party—or, Sahapracha-Thai (The United Peoples' Party)

2.) The major opposition party—or, Prachaatibut (The peoples' Democratic Party)

The current prime minister, Thanom, is the nominal head of the government party, but during the election proceedings his official title was held in abeyance until the votes were all in. He may only be unseated if the PDP defeated the UPP by a substantial majority in the race for representative seats in the lower house. The leader of the PDP was Saynii Pramoth, now running as a representative from a Bangkok district. His brother was Kukrit, the well-known writer-publisher of Siam-Rath Newspaper and the Siam-Rath Magazine (editions in Thai and English). Kukrit has for some time been a political gadfly of the present leadership. He was his own man and has enough power and prestige (he's related to the Royal Family) to be assured a platform. He was recently censored by the army for stepping out of line. Most of Kukrit's problems were associated with his taking issue with UPP platforms, rather than openly boost his brother's candidacy. Before anything else, he viewed himself as a strong patriot and spokesman for the kind of democratic country he believed Thailand could become. A blistering editorial he wrote attacking Peace Corps gave him headlines even in Buriram and some coverage in the Western press. He wrote that he believed the agency had lost much of its earlier altruistic ideals and had shifted to an evangelic position of preaching what was right and what was wrong with Thailand. He concluded that too many B.A. generalists were being sent over and not enough volunteers with technical know-how. Some highly-placed Thais resented what they called the Peace Corp's holier than thou attitude. One area in which the brothers agreed on was a need for change in the current political hierarchy. If their party made a strong win, some sweeping changes could be expected—possibly even the dropping of General Prapas from some of his many appointed positions. A school teacher in Buriram who was fluent in English talked with me about the election issue causes. He admitted many people were skeptical over the ground rules. They remembered during previous elections, members of the so-called opposition who did win seats, suddenly changed party allegiance or were forced to resign by the military in the interests of national security. He smiled when he said he believed the expression for this sort of government was *guided democracy*.

When I wrote this entry, the government parties were winning heavily up-country in the remote provinces and losing in Bangkok. That same teacher told me that people in Thailand's northeast will either not vote at all, or will vote to retain the current powers or, whomever their local bosses tell them to vote for.

A few days before the election Nang Rong was visited by small fleet of army helicopters and a contingent of police officials and army generals who spoke at the local hall and basically told everyone there it would be in their best interests to support the current government. I've heard the citizens of Bangkok and its sister city of Thonburi, will likely support the opposition. There, large centers of intellectuals, would-be unionists, students and a healthy percentage of the middle class may opt for change. Thamasat University, a center of political science, had organized teams of students to campaign for PDP (with, it is rumored, some volunteers supported).

The radio commentaries said that the percentage of the population turning out to vote ranged anywhere from the high 60's in Bangkok to below 10% in outlying districts. One of Nang Rong's barbers told me that the people outside the capital will vote for the man, while the people inside Bangkok will vote for the party. At this time, with 140 out of 800 precincts reporting, the government party was being beaten by a margin of 3–1 in Bangkok. Up country, the government piled up substantial majorities.

In Buriram, Mr. Tam was supposed to sweep the # 1 spot without trouble, but was outdistanced by Mr. Suwat. Suwat's also a government man, but independent in his own fashion, probably due to his vast wealth through ownership in bus lines, rice fields, mills, shops and family connections in car dealerships, insurance companies and banks. Wisut seemed to feel some degree of support for him, but usually he's seemed ambiguous about where he stood.

One major problem Wisut ran into at his polling station was that although many people came to vote, they could not do so because they were registered on old census lists in other districts.

There was overall chaos as to voting procedures. In some instances voters were not only told how to vote but who to vote for. There was no rule about checking IDs and anyone who came in to vote, whose name was on the list, was simply checked off with no proof asked. Later in the day, a number of people appeared to vote only to discover their names had already been checked off.

Prior to Thanom, the government party was headed by Sarit. This was in the era pre-dating the rise to power of General Prapas. He was also the son-in-law of Prime Minister Kittikachorn! At Sarit's height, he was as powerful as Prapas was today. He had a rather intolerant view of dissidents and reacted with military vigor to even a hint of insurrectionist activity on the borders. About seven years ago, a district leader was ambushed in a small town not too far from Nang Rong. Sarit sent out a commando force to the area which issued an ultimatum to the population. Either the assassins were turned over to them or the town would suffer severe consequences. When the time table passed without anyone being named, the commandos burned the village to the ground and relocated the people.

Following Sarit's leadership, came Thanom, a relatively weak ruler. Feuding personalities who had been held in check by Sarit's iron grasp, were free to return to the infighting to which they'd been accustomed. Within the power vacuum that arose, Prapas' strength increased until he became General of all the armies. All in all, the history of democratic process in Thailand is an intriguing business and worth a few dozen Ph.D. theses.

....

February 11, 1969

Morning election returns: the government party is trailing in Bangkok by 4–1. Saynee himself is leading his government opposite by even more than that. In Buriram, Tam not only lost to Suwat, but didn't even manage to finish within the top five candidates. Suwat came in second. Two of the five government men came in within the top five, the rest were independents who, rumor again, may well swing over to the government side after the votes were made official.

I saw my headmaster sitting by himself in the teachers lounge at the end of election day.

I greeted him, politely and asked if he was comfortable.

"No, Khun Burgess, I am not comfortable. I am very sorry that Mr. Tam lost."

He did not seem eager to continue, although it was only a few hours ago he approached me near my room and asked me a few questions about the election and my own feelings concerning his country's new willingness to have elections at all. Right there, with the sinking sun's rays in his face, his appearance shocked me. I had not seen him up close since his hospitalization. He seemed at least ten years older, his body was no longer muscled and taut, but slightly bowed and thin. His face now showed distinct wrinkles. During previous meetings he always gesticulated with vigor and spoke in strident tones, but now before me, he kept his hands in his pockets and his voice was raspy and almost inaudible.

"I am sorry Mr. Tam lost, too," I said.

Smiling slightly, he waved me over to a chair near his. Rubbing his forehead before he spoke, he asked me how things were going for me at the school, how the students were doing, and what I thought my memories of Thailand would be once I was back in my own country.

I found myself lowering my own voice as if experiencing a vicarious sense of debilitation.

"I am sorry my students did not do well in the grammar exam. Gerunds are…"

"Never mind about gerunds," he waved a hand, then dropped it on an arm of his chair.

The conversation turned to my own family and my personal plans for employment once I returned. As he spoke, he turned his head and stared out at the green field in front of the school, the wall of palm trees and the sun's rays turning pink and purple as it dropped behind the water of Lake Nong Tamue.

"Do you see that?" he pointed. "Tell America about that."

He folded his hands on his lap, sighed and told me he could no longer drink alcohol, smoke cigarettes, nor eat heavily-seasoned food. I sensed he felt free to say anything to me because I was only a visitor.

"I will always do my duty to my school!" he suddenly declared, in a voice reminiscent of the old leader.

Then, his head fell forward a little and he started muttering to himself in Thai. I had no idea what he was saying. I wondered if it had to do with his sense of lost strength, to the possibility that the allegiance accorded him now was really toward a man who no longer existed.

I wondered what he saw when he looked out at the field and trees. Did he see the land the way it used to look before he arrived to work in Nang Rong? What had life in the district been like then? Then, I realized how fortunate he was to live in Thailand and not the United States, where his life's accomplishments would be quickly forgotten and the honors accorded Adjan Suraporn Kamonchai, would be forgotten. If I hadn't learned anything else in this country, it was how important it was to honor the elderly and the educated.

"Adjan Suraporn?" I said.

"Khun Burgess. Yes, yes, I am awake. What is it?"

"You know I will be leaving Nang Rong next Month?"

"Yes, next month. We must plan a party. You must tell your friends from Buriram to be here."

"Yes, Adjan. Thank you."

He nodded me away.

February 20, 1969

It was a quiet Thursday evening and I enjoyed a final inhale from a Falling Rain cigarette after a pleasant meal of fried rice with a few eggs on top along with a slosh of spicy fish oil and soy sauce. I could not remember what used to be a satisfying meal in the states.

Last night I stayed at Thom's because there were too many parties and drinking scenes in Nang Rong for my stomach to handle. After a day of not doing anything and sipping warm tea, I went out and spent a tenth of my entire month's living allowance on a large meal I shared with Thom. He asked me if I'd like to accompany him to a night class he taught with students who were all teachers at the Agriculture School. He described them with such superlatives, I couldn't resist, even though it meant borrowing a bicycle from someone and pedaling through the city. One of the students who lived with Thom offered his bike and we wobbled off. The side streets of Buriram were well lit. After a few hundred yards, my chain broke, the brake connection snapped, the headlight popped into the air and smashed on the pavement, the rear tire went flat and the right fender was disconnected and began to scrape against whatever was left. We stopped at a new gas station and I tried to pump air into the tire. Turned out the pump I used was for truck tires and within a second of making a connection, the tire blew up in my face. When I returned the remains of the bike, I promised the student I'd send him money for repairs and we walked on to meet the students.

The two men and two women who greeted us impressed me as far more sophisticated and fluent in English than anyone I'd met in Buriram. The grammar review Thom had prepared, which I thought was quite complex, gave them no trouble at all, and the rest of the evening was spent reviewing reading assignments and testing them on comprehension of spoken passages. At one point, I noticed one woman had doodled something beside an answer that had to do with TNT. I looked over her shoulder and asked her what the drawing represented. She gave a small shrug and explained it was the chemical linkage for TNT which popped into her head when she heard it pronounced. I later found out she was waiting to hear from the Fulbright Foundation about a work-study grant in the states.

Later, back in Nang Rong

Last night I dreamed of traveling home by way of the foothills of the Himalayas where the air was cool enough to crystallize my breath.

The following morning, I heard about the final election returns. The government party wound up with seventy-five reps, the majority opposition received sixty-seven and the independents got sixty-nine or seventy depending on the final count. The government lobbyists and those of the opposition were trying to woo the independents over to their side, but because the government had so much patronage, it will inevitably come out on top. Mr. Tam, running in Buriram Province, and Sanguan's favorite, came in seventh. Since there were only five openings, he's totally out. Still, there were twenty-six candidates, so coming in seventh wasn't all that bad. Sanguan told me that in his opinion Mr. Tam was a real gentleman who had been much maligned. I told him I hadn't heard any specific rumors about him. Had he? Sighing, he volunteered the information that many of Tam's enemies said he made a lot of money through his job in Bangkok. And, what, I wondered, was Mr. Tam's job in the capital? He said he was in charge of license renewals for certain parts of the liquor industry and also had a small interest in an agency that approved sites for construction of new distilleries. Sounded awfully tempting. After Sanguan left, Wisut came in with a big smile because he was delighted Tam had lost. He only regretted that the opposition did not do as well in the provinces as it had in Bangkok. The differences between Sanguan and Wisut's backgrounds impacted their points of views. Wisut, whose father was Chinese, was much more aware of the distinction between the theory and practice of constitutional monarchies. Sanguan, whose extended family had connections and vested interests in the current regime, wanted nothing more than the status quo. Sanguan's parting shot to me was that the entire general assembly so recently elected should be dismissed, en mass, and then new elections should be held in which, "…bad men…" would not be allowed to run.

My students were nervous about their general exam which will be given in early March. I've been drilling them on verbs, syntax, word usage and, of course, the bane of my existence, gerunds.

Next day

I received two old copies of the *Village Voice* from my friend, Roger, in Wapipatum. Photographs inside showed nude men and women congregating outside a church in the East Village. Now that I'm acclimated to Thailand, how long will it take me to be reacclimated to my own country?

February 26, 1969

Wisut showed me a copy of a newspaper from Bangkok that had a full page spread on the capture of many communists in Nang Rong District. I laughed. Truth was, the Nai Amphur had simply echoed Captain Louis Renault, in Casablanca, when he said *Round up the usual suspects.* Soon enough, all *suspects* were brought in for interrogations. Soon after, two dozen more people presented themselves at the district court office, declared themselves to be suspects and announced they wanted their interrogations over first so they could get back to their farms. Everybody was happy.

Since Thom is planning to leave for Bangkok on March 4th, I decided to go with him. I only mentioned my departure time once to the headmaster, but I think one week's official notice should be enough time. Unfortunately, some of my students will be in the middle of their exams, but these were tests made up by other teachers in Korat and I will not be responsible for grading them. According to my Peace Corps contract, I will be theoretically able to leave Nang Rong this Friday, but that's only because all formal classes will be over. This Saturday, there is a party planned by Wisut, myself and close friends. The headmaster will probably plan something bigger involving everyone in the school and maybe some local officials. I will be taking my own language test, in Thai, on March 8th and begin my last physical exam the same day. After three months of training and studying Thai, I only scored 0+ on the Federal Language Test (out of a possible 6). I hope I'll at least be able to score a 2+ this time around. The termination meeting will be on the

15th and after that there will be visas to collect and I will need to finalize my travel plans with an airline. My departure date from Thailand will be March 20th, 1969!

Every night, I worry about my farewell speech. Wisut and I have been working on it for days now and all my waking hours are spent saying it over and over again in front of a mirror. I told him what I planned to say and asked for help translating it into Thai. Sensitive as always, he nodded and began to make suggestions. Obviously he has much more sense of what should be in a farewell speech for a Thai audience. It sounded extremely stilted to me, with grand thank you's here and eloquent blessings there, but I accepted all of his advice. Because I have a very hard time actually reading Thai, he helped me write everything down phoenetically.

Another joint venture of ours has been a brief comedy skit involving only the two of us. Wisut plays the role of a helpful Thai citizen to my American tourist, who knows only a few fractured Thai phrases. The climax of the skit begins with Wisut asking me if I've ever been to Bangkok. I reply, "Yes, I have been to Bangkok…" but, instead of using the usual abbreviated word for the capital, I pronounce its full name, which goes on for several lines, thus demolishing my earlier image of a bumbling tourist and stands revealed as a Thai speaker extraordinaire! For what its worth, here's what it looks like phonetically:

Wisut: Khun koey pai Grunteyp mai? (Have you ever been to Bangkok?")

Me: Chai. Pom khoey pai Gruntep pramahanakhorn amorn ratana gosin ma hiintara yutayaa mahadilok pop noparat rejatanii buriirom odom rejaniiwayt ma hassatan tidya wiganugam prasit (Yes, I've been to Bangkok).

The name, composed of *Pali* and *Sanskrit* root words, translates as: *City of angels, great city of immortals, magnificent city of the nine gems, seat of the king, city of royal palaces, home of gods incarnate, erected by Vishvakarman at Indra's behest.*

Oh well, I guess you had to be there. My students thought it was hysterically funny.

....

March 4, 1969

I'd convinced myself I hadn't done anything wrong by not mentioning to the headmaster, again, when exactly I planned to leave. But, when I found him alone today in the teachers lounge and I just straight out repeated that I'd be leaving town on March 7th. He went through the roof.

"Khun Pandit, this is very bad for you to tell me this so late. How will I have time to create a going-away present for you? This will upset all the people who should be at your going-away party."

"I did tell you before I was leaving soon, Adjan…"

"No! You never did!" he exclaimed. Then, seeing that a few teachers had entered the room he lowered his voice. "I am very sorry Khun Pandit, but if that is when you will go then I will try to arrange something."

He looked miserable, but not as miserable as I felt.

Wisut told me that right after I had that conversation, the headmaster called in several women on the staff and told them to start cooking for the *foreigner's* going away party. He said everyone was shocked. They had no idea I was about to suddenly leave the village forever. I also heard the janitors were instructed to start brewing a large batch of sato. Orders went out to the Raxana Restaurant for a few cases of Mekhong whiskey, several dozen bottle of soda water and tubs of crushed ice. It brought back memories of my welcoming party.

John, from the malaria group, arrived on Friday and the two of us walked over to the Raxana for a drink. The village had changed quite a bit since my arrival. First, the road was paved; second, electricity now flowed twenty-four hours a day: and, third, taxi cabs now zipped back and forth to Buriram at half the old bus time. We sat at a back table and commiserated on all that had happened in the past few years, especially memories of Fred's drunken spree when he helped Cambodians unload bags of jute and that wonderful picnic with women from the red light district.

Fred and Thom showed up the following afternoon. We wandered through the school grounds. The aroma of food cooked for my party drifted over the campus. I noted there was plenty of *som tam*, the powerful green papaya salad that had made my eyes water during my first big meal with everyone. Boiling away in a large cauldron was my favorite soup, *tom saab moo* (sour soup with pork). Of course, the town's classic dish was on order: whole roast pork. Several teachers were working on layers of *gai yang* (grilled chicken) and, of course, there was plenty of *khao meow* (sticky rice) to be served with everything.

Students clustered around us wishing me tender goodbyes and presented me with small photos of themselves, all lovingly inscribed with such lines as: Dear Burgess, I give my this for you. You will happy at have my picture. Please keep and give well. My quiet student, Tassania, wrote: *This picture for my teacher. I don't forget you because I love you.* Pian wrote: *For my teacher, to sir with love. If you marry I think you can make three children.* It was all I could do not to hug and cry over each and every one of them.

At twilight, we gathered at my house to dress more formally in sport shirts, slacks and clean loafers. In front of the school, a double table was set up with trays of food and drinks. Lights had been strung from the school's porch down to the tables and out over the small pool that encircled the flag pole. Mayor Somchai was there along with most of the teachers and friends of mine from the town. Off to one side a special table held: soda water, quarts of Mekhong whiskey, unlabeled bottles with a milky fluid that indicated sato, quarts of frosty Thai beer and many buckets of crushed ice.

There was just enough light to outline coconut palms against a darkening sky as we walked to our assuaged seats. There was no small talk. Everyone ate softly with polite glances down at the tablecloth. Awkward beginnings of chit-chat quickly petered out. Then Fred, who generally got drunk faster began to make jokes with the Nai Amphur and at the first sound of the Mayor's belly-laugh the rest of the party joined in. Soon glasses clinked in toasts and even Headmaster Suraporn smiles, although I could tell by his occasional grimace his stomach was giving him trouble.

My farewell speech, so carefully prepared by myself and Wisut, was folded on my lap. I'd desperately tried to memorize it, but there were simply too many unfamiliar Thai phrases. After most of the food was gone (rice, soups, pork and beef dishes, salads, plates of condiments and friend morning-glory leaves) the headmaster gave a signal to the mayor and suddenly it was silent. The Nai Amphur, a product of Thai grade schools and Scandanavian universities, arose holding my going-away present — an engraved silver bowl. He raised his eyebrows at me and we both laughed at the obscene implications such a gesture meant in Thailand. I managed to stand, giddy from whiskey, and leaned my pelvis against the edge of the table.

"Do you want me to speak in Thai or English?" the mayor asked me, grinning.

"In Thai, of course."

Ignoring my answer, he looked up at the assemblage and spoke in English: Ladies and gentlemen, we are here today to pay honor and give thanks to Mr. Burgess Needle who always did his duty and…"

The table wavered before me as his words described all too kindly the contribution I had made to his small village and to his country, then he went on to the parallels between Thai and American history, our current political situation, Peace Corps' work around the world, back to me again, himself, Nang Rong School, other Americans present, Nang Rong teachers and, finally, Headmaster Adjan Suraporn who sat beaming by my side.

With a half-stiff bow, Adjan Suraporn arose and carefully handed me a silver bowl inscribed with the words PEACE CORPS, my name and the years I'd taught at Nang Rong School. I accepted it with a bow, then we shook hands. The entire scene felt rapid and slow all at once. My own speech said many of the same things that the mayor had said about me, but in the high, flowery language of formal Thai. I only new what I was saying because of Wisut's word-by-word explanations. I'd practiced reading it alone, then to John and Fred who did not understand it either and finally, foolishly, to a student who freaked and ran away the instant he comprehended what I was saying.

And so I read on, getting my laughs, pausing when I remembered to pause, and smiling inside when I heard a teacher near me whisper to a colleague. *He speaks so clearly! I never heard him speak this well before.*

At the end, I bowed, straightened up, and wondered what in God's name was supposed to happen next. As the applause died, Fred, red-eyed, veins popping, leaped to his feet, glass in hand, and shouted, CHAY-YO! A cheer quickly picked up by the others. John and Fred's automatic camera flashes punctuated the night. When the men began uncorking bottles of sato, the women quietly arose, took me aside, one by one wished be good luck, and departed. We began to sing. The headmaster got to his feet, rubbed his stomach, looked over at the quarts of whiskey somewhat ruefully, carefully walked over and bid me pleasant dreams, and roared away on his gleaming, new Yamaha bike. Only the young male teachers and the Americans remained. Sensing things were beginning to get out of control, the mayor edged out of the area, got into his jeep and waved goodbye. The whiskey, sato and beer were swallowed with abandon (along with a few leftover pieces of salted, dried squid). A few teachers stood over the goldfish pool and tried to brain the fish with pieces of decorative marble. A visiting teacher from Surin fell over backwards in his chair, banged his head on concrete, and remained that way until discovered by janitors hours later when they came to clean up. Even the soda water disappeared. A few stray bottle of Mekhong were discovered and quickly dispatched. Wisut tried to jump into the pool, but was stopped just in time by Fred, who wanted to get in ahead of him. John held Wisut in his arms, both their bodies dangerously swaying back and forth. Ponchai, a new arrival from Bangkok, young and impressionable, quietly and politely threw up beneath the table. Mr. Anan fell asleep on top of his plate. Mr. Zwie fell asleep on the ground against a tree. Fred sat by the water's edge trying to catch fish with his feet. The school building seemed to advance and retreat from me. Suddenly, everything went black. The electricity had shut off. Some thought they'd gone blind and began to moan. The party, slowly, inexorably began to die. Teachers tried to pedal away on their bicycles, and the crash of metal on concrete was heard as they rebounded off the school's walls, and they remounted only to ram trees and bushes until they finally found their way to the road. Some decided to hang around and crawled up the stairs to the teachers' lounge where they collapsed. I heard a motorcycle smash the far corner of the outer-most building. I heard a yell, an engine re-starting, and a roar as whoever it was skidded off the gravel driveway into a supplementary reservoir. Havoc, chaos and cheers as Wisut, on his feet again, made one final attempt to jump into the pool. John caught him in mid-air. I danced back to the house with John, Wisut and Fred (who valiantly tried to finish off the remaining bottle of sato. From the shadows crept the janitors to clean up. Mr. Chop slapped me heartily on the back over and over again, telling me how proud he was to drink with me and how wonderful it was that there were so many Americans here all drinking Thai whiskey and hadn't it been a fine party!

Back at my house, Fred became manic. We tried to calm him down, get him to take deep breaths, forced him to lie down on the floor all the time telling him he needed to be quiet because he was at someone else's house and he was attracting attention. Someone pounded on the front door! We looked at each other in paranoid suspense and then the door flew open to reveal a very tardy border patrol policeman, smiling, still sober, holding forth an unopened bottle of Mekhong. John and I groaned. Wisut and Fred cheered.

Next morning I struggled free from the torn strands of my mosquito net to examine the total shambles of my house's interior. I fell back asleep on top of my mesquito net.

By mid-morning we had to offer penance for our sins. We walked together, me blindingly stumbling from one telegraph pole to the next, Wisut turning in circles as he walked, Fred walked with his eyes shut and John stumbled backwards so the sun wouldn't hit him in the face…on we trekked to the market for the all-purpose, hangover cure-all… boiled rice. Freshens your mouth, whitens your teeth and stops the runs.

March 5, 1969

Finally, some peace. Once again I was the only American in Nang Rong. By evening, my stomach had settled enough for me to walk slowly to the Raxana Restaurant and try a little fried rice. The district police captain was there with the provincial chief, his boss, having a good time. They nodded me over for a beer. Gagging, I sat down and chatted for a bit until the captain casually asked me when I planned to leave. I said it would be in a few days and I apologized for not having invited him to my farewell party at the school. He laughed, slapped his knee, and said, "No, really, when are you going to leave?" Big breath. I again told him I was almost on my way. The two of them appeared stunned. The chief looked at the captain angrily.

"The captain just finished telling me," the chief said softly, "that he planned to give you a big going-away party and he would begin to make he arrangements when he knew for sure what your departure date would be. Hasn't he said anything to you about that party?"

"I…I…" really did not know what to say and tried not to look at the hurt and angry face of the captain.

"I did not know you would be leaving so soon. Everyone knows you are my friend. They must think I will give you a big party. And, I want to do that anyway!"

"I am very sorry if I am going to give you trouble…" I began, but he interrupted me.

"No trouble! Never mind. But, you *must* come to the police station this Monday evening and we will all have something to eat and drink and maybe you will song a song for everyone. What do you think about that?"

"Wonderful," I said, notifying my stomach to start lining up extra tissue for an onslaught of alcohol.

"But, for now," the chief said, "time for some more Thai beer. And food! What can we order for you?"

March 6, 1969

I strolled around town today with Wisut, giving final handshakes to shopkeepers and people on the street who had just heard I was leaving. We continued on to the headmaster's house. He was outside, lying down beneath the shade of coconut palms, surrounded by three generations of his family. The closer we got the slower Wisut moved, until I got the hint it was up to me to approach on my own. For once, my shadow translator and go-between would be left behind and my own words would have to do.

I pressed my palms together and deeply bowed my head, causing him to smile. He waved me to sit and I sank to the ground, careful to keep my own head lower than his. He noted the effort and smiled. I said something about what the past two years had meant to me. He listened quietly and made his own comments about my acceptance of Thai culture, language and, with a laugh, its food and drink. I promised to write and he shook my hand. I bowed again and backed carefully away. Just before I turned to join Wisut by the side of the road, the headmaster threw me a weary salute.

As we walked away, Wisut said we should drop by and say a few words to his uncle. As we walked over there something kept itching in my head about appointment. The old man had a bottle of *sato* ready and waiting. His wife and daughters came out from under the cool shade of his home to say their goodbyes. We laughed softly in the early haze of evening's dust and dark. Uncle came up with a few more questions for me he must have been savoring for days.

"Who or what do you think you were born before? Do you believe in Buddha, yet? What do you really want out of life?"

Really, the kind of questions I asked myself every day. Suddenly, a member of the border patrol police roared up in a motorcycle, marched directly toward me in his stared khaki uniform with bright, white cross-stripes and a holstered .45 and announced, "My captain is waiting for the American to attend his going away party."

Oh shit. That was what I was trying to remember. From the expression on Uncle's face, it was a very bad time to initiate negotiations. I began to speak at the same time as Wisut, when Uncle angrily looked up and told the cop to go to hell. The policeman's chest visibly swelled and, in a firm, unwavering voice, he repeated his earlier message. Wisut spoke a few fast words to his uncle, who in turn told the cop that the American would be along soon, perhaps ten minutes. The policeman replied that I was wanted at once! Uncle scowled and began to rise. Wisut once more interceded and told the cop to return to his boss and tell him I was on my way, and as he spoke, quickly poured a shot of drink for his uncle and myself, indicating a final toast. Uncle gave a massive sigh and we all hoisted the bile-tasting drink up, then down the hatch. I shook hands one more final time with Uncle, feeling his cracked, warm, enormous hand engulf mine tightly.

"America...dee maak (America is good)," he said.

I nodded, we stood and hugged. Two little kids ran out and hugged my legs.

"I won't forget," I said. "I can't forget."

Then, we left at a fast trot, crashing through thick foliage and brushing aside dragonflies. The young trooper who accompanied us back was uncommunicative until just before we reached the outer perimeter of the police compound when he began to apologize for interrupting our little party. Wisut kept his eyes down and didn't comment.

"Please do not be angry with me, " he pleaded. "The captain has many men out looking for you. He said if we did not find you shortly there would be trouble. Do you know what that could mean? I am married and have children. I must not lose this job. Do you understand me?"

"Yes, I understand."

He left us at the gate and we walked ahead to a low, long table set up alongside the captain's house. It was covered with plates of food and bottles of liquor. Police from the entire district, who were in favor with the captain at the time, were all there with their wives alone with the Nai Amphur who seemed to have recovered from the previous party. Many of those standing around already seemed a little drunk. Wisut, myself and the Nai Amphur were gently twitted by the captain for being the only single men present. The ladies looked down into their soup. The captain made jokes about women who worked in the red light district. That's when I realized he was totally sloshed. He and the Nai Amphur began to get personal about their experiences and the ladies at the table suddenly found new interest in their toothpicks, shreds of lettuce and piles of rice. A sub-lieutenant across from me asked who my favorite girl was and I, already a little high from Uncle's sato, was giddy enough to tell him, shouting her name across the table. He slipped into paroxysms of laughter and had to leave the room for the safety of he bathroom. He began to vomit just before he reached the door, holding his sides laughing between heaves.

I finally stopped laughing and nibbled on some of the food. It was delicious, but because I'd only recently eaten and also had a few cups of sato in me, I was unable to eat my portion and made castles with my curried rice. Wisut and I signaled each other with our eyes.

Wisut: I'll try to get us out of this.

Me: Anything! I'm dying!

Wisut: I'm only a poor teacher. But, I'll try. (shrug)

Me: Pretend you're sick and I'll have to take you home.

Wisut: No, they'll just let me die under the table.

The Nai Amphur interrupted our silent dialogue.

"I am expected to travel to Nongki Village this evening for a big fair; but I have other business at hand and will not be able to go. Would you like to represent me and join the captain? I am sure he will be pleased to have you along."

Wisut slid from his seat and began to glide toward the exit when he heard the Nai Ampur say, "Of course, you will go with Mr. Wisut along with some of the young women here this evening. They have never seen a beauty contest before. What do you think? As a judge, you may be rewarded."

"A beauty contest?"

"Yes! I thought that would get your attention. They asked me to judge, but I will send you as my emissary. I'm sure the two of you will have a good time. Captain?"

The captain tried to say something, made a gurgling sound, and ended up shrugging what seemed to be an acceptance.

"Excellent. You will go in my jeep," the Nai Amphur said. "It's in top shape and I'm sure you all will have a wonderful time."

None of us wanted to go at all. Drive at night over side roads? In the Nai Amphur's jeep? The one with glowing lettering on each side with government emblems? Without guards? In the direction of Korat? Rampant insanity.

The captain accepted his duty as fatally as rain and sent his wife to his home for his .45. The rest of us got up, bid the sadistic Nai Amphur farewell, and piled into his jeep. As we backed out of the field, the Nai Amphur stood at attention with a big smile and waved.

I knew Cambodian irregulars or dissident Thais were just waiting for government jeeps in the forest. What a coup it would be for them to kill, wound or capture a police captain, an American spy and a stray art teacher who'd be seen as one of those running dog Thai government collaborators.

The road was terrible and the captain did not seem inclined to slow down for ruts, people or water buffalo. He drove speedily across shaky wooden bridges, one arm out the window, banging time on his door to some obscure Thai music. The women squeezed into the back remained silent. Knowing Wisut to be one of the most optimistic people I've ever known, his obvious nervousness scared the shit out of me. Nongkhi Village's night lights finally broke through the foliage. Up ahead was a stage with women holding multi-colored balloons. The captain swerved in for a fast stop. The men exited first and then the women, giggling and holding hands over their faces, got out last. I turned to Wisut.

"Why do the women have balloons?"

"I don't know. I think the one with the most balloons wins. Not sure. Maybe the man with the gas tank who is filling all the balloons knows."

Sure enough there was a decrepit metal tank by the edge of the stage operated by a guy who kept filling one balloon after another. He had a cigarette hanging from his lips and a fairly large knife stuck in his belt. I decided there had to be someone safer to ask. Meanwhile, the women were slowly disappearing behind a wall of multi-colored balloons.

The captain disappeared in the crowd so I struck up a conversation with an old man. If I hadn't learned anything else during the past two years it was that older people were the easiest to talk with because they always made more of an effort to be understood and other Thais respected me for talking with my elders. Since Wisut had joined the captain at the open bar, I asked the old man about the balloons.

"The woman with the most balloons wins!" he exclaimed, as if talking to a child.

Contestants on stage crowded together, nibbled oranges and looked frightened. The old man reached out to feel my skin and asked me if I came from *Shi - kha - go!*"

"No," I said. "I'm not from Chicago. I'm from Boston."

He brightened up at that. Most Thais had heard of Boston because the king, Bhumibol Adulyadej, also known as Rama IX, the ninth monarch of the Chakri Dynasty, had been born there and had attended Harvard. So, I had something in common with Thai royalty.

"How long have beauty contests been held with balloons as points?" I asked him.

"Not too long," he said. "I think about ten years that I can remember."

"Do people ever think the contest could be unfair?"

"What do you mean?"

"I mean, couldn't a rich man buy a lot of balloons to make sure his girl friend wins?"

"Yes," he nodded. "That is how it works. That big man over there is very rich so he buys the most balloons and makes sure his girl friend will win. Just like you say. Is democracy!"

"Democracy?"

"Yes," he nodded, emphatically. "Isn't that the way it works in America?"

The more I thought about it the more I realized the old man was right. Strip away the political parties, the promise of patronage, the phony conventions and what do you get? The candidate with the most balloons wins!

The MC called down to me to join him on stage and sing a song. Around me, other judges scribbled numbers on piece of paper and counted balloons. Men on stage counted balloons and shouted out numbers. The women continued to nibble on oranges and giggled. Someone tapped my shoulder and when I turned around the captain handed me a glass of whiskey. Balloons began to drift on to and away from the stage. I nodded back at the MC. Sing a song? Sure! The very least of my talents! Over to my right I noticed another stage had been set up with heavily made-up women from Korat who were there to dance with customers for only two baht. Behind that stage I could barely hear a local band playing American rock and roll music. They were waving at me frantically to join them and sing. I nobly leaped up to their stage, nodded to the leader, and asked what they wanted me to sing.

"Simon Says!" he shouted.

I nodded. The audience cheered.

I detached the mic from the stand, looked down briefly, gathered my breath and burst forth with:

Simon says put your hand on your head
On your head on your head Simon says
Simon says put your hand on your head
On your head on your head Simon says

I didn't muff the lyrics and danced around the stage until I ran out of breath. The amplification was so poor most people couldn't hear me, but they applauded my élan. Next, came *Ta nun hua djai* (Heart Road) a song about a young man comparing his heart to a road that's being stepped on by his lover. Wisut had rehearsed me on it for hours. That one, most of the people apparently heard and understood. The MC beamed at me. Someone handed me ten dance tickets. I glanced over at the women from Korat. Some of them looked very nice, even though Wisut had warned me that they really were nice and not to suggest anything improper. I thanked the donor for the tickets, bowed again to the audience, and walked over to the ladies-in-waiting. I must have been on my fifth or sixth ticket when my dance partner asked me how I liked Thai food. I told her I loved it and we discussed a few other things we had in common, then it sounded like she said something to me about twenty baht. She would do *what* for twenty baht? Oh my, Wisut didn't know everything. Not exactly the best time to hop behind a stage for hanky-panky, but thanks for the offer. I spotted Wisut waving madly in my direction. I jumped off the stage and tried to hand him a dance ticket, but her nervous pushed it away.

"Don't you want to dance?"

"Not dance," he said. "Time to go. But, maybe we cannot go. You must tell me this. Can you drive the jeep? The captain is very drunk and he say he cannot drive and the foreigner, you (!), must drive us home. The jeep must not stay here because it belongs to the Nai Amphur. Captain must get home with jeep or he lose his pride or something like that. So, you must drive. You know how? You tell me before, I remember, that you can do the drive. Is true?"

I was so drunk myself I was practically embalmed. I could hardly stand straight. Could I drive the jeep? Hah! Push any worry from your mind. Oh, turned out the vehicle had been made in England with steering on the wrong side. Wrong side to me, that is! Drive this baby over unknown roads, through woods, no lights, past lurking irregulars all the way back to Nang Rong Village? Sure!

It was two in the morning. I walked back to the contest where judges were still adding points. The captain, propped up by three women, lurched in the direction of the jeep when a fight broke out. Ruddy-faced with anger, he screamed at the young men kicking each other, clutching the .45 on his hip, and looking plain mean. They quieted down and in a fit of sobriety he demanded to see their I.D.s They all turned out to be off-duty police. The captain appeared very close to shooting them on the spot. He spat on the ground and sent them away with a violent swing of his arm, then swung over to vomit on his shoes. The women retreated. Wisut clutched by arm.

"We must go now," he said.

"We can't go now! We don't even know who won!"

"No fun now. We must go before captain die."

"He won't die!" I insisted, but then I saw the captain's glassy eyes and the yellow whites of his eyes.

Shit, maybe was going to die. We quickly explained the situation to the women and they nodded in agreement. Time to go! We managed to ease the captain into the back of the jeep and Wisut shouted to anyone who could hear that we would trust the results of the other judges.

"Must get out…."I heard the captain's plea.

We struggled to squeeze him back out and pointed in the right direction as he pee'd profusely into the foliage. The women remained huddled inside. I had no doubt they needed to go as well, but there was no way they were going to say anything.

Finally, the captain was crushed back into the furthest recess of the jeep, Wisut handed me the key and I slid it into the ignition. Wisut looked very nervous. He only had my drunken word I knew what I was doing. The key turned easily, engine started, coughed, died. There was a manual choke. I pulled it out, the engine roared to life and we jumped ahead so fast the captain slammed back even further into his little space, breaking wind occasionally to remind us of his presence.

Uncoordinated as I was, dealing with a stick shift on the wrong side of a steering wheel that was itself on the wrong side of the jeep, made driving all the more difficult for me. Every time I had to down shift there was an ominous grinding of gears. From the corner of my vision I could see Wisut's expression read: I thought you said you could drive! We moved along at a steady nine kilometers an hour, according to the dash board, and every small bridge we crossed gave me goosebumps. Were the machine guns located on either side as we went by, or centered beneath us to shoot up and blow us all against the roof? Would I live through it only to become a crippled hero in Boston? Would the lousy bridges themselves collapse under our weight and draw us into the Thai version of some LaBrea Tar pit? Would our remains be found by Chinese archeologists 10,000 years from now doing ancient Thai digs?

"*&^%%$#%*)*&^%^%&^%&%&" (Oh, look! What's this caucasian skull doing mixed up with Thai bones?)

The bumpy road was barely illuminated by the jeep's weak headlights. We finally reached Paak Wan Village where the women lived. That was where Sanguan lived as well, and, for a second, I considered stopping there to crawl through his bedroom window (as he had often crawled through mine) waking him up (as he had often done to me) to tell him what a wonderful time I was having. But, human kindness prevailed and I let him sleep.

Approaching Nang Rong Village felt as if we were on the outskirts of a real city, compared to Paak Wan, with real electric lights illuminating the highway. Wisut shook the captain awake. Dawn was breaking over the school as the captain took command of his jeep and swerved off into the morning with his hand heavily on the horn.

··

March 7, 1969

Weather in the low 100's for a change. I've made so many farewells that everything else will seem anticlimactic. My trunk and bags weigh so much Wisut had to borrow a cart from one of he janitors. We slowly lugged everything over to the bus depot. A mob of teachers and students stood around in the dust and waved goodbye.

Adjan Suraporn stood tall and dignified, glancing around at the multitudes in mild distaste. The scene must have appeared far too chaotic for his sensibilities. He drew me to him with his eyes and gave me a warm handshake. We stared at each other for a full minute, then he squeezed my hand really hard and told me to "…continue to do your duty."

Sanguan must've emptied his own building because the area was also filled with students from the private school who were crying, laughing, peeing in their pants, brushing flies away from sweet balls of rice they nibbled like candy. My own students, faces so familiar to me from day-to-day contact, hung on me, stroked my arms and murmured not to forget them and they would not forget me. My old friend Mr. Pbreeda who used to work with me at the school came in from Prakhonchai to say goodbye. Even Mr. Prayun, who tutored me in Thai when he also worked at the school, came in from distant Satuek. Wisut zipped in and out of the crowd snapping final photographs of the people and scenery of Nang Rong Village.

I was suddenly overwhelmed by a rush of regret. Had I really tried to teach them the English language as hard or as creatively as I could have? I thought of my old student Wisai when he walked with me through the moonlit shadows of the monastery, the fragrance of the lush greenery around us, telling me that he couldn't wait to get to an American city where the buildings were so tall they blocked out the sun. All those smiles of gratitude were too much for me to accept. For all those parties I attended? And, what about the temples? I only went to a few Buddhist ceremony because Wisut took me. What other opportunities had I blown?

The bus, *my* bus, swirled into its spot with a wave of red dust, making the crowd cough and choke. Every square inch of clothing I wore was drenched with sweat and sticking to me like tar. It was all sort of like the first day I arrived. Standing there in Nang Rong's heat, drenched in my new, ridiculous silk suit, looking around for my future, suddenly the scene before me had become my past. My suitcase, trunk and book locker were thrown on top of the bus and tied down. I'd been anticipating this moment for so long, the actuality made me dizzy. I looked around one last time before turning my back on everyone and walked to the bus door. I saw the headmaster staring at me, his head higher than the others, staring right into me above the crowd, worry lines etched on his forehead. He wore a fixed smile, that Thai smile I now knew could mean everything or nothing. Wisut, my roommate, friend, companion, my living connection to so many people in the town, kept nodding his head and brushing away tears. We grabbed each other in a fierce hug. I felt just as foolish as ever to look down and see the top of his head with its shiny black hair moving below my chin. He stepped away. Sanuan came over, clasped hands with me and whispered goodbye.

I climbed inside the bus, settled on to a wooden seat and looked out and down at all the teachers and students. Sanguan climbed on to the running board and clung there for a few hundred yards, reaching over to squeeze my knee and telling me words I could not hear over the bus's roar, then he jumped free into a flash of foliage.

Something moved beneath my left foot. I twitched as if an insect had landed on my neck. Was I on a snake? Then, I saw my shoe rested on a section of saffron cloth. I was sitting next to a monk who was trying to get into a more comfortable position, but could not because my foot pinned his robe to the floor. I hastily apologized and offered him a cigarette from my pack of Falling Rain. He accepted it with a rueful expression.

"You are still smoking Thai cigarettes," he said, softly. "You must really like them."

Was the same monk who sat next to me on my arrival two years ago? He spoke to me as if no time at all had passed. Where had *he* been for the last twenty-four months? What else had I missed? Such a small village, and yet I had obviously lived my life on the most superficial strata of Thai culture and society.

And then, briefly, I admit it was very brief, I wanted to get off at the next stop and return to Nang Rong. Now was the time to just *begin* to discover what this country was about. The feeling went away. Why? Because I had not changed? Because I was still an out-of-place American, unable to transient my own culture? This tangential dip into another land was over for me and nothing had changed, had it?

"Look at all these people?" I wondered. "They seem so *familiar* to me now. Their faces no longer look foreign. I understood everything the monk said now, and he no longer appeared exotic. My own horizons had somehow been smashed open just by having lived here; perhaps some aspect of my presence has opened up a glimpse of another world to some of my students, a few of the shopkeepers, Thais I've spoken with have perhaps changed however slightly their perception of America. Hopefully, for the better, the same way I hope I have changed for the better after two years in this place called *Sit and Cry*.

I inhaled deeply on my cigarette and felt the sharp menthol hit my lungs. Faded pagodas hovered over grasses some hundreds of yards away from the road. Sunlight glittered off the surface of the ride paddies. I thought of Boston and wondered if the Swan Boats were still gliding across the lake in the Public Gardens.

When I thought of the swans I remembered my students asking," Mr. Burgess, who collected the duck eggs? Why did the people feed other peoples' ducks? Why didn't anyone come and take the ducks away at night?"

Why *didn't* anyone come at night to steal the ducks? I must have answered that question a long time ago, but I could no longer recall what I said. There simply was no good reason to take the ducks. The average American already had all the ducks he needed.

I felt the monk shift in his seat. He smiled at me.

"You will not forget," he said.

"Forget what?" I asked, feeling scared.

"That!" he said, pointing out at the rice paddies, the distant pagodas and the vast stands of coconut palms at the edge of the sky. "You will not forget *that!*"

Closing my eyes, I nodded. He was right. I would never forget.

Reading Thai comic books to local children.

PEACE CORPS
242 Rajavithi Road, Sam Sen
Bangkok, Thailand

DESCRIPTION OF PEACE CORPS SERVICE

Burgess S. Needle – Volunteer No. 185923 – Thailand

Burgess S. Needle entered training on February 6, 1967, at the Peace Corps Training Center, Hilo, Hawaii, and on May 5, 1967, completed an intensive 13 – week program. Included in the subjects studied were Thai language, TEFL, cross-cultural studies, English syntax (grammar et al.). He was enrolled as a Peace Corps Volunteer on May 5, 1967.

Mr. Needle was responsible to the Ministry of Education, Secondary Education Department, during his service in Thailand. He served as a teacher assigned to Nang Rong School, Amphur Nang Rong, Buriram, where he was one of 16 faculty members. The school offers three grades of study and has an enrollment of approximately 300 pupils. Mr. Needle reported directly to the principal of the school, Suraporn Camonchai, and was responsible for teaching the following courses:

Dates	Subject	Grade	Students	Hours Per week
5/67 – 3/68	English	MS-1	110	18
5/68 – 3/69	English	MS-3	108	21

Additionally, Burgess Needle was involved with the English Club of Nang Rong School and helped the students to produce their own newspaper, attempt several plays (adapted by him for their use), and gave special classes at his home for those students who needed extra help and those students who wanted advance lessons beyond the scheduled curriculum. For three days a week, he taught at a primary school (Sangkagrit School) where he personally presented theories of TEFL methodology. On a number of occasions he traveled to nearby villages to watch teaching on a primary level as presented by Thai teachers and attended numerous festivals as a point of interest in the local culture. With the exception of two of his vacation periods, he traveled extensively to Thailand's north and northeast regions to compare them against his own area with regard to language, social and food differences. On one vacation period he was part of a summer camp for Thai students from the Northeast region. "Camp Thai-Am," as it was called, involved slightly more than 110 Thai students, twelve peace corps volunteers, and ten Thai teachers. The motivation behind the camp was to simultaneously teach Thai students some aspects of the English language they may have had only slight contact with and to involve Thai teachers in the presentation and planning of TEFL-oriented lesson plans. During the second term break of his second year, Burgess was invited to attend a seminar for Thai primary school teachers in Buriram Province, along with two other Volunteers, and presented model lesson plans and discuss TEFL methodology with the participants. He took an active interest in the social life of his town (Nang Rong) and was a frequent visitor of the meeting hall celebrations for various national holidays and locally celebrated events. With the help of his roommate, Mr. Wisut Pinyowanitchka, he soon became an active participant himself in the social activities near him.

Pursuant to section 5(f) of the Peace Corps Act, 32 U.S.C. 2504 (f), as amended, any former Volunteer employed by the United States government following his Peace Corps Volunteer service is entitled to have any period of satisfactory Peace Corps service credited for purposes of retirement, seniority, reduction in force, leave and other privileges based on length of Government service.

This is to certify in accordance with Executive Order No. 11103 of April 10, 1963, that Burgess S. Needle served satisfactorily as a Peace Corps Volunteer. His service ended on March 16, 1969. His benefits under the Executive Order entitlement extend for a period of one year after termination of Volunteer service, except that the employing agency may extend the period for up to three years for a former Volunteer who enters military service or pursues studies at a recognized institution of higher learning.

10/69
Kevin Delany
Director
Peace Corps/Thailand

OTHER BOOKS by BURGESS NEEDLE

Every Crow in the Blue Sky & Other Poems.
  Diminuendo Press. ©2009.

Thai Comic Books: Poems From My Life in the Peace Corps: 1967-1969.
  Big Table Publishing. ©2013

Faded Photo Brings It Back & Other Poems.
  ©2013

PUBLISHED FICTION
  http://www.burgessneedle.com/fiction.html

FOR ADDITIONAL THAILAND PHOTOS, POETRY, ETC
  burgessneedle.com

70056306R00179

Made in the USA
Columbia, SC
29 April 2017